Praise for *The Remote System Explorer*

"I thought I knew a lot about RSE, having been a user, a teacher, and an avid fan of the tool for years. While reading this book, I found there was still a lot for me to learn! Don and Nazmin have done a great job of providing guidance, details, and tips in a way that allows beginners and experienced users alike to find what they need to know. They write in a conversational tone—not IBMeze—and focus specifically on the needs of the typical RPG or COBOL developer. They have also made the book product agnostic, so that it is equally applicable whether you have WDSC V7.0 or RDi V7.1 installed. When you're ready to give up SEU and PDM, this is definitely the book to read!"

Susan Ganter
Co-founder of SystemiDeveloper and Partner400

"I've been a user of the WDSC family of tools since the original OS/2 release of CODE/400-and I've been teaching others about them for almost as long. Even so, I knew there were some areas of RSE that I was a little thin on, such as filter pools. So, when I was offered the opportunity to read an advance copy of this book, I jumped at the chance. I'm happy to say that I've learned a lot, but I'm surprised that I had *so much more* to learn than I had imagined!

"Not only have Don and Nazmin done a great job with this book, but they have done so without lapsing into IBM jargon. The topics they cover are those that will be of interest to the majority of programmers, and they have avoided the traditional IBM mistake of focusing too much on esoteric functions that few will ever use.

"If you can't spare the time or money for a hands-on class in RSE, buy this book. You'll learn a lot!"

Jon Paris
Co-founder of SystemiDeveloper and Partner400

"If you want complete coverage of RSE in a single source, this is the book to get!"

Jef Sutherland
Vice President, Information Services, Kampgrounds of America

The Remote
System Explorer

The Remote System Explorer

Modern Developer Tools for the System i

Don Yantzi
&
Nazmin Haji

MC Press Online, LLC
Boise, ID 83703

The Remote System Explorer: *Modern Developer Tools for the System i*
Don Yantzi & Nazmin Haji

First Edition
First Printing—September 2008
Print on Demand - May 2020

MC Press offers excellent discounts on this book when ordered in quantity for bulk purchases or special sales, which may include custom covers and content particular to your business, training goals, marketing focus, and branding interest.

For information regarding permissions or special orders, please contact:

MC Press Online, LLC
3695 W Quail Heights Court
Boise, ID 83703-3861 USA

For information regarding sales and/or customer service, please contact:

Tel: 208-629-7275
eMail: operations@mcpressonline.com

ISBN: 978-158347-081-7

To my husband, Al-Karim, and my three lovely children, Meera, Ashna, and Adam,
for allowing me to "steal" the precious time away from you to chase my dream.
Thank you for your understanding, unconditional love,
and constant encouragement; with your support, this dream has become a reality!

—Nazmin Haji

To Jennifer, Nathan, and Corinne.
Thanks for all your love and support.
Having you around to encourage, humor,
and distract me kept me going. Thank you!

—Don (Dad)

Acknowledgments

We'd like to start by thanking the many WDSC users who kept asking us for a book on the RSE. Ultimately, this is what initiated this project. However, the idea would not have gone far without having George Farr as both a motivator and author role model.

Being first-time book authors, we are eternally grateful to Merrikay Lee at MC Press for not only publishing the book, but for guiding us through the publishing process and answering our many questions. Thank you to our editor Marianne Krcma, who took our raw chapters and transformed them into something much more readable.

A special thanks to our reviewers Tarcholan (Tosh) Bimbra, Susan Gantner, Jon Paris, and Jef Sutherland, who were given a slightly larger than expected book to review in a very short period of time. We truly appreciate your comments.

And last, but not least, thank you to the rest of the RSE team at the IBM Toronto Lab for all the hard work you put into the RSE, and for answering our questions while we were writing. A book about the RSE would not have been possible without the RSE!

Contents

Foreword

Of all the subjects that Don and Nazmin could write about, the Remote System Explorer (RSE) suits them the best. They've devoted a good part of their careers at IBM to working on the RSE since its inception. They have the perfect combination of RSE development skills and experience to explain hard technical topics in a simple format. Who else would have greater technical expertise on this subject than them? (I might have something to do with their expertise, since I managed both of them for many years. Ahem.)

I can assure you that you are in for a real treat! You have here two of the most qualified developers in this topic. Now, they've joined to deliver this one-of-a-kind book to you.

I am incredibly thrilled to have been asked by Don and Nazmin to write the foreword for their first book. Don and Nazmin are great educators. Having them team up to put this book together makes it that much more precious. Don't get me wrong; the RPG and COBOL development tools in the RSE are not hard to learn. However, having a book such as this one, written by the subject matter experts, will expedite your learning and get your productivity up to its best in the least amount of time.

As I read the book, I see they have done a remarkable job guiding you through the different combinations and permutations that you face day to day in developing RPG and COBOL applications in your shops. I haven't been so engaged by material of this sort for a long time. Once I started reading their first draft, I just couldn't put the book down. The book they deliver here is well-written and engaging; it walks you through the RSE and related tools at just the right pace. Whether you are new to the RSE or an experienced user, I strongly recommend you adding this book to your library.

Ultimately, you have a job to get done, and this book shows you how to use the tool that is at your disposal. It is full of examples that can help you get started. It is also an excellent reference that you will surely want to keep close at hand. You'll learn solid techniques that will help you code faster, be more productive, and therefore get home earlier at the end of the day! So, even your wife/husband and the kids will be proud of you for reading this book.

So, come on in! It's very safe in here! Let Don and Nazmin be your guides as you dive into the latest Eclipse-based technology in application development on IBM i. You are going to enjoy it!

—George N. Farr

George N. Farr has been a tester, developer, team leader, technical planner, and development manager for AS/400 compilers, RSE, and others. In 2005, he took over the management of the total Application Development solution for System i. George has recently been named the worldwide product line manager for all IBM i tools and compilers.

George is an award-winning speaker and prolific author of articles on IBM i application development. He holds a specialized honors degree in computer science and mathematics from York University in Toronto. He is the author of many books, including *Java for RPG Programmer, Java for S/390 and AS/400 COBOL Programmers*, as well as *ILE: A First Look* and *RPG IV by Example*.

You can reach George at *farr@ca.ibm.com*.

Introduction

This book is written for application developers using RPG, COBOL, CL and DDS on the IBM System i. This includes existing Source Entry Utility (SEU) and Program Development Manager (PDM) users who are thinking about moving to the Remote System Explorer (RSE), as well as those who have been using the RSE for many years.

Through our many discussions with SEU, PDM, and RSE users, we have gained a rich knowledge and understanding of the challenges faced by developers using these tools and transitioning from SEU and PDM to the RSE. We've learned the common questions all users have, the features they find most useful, and the features that are often misunderstood.

Our goal was to write a book that leveraged this insight and the technical knowledge we have gained from being developers on the RSE team. We've tried to include information that will be important for new RSE users, as well as the deep technical information that experienced users have been asking for.

The chapters are written in such a way that you don't have to read the book from front to back. You can pick and choose the topics you are interested in or need to learn quickly.

Chapter 1 provides introductory, high-level information that answers some of the common questions we get when talking with SEU, PDM, and IBM WebSphere Development Studio Client for System i (WDSC) users, as well as some background information on the application development tools.

The first thing you have to do is install the product, so chapter 2 covers installation-related topics, like installation, setup, and applying updates. Then, since you are probably eager to get down to business, chapter 3 is a "getting started" chapter that covers creating a connection; finding your libraries, objects, and members; editing a member; and compiling and debugging.

Chapter 4 covers the basics of the Eclipse Workbench. The word "basics" is not meant to imply this is a simple chapter. Instead, it's meant to convey how fundamental this chapter is to using the Workbench. There are commonalities in the Workbench, regardless of whether you are doing RPG, COBOL, Java, Web, or Web services development. Understanding these commonalities is key to using the Workbench effectively.

Chapter 4 is kind of a chicken-and-egg problem: understanding the Workbench is key to using it effectively, but you will get the most out of chapter 4 if you have some experience using tools inside of the Workbench. So, if you are new to WDSC or Rational Developer for System i, we recommend you read the chapter twice! Read it once before reading the rest of the chapters, and don't worry if some of the things don't make sense yet. Then re-read it after you've had a chance to play around and get comfortable with the Workbench.

Chapter 5 covers the core of the RSE: how to create connections; work with your libraries, objects, and members; perform actions; and run commands. If you are an experienced RSE user, you might be tempted to skip this chapter, but do so at your own peril! Many useful, but hard to find, features in the RSE are covered here. (We even found some we didn't know about while writing the book!) This chapter also includes some of our thoughts on how to effectively set up and use the RSE.

Editing source code is a major part of developing or maintaining any application, and the RSE has lots of great features here. There are so many great editing features, in fact, that we had to divide this topic into two chapters. Chapter 6 covers the fundamentals of the Remote Systems LPEX Editor and using it to edit i5/OS source members, regardless of the programming language. Chapter 7 covers the language-specific features of the editor (for RPG, COBOL, CL, and DDS).

Launching compiles, using the Error List view, and customizing compile commands are covered in chapter 8. Chapter 9 covers running and debugging applications in the Workbench. Running an application is very similar to starting an application for debug, so the chapter focuses on debugging and explains at the end what is different if you only want to run your application.

There are many smaller, but still very useful, features in the RSE that didn't fit into any of the previous chapters and are not big enough to justify chapters of their own. We grouped these features into chapter 10. This includes things like user-defined actions, remote searches, working with jobs, and accessing the Integrated File System from the RSE.

i5/OS projects are a way to continue to edit your source members while disconnected from the remote system. They also provide a way to manage your RPG, COBOL, CL, and DDS source code in a stream file change-management system such as Concurrent Versions System (CVS), Subversion, or IBM Rational ClearCase. This is all covered in chapter 11.

Chapters 12 and 13 cover the newest tools added to WDSC Advanced Edition and Rational Developer for System i: the Application Diagram and Screen Designer. The Application Diagram builds a graphical representation of the structure of an RPG, COBOL, or CL application. Screen Designer is a visual editor for display-file DDS source.

In case you still want to learn more after reading this book, we have included chapter 14, which lists a whole bunch of additional resources.

What Is the RSE and How Do I Get It?

The Remote System Explorer (RSE) is a set of tools for developing RPG, COBOL, CL, and DDS applications, or what we often refer to as *native* IBM i5/OS applications. These could be 5250 applications, batch applications, stored procedures, or RPG and COBOL programs that are used in a Web application. (Tools for working with the Web part of an application are not included in the RSE.)

At a high level, the tasks that can be accomplished using the RSE include the following:

- Working with libraries, objects, members, jobs, and integrated file system files
- Editing
- Compiling
- Debugging
- Searching
- Performing user-defined actions
- Visually designing display files
- Generating graphical diagrams of an application's structure

At a low level, there's a whole lot more to the RSE, as you will find out through this book.

Trying to learn and understand the RSE and its related tools can be quite overwhelming at first, especially if you are jumping into it with little or no background with workstation development tools. To realize the benefits of the RSE, you need to understand its capabilities and how to use them effectively.

In today's environment, getting up to speed quickly and becoming productive with any new application development tool has become a necessity. You have to do this while still doing your day job, so there isn't the luxury of being unproductive while learning. If you're going to invest the time to learn the RSE, you likely want some pretty concrete reasons for doing so. Here are what we consider the three main reasons:

- *The RSE improves productivity.* The integrated nature of the RSE tools, their additional capabilities in helping you understand your source code, the ease of debugging your programs they provide, and their many other features ultimately lead to improved productivity. You will be able to prove this to yourself as you read this book.

- *It's fun and exciting.* Sure, it's your job, but you might as well have some fun and enjoy it!

- *Learning the RSE lowers the next learning curve.* Learning the RSE lowers the curve for learning other new technologies and tools in the future. The RSE is just one of many tools integrated into the Eclipse Workbench. Most of these tools share a common Workbench user interface, help system, editing behavior, views, and debugger. While using the RSE, you will learn all of these things, which can then be applied when you have to learn a new technology such as Java, Web services, XML, Enterprise Generation Language, or PHP. All of these technologies have corresponding Eclipse-based tools.

The RSE is the strategic tool for i5/OS application development and is the replacement for SEU, PDM, and the IBM Cooperative Development Environment (CODE). We didn't include this in the list of reasons above, however, because we think you should choose a development tool based on its merits, not because someone told you it's strategic.

The RSE is not a product, so you cannot call IBM and buy it directly. The RSE is a set of tools for developing native i5/OS applications using RPG, COBOL, CL, and DDS. IBM WebSphere Development Studio Client for

System i (WDSC) and IBM Rational Developer for System i are IBM products that include the RSE.

WDSC and Rational Developer for System i are separate IBM products. WDSC has many features that are not included in Rational Developer for System i, such as the Web and Web services development tools, WebFacing, and Host Access Transformation Toolkit (HATS). On the other hand, Rational Developer for System i has some features that are not in WDSC, such as the Application Diagram and Screen Designer. (These were only shipped in WDSC Advanced Edition.)

Rational Developer for System i is the strategic tool for i5/OS application development going forward. This is where all new development is focused. WDSC is now in maintenance mode, with version 7.0 being the final release.

Both WDSC and Rational Developer for System i include the RSE, Remote Systems LPEX Editor, Integrated i5/OS Debugger, and i5/OS Projects. These features are the main subject of this book, so you can use the information here regardless of whether you are running WDSC or Rational Developer for System i. Specifically, this book is written to the Rational Developer for System i 7.1 version of these features. This means some new features described here are not available in WDSC; the Application Diagram and Screen Designer are the biggest ones. There are also some minor differences between the screen shots shown in the book and what you will see in WDSC; mainly, there is the renaming from iSeries to i5/OS. Appendix B summarizes the differences between WDSC 7.0 and the content of this book to assist you if you are using WDSC.

The Recent Evolution of RPG and COBOL Tools

The year is 1988. The Chicago Cubs play their first night game at Wrigley field, *Rain Man* wins the Academy Award for best picture, and IBM first releases the IBM AS/400. Along with it is a new release of RPG and COBOL development tools from IBM: Source Entry Utility and Program Development Manager, more affectionately known as SEU/PDM.

Move on to 1992. IBM introduces the Cooperative Development Environment for AS/400 (CODE/400) on IBM OS/2. (Eventually, CODE/400 was ported to

Microsoft Windows.) CODE/400, which has since been renamed just CODE, is a suite of tools that includes the following:

- *CODE Editor*, a workstation editor for remote editing of RPG, COBOL, CL, and DDS source members. CODE Editor included many SEU features, such as prefix commands, prompting, and syntax checking. It also included many new workstation features, such as color tokenizing, undo/redo, and program verification.

- *CODE Designer*, a graphical editor for DDS. CODE Designer included a palette of DDS records, fields, and constants that could be added to the graphical design area. You could then use the mouse to graphically lay out the screen or printer file.

- *CODE Navigator*, a graphical tool that could take a selection of open editors (RPG and COBOL) and build a call graph for the source, showing subroutines and procedures and the calls between them.

- *Program Generator*, a graphical user interface for launching compiles and retrieving and displaying the compiler messages.

- *Code Project Organizer*, a central tool for defining development projects, filters of remote libraries, objects, and members, and launching the other CODE tools from them.

CODE was IBM's first workstation application development tool for RPG, COBOL, CL, and DDS development. It had a small but fairly loyal set of users. Unfortunately, it never gained widespread adoption. The same development team that produced CODE produced WDSC. As such, the CODE tools, and the customer feedback IBM received on them, had a big impact on the initial designs of the Remote System Explorer in WDSC and now Rational Developer for System i.

Now, fast-forward to around 1999. Java is becoming popular, the Internet is starting to take off, XML is appearing on the horizon, and RPG and COBOL are still going strong. IBM (and the industry in general) has created separate development tools for each one of these languages or technologies. The problem is that developers are creating applications that leverage many of these tools, but each one looks and behaves differently, and they don't integrate that well.

Consider a typical Web application that uses HTML for the user interface, RPG or COBOL for the business logic, and Java to tie it all together. A developer would have to use all of these:

- SEU/PDM or CODE for the RPG/COBOL business logic

- VisualAge for Java for the Java code

- WebSphere Studio (the predecessor to the WebSphere Studio products based on Eclipse) for the Web site design

These are all IBM tools, but they are so different that they might as well have been created by different companies.

At this point, IBM realized it had a problem and started down the road of creating an integrated tooling platform that any development tool could be plugged into. This platform would provide lots of frameworks, so tool writers could quickly create new tools. Eventually, IBM open-sourced this platform, which is now known as Eclipse.

This started the process of most IBM application development tools teams rewriting their standalone development environments to be integrated into Eclipse. The CODE development team was no different. The redesigned and rewritten CODE suite of tools was released in 2002 as WDSC.

WDSC was originally a bundle of IBM Rational Web Developer, i5/OS extensions to the Web, Java and Web services features in Rational Web Developer, and RPG and COBOL development tools (the RSE, Integrated i5/OS Debugger, and Remote Systems LPEX Editor).

Rational Web Developer was a product targeted at Web developers, not Java 2 Enterprise Edition (J2EE) developers. A different product called IBM Rational Application Developer was targeted at J2EE developers. Eventually, IBM came out with a product called WDSC Advanced Edition (WDSC AE) that included Rational Application Developer instead of Rational Web Developer. WDSC AE was targeted at developers who wanted to do J2EE development, and RPG and COBOL development.

Over time, some of the new i5/OS related features were added only to WDSC AE. This included things like portal support and single sign-on for

WebFacing, the i5/OS J2EE Connector Architecture (JCA) Adapter, and the wizards for converting i5/OS job logs and message queues to Common Base Event (CBE) format for use with the log and trace analyzer tools. The tipping point seemed to be when IBM shipped the Application Diagram and Screen Designer technology preview only in WDSC AE for the 7.0 release. There was a loud community backlash, to say the least!

At this point, it was becoming obvious that the packaging model wasn't fitting the market requirements. In addition to the WDSC versus WDSC AE criticisms, users often raised concerns that WDSC was too big (to install, run, and download updates) and too complicated to understand and use with all the Web, Web services, WebFacing, HATS, XML, and database tools bundled together along with the native i5/OS application development tools.

So, in 2008, IBM released Rational Developer for System i, a new product focused solely on RPG, COBOL, CL, and DDS application development. Rational Developer for System i includes the Remote System Explorer, Remote Systems LPEX Editor, i5/OS Projects, Integrated i5/OS Debugger from WDSC, and the Application Diagram and Screen Designer technology preview from WDSC AE, along with some new features such as V6R1 support.

WebSphere, Rational, and System i, Oh My!

Consider the following scenario:

IBM   : Hello, how may I help you?

Customer   : Hi, I'd like to order WebSphere 7.1.

IBM   : Okay, do you mean WebSphere Application Server, WebSphere Process Server, WebSphere Integration Developer, or WebSphere Business Modeler?

Customer   : Um, do you have anything just called WebSphere?

IBM   : No, WebSphere is an IBM brand that covers lots of products.

Customer   : Okay, how about Remote System Explorer 7.1? The replacement for SEU and PDM?

IBM   : Sorry, we don't have anything by any of those names.

Customer   : Oh, right, it's now called Rational 7.1.

IBM   : Great. Would you like IBM Rational Software Architect, IBM Rational Application Developer, IBM Rational ClearCase, IBM Rational ClearQuest, or IBM Rational Functional Tester?

Customer   : Hmm, how about Eclipse? Do you sell that?

Okay, you get the idea that there is some confusion out there in the i5/OS application development community. Hopefully, this section will start to make some sense of the various names and version numberings IBM uses.

Let's start with Rational and WebSphere. IBM has five major software brands that it sells software under, each with its own focus area:

- *WebSphere*: The WebSphere brand focuses on application runtimes and development tools specific to those runtimes. WebSphere Application Server is an example.

- *Rational*: The Rational brand focuses on application lifecycle tools, such as requirements gathering (IBM Rational RequisitePro), application development (Rational Developer for System i), testing (Rational Functional Tester), and change management (Rational ClearCase).

- *Lotus*: The Lotus brand focuses on collaborative software, such as Lotus Domino, Lotus Notes, and Lotus Sametime.

- *Information Management*: The well-known Information Management brand is led by its flagship DB2 database product.

- *Tivoli*: This is the services-management brand.

When IBM first released WDSC in 2002, Rational was a separate company, and the WebSphere brand covered both application development tools and runtimes. So, IBM released the Remote System Explorer and associated i5/OS application development tools in a product called IBM WebSphere Development Studio Client for iSeries.

In 2003, IBM acquired Rational Corporation, which focused on application development lifecycle tools. Over time, Rational evolved into the IBM brand for application development tools. In 2007, the i5/OS application development tools team in Toronto was moved from the WebSphere organization to the Rational organization. This ultimately led to the Rational branding for Rational Developer for System i.

What's in a Number?

Although WDSC and Rational Developer for System i are closely tied to i5/OS, their version numbers having nothing to do with i5/OS version numbers. In the past, the application development tools linked their version numbers with the version of WebSphere Application Server they supported. The first release of WDSC was version 4.0 (not version 1.0) because it supported WebSphere Application Server 4.0.

In addition, the application development tools all tried to ship roughly around the same time, with the same version numbers. This is important for users who want to install multiple application development tools into the same copy of the Workbench. Generally speaking, Rational application development tools with the same version number can be installed into the same Workbench.

The approach of linking application development tools and WebSphere Application Server versions broke down in version 7 of the tools. At the time of this writing, the Rational application development tools are at version 7.0 (7.1 for Rational Developer for System i), but WebSphere Application Server is only at 6.1, which is the version supported by the 7.0 tools.

There are two important things to get out of this. First, WDSC and Rational Developer for System i version numbers have nothing to do with i5/OS version numbers. When a new version of WDSC or Rational Developer for System i is shipped, it can be used with any of the versions of i5/OS that are currently in service. Second, if you want to install multiple tools and have them use the same Workbench instance, you should get tools at the same version number. (Rational Developer for System i 7.1 can be installed into a Workbench with the other Rational 7.0 tools.)

How Do I Get It?

Prior to V6R1, there was only one package: IBM WebSphere Development Studio. This is the i5/OS licensed program (5722-WDS) that included the host compilers (RPG, COBOL, C, C++), ADTS (SEU, PDM, RLU), and unlimited licenses of WDSC. Every time IBM released a new version of WDSC, a 5722-WDS refresh code would also be issued for ordering it. Customers on software subscription or software maintenance could use the refresh code to get the latest release.

WDSC could also be purchased separately, through the IBM Passport Advantage site. This was primarily for consultants who wanted WDSC, but didn't own their own System i. IBM Passport Advantage is the only way you can purchase WDSC AE.

In V6R1, the entire WebSphere Development Studio package has been broken down into the following separately purchasable features: ILE compilers, heritage compilers (OPM, S/38, S/36), and ADTS. With the move to user-based pricing for the WebSphere Development Studio features, there are no unlimited licenses for Rational Developer for System i. A license of Rational Developer for System i needs to be purchased for each developer using it. This can be done in one of two ways:

- As a priced feature of WebSphere Development Studio (5761-WDS) when ordering V6R1

- Through the IBM Passport Advantage Web site

When ordered as part of WebSphere Development Studio, WDSC and Rational Developer for System i are shipped in a package of CDs that are included with the rest of the host software. The person unpacking the system might not know what the CDs are for, and just put them on a shelf somewhere. Finding these CDs is often one of the biggest challenges for developers getting started with the RSE! For WDSC 7.0, IBM even put a bright orange sticker on the back of the CDs that says "Forward to iSeries application development team."

The Building Blocks Behind the RSE

Building the i5/OS application development tools included in Rational Developer for System i and WDSC is an interesting example of a component-based development project. We thought we'd share a little background from behind the scenes for those who are interested.

The main development team that builds and ships the RSE, Remote Systems LPEX Editor, and Integrated i5/OS Debugger are located at the IBM Toronto Lab in Canada. However, there is no way this team could have developed and shipped a product like Rational Developer for System i on its own. Two things have made this possible: open source and component-based software development.

The most obvious piece of open source used in Rational Developer for System i and WDSC is Eclipse. Eclipse provides the things like the Workbench, wizard frameworks, editor frameworks, preferences, help system, debug framework, and a large part of the user interface (menus, views, and frameworks for things like tables and tree views).

Many other open source components are used in Rational Developer for System i and WDSC, such as these:

- *JTOpen (IBM Toolbox for Java)*: Originally from the Rochester lab, this is now maintained as an open source project on SourceForge. net. With the exception of the debugger, JTOpen is used for all underlying communications between the Workbench and i5/OS.

- *Apache Xerces and Xalan*: Xerces is used for XML parsing. Xalan is used for Extensible Stylesheet Language Transformations (XSLT).

- *International Components for Unicode (ICU4J)*: This is a Java class library for supporting internationalization and globalization.

The RSE also uses a lot of software components from other development teams within IBM. Here are some examples:

- *i5/OS*: The RSE does not have its own server (with the exception of the debugger). Instead, the Toolbox for Java and i5/OS host servers are used for communications. A lot of the information needed by the RSE is available directly from the Toolbox. The remainder of the information is retrieved by calling i5/OS APIs (via the Toolbox's program call support).

- *Debugger*: The workstation debugger was developed by another team at the IBM Toronto Lab and is used by Rational Developer for System i and other IBM products. Our team adds the i5/OS capabilities to the workstation debugger.

- *LPEX*: The base LPEX editor is also used by a few IBM products, such as Rational Developer for System i and IBM Rational Developer for System z. Each team extends the LPEX editor by adding their own parsers for the programming languages each supports.

- *Program verifiers*: The program verifiers are ports of the RPG and COBOL compilers to run on the workstation. (The part of the compiler that generates the module object is stripped out.) The RPG program verifier is subsequently reused to populate the outline view, provide content assist, and build the application diagram for ILE RPG source.

- *Install*: IBM Installation Manager and the associated install code comes from a separate team and is reused by most Rational application development products.

The RSE itself was designed to be a reusable component. When the RSE was being designed, the development team divided it into two main components: a base component and an i5/OS component (iSeries, at the time). The base component includes the framework, model, and user interface, but no connection types. The i5/OS component adds an i5/OS connection and tools related to developing RPG, COBOL, CL, and DDS.

The base RSE component is reused by two other IBM products: Rational Developer for System z and the IBM Transaction Processing Facility (TPF) toolkit. If you install Rational Developer for System i and Rational Developer for System z on the same machine, the RSE will show a connection type for i5/OS and a connection type for z/OS.

In 2006, the base RSE component was open-sourced on Eclipse.org. It goes by the project name *Target Management (TM)* inside the top-level Device Software Development Platform (DSDP) project. This project is lead by Wind River Systems, with committers from IBM and Symbian Software. Between the open source and IBM internal versions, the RSE is being used as a development environment for everything from cell phones to mainframes.

Also Brought to You by Rational

Rational is an IBM software brand that focuses on tools for the entire software development lifecycle. Below are some additional Rational products that might be of interest. More information on each one is available from the Rational web site (*www.ibm.com/software/rational*):

- *IBM Rational Software Architect and IBM Rational Software Modeler*, for software modeling using the Unified Modeling Language (UML)

- *IBM Rational Application Developer*, an application development tool for J2EE development

- *IBM Rational Business Developer*, an application development tool for writing business applications using Enterprise Generation Language

- *IBM Rational Developer for System i for SOA Construction*, a bundling of Rational Developer for System i and Rational Business Developer

- *IBM Rational RequisitePro* for managing requirements

- *IBM Rational ClearQuest* for defect tracking, process automation, and reporting

- *IBM Rational ClearCase* for software configuration/change management

- *IBM Rational Manual Tester* for manual test authoring and execution

- *IBM Rational Functional Tester* and *IBM Rational Functional Tester Extension for Terminal-based Applications*, for automated software testing with an extension product for testing 5250- and 3270-based applications

Jazz and IBM Rational Team Concert

We would be remiss if we didn't at least mention IBM Jazz and IBM Rational Team Concert here. Jazz is an extensible team collaboration platform that is designed to integrate all aspects of the software development lifecycle, including requirements, design, development, testing, and defect tracking. Eclipse is designed as an integrated development environment to make the individual developer more productive. Jazz is designed to make the whole team more productive. (And, of course, it has an integrated Eclipse client.)

At the time of this writing (early 2008), Rational Team Concert is only in beta and has not been officially released. You can find additional information and future announcements on *www.jazz.net*.

CHAPTER 2

Installation and Setup

Congratulations, you've got your hands on a copy of WDSC or Rational Developer for System i, a copy of this book, and you're rarin' to go! Let's get the software installed so you can move on to the fun stuff.

Workstation Requirements

You can find the exact technical hardware and software requirements for each release of WDSC and Rational Developer for System i in the corresponding announcement letter. Here is a more practical list of what you should have for your workstation, assuming you are installing Rational Developer for System i, or just the i5/OS Development Tools with WDSC 7.0:

- *Memory*: For WDSC, memory was always the killer; you needed lots of RAM to get good performance. This problem has largely been solved with WDSC 6.0.1 "Lite," WDSC 7.0 with only the i5/OS Development Tools, and Rational Developer for System i. However, any Windows workstation pretty much requires a minimum of 500 MB to run, and at least 1GB is recommended.

- *Disk space*: In general, you need lots of disk space. You need disk space for the actual product install (1GB), to apply updates as they become available (1GB), and for your Workspace (200–500 MB). So, we recommend you have at least 3 GB of free disk space. Keep in mind, however, that the Workspace and product install can be on different drives.

If you are in the enviable position of getting a new workstation, order as fast a hard drive as possible. The Workbench reads and writes a lot of files as it runs, and the faster hard drive should make a noticeable improvement in overall performance (other things being equal).

- *Monitor and screen resolution*: As you will see throughout this book, WDSC and Rational Developer for System i are very flexible in the way you can arrange your Workbench layout. You can have multiple members open at the same time side by side, along with the outline view and a graphical diagram of the source (the Application Diagram). The more screen real estate you have, the more information you will be able to view at once without having to switch between editors and views. So get a big monitor and crank up that screen resolution as high as your eyes will allow!

- *CPU*: Of course, faster is better, but we don't have any specific advice here. Our feeling is that if you have a fairly recent CPU, then the first three things in this list are more important.

- *Operating system*: WDSC and Rational Developer for System i currently only run on Windows. Windows 2000, XP, and 2003 are all supported. Rational Developer for System i supports Windows Vista, but WDSC does not.

Server Requirements

The RSE and Integrated i5/OS Debugger have very few requirements on i5/OS. The rule of thumb is WDSC and Rational Developer for System i support all versions of i5/OS in service at the time the client tool is released. So, the latest version, Rational Developer for System i 7.1, supports i5/OS V6R1, V5R4, and V5R3 (until V5R3 goes out of service).

No specific RSE server needs to be installed on i5/OS. Instead, the RSE uses the host servers included with i5/OS for all communications. This includes the sign-on and remote command host servers, as well as the DDM TCP/IP server. For more details on this, see the communications section of chapter 10.

If you will be compiling and debugging on the remote system, you will need to install *BASE and option 60 of WebSphere Development Studio

(5722-WDS for V5R3 and V5R4; 5761-WDS for V6R1). Option 60 includes some programs that are used by the RSE for launching batch compiles and retrieving the compiler messages. It also includes a service program used for starting debug sessions.

Coexistence

WDSC and Rational Developer for System i can coexist on the same workstation. Different versions of WDSC can also coexist on the same workstation. You could even have WDSC 6.0.1, WDSC 7.0, and Rational Developer for System i 7.1 all installed on the same workstation. You'd be wasting a lot of disk space, but you could do it.

If you have multiple versions of WDSC and Rational Developer for System i installed, you need to be careful about how you handle Workspaces. In general, a Workspace created by a previous release can be opened in a more recent release, but not vice versa (that is, forward migration is supported, but not backwards migration). See the section on Workspace migration later in this chapter for more details.

Running the Install

WDSC 7.0 and Rational Developer for System i 7.1 both use the IBM Installation Manager, a separate program that is installed on your workstation before installing WDSC or Rational Developer for System i. Since both WDSC and Rational Developer for System i are installed via Installation Manager, their installs are very similar. This section describes the installation process for both products, highlighting differences where they exist. Screen shots are taken from Rational Developer for System i.

You have to be an administrator on the local workstation to install WDSC or Rational Developer for System i.

The Launchpad

The launchpad provides a central place to start the install, install optional products, and view the readme and installation guides. Figure 2–1 shows the launchpad for Rational Developer for System i 7.1.

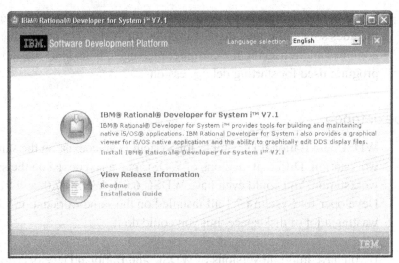

Figure 2–1: The launchpad for Rational Developer for System i 7.1.

The launchpad normally starts when you insert the first CD into the drive. (If it doesn't, run launchpad.exe from the CD.) The text in the launchpad is hyperlinked to launch the install or open the readme or installation guide. Click the **Install** link to start the installation.

Main Installation

The installation first checks to see if Installation Manager is installed. If not, it has to be installed first. This is where WDSC and Rational Developer for System i installs differ. WDSC requires you to go through a short install wizard to install Installation Manager before proceeding with the WDSC install. Rational Developer for System i includes Installation Manager as a required package to install as you go through the regular product install.

Rational Developer for System i requires a specific level of Installation Manager. If you already have Installation Manager (perhaps from a previous WDSC installation), you might be prompted that it needs to be updated before proceeding. Click **OK**, and the install updates Installation Manager, and then continues with the normal install.

As you can see in Figure 2–2, the first page of the install for either
WDSC or Rational Developer for System i shows the package to install.
Installation Manager refers to everything it installs as a *package*.
This could be a full product like WDSC or Rational Developer for
System i, or it could be an extension such as Rational Business
Developer Extension 7.0. (Rational Business Developer Extension was
turned into a standalone product in 7.1.)

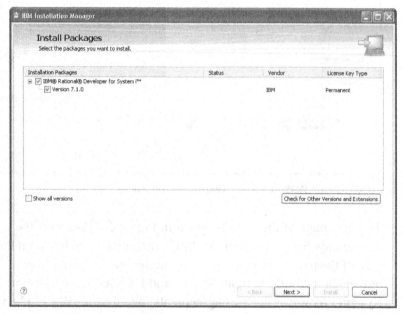

Figure 2–2: The package selection screen.

Updates are probably available for the package you are installing.
Instead of installing the product and then having to check for updates,
have the install check the IBM site for the latest updates by clicking the
Check for Other Versions and Extensions button. (This button was
labeled "Check for updates" in earlier versions of Installation Manager.)
Any available updates are listed as more recent versions underneath the
package, as shown in Figure 2–3. Select the checkbox beside the
version you want to install and click **Next**.

Figure 2–3: A WDSC install showing available updates.

The next page of the install, shown in Figure 2–4, presents the license
agreements for the product. Multiple agreements are listed on the left
side of the page. Selecting an entry on the left shows its license
agreement text on the right. WDSC and Rational Developer for
System i have two licenses agreements: one for the IBM product and
another for the third-party components included in the product.
One radio button at the bottom of the page represents acceptance
of all listed license agreements.

Installation Manager installs most of the files for packages into a single
directory called the *shared resources directory*. This directory is shared by
all packages installed by Installation Manager (hence the name). The
reasons for this will become apparent on the next page of the install
(so hold that question for just a minute). The first time you install a
package with Installation Manager, you will be prompted for the
location of the shared resources directory, as shown in Figure 2–5.

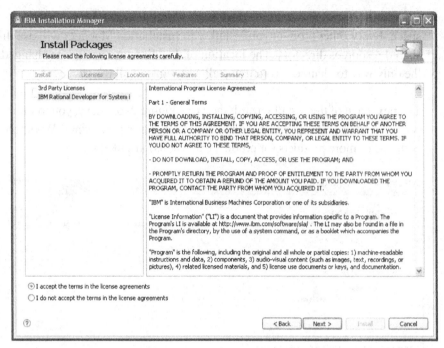

Figure 2–4: License agreements.

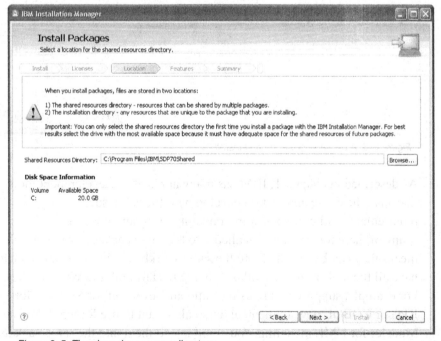

Figure 2–5: The shared resources directory.

Choose this location carefully, ideally on a drive where you have lots of space. Every other product you install with Installation Manager will use this shared resources directory. The location of this directory cannot be changed; the only way to change it is to uninstall and reinstall all the packages.

The next page of the install wizard, shown in Figure 2–6, allows you to install packages into a *package group*. Think of a package group as a single Workbench with one or more products (or product extensions) installed into it.

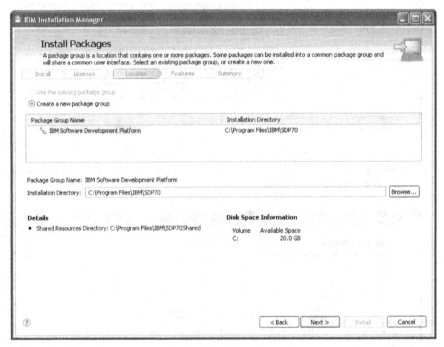

Figure 2–6: A package group on first install.

As described in chapter 1, IBM has many application development tools that span the entire application development lifecycle, such as requirements gathering, software modeling, programming, and testing. Many of these tools can be installed into the same package group, which means they can be installed into the same Workbench instance, so you can have all the tools available without having to start multiple Workbenches. For example, suppose you're using Rational Developer for System i for RPG or COBOL development, and you also want to use Rational Software Modeler for UML modeling. You could install them into the same package group, so both products are available from the same Workbench.

You can also run the install for a single product multiple times, so that the same product (or features of the product) is installed into multiple package groups. In the previous example, you might want one Workbench that has the RSE from Rational Developer for System i and the UML modeling tools, as well as a second Workbench that has just the RSE installed. Then you could use the lighter RSE Workbench when you are just using the RSE, and the heavier Workbench when you are using the RSE and doing UML modeling.

This is why there is a shared resources directory. Instead of each package group having its own copy of the resources (plug-ins) and wasting disk space because of duplication, the resources for each package are installed into the shared resources directory. Then, each package group just points to the resources it requires.

As you saw in Figure 2–6, only the option to create a new package group is enabled the first time you install something with Installation Manager. Subsequent installs give you the option to add the package to an existing package group or create a new one, as shown in Figure 2–7.

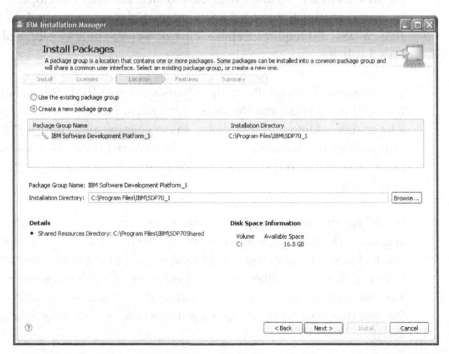

Figure 2–7: A package group on subsequent installs.

Each package group has its own installation directory where information specific to the package group is stored, such as configuration details, the Java Runtime Environment (JRE), and plug-ins that are installed into that Workbench via the Eclipse update mechanism.

Some packages are not compatible with each other. For example, Rational Developer for System i cannot be installed into the same package group as WDSC. In these situations, an error message appears at the top of the page. You will not be able to continue until you either select a different package group that is compatible, or create a new package group.

Conversely, some packages require other packages. In that case, you must select a package group that contains the prerequisite before proceeding. An example of this is the HATS toolkit.

The next page of the install, shown in Figure 2–8, gives you the option of using your own copy of Eclipse and Java Virtual Machine (JVM) if you already have them installed. Otherwise, a copy of Eclipse and the IBM JVM are installed with the product. Rational Developer for System i requires Eclipse 3.2.2 or a compatible version and a Java 5.0 JRE. WDSC 7.0 requires Eclipse 3.2.1 or a compatible version and a Java 5.0 JRE.

We recommend you use the Eclipse Workbench and IBM JRE included with WDSC and Rational Developer for System i unless you have spent a lot of time adding third-party plug-ins to your existing copy of Eclipse. This ensures you are using the copy of Eclipse and IBM JRE with the latest updates that WDSC and Rational Developer for System i were tested with.

WDSC and Rational Developer for System i are translated into nine different languages. The install page shown in Figure 2–9 gives you the option to choose which of these languages you would like to install. Don't spend a whole lot of time struggling over whether you should install, say, Spanish in addition to Japanese. All translated languages are packaged together in WDSC and Rational Developer for System i, so if you select one of them, all of them get installed.

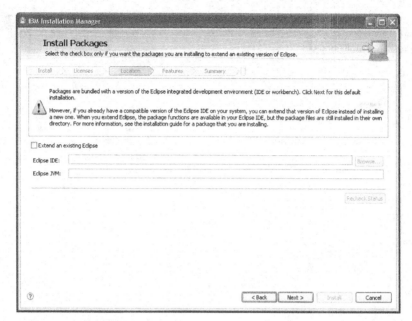

Figure 2–8: Choosing an existing Eclipse Integrated Development Environment.

Wait a minute. The install lists 13 languages in addition to English, but we just said WDSC and Rational Developer for System i are only translated into nine languages. This is true; WDSC and Rational Developer for System i are not translated into Hungarian, Russian, Czech, or Polish. However, some of the components they include are translated into these languages. If you install one of these languages, most of the user interface will appear in English, with only parts appearing in the translated language.

Prior to WDC 7.0, you had two options for installing: everything or nothing at all. WDSC 7.0 and Rational Developer for System i both provide a selective install, where you choose which parts of the product you want. This is shown in Figure 2–10 for Rational Developer for System i 7.1 and Figure 2–11 for WDSC 7.0.

For Rational Developer for System i, you will likely want to install everything, since it's already a lightweight package targeted specifically for RPG, COBOL, CL, and DDS development. For WDSC 7.0, you might want to make use of package groups, and install one package group with only the i5/OS Development Tools and another package group with everything installed.

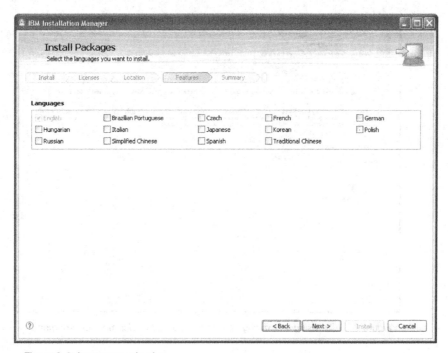

Figure 2–9: Language selection.

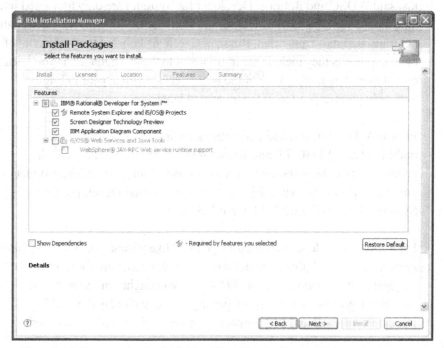

Figure 2–10: Feature selection for Rational Developer for System i 7.1.

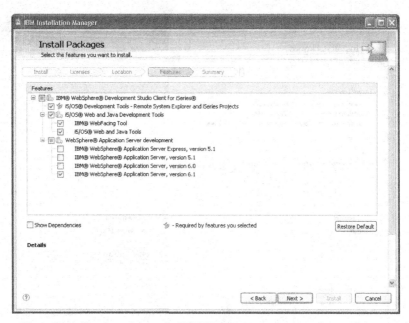

Figure 2–11: Feature selection for WDSC 7.0.

The last page of the install, shown in Figure 2–12, provides a summary of which features will be installed, where they will be installed to (the package group's install directory and the shared resources directory), and where they will be installed from. If you selected to install updates while installing the product, you will see two locations in the Repository Information section. One will be your product CD location and the other will be an HTTP URL where the updates will be downloaded from.

After the installation completes, you will have a new path in your Start menu for launching the product. It will look something like this:

```
IBM Software Development Platform > IBM Rational Developer for System
i > IBM Rational Developer for System i
```

If you created a new package group, the first part of the path will have an underscore number, such as _2, appended to it. This represents the package group name. Installation Manager doesn't allow you to name your package groups, so we usually rename the folder in our Start menu after installing.

Figure 2–12: The install summary.

Installing from a LAN Drive

You will likely want to copy the install image to a shared LAN drive if you
have multiple workstations to install, instead of continually swapping CDs.
To copy the CDs to a LAN drive, first create directories named "disk*X*,"
where *X* is the CD number. Then, copy the contents of each CD into the
corresponding directory. For example, create a directory called "disk1,"
and copy the contents of the first CD into that directory.

On each workstation, map to the LAN drive and run the launchpad.exe
executable from the disk1 directory to start the install.

Installing from an Electronic Download

With Rational Developer for System i 7.1 being only two CDs, you might
choose to download the electronic images when purchasing from the
IBM Passport Advantage site, instead of waiting for CDs to be shipped.

The files downloaded from the Passport site are compressed and need to be extracted to the same root directory. After extraction, you will see directories labeled "disk1," "disk2," etc. Run the launchpad.exe executable from the disk1 directory to start the install.

Silent or Automated Installs

WDSC and Rational Developer for System i support silent install using a response file. Instructions on setting this up can be found in the installation guide, which is available on the first CD (click the "Installation Guide" hyperlink from the launchpad).

Installing the Other Stuff in WDSC

WDSC includes a bunch of tools that are not installed as part of the main installation process. The main ones are HATS, CODE, and VisualAge RPG. You can install HATS by clicking on the link from the WDSC launchpad. CODE and VisualAge RPG install together without using Installation Manager. They also don't use package groups; they are installed into their own directory. To install CODE and VisualAge RPG, insert the CODE and VisualAge RPG CD into the CD drive and run setup. exe if the install does not start automatically.

IBM Installation Manager

In addition to installing WDSC and Rational Developer for System i, Installation Manager is used for applying updates, adding and removing features after installing, and uninstalling. To start Installation Manager, click the Windows **Start** button, and select **IBM Installation Manager > IBM Installation Manager**. This opens up the Installation Manager window, which provides links to each of the Installation Manager features, as show in Figure 2–13.

Getting Updates

Each IBM product has a Web site where product updates are stored. This Web site is not intended for mere mortals to view; instead, it is used by Installation Manager to download and install product updates.

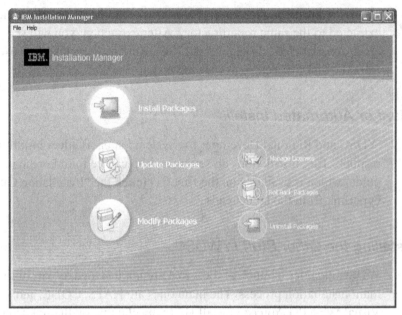

Figure 2–13: IBM Installation Manager.

WDSC and Rational Developer for System i (along with most
other IBM Rational products) use Installation Manager for
finding and applying updates. They do not use the Eclipse
update manager.

If your company uses a proxy server for HTTP access, you will need
to specify it in the Installation Manager preferences. Select **File >
Preferences** from the main window and then enter the proxy settings
on the **Repositories > HTTP Proxy** page. There is a proxy page for FTP,
but this is not required because WDSC and Rational Developer for System
i only use HTTP access for updates.

Click the **Update Packages** icon in the Installation Manager window to
start the update wizard. On the first page of the wizard, select the
package group(s) that you want to update. (You can select multiple
package groups.)

Click **Next**. Installation Manager goes off and searches the product site for applicable updates. It displays any available updates on the next page, shown in Figure 2–14. Select the updates you want to install, and continue through the license acceptance and summary pages of the wizard.

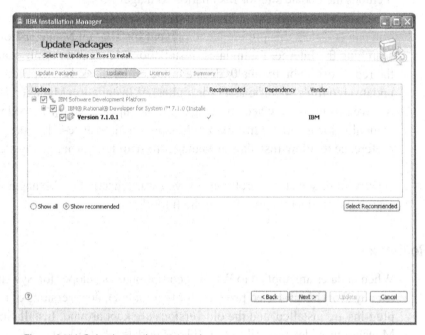

Figure 2–14: Selecting updates to apply.

Manually Downloading Updates

Updates can be manually downloaded from the product support sites (see chapter 14) if your workstation is not connected to the Internet (gasp!) or if your company firewalls blocks Installation Manager from accessing the Internet.

Installation Manager uses the term *repository* for the location where it searches for updates. If you are manually downloading updates, you will have to download and extract the update to a directory on your workstation (or a LAN drive), then add that directory as a repository in Installation Manager. Select **File > Preferences** from the main Installation Manager window and add the location on the Repositories preference page. Then, click the **Update Packages** button on the main page.

This preference page includes an option for Installation Manager to *Search service repositories during installation and updates*. When selected (the default), Installation Manager automatically searches the predefined product updates sites when the Update Packages button is clicked. This includes the update site for Installation Manager itself.

You can de-select this preference to prevent Installation Manager from searching the Internet for updates. Installation Manager will only search the repositories you manually define in the preferences. Some product updates require a specific level (or higher) of Installation Manager. If you receive this message when applying a product update, you will need to manually download the Installation Manager update or re-select the preference to allow Installation Manager to search its own update site.

Be sure to re-select this preference if you want Installation Manager to search the product update sites in the future!

Rollbacks

When updates are applied to WDSC and Rational Developer for System i (or any Workbench-based product, for that matter), new versions of the plug-ins are installed, and the old versions are kept around. Installation Manager provides the ability to roll back updates, but WDSC and Rational Developer for System i do not support this feature. Consequently, the older plug-in versions build up over time, and waste disk space. To delete these old plug-ins from Installation Manager, open the **Preferences** dialog, switch to the **Files for Rollback** page, and click the **Delete Saved Files** button, shown in Figure 2–15.

Adding and Removing Features

So, you just installed Rational Developer for System i and deselected the IBM Application Diagram component because you had no idea what that was. Now, though, you've just seen the cool Application Diagram demo on the Rational Developer for System i Web site, and you wish you hadn't deselected it. No problem! You can go back and add (or remove) features after the install.

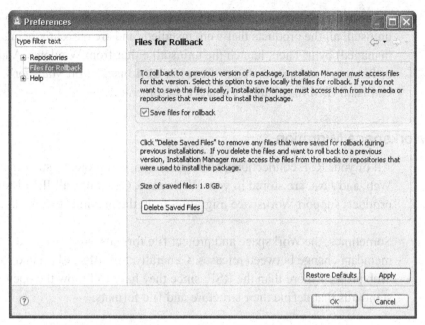

Figure 2–15: Setting the preference to delete rollback files.

From the Installation Manager main window, select **Modify Packages**. The subsequent wizard guides you through selecting which package group you want to modify, which languages you want to add or remove, and which features you want to add or remove.

Uninstalling

Uninstalling products is also done from Installation Manager. You can select a package group to uninstall from Windows' regular Add or Remove Programs dialog, but it just launches Installation Manager in uninstall mode.

To uninstall a product, select the **Uninstall Packages** link from the Installation Manager main window. This page shows all of the package groups, with a list of all the products installed in each one. Select the products (or entire package groups) you want to uninstall, and click **Next**. This goes directly to the summary page of what will be uninstalled and from where. Click the **Uninstall** button to proceed with the uninstall.

If you want to uninstall Installation Manager itself, you first need to uninstall all the products that were installed (and are currently being managed) by it. Then, launch the uninstall either from Windows' Add or Remove programs dialog or from the IBM Installation Manager's Uninstall IBM Installation Manager Start menu item.

Workspace Migration

All of your RSE connections, customizations, and projects, such as i5/OS, Web, and Java, are stored in your Workspace. Generally, all IBM Rational products support Workspace migration from the previous two releases.

Sometimes, the Workspace and project file formats, structure, and metadata change between releases. Generally, this affects Java and Web projects more than the RSE, since they have to follow the open standards that define their structure and file formats.

In the best migration case, you just start up the new version of WDSC and Rational Developer for System i, point to the old Workspace, and the Workbench automatically performs any required migration. In the worst case, you might need to perform some manual migration steps.

Always check the migration guide for the release you are installing to understand what manual steps need to be done to migrate a Workspace. Don't be intimidated by the size of the migration guide when you first open it. The guide covers migration steps for all scenarios of all features in WDSC and Rational Developer for System i. In most cases, you will likely only need to read the small subset of the migration guide that applies to your situation.

TIP
Migration is forward only. Once you open a Workspace in a more recent version of a product, you might not be able to open it in a previous version. Make sure you back up your Workspace before opening it in a new version, as some migrations are performed automatically as soon as you open a Workspace in a new version.

Troubleshooting

Many of the chapters in this book include a troubleshooting section that contains common questions and suggested fixes, along with background information to assist in narrowing down the problem. Below are some common problems installing the RSE:

» *I can't get WDSC to install on Windows Vista.*

Only Rational Developer for System i is supported on Windows Vista.

» *I know there are updates available, but Installation Manager can't find any.*

Make sure that your workstation firewall software is not blocking the HTTP connection from Installation Manager to the Internet. You might need to configure a firewall rule to allow this.

Also, make sure you enter the proxy information for your company on the Repositories > HTTP Proxy preference page in Installation Manager, if this is required by your company's network configuration.

Alternatively, you can manually download the update from the product support pages and install it locally. See the "Getting Updates" section of this chapter for additional details.

» *I got a message that Installation Manager needs to be updated.*

This is normal. When you install packages and updates, Installation Manager checks the IBM Web site to see if there are any updates for itself. If there are, it will prompt you to install these updates first, and then proceed with the product or package updates.

3.5 RSE Perspective

CHAPTER 3

Getting Started with the RSE

Are you feeling stuck with antiquated development tools while the modern tools are passing by? Do you want to do something about it, but don't know where to begin? Well, look no further. This chapter is for you. Once you go through the learning process, you will be able to do things that you never dreamt were possible as an SEU/PDM user. You will also be able to appreciate the power of new development tools built on Eclipse technology. Don't get us wrong; SEU and PDM were great, in their era. It is now time to move on, however.

You have just had the joy of installing the product (as explained in chapter 2). All you want now is to prove to your boss that you can learn this development tool quickly, be more productive in no time, and deserve a raise. Great! You are in the right place. The RSE might look a bit complicated to operate, with all its bells and whistles. You are right; it can be complicated at first—unless you have this book! We are here to guide you, provide tips and techniques to get you started, and relate the RSE to what you already know in SEU/PDM.

This chapter walks you through the basic steps to quickly get you started using the RSE. It covers the key features of the RSE, in terms of moving from green-screen programming tools to using modern tools to accomplish your daily tasks. Subsequent chapters dive into details and cover additional features.

The RSE Perspective

When starting Rational Developer for System i, the first thing you will need to provide is the location for your Workspace, as shown in Figure 3–1. The Workspace holds and maintains the information needed by you, the developer. The Workspace is located on your workstation. When you first start, you will see the default location for the Workspace as determined by Rational Developer for System i. Feel free to change this location to anywhere you would like your Workspace to be. (For details on this, refer to chapter 4.)

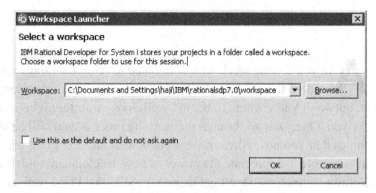

Figure 3–1: Selecting a Workspace location.

Once you specify the location of the Workspace, click **OK**. If this is the first time you are starting Rational Developer for System i, or if you are starting with a new Workspace, you will see the welcome page in Figure 3–2.

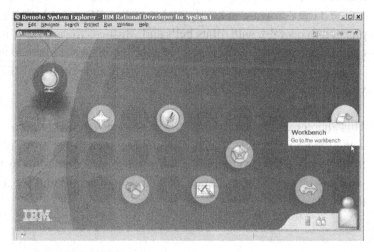

Figure 3–2: The welcome page.

The purpose of this page is to introduce the product. It contains links to an overview of the product and its features, tutorials to guide you through some basic tasks, and samples to get you started. Position your mouse over any of the icons on the page, and you will see some text indicating what will be presented if you click that icon. For example, clicking the "Tutorials" icon ( ) will take you to the tutorials page, where you can learn how to use the key features of the product.

Click the **X** in the tab for the welcome page (shown directly below the Navigate menu in Figure 3–2) to close the page, or click the "Go to the workbench" icon ( ). To reopen the welcome page at any time, select **Help > Welcome** from the Workbench menu.

The Remote System Explorer perspective shown in Figure 3–3, which is the default perspective for WDSC and Rational Developer for System i, will open when the "Go to the workbench" icon is clicked. This is where you use the RPG and COBOL programming tools from inside the Workbench. The RSE perspective is the default perspective when you start the product with a new Workspace.

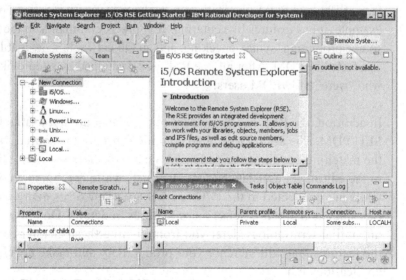

Figure 3–3: The default RSE perspective.

A *perspective* is a collection of views and actions based on the notion of a task-based grouping. For example, a Java programmer will most likely work with the Java perspective to create Java-based applications, while an RPG or COBOL programmer will work with the Remote System Explorer (RSE) perspective. The name of the current perspective displays on the left side of the Workbench window's title bar. The perspective is customizable to one's need. (Chapter 4 covers the details on perspectives and Eclipse technology.)

If the RSE is not your current perspective, you can open it by selecting the **Window > Open Perspective** menu. If the Remote System Explorer perspective does not show in the list to select, click the **Other** menu. If it does not show in that other list either, click **Show all**. Once you have located the Remote System Explorer perspective, double-clicking it will open the perspective.

The RSE perspective is the modern, graphical, workstation-based application development tool for RPG and COBOL programmers. It contains a tightly integrated set of tools that enable RPG and COBOL programmers to perform their daily tasks, and much more. It contains many SEU- and PDM-like features to make the transition easier. For example, it has features like entering SEU prefix commands in the editor, source prompting, syntax checking, and an Object Table view that looks and feels like PDM. After all, the RSE was developed by people like you, who "were" SEU/PDM users!

In addition, the RSE has many cool features that are not available in SEU/PDM. The ability to embed compile errors in the source, find the matching beginning or ending of a code block (such as *If...End*) in the editor, get assistance (content assist) while coding, and code while not connected to the i5/OS server are a few of its many features. Subsequent chapters discuss these features in details. Do not let the unfamiliar terminology deter you from visiting these chapters to learn the features that will increase your productivity and make developing applications fun.

Creating a Connection

To start working in PDM, you would normally start the emulator, sign on, and issue one of the WRKxxxPDM or STRPDM commands. To begin using the RSE, you do similar things in a different way. It might seem unconventional at first, just because you are used to the "green" look. Do not get discouraged by the jazzy words and splashy graphical interface. An object on i5/OS is still an object on i5/OS, regardless of the development tool!

A connection in the RSE represents a remote system. When creating a connection, you specify the TCP/IP hostname and give the connection a meaningful name that appears in the RSE. This is no different from creating a new 5250 emulator session, when you have to specify a hostname to connect to and a filename to save the emulator settings.

Because of its graphical user interface, users often expect the RSE to behave totally differently from a regular 5250 emulator job. When trying to figure out how things work, or what to expect, it is important to remember that the RSE follows standard i5/OS job processing.

For example, before connecting your RSE connection to the remote server, you will need to first authenticate with a valid i5/OS user profile and password. Each RSE connection has its own i5/OS server job. You can configure the library list in that server job from the RSE connection. All commands and compiles submitted from the RSE are run in the server job and follow standard library list processing. Therefore, it really is a familiar environment; it just has a lot of really cool and productive programming tools built on top.

When you first open the RSE perspective, you are not connected to any system except your local workstation. (The RSE can connect to your local workstation, AIX, Linux, and Windows, in addition to your i5/OS server.) This local connection is predefined. To connect to a remote i5/OS server, you need to define an i5/OS connection.

The Remote Systems view in Figure 3–4 is the main view in the RSE perspective. This is where you manage your connections, and work with your libraries, objects, members, and jobs. By default, this view is located on the top left side of the RSE perspective. It works much like Windows

Figure 3–4: The Remote Systems view.

Explorer, where you drill down by clicking the plus sign (+), to list nested items or perform an action.

RSE connections are created using the New Connection wizard. You can open this wizard by expanding the **New Connection > i5/OS** entry or by clicking the "New connection" icon ( ) in the Remote Systems view.

This launches the New Connection wizard, used to configure a connection to your i5/OS server. If this is your first time creating a connection, you will need to provide a profile name, as shown in Figure 3–5, before the new connection dialog appears.

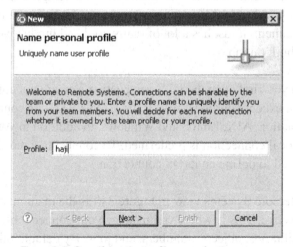

Figure 3–5: Specifying the profile name for the new connection.

Do not confuse this profile name with your i5/OS user profile. It has nothing to do with that profile. The profile name here is just a unique name that identifies you within a group of users who can share RSE configuration information. (Profiles are discussed in details in chapter 10.) The profile will be pre-filled with your local workstation name. Click the **Next** button to define the connection, as shown in Figure 3–6.

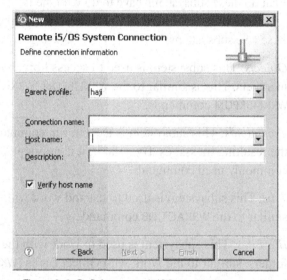

Figure 3–6: Defining a new i5/OS connection.

You need to supply the following:

- *Profile name*: The profile name you entered in the previous page.

- *Connection name*: Any name you want to give your connection. It is useful to give a name that can be associated with your connection. This name will appear for your connection in the Remote Systems view. If you do not specify a name here, it will be filled with the host name specified in the next field.

- *Host name*: The TCP/IP host name or address of your i5/OS server.

- *Description*: This is an optional field. You can put any text here, and it will appear in the Properties view after the connection is created.

- *Verify host name*: This checkbox ensures that you have specified a valid TCP/IP hostname. By default, this is checked, and we recommend that you leave it that way. An error message is issued if the host name you specified cannot be resolved to a TCP/IP address.

Click **Finish** to create a connection to your i5/OS server. Your connections, identified by the connection names you specify, appear in the Remote Systems view.

When you expand your connection, you see entries under it that allow you to access different i5/OS resources. These entries are called *subsystems* in the RSE. What do these subsystems have to do with the i5/OS job subsystems? Nothing, so try not to confuse them. It is time to put on the RSE hat and talk about these five subsystems:

- *Objects*: This subsystem is used to access libraries, objects, and members. This is similar to the WRKLIBPDM, WRKOBJPDM, and WRKMBRPDM commands.

- *Commands*: This subsystem is used to run commands and view the resulting messages. By default, it is pre-populated with a set of commonly used commands.

- *Jobs*: This subsystem is used to list and work with jobs. This is similar to the WRKACTJOB command.

- *IFS Files*: This subsystem is used to work with the IFS files and folders, similar to the Work with Object Links (WKRLNK) command.

- *Qshells*: You can use this subsystem to start a Qshell. This is also used to access active running Qshells for the connection. This is similar to the STRQSH command.

At this point, it is important to mention that having created a connection does not mean you are connected to the i5/OS server. After all, you have not provided a user ID and password to connect to the i5/OS server yet! Maybe you thought you could get away without a user ID and password in RSE? No way. A connection is simply a saved copy of the information needed to access a particular remote host. Therefore, creating a connection is equivalent to defining an emulator session. You can define multiple connections to the same i5/OS server. You can also include different configurations for the startup of your connection, such as saving different user IDs and passwords, initial library lists, and so on.

If this is the first time you are accessing this particular i5/OS server, we recommend you make sure that all the required host servers are started and

all required PTFs for the RSE are applied. You do this from the connection
you just created. Right-click any one of the subsystems, such as the **Objects**
subsystem, and select **Verify Connection**. You will be prompted for your
i5/OS user ID and password, as shown in Figure 3–7.

*Figure 3–7: Prompting for a user ID and
password.*

Click **OK** after entering your user ID and password. At this point, the RSE
checks that all required host servers are started and that all required PTFs
are applied. A Verify Connection dialog, shown in Figure 3–8, is displayed
with the results.

If you have any missing Remote System Explorer or Integrated i5/OS
Debugger PTFs, as shown in Figure 3–8, it would be a good idea to install
them on your i5/OS server before proceeding with using the RSE. Do not
worry at this point if the "Checking server callbacks" section fails. (The
background on this, along with troubleshooting tips and a recommended
workaround, are covered in chapter 8.)

The RSE requires WebSphere Development Studio (5722-WDS
for V5R4 and earlier and 5761-WDS for V6R1) option 60 to be
installed in order to compile in batch and debug applications.
We find this is normally installed on most systems. The Verify
Connection action will tell you if it is not installed.

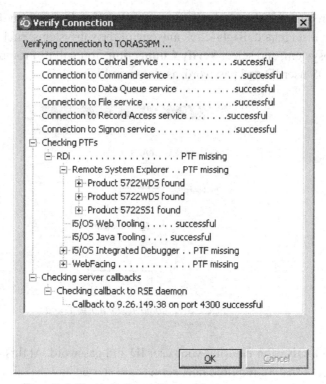

Figure 3–8: The Verify Connection results.

Setting the Library List

First, you want to ensure that the library list for the RSE connection is correct. Expand the **Objects** subsystem, and then expand the **Library List** filter, as in Figure 3–9. This will show the library list currently used by the RSE connection.

The RSE connection is connected to the i5/OS server the first time information from the i5/OS is requested; the library list, in this case.

Where does this library list come from? It is based on the job description associated with the i5/OS user profile that you used to connect. This is the same as what you get when connecting in an emulator session.

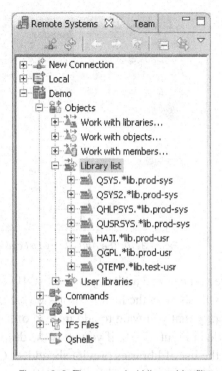

Figure 3–9: The expanded Library List filter.

Of course, you might want to modify this library list, depending on the tasks you want to perform on the system. We will discuss here one of the ways to change the library list for the connection. Chapter 5 covers this in more detail, along with a way to save these library list settings.

To modify the library list, use the actions from the Library List filter's pop-up menu. Right-click the **Library List** filter and you will see two actions: Add Library List Entry and Change Current Library.

If an action ends with ellipses ("..."), clicking it will always prompt for additional information.

Click the **Add Library List** action to open the Add Library List Entry dialog shown in Figure 3–10. This is equivalent to running the ADDLIBLE CL command. You will see the command as it is being modified at the bottom in the dialog.

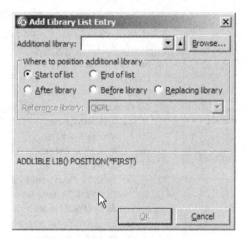

Figure 3–10: The Add Library List dialog.

This is where you can add a library to the list. If you have added libraries before, they will show in the history drop-down combo box. It is easier to select the library that you want to add instead of having to type it again. In the example in Figure 3–10, if you click the drop-down button (▾), you will see the list of libraries previously added. Click **OK** to run the constructed ADDLIBLE command on the i5/OS server.

In the Remote Systems tree view, you can change the order of the libraries within the library list by right-clicking the library you want to reposition. You will see various actions related to the options of moving the library within the library list, as shown in Figure 3–11. You can use these actions to changes the library list for the RSE connection. This is equivalent to using the Edit Library List (EDTLIBL) command in a 5250 session.

Added libraries are not saved when you disconnect from the i5/OS server, so when you reconnect, your added libraries will no longer be there. This is the same as adding libraries in the emulator using ADDLIBLE CL command, then signing off and signing back on. You can customize your RSE connection to always add certain libraries to the library list when it is connected. Chapter 5 covers this in detail.

Figure 3–11: Library list options.

Locating a Member

Once you have established the RSE connection and set up the library list, you want to locate members to edit. If the library in which the member resides is in the library list, you can expand the library, then expand the source physical file and locate the member. However, this is not an efficient way of locating a member, especially if the library contains hundreds of source physical files and the source physical file contains hundreds of members. Of course, RSE has a better and faster way of locating a member. (Do not think of going back to PDM!)

Allow us to introduce the notion of *filters* in the RSE. In PDM, you might have created a subset of member list. The notion of filters in RSE is similar, but more powerful. In this chapter, we will just touch on member filters, to get you started. Chapter 5 covers filters in detail.

Filters are named lists that you can easily access. Filter names are stored with the RSE connection and saved between sessions. To create a filter to locate a member, expand the **Objects** subsystem, and then expand **Work with Members**. This opens the Member Filter dialog in Figure 3–12.

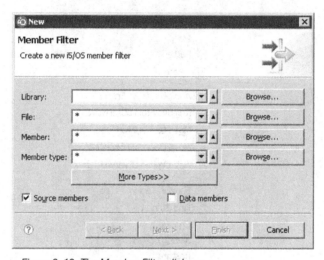

Figure 3–12: The Member Filter dialog.

Enter the library, file, and member names in the dialog. Any of the names can be generic. For example, enter **cus*** as the member name to list all members that begin with cus.

If you enter a generic file name, you have the option of specifying if you want just source members, just data members, or both. By default, the "Source members" checkbox is selected, meaning only source members will be displayed. However, you can select data members as well by clicking the "Data members" checkbox.

Click Next to display the next page of the dialog, shown in Figure 3–13, where you can enter the name of the filter. This name will appear under the subsystem the filter was created from; in this case, it is the Objects subsystem. Check the "Only create filter in this connection" checkbox if you want the filter to display only under your current connection. Otherwise, it displays under all of your connections.

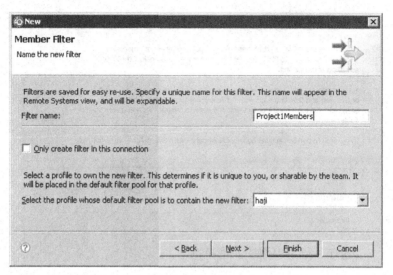

Figure 3–13: Entering a new member filter name.

Click **Finish** to create the filter, which can be expanded to locate the members. This filter is saved and will appear under the Objects subsystem even after you shut down and restart the Workbench.

The Object Table View

If you are not yet comfortable using the Remote Systems view, you are not alone. Many PDM users find the tree view awkward to use at first. Do not worry. The RSE is designed to accommodate all kinds of users, including those who are accustomed to PDM and want a gradual transition to the new application development tools, as well as those who want to dive right away into the new user interface options.

Remember, a perspective is just a collection of editors and views. So far, we have been using the Remote Systems view in the RSE perspective. There is another view, called the Object Table view, in the RSE perspective. The Object Table view allows you to look at artifacts in a table format, much like PDM. This view provides a rapid springboard for PDM users to move to the new tools while having a familiar look and feel. By default, this view, shown in Figure 3–14, is located in a tabbed notebook of views at the bottom right corner of the RSE perspective.

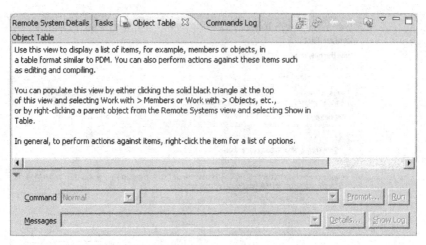

Figure 3–14: The Object Table view.

Members can be populated in the Object Table view in one of two ways:

- Right-click the new member filter you just created in the Remote Systems view and select **Show in Table** from the pop-up menu.

- Open the pull-down menu inside the Object Table view (using the upside-down triangle in the top right corner, ▽) and select **Work With > Members**. This opens the Work With Members dialog, where you can enter the library, file, and member names (including generic names) used to populate the table.

Opening and Editing the Member

You have navigated through the Remote Systems view or the Object Table view and located the member. Now you want to edit it. This is done using the Remote Systems LPEX Editor, the RSE's source editor for RPG, COBOL, C, C++, CL, and DDS.

Opening the Member

To open a member for editing, right-click the member and select **Open with > Remote Systems LPEX Editor.** This checks if you have authority to edit the member, locks the member on the host, and then opens it in the editor. This is equivalent to performing the WRKMBRPDM CL command on the host, and then choosing option 2 on the member you want to edit, or using STRSEU.

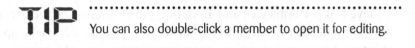

You can also double-click a member to open it for editing.

While you are editing a member, it remains locked on the i5/OS server. The lock is released if any one of the actions is taken:

- The editor is closed.

- The RSE connection is disconnected.

- The Workbench is closed.

To browse a member, right-click it, and select the option **Browse with > Remote Systems LPEX Editor.** This allows you to browse the contents of the source member, but does not allow you to change the contents. This is equivalent to performing WRKMBRPDM CL command on the host, and then choosing option 5 on the member you want to browse.

You can tell whether the member is open in edit or browse mode by looking at the top of the editor. If it is opened in browse mode, it will have the word "Browse" in the status line, as shown in Figure 3–15.

```
 VERIFY.CBLLE    ALIAS2.PRTF    CALLG5A1.CBLLE    EVALCORR.RPGLE  ×
   Line 7        Column 1     Replace              Browse
              ....DName++++++++++ETDsFrom+++To/L+++IDc.Keywords++++++++++++++++++++++++
   000100      H DEBUG(*INPUT)
   000102
   000103      D ds1           ds                     qualified
   000200      D  charfld                     10a
   000300      D  numfld                      5p 0
   000400      D  other                       5p 0
   000500      D ds2           ds                     qualified
   000600      D  numfld                      5p 0 inz(12345)
   000700      D  other                       5a  inz('98765')
   000800      D  charfld                     10a inz('abcdefghij')
   000801      D  extra                       5a  inz('20050')
   000802
   001000      C                     eval-corr ds1 = ds2
   001100      C                     eval      *inlr = '1'
   001101
   001102        /free
   001103         eval-corr ds1 = ds2;
   001104        /end-free
```

Figure 3–15: Determining that the member is opened for display (browsing) only.

By now, you are probably thinking that this was a lot of steps just to get the member open for editing. We agree that it is more steps and will take slightly longer than opening the member in SEU. However, we also believe that performance gains from the editor features and the overall edit, compile, debug integration of the RSE will more than make up for this little bit of extra time required to open the member. Also, we are only covering the most straightforward way of doing things in this chapter. As you progress through the book, you will learn lots of time-saving tips, techniques, and shortcuts.

For example, there is a faster way to open a single member if you know the library, file, and member name. Right-click the **Objects** subsystem, and choose **Open Member.** The Open Member In Editor dialog will open, with the fields pre-filled based on the current selection or the previously used values, as shown in Figure 3–16.

This dialog allows you to select the connection where the member resides or create a new connection. For the library, file, and member, you can simply type the names in their respective fields or select previously used values. You can choose to open the member for editing or browsing by selecting the corresponding radio button.

Figure 3–16: The Open Member In Editor dialog.

You can also invoke the Open Member In Editor dialog by using the shortcut key combination Ctrl+Shift+A. This can be invoked from anywhere within the RSE perspective.

Multiple members can be open at the same time; each one will have its own editor tab in the form of a notebook. You can also open multiple members in one open action. To do this, select all the members you want to open from Remote Systems view or Object Table view, right-click, and choose **Open with > Remote Systems LPEX Editor.**

Editing the Member

We will first describe the editor pane and introduce the terminology used for referring to different parts of the editor, shown in Figure 3–17.

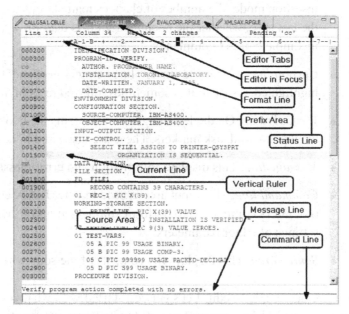

Figure 3–17: The Remote Systems LPEX Editor layout.

For every member that you open using the Remote Systems LPEX Editor, the default layout is the same as in Figure 3–17. You can customize the editor's appearance and function to suit your preferences or project needs. Chapters 6 and 7 cover this in detail.

For now, let's look at what these control and information areas display in the LPEX Editor pane.

- *Editor tabs*: Each open member is represented in the editor area by an editor tab.

- *Active editor or Editor in focus*: The source member you are currently editing. The editor tab is darker in color to distinguish it from other open editors.

- *Format line*: This displays the column positions in the editing area, as well as the current cursor position. This is to help column-sensitive editing.

- *Prefix area*: This displays sequence numbers. This area is used to enter prefix commands, similar to SEU.

- *Status line*: This shows the current line and column location, the insertion mode, the number of changes made to the document since the last save, whether the document view is read-only, and any incomplete prefix commands.

- *Current line*: This is the current line being edited, and it is highlighted. As such, it is sometimes referred to as highlighted line.

- *Vertical ruler*: On the left margin, this contains the bookmark, breakpoint, and task markers. These are discussed in later chapters.

- *Message line*: This displays information and error messages.

- *Command line*: This input area is used to enter LPEX commands (not i5/OS commands) to perform editing actions, or modify the settings of editor parameters.

- *Source area*: This displays the contents of the source member.

You are now ready to edit. Let's get you started with what you already know from SEU. You can perform all the basic editing functions, such as insert, delete, copy, and paste. You can also perform SEU commands in the prefix area. Yes, that is correct! The prefix area, the same old prefix area, which contains the sequence numbers of the member, supports all the same commands as SEU, such as CC, B, A, and LL. Figure 3–18 shows SEU commands entered in this area.

If you enter a statement that contains a syntax error, you will notice that RSE has live syntax checking. A syntax error is inserted below the line containing the error. The lines in the editor containing errors are not part of the source, so they are sometimes referred to as *show lines*.

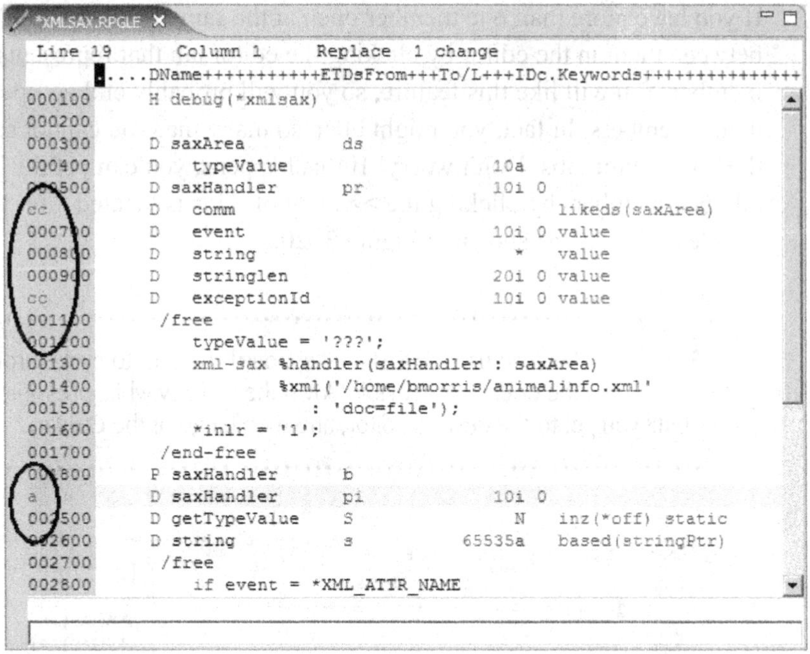

Figure 3–18: Entering SEU commands in the prefix area.

Once the syntax error is fixed, and the line is syntax checked again, the error will be removed from the source. Alternatively, you can remove the error message by going to the Source menu and selecting Remove Messages, as shown in Figure 3–19.

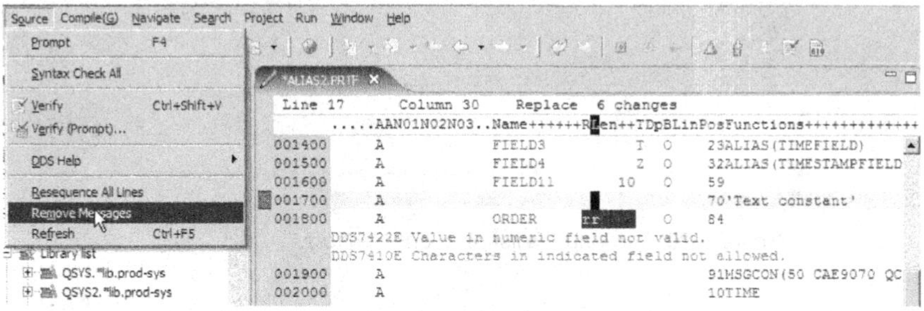

Figure 3–19: Removing the error messages from the source.

Some people find that the live syntax checking drives them crazy! If this sounds like you, you can disable the automatic syntax checking and invoke it manually on either a selected area in the source or the entire source. Chapter 7 explains how to do this in detail, and how to configure your editor preferences.

If you have more than one member open at the same time, you can switch between them in the editor by clicking the editor tab that represents the member. You will like this feature, so you will probably end up opening many members. In fact, you might open so many that you cannot see all the open editor tabs. Don't worry! If this happens, you can get the list of all open members by clicking the >> symbol. This is located after the last visible editor tab, as shown in Figure 3–20.

TIP You can use the Ctrl+F6 keyboard shortcut to cycle through the open editors. Hold down the Ctrl key while pressing F6 until you get to the desired editor, and then let go of the Ctrl key.

```
 CALLG5A1.CBLLE     *XMLSAX.RPGLE      EVALCORR.RPGLE  X    >>
                                                             4
    Line 1        Column 1        Replace
              ....HKeywords++++++++++++++++++++++++++++++
   000100        H DEBUG(*INPUT)                                ALIAS1.PF
   000102                                                       ALIAS2.PRTF
   000103        D ds1            ds              q             COMMDSPF.DSPF
   000200        D  charfld                    10a             VERIFY.CBLLE
   000300        D  numfld                     5p 0            CALLG5A1.CBLLE
   000400        D  other                      5p 0            EVALCORR.RPGLE
   000500        D ds2            ds              q             *XMLSAX.RPGLE
   000600        D  numfld                     5p 0 i
   000700        D  other                       5a   inz('98765')
   000800        D  charfld                    10a   inz('abcdefghij')
   000801        D  extra                       5a   inz('20050')
   000802
   001000        C                    eval-corr ds1 = ds2
   001100        C                    eval      *inlr = '1'
   001101
   001102        /free
   001103          eval-corr ds1 = ds2;
   001104        /end-free
```

Figure 3–20: Showing the list of all open editors.

The number beside the symbol indicates the number of open editors not visible. After you open the list, you can click the source member you want to edit. This will now be the editor in focus. Figure 3–20 shows that four open editors are not visible. These four appear in bold at the top of the list.

TIP
You can tell from the editor tab if you have any unsaved changes for the member. The editor tab adds an asterisk before the source member name. In Figure 3–20, for example, XMLSAX.RPGLE contains unsaved changes.

Language-sensitive help is available by pressing the F1 key anywhere in the editor. This help is context-sensitive. For example, when editing an ILE RPG source member, if you press F1 on the opcode, information about the opcode will be displayed in the Help window, as shown in Figure 3–21.

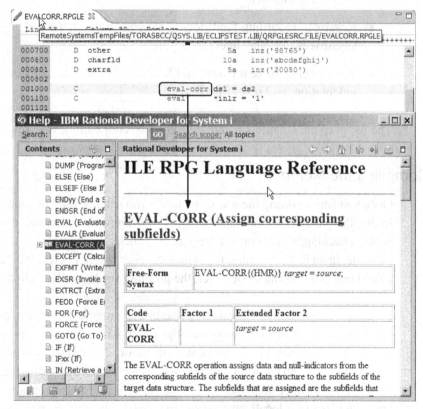

Figure 3–21: Pressing F1 to provide context-sensitive help.

You might find that the size of the editor window is too small, depending on your monitor size. You can maximize the editing window by double-clicking the editor tab that shows the source member. In fact, you can maximize any one of the views by double-clicking the view. To restore the editor or view back to its original size, double-click the tab again.

In addition to basic editing functions, the Remote Systems LPEX Editor offers many additional features that are not available in SEU. These features are designed to speed up and improve your editing experience. Here are just a few of these features:

- The Outline view displays the outline of your program. This helps to navigate within your program.

- Content assist provides assistance while you are entering your code.

- The ability to define bookmarks helps you move quickly from one location to another.

- Keystroke recording facilities enable you to record a set of keystrokes to replay later.

- You can customize the look and feel of the editor, in terms of color, indentation, and text effects.

The list goes on. Chapters 6 and 7 cover these cool editing features.

Compiling the Member

Once you finish editing the source member, you usually want to compile it. In the RSE, there is a functionality called *program verification*. In addition to syntax checking, a program verifier can also check for semantic errors. For example, in an RPG program, the syntax checker will not detect the usage of a field that is not defined. However, the program verifier will report an error.

Program verification is equivalent to compiling a member with the option of not generating a module or program object. The advantage of the program verifier is that it runs locally on your workstation. The remote server is accessed only when external descriptions, like externally described files, are needed for the first time. Once these external descriptions are obtained, they are *cached* (stored) locally and reused in subsequent program verifications.

You might want to run your source through the program verifier before compiling, to ensure that your program is syntactically and semantically correct before submitting it to the host for compilation. This feature can also be used when you are not connected to the host. For more details on program verification, refer to chapter 7.

With graphical menu actions, you do not have the ability to press F4 to prompt the action. Therefore, you will often see places in the RSE where menu actions are duplicated, with one set running the action and the other prompting the action before it is run. This is true of the RSE compile actions, which are grouped into two menus: Compile and Compile (Prompt).

From the RSE, you can invoke the compiler in various ways. From the Remote Systems view or the Object Table view, you can right-click a member, and choose either the Compile or Compile (Prompt) action, as shown in Figure 3–22. Use the Compile (Prompt) menu if you want to prompt the compile command before it runs. Each of these menus cascades to show the standard IBM compile commands associated with the member's source type.

You can use the Work with Compile Commands action to customize the compile commands or add your own. Chapter 8 covers this in detail.

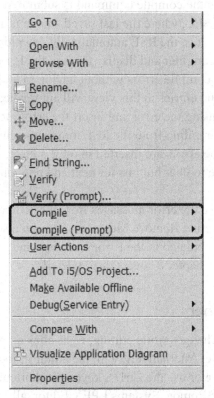

Figure 3–22: The Compile menus from the
Remote Systems or Object Table view.

You do not need to close the source member in order to issue compile commands. You can use one of the following ways to invoke a compile right from within the editor:

- Use the Compile menu in the Workbench menu bar. This contains two cascading menus, Compile and Compile (Prompt). These are the same as the ones available from the Remote Systems and Object Table views.

- Use the Toolbar button (▤). This uses the last compile command for the member type to compile without prompting.

- Use the shortcut key combination, Ctrl+Shift+C. This also uses the last compile command for the member type to compile without prompting.

If you have not saved your source prior to compiling, you will be prompted to do so before the compile command is submitted. This is a different behavior than SEU, where the last saved source is always used. After the compile completes, the RSE automatically downloads a list of all messages issued by the compiler and display them in the Error List view. This allows you to see the compile errors without having to look at the spool file. Double-clicking entries in this view will automatically position the editor on the line causing the error and insert the error messages into the editor. This makes compiling from the RSE more appealing than compiling from PDM. Once the errors are inserted into the source, you can move between them using the toolbar buttons for next and previous errors (▤   ▤).

You can remove the error messages from the source by going to the Source menu and selecting Remove Messages. You can also select which severities of errors are populated in the Error List view and which errors are inserted in the source. Chapter 8 covers this in detail.

Saving the Member

To save your changes while editing, right-click anywhere inside the editor and select **Save**. Alternatively, with the editor in focus, go to the **File** menu and select **Save** or use the Ctrl+S keyboard shortcut. When you save the member in the Remote Systems LPEX Editor, all the changes in the editor are saved to the remote member.

You can also save the member with a different name using the **File >
Save as** action. This opens the dialog in Figure 3–23, from which you can
choose the location and name of the new member. When running the Save
as action, the original member is closed, and a new member is created and
opened in the Remote Systems LPEX Editor. As you can see from Figure
3–23, the member can be saved to another server, as well.

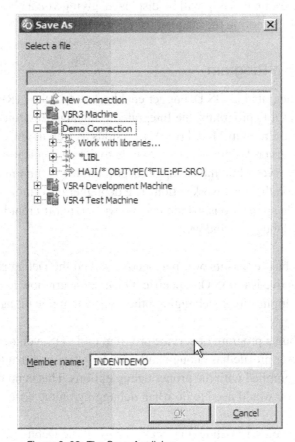

Figure 3–23: The Save As dialog.

TIP ··
        If you have multiple members open, you can save all of
        them with one action. Go to the **File** menu and choose the
Save all option, or use the Ctrl+Shift+S key combination.
··

Once you are done editing or browsing the member, close the member by clicking the **X** on the editor tab. Alternatively, with the editor in focus, go to the **File** menu and choose the **Close** option, or use the Ctrl+F4 keyboard shortcut. You can close all open members in one action by choosing the **Close All** action from the **File** menu or using the key combination Ctrl+Shift+W. If you have any unsaved changes while closing members, a Save Resource dialog will be displayed, giving you a choice of saving your changes, ignoring the changes, or returning to editing.

Debugging a Program

The Integrated i5/OS Debugger enables you to debug (RPG, COBOL, C, and C++) programs, the Integrated Language Environment (ILE) and Original Program Model (OPM) versions as well as Java. The debugger's client/server design makes it possible to debug applications running on the i5/OS server while the debugger user interface is running inside the Workbench on the local workstation. The debugger user interface lets you debug multiple applications, which may be written in different languages, from a single debugger window.

The debugger has its own perspective, called the Debug perspective. This perspective is not i5/OS-specific. Once you learn how to use it to debug i5/OS applications, debugging other types of applications will be a snap.

To debug a program or service program on i5/OS, you need to ensure that your user profile has enough authority to debug and that the object has been compiled with the proper debug options. This is no different from what you would need to do when debugging on the host.

Before you start debugging, make sure that the Debug server is started. In the Remote System Explorer, right-click the **Objects** subsystem and select **Remote Servers > Debug**. If the Start action is grayed out as shown in Figure 3–24, the Debug server is already started on the server. Otherwise, click it to start the Debug server.

There are many ways to launch your application for debugging with the Integrated i5/OS Debugger. One of the easiest ways is to use *service entry points* (*SEPs*). This is the one we will discuss here.

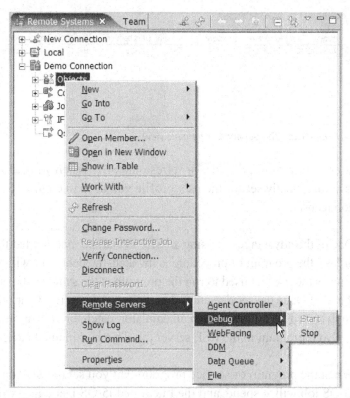

Figure 3–24: Starting and stopping the Debug server.

Let's start by introducing the SEP. A service entry point is a special kind of system-wide breakpoint that can be set directly from the Remote System Explorer. It is triggered when the first line of a specified procedure is executed in a job running under your user profile that is not already under debug. SEPs allow you to start debugging the job from that point. A new debug session gets started, and execution is stopped at that location.

You can set SEPs from the Remote Systems view or from the Object Table view. Select the program or service program that you want to debug. You can view modules and procedures by expanding the program and service program objects in the Remote Systems view. To see the modules and procedures in the Object Table view, right-click the program or service program, and select **Show in Table**. Once you have located the object to debug, right-click it and select **Debug (Service Entry) > Set Service Entry Point**. This sets the SEP and adds it to the i5/OS Service Entry Points view, shown in Figure 3–25. You can use this view

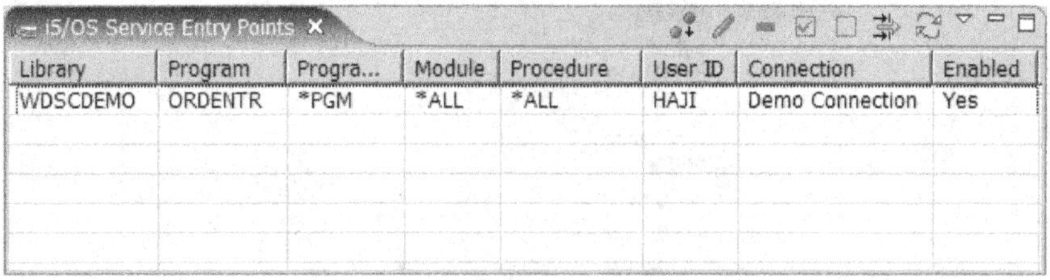

Figure 3–25: The Service Entry Points view.

later on to remove, disable, or refresh the SEP. When you set an SEP, it is automatically set for the user profile you used to connect to the RSE connection.

One of the advantages of using an SEP is that, no matter what the type of job or how the program or procedure is invoked, the debugger will get control as long as the user ID used to run the program is the same as the one used to set the SEP. Once the service entry point is set, you can run your program from anywhere. This could be from an emulator, batch, or Web application. Do not run your program in the RSE server job. This is explained later, in chapter 9.

When the program or service program that you set the SEP on is called, the i5/OS job will suspend, and the Integrated i5/OS Debugger will get control and attach to the job. At this point, the Debug perspective will open. The RSE perspective stays active while you are in the Debug perspective. All open perspectives appear in the top right corner of the Workbench. You can click the >> symbol to see the complete list of open perspectives. Clicking any one of them will switch to that perspective. Alternatively, you can use the Ctrl+F8 key combination to toggle between open perspectives.

Now that the Debug perspective is active, and the job is suspended at the SEP, you can start debugging the source. You will see the Debug view at the top left corner. It shows all of your active debug jobs and the current call stack for each of the jobs that is currently suspended. If the Debug view is not displayed as the top view, click the **Debug** tab.

The source view or listing view for the current call stack entry appears in the editor section of the Debug perspective, with the current line highlighted. In the case of SEPs, the current line is the first line of the source. To toggle between the source and listing views for your program, right-click in the debug editor and select **Switch View.**

You can now perform the debugging tasks. Under the Run Workbench menu item, you can find actions for controlling how the debugger steps through the execution of your program. These items also appear as toolbar icons in the Debug view. For example, to step over the current line, select **Run > Step Over**, or click the "step over" icon (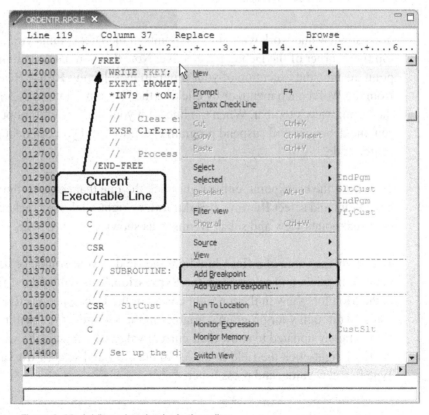) in the Debug view's toolbar. If you have a procedure or program call in your code, you can also try the Step Into action, by selecting **Run > Step Into**, or click the "step into" icon ( ) in the Debug view's toolbar.

To set a breakpoint, right-click the executable line and select **Add Breakpoint,** as shown in Figure 3–26. A line in the source that has a breakpoint set on it will have a blue dot in the vertical ruler area. In addition, if the breakpoint is active, there will also be a checkmark beside the blue dot, as shown in Figure 3–27. A breakpoint will be active if it is set while the debugger is running.

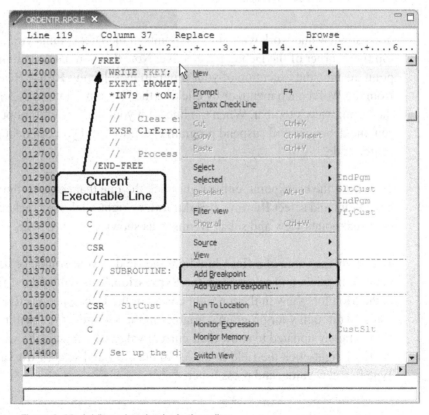

Figure 3–26: Adding a breakpoint in the editor.

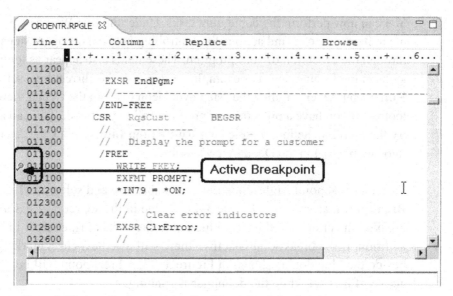

Figure 3–27: An active breakpoint, with a blue dot and checkmark.

You can view and work with all breakpoints in the Breakpoints view, in the top right corner of the Debug perspective. Now that you have set a break-point, resume the execution of your program by selecting **Run > Resume** from the Workbench menu, or by clicking the "Resume" button (▶) in the Debug view's toolbar. When the line with your breakpoint is about to run, the debugger will suspend program execution, and you can debug the source code.

To remove the breakpoint, either right-click the line that contains the breakpoint and select **Remove Breakpoint**, or right-click the breakpoint in the Breakpoints view and select **Remove**, as shown in Figure 3–28.

To display the value of a field, highlight the field in your source or listing view, right-click, and select **Monitor Expression**. This will add the field to the Monitors view in the top right corner of the Debug perspective. As you step through your program, variables in the Monitors view will be automatically updated to show their current values. To change the value of the field, right-click the field in the Monitors view and select **Edit value**. Type in a new value, and press Enter.

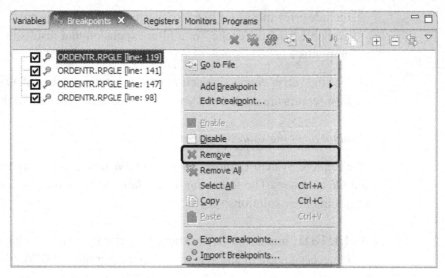

Figure 3–28: Removing a breakpoint using the Breakpoints view.

If you recompile the source, you will need to refresh the SEP. You do this from the Service Entry view. Right-click the SEP and choose **Refresh**, as shown in Figure 3–29.

When you have completed debugging and fixed the problems (bugs), it is important to remove all the SEPs. While you have set a service entry on an object, no one else can set a service entry point on the same object.

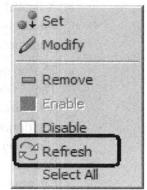

Chapter 9 covers other ways of debugging i5/OS objects. It also covers details on the Debug perspective and its views.

Figure 3–29: Refreshing an SEP after recompiling the source.

Troubleshooting

Finally, here are some common problems you might encounter while getting started with the RSE, together with their likely causes and solutions:

- *The connection will not connect.*

  » Right-click the connection and ensure the Work Offline action is unchecked. Other symptoms that Work Offline is checked

include error messages like "Requested information is not
available from the cache," or a filter expansion that results in
empty list.

» Use the verify connection action to test that the required i5/OS
host servers are started and your workstation can connect to them.

- *I cannot open the source member in the editor.*

The Remote System Explorer uses the DDM server to read and write
remote members. The following list explains some of the possible
cause and their solutions:

» The DDM host server is not started. Start it by right-clicking the
Objects subsystem and selecting Remote Servers > DDM > Start.

» The i5/OS user profile is not authorized to use the DDM host
server. Contact the system administrator to obtain authorization.

» An exit program associated with the DDM host server is
blocking read and write requests.

» A firewall is blocking the TCP/IP connection from your
workstation to port 446 on the i5/OS server. You need to
configure a firewall rule to allow this communication.

» The job description specified in your user profile does not exist.
The i5/OS Remote Command host server allows you to connect
with a user profile that is associated with a nonexistent job
description. However, the TCP/IP DDM host server does not
allow you to connect without a valid job description. Hence, the
RSE can "connect" without a valid job description, where you
can resolve filters and run commands but cannot edit. To resolve
this, create the job description associated with your user profile or
update your user profile to use an existent job description.

» You cannot edit members from QTEMP. The reason is RSE runs
commands in the Remote Command server job, but read/write is
done through a DDM server job. So, you have two jobs with two
different QTEMP libraries.

- *When I click the Source or Compile menu, the actions pertaining to the source member are grayed-out (disabled), as in Figure 3–30.*

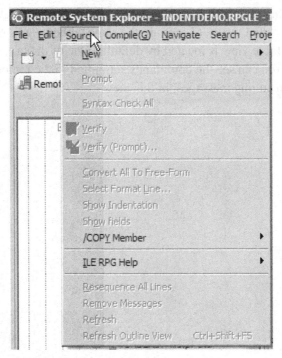

Figure 3–30: Grayed-out options.

Ensure that the source member for which you want the actions is in focus. When you move away from the editor to another view, you need to bring the focus back on the editor by clicking the editor pane. You can tell that the editor is in focus by the color of the editor tab, as discussed earlier in this chapter and shown in Figure 3–17.

- *When I compiled my program, it completed successfully with no errors. I had the library where the *pgm object was to be created already expanded in RSE Tree view and I do not see this program.*

You need to refresh the contents of the library, which are not always automatically refreshed, for performance reasons. To do this, right-click the library and choose **Refresh**, or click the library to give it focus and press the F5 shortcut key.

- *When submitting commands from the RSE, where can I see what was submitted and the results of the execution?*

  In the default RSE perspective, on the bottom right side, there are tabbed views. (These are the same tabbed views where the Object Table view is located by default.) One of the tabs is Command Log. You can see the commands submitted to the remote server, and the resulting messages, in this view.

4

Workbench Basics

In any Eclipse-based application development tool like WDSC or Rational Developer for System i, you will come across common terminology, such as *Workbench*, *Workspace*, *perspective*, *view*, and *active editor*. You need to be familiar with the common concepts, user interface, and terminology of Eclipse, so that you can navigate with ease in the Remote System Explorer, Integrated i5/OS Debugger, and other Eclipse-based tools you might use in the future.

This chapter covers the building blocks necessary to understand any Eclipse-based tool. When you are finished with this chapter, you will have a strong base from which to explore further.

If you are a PDM/SEU user, this chapter will introduce you to a richer, powerful, more robust, and integrated application development environment. If you're an experienced RSE user, this chapter will help raise your awareness of some common behaviors across views and tools, and show you ways to customize your Workbench.

The Workbench

Let's begin with the term *Workbench*. This refers to the overall graphical user interface and tools that make up the development environment. Each Workbench window contains one or more *perspectives*. Perspectives contain views and *editors*, and control what appears in menus and toolbars.

The Workbench toolbar is displayed at the top of the Workbench window, directly underneath the menu bar, as shown in Figure 4–1. The toolbar's contents change based on the editor currently being used, also known as the *active* editor. Actions in the toolbar may apply to a particular editor, so these actions may be enabled or disabled based on the state of the currently active view or editor.

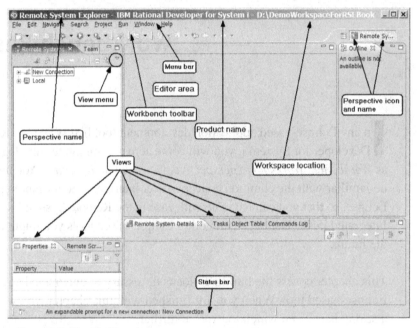

Figure 4–1: The Workbench.

More than one Workbench window can be open on the desktop at any given time.

Perspectives

A perspective defines the initial set and layout of views shown in the Workbench window, along with the menu actions that are available. Each perspective is designed to perform a particular set of tasks, and is identified by a name and an icon. For example, when you open the Remote System Explorer perspective, you will find tools to connect to i5/OS servers and edit and compile source members on those servers. However, if you want to debug a program, you switch to the Debug perspective.

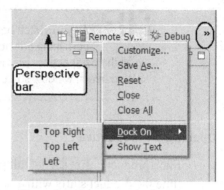

Figure 4–2: The perspective bar.

The name of the current perspective is shown in the title bar for the Workbench window. You can have many perspectives open at the same time in a single Workbench window. Often, you will be switching between perspectives depending on the tasks you are performing. The perspective bar, shown in Figure 4–2, lists the current open perspectives, allowing quick access to open ones. Click on a perspective's name and icon to switch to that open perspective.

TIP The Workbench provides a shortcut key for switching between open perspectives. Press Ctrl+F8 once to switch back to the last opened perspective. Alternatively, hold down the Ctrl key while pressing and releasing F8 to open a dialog that shows a list of open perspectives. Continue pressing F8 while holding down the Ctrl key until the open perspective you want is selected. Then, release the Ctrl key. This same behavior works for views using Ctrl+F7, and for editors using Ctrl+F6.

The perspective bar may be docked in three different positions: the upper right corner (the default position), the upper left corner (under the main toolbar), and to the far left. Right-clicking the perspective bar shows you the operations available for the perspective. Click the double arrow in the perspective bar to list additional open perspectives.

To change the size of the perspective bar, position the mouse on the edge of the perspective bar (the mouse pointer changes to a two-sided arrow), click the left mouse, hold, and then drag the perspective bar. Release the mouse when the desired size is achieved. Once you are familiar with the icons for each perspective, you will likely want to deselect the Show Text option so more open perspectives can be shown in the perspective bar.

TIP   As you switch between perspectives, you will see views
       pertaining only to that perspective, but all the editors open
in all the perspectives are visible. This is because all perspectives within
a Workbench window share the same editor pane.

Opening a Perspective

Each product defines a default perspective, which is opened the first
time the product starts with a new Workspace. For WDSC and Rational
Developer for System i, the default perspective is the Remote System
Explorer perspective. This perspective is opened the first time you start
the Workbench.

To open a new perspective, click the "open perspective" icon (▤) in
the perspective toolbar, or select **Window > Open Perspective** from the
menu bar. This shows a list of perspectives that are closely related to
the current one. Click **Other** if you do not see the perspective you want
in this list. This opens a dialog with a list of all perspectives from all
enabled capabilities. If you still do not see the one you want, select the
Show all checkbox to include perspectives from disabled capabilities.
(You'll learn more about capabilities later in this chapter.)

Once you select a perspective to open, the title bar of the Workbench
window changes to display the perspective name. An icon and the name
are also added to the perspective bar, allowing you to quickly switch back
to the perspective from other perspectives in the same window.

By default, new perspectives open in the same Workbench window.
There is a preference to change this behavior so perspectives open in a
new Workbench window. Workbench preferences are discussed later in
this chapter.

Customizing the Perspective Layout

Perspectives can be customized to suit the needs of you, your project, and
your screen size. Depending on the size of your screen, you might not want
to see all the views at once. Views can be added, deleted, and moved within
a perspective. (This is covered in the next section.)

When you get to the point where the layout of your perspective is a work of art, be sure to save it for future use. You can either save the changes to the current perspective or create a new perspective. (We recommend the second option.) To save the perspective, select **Window > Save Perspective As** from the Workbench menu. This opens a dialog box where you can enter a new name for the perspective or select an existing perspective that you want to overwrite. If you create a new perspective, it will be included in the list of Workbench perspectives.

If your perspective doesn't turn out to be such a work of art after all, reset it back to the original layout by selecting **Window > Reset perspective**. To reset modified perspectives that were installed as part of the Workbench, use the **General > Perspectives** preference page. Select the perspective from the list, and click **Reset**. Perspectives can also be deleted from this preference page.

The idea behind customizing a perspective is that you can choose the views that pertain to your development environment. It is a good idea to customize the perspective so your Workbench is not cluttered up with views you don't use. Try it; you have nothing to lose. If you delete or add something you don't want, you can always go back to the original layout and start again.

TIP   Some users create their own custom *editing* perspectives that have no views open, or all views set up as fast views (more on this later). Since there are no views, any open editors automatically expand to take up the whole Workbench window. Then, the Remote System Explorer perspective can be used to open members, and the custom editing perspective can be used for editing source members.

Views

Views and editors are the main visual components that make up the Workbench. In any given perspective, there is a single editor area, which can contain multiple editors, and a number of surrounding views. Views are usually used to navigate a hierarchy of resources and to display information about the resources. Views can provide actions to work with the resources, such as opening an editor or searching. Some views are read-only, while others allow modifications to the resources.

A view might appear by itself or with other views in a group. A view group shows multiple views in a section of the Workbench using a tabbed notebook, with each view represented as a tab. To activate a view that is part of a tabbed notebook, simply click its tab.

Some features are common to both views and editors, sometimes referred to as *parts*. Only a single part can be active at any time. The active part is the one whose title bar is highlighted. It is the target for common operations like cut, copy, and paste. Pressing Ctrl+C to copy and Ctrl+V to paste have very different results, depending on whether, say, an editor or the Remote Systems view is active.

The active part also determines what information is displayed in the Workbench status bar (Figure 4–1), which is located at the bottom left corner of the perspective. If an editor tab is not highlighted, the editor is not active; however, views related to editing (the outline view, for example) may still show information based on the last active editor.

Each view has its own title bar that contains the view's name, its icon, and optionally a toolbar. Views do not use the Workbench toolbar; this is reserved exclusively for editors. Each view can have its own toolbar containing actions that apply only to that particular view.

Right-click a view's tab to display a menu that contains actions to control the size and location of the view, as shown in Figure 4–3. This is referred to as the view's System menu. Some of the items on the System menu are familiar Windows actions, like move, size, minimize, and maximize. Others, like Fast View and Detached, are specific to the Workbench and will be covered shortly. You can also access this menu using the key combination Alt+- (the minus key).

Many views also contain a pull-down menu, which is accessed by clicking the upside-down arrow (▽) in the view's toolbar. This pull-down menu, also referred to as the view's menu, typically contains operations that apply to the entire contents of the view, as opposed to individual items shown in the view. Operations for sorting and filtering are normally found in the view's menu. This menu can also be accessed through the key combination Ctrl+F10.

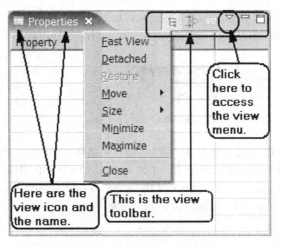

Figure 4–3: The Properties view with its System menu open.

You can maximize a view or editor so that it fills the entire Workbench window. Right-click the title bar and select **Maximize** from the view's System menu. To restore the view or editor to its previous position and size, open the menu again and select **Restore**.

TIP   You can maximize or restore a view or editor by double-clicking its title bar or using the Ctrl+M keyboard shortcut. This keyboard shortcut does not work for the Remote Systems LPEX Editor, however, because the editor assigns a different action to this key combination. Later in this chapter, you will learn how to assign different key combinations to the maximize and restore actions for the Remote Systems LPEX Editor.

Adding and Removing Views

Perspectives predefine the combination and location of views they initially show. To open additional views, select **Window > Show View** from the main menu bar. The current perspective determines which views may be of interest and displays these on the Show View submenu. For additional views, select **Other** from the Show View submenu. Selecting one of the views will add it to a default location in the current perspective. You can then move the view to any location you want.

Click the **X** in the view's tab, next to the view's name, to close the view
from the current perspective, as shown in Figure 4–4.

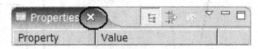

Figure 4–4: Closing the view.

Normally, only one instance of a view exists within a Workbench window.
That view instance may be open in multiple perspectives at the same time.
So, changing the contents of the view in one perspective will be reflected
in all perspectives that have the view open.

Resizing and Moving Views

You can resize editors and views by dragging the sashes that separate them.
When you position the cursor on a sash, a double-headed arrow appears, as
shown in Figure 4–5. Drag this arrow by holding the left mouse button and
release the mouse button once the part reaches the desired size.

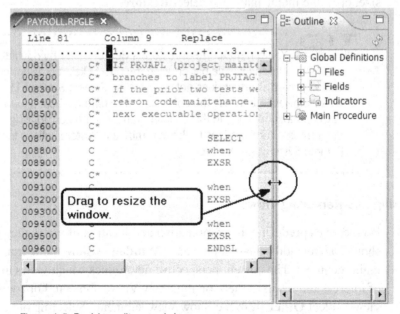

Figure 4–5: Resizing editors and views.

The layout of the Workbench can be rearranged by dragging views to
different positions within the Workbench window. To change the location

of a view in the current perspective, drag the view by its title bar by holding down the left mouse button. As you move the view around the Workbench, the mouse pointer will change to one of the *drop cursors* shown in Table 4–1. Drop cursors indicate where a view will dock when you release your mouse button. This indication is relative to the part currently underneath the mouse pointer. Release the left button once the view is in the location you want.

TIP

A group of stacked views can be dragged using the empty space to the right of the view tabs.

You can also drag a view outside of the Workbench to turn into a *detached* view. Alternatively, detach a view by right-clicking the view tab and selecting **Detached**. To re-attach the view to the Workbench, right-click the view and select **Detached** again.

Detached views can be handy if you are lucky enough to have two monitors connected to your workstation. You can display the main Workbench window on one monitor and some key detached views on the other.

Another advantage to detached views is they stay on top of editors that are maximized. So, you can maximize the editor and have the Outline view or Source Prompter floating on top. (Actually, for source prompting, it is likely easier to create a custom perspective that only shows the Source Prompter view at the bottom of the perspective and leaves the rest of the area for the editors.)

Table 4 1: Drop Cursors		
Cursor	**Name**	**Description**
↑	Dock above	The part will appear above the part underneath the cursor.
↓	Dock below	The part will appear below the part underneath the cursor.
→	Dock to the right	The part will appear to the right of the part underneath the cursor.
←	Dock to the left	The part will appear to the left of the part underneath the cursor.
⧉	Stack	The part will appear as a tab in the same pane as the part underneath the cursor.
⊘	Restricted	You cannot dock the view in this area.

Fast Views

Fast views are views that are hidden, but can quickly be made visible to work with the view and then hidden again. They work like other views, except they do not take up space in the Workbench window.

A fast view is handy when you want to use the view occasionally, but do not want it to take up space or clutter up the Workbench. Fast views are also handy because they can be shown when an editor is maximized, without having to restore the editor. This makes the Outline view an ideal candidate for use as a fast view.

Fast views are docked on the fast view bar, which is the horizontal toolbar initially at the bottom left of the Workbench window. Views in fast view mode are shown as icons on the fast view toolbar. You can make a view a fast view in one of three ways:

- Drag the open view to the fast view toolbar.

- Right-click the view's tab, and select the **Fast View** option.

- Click the "Fast view" icon (🗔) located on the left side of the fast view bar. This pops up a list of views, as shown in Figure 4–6. Select a view from the list to add it to the fast view bar.

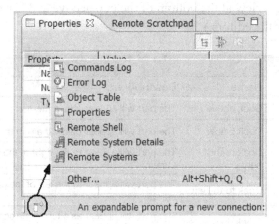

Figure 4–6: Creating fast views.

In Figure 4–6, at the bottom of the list of views, you see **Other** assigned to the key combination Alt+Shift+Q, Q. Let us explain this here, and then we will come back to fast views. Eclipse supports key bindings that contain more than one keystroke, and this is an example of it. Therefore, to see the list of other views, you need to press Alt+Shift+Q together, let go, and then press Q.

It's difficult to memorize these shortcuts, especially if you do not use them often. To help, when you press Alt+Shift+Q, a pop-up appears showing the possible completions for this key combination, as shown in Figure 4–7. Choose the one you want from the list using the mouse, or type the next letter (in this case Q), to complete the action.

Breakpoints	Alt+Shift+Q, B
Cheat Sheets	Alt+Shift+Q, H
Console	Alt+Shift+Q, C
Java Declaration	Alt+Shift+Q, D
Java Package Explorer	Alt+Shift+Q, P
Java Type Hierarchy	Alt+Shift+Q, T
Javadoc	Alt+Shift+Q, J
Search	Alt+Shift+Q, S
Show View	Alt+Shift+Q, Q
Show View (View: Outline)	Alt+Shift+Q, O
Show View (View: Problems)	Alt+Shift+Q, X
Synchronize	Alt+Shift+Q, Y
Variables	Alt+Shift+Q, V

Figure 4–7: Key bindings with more than one keystroke.

Back to fast views. Figure 4–8 shows an example of the fast view bar with four views docked as fast views. Clicking the icon for a view in the fast view bar temporarily opens the view in the current perspective. Clicking outside the view causes the view to be hidden again.

Figure 4–8: The fast view bar with icons.

By default, the fast view bar is docked on the bottom left corner of the Workbench. However, you can choose to dock it on the top, left, or right of the Workbench. Position the mouse on the small vertical line immediately before the fast view icon. (This line may be solid or dotted.) The mouse cursor will change to a four-sided arrow, as shown in Figure 4–9. Hold

down the left mouse button, drag the four-sided arrow to where you want
to dock the fast view bar, and then release the mouse button. Alternatively,
you can right-click the small vertical line and select one of docking
positions from the pop-up menu shown in Figure 4–10.

*Figure 4–9: Dragging the four-sided
pointer to reposition the fast view bar.*

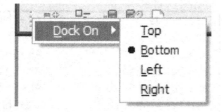

*Figure 4–10: The fast view bar's docking
options.*

Depending on where the fast view bar is docked, the views will be opened
in different locations in the Workbench. You might want to experiment
with this, so you have the views opening where they suit you best. The
orientation of each fast view can be set to either horizontal or vertical by
right-clicking the view's icon and selecting one of the options from the
Orientation submenu. Some views, like the Remote Systems view, are
more usable with a vertical orientation, while others, like the Object Table
and Source Prompter, are better with a horizontal orientation.

Editors

The Workbench contains many different types of editors; each specialized
for a specific resource type. Rational Developer for System i has over 50
editors registered. WDSC has more than that. For the most part, you will
only be using the Remote Systems LPEX Editor for editing RPG, COBOL,
CL, and DDS source. If you are using WDSC AE or Rational Developer
for System i, you might also be using the Screen Designer for editing DDS
display file source, as well as the Application Diagram editor.

Each perspective typically reserves an area where editors appear. This area
appears with a grey background when no editors are open. Open editors are

shared by all perspectives inside the Workbench. If you open an editor in one perspective, then switch to a different perspective, the editor will still be visible.

Multiple instances of an editor type can be open within a Workbench window. This could be from either editing multiple files (members), editing the same file multiple times, or a combination of both. Multiple editors show up as tabs in the editor area, as shown in Figure 4–11.

If all the open editor tabs are not visible, you can get the full list by clicking the » symbol or using Ctrl+E key combination. Select the file you want to make active using the Up and Down arrow keys, and press Enter.

TIP

To close a file, you can right-click it in the list of open files and select **Close**.

You will come across the terms "dirty editor" and "clean editor" when working with editors. There is nothing dirty about it! A dirty editor is just an editor that contains unsaved changes. This is visually represented in the editor tab by an asterisk (*) before the name of the file, as shown in Figure 4–11. A clean editor has no unsaved changes.

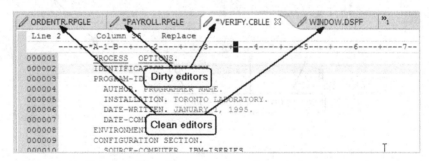

Figure 4–11: Clean and dirty editors.

You will also come across the terms "editor in focus" or "active editor." (We used these terms earlier, as well.) They both mean the same thing. As described earlier during the discussion of views, the active part (editor or view) is the one currently being used. The title bar of the active part is highlighted.

Some Workbench views, such as the Navigator and Remote Systems views, can be linked to the active editor. This means that closing or switching editors changes the selection in the view to match the file open in the active editor. You can use the "Link With Editor" icon ( ) found in the view's toolbar to toggle the view to automatically select the current file being edited.

Tiling Editors

Open files can be grouped into sets of editors. Each editor set can contain one or more open files. The Workbench allows more than one editor set in the editor area at a time by tiling the sets, as shown in Figure 4–12. This allows you to see the contents of two or more editors at the same time. It is often referred to as "split-screen editing." (Split-screen editing of a single member is covered in chapter 6.)

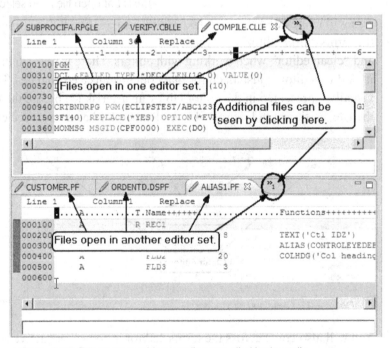

Figure 4–12: Editors open with two editor sets tiled horizontally.

Tiling editors is accomplished the same way as moving views. Drag an editor by clicking its editor tab and holding down the left mouse button. Move the mouse to the left, right, top, or bottom of the editor area, and release the left button when the mouse changes to a black arrow. The editor will be dropped into a new editor set in the designated area.

To tile editors vertically, drag and drop to the left or right of the editor area. To tile horizontally, drag and drop to the top or bottom. You are not limited to tiling only vertically or horizontally. You can mix and match until you run out of screen space!

The list of open editors only shows the list in that particular editor set. For example, pressing the double arrow (or using Ctrl+E) in the first editor set in Figure 4–12 will show only the open editors in that editor set. Pressing Ctrl+E in the second editor set will show only the open editors in that editor set, as shown in Figure 4–13.

Can you get the list of all open editors in all editor sets? Yes, you can, by using the Switch to Editor dialog. This can be invoked using the key combination Ctrl+ Shift+E. Figure 4–14 shows the Switch to Editor dialog for the example in Figure 4–13.

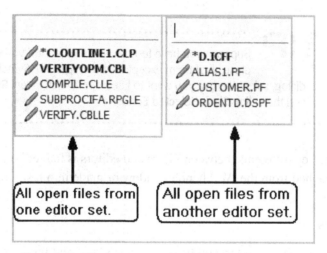

Figure 4–13: The open files in one editor set.

The Switch to Editor dialog displays all open editors, allowing you to choose the ones you want to close, save, or activate. Notice that we said *all* open editors, meaning that you can actually list not only editors from all editor sets within one Workbench window, but editors open from all open windows (from the same Workspace). To obtain this list, check the box **Show editors from all windows**.

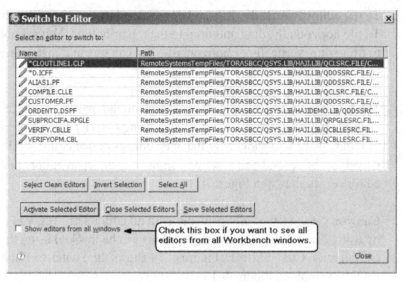

Figure 4–14: All open editors.

TIP

Suppose you have ten members open, and you want to close all of them except for two. Open the **Switch to Editor** dialog, select the two you want to keep open, click **Invert Selection**, and then click **Close Selected Editors**.

One key difference between views and editors is that editors cannot be detached from the Workbench window or made into fast views.

Toolbars

In this chapter so far, you have seen many different toolbars in the Workbench. Let's summarize them here and put them together to see the big picture. There are four main toolbars in the Workbench:

- *Workbench toolbar*: This displays at the top of the Workbench window, directly beneath the menu bar. The contents of this toolbar change based on the current perspective and active editor. Items in this toolbar may be enabled or disabled based on the state of either the active view or editor. You can rearrange the sections of the main toolbar.

- *Perspective toolbar*: This allows quick access to open perspectives and has a button to open new perspectives.

- *View toolbars*: These are individual toolbars that appear in the title bar of a view. Actions in a view's toolbar apply only to the view in which they appear. Some view toolbars include a view menu that contains additional actions for the view. The view menu can be accessed by clicking the upside-down triangle.

- *Fast view bar*: This contains icons representing the current set of fast views.

You can rearrange the items in the perspective and fast view bars by dragging and dropping them. The Workbench toolbar is broken down into sections that can be rearranged using the mouse, but the individual items within a section cannot be rearranged. A vertical line divides the toolbar sections. (Depending on the operating system settings, this line may be dotted or solid.)

You can lock the main toolbar to prevent accidental changes to it. When the vertical line dividing the sections is visible, as in Figure 4–15, the toolbar is unlocked. Otherwise, the toolbar is locked, as shown in Figure 4–16. To lock and unlock a toolbar, right-click anywhere in it and select the **Lock the Toolbars** menu item.

Figure 4–15: An unlocked toolbar.

Figure 4–16: A locked toolbar.

Eek, It's a Mouse

We have come to learn that SEU and PDM users don't like mice. At first glance, you might think the only way to navigate through this seemingly overwhelming Workbench is by using the mouse. However, you can maneuver just as easily around the Workbench using the keyboard. It jus takes a bit longer to memorize all the keyboard shortcuts.

Table 4–2 contains some helpful keyboard shortcuts for navigating around the Workbench, from views, to editors, to menus, and to other perspectives.

Table 4–2: General Workbench Keyboard Shortcuts	
Keystroke(s)	**Action**
F10	Access the menus on the Workbench menu bar. (In Microsoft Windows, Alt does the same thing.) You can traverse actions along the menu bar using the Left and Right arrow keys. Use the Up and Down arrow keys to traverse through the menu actions.
Alt+mnemonic	Instead of using F10 and then traversing, you can use this to easily activate the Workbench menu for a particular entry. For example, Alt+W opens the Window menu.
Shift+F10	Pop up the context menu for the current view, editor, or selected item. This is the same as right-clicking.
Ctrl+F10	Open the pull-down menu for the current view, if there is one. For editors, it will open the menu for vertical ruler (also known as the marker bar) on the left of the editor area.
Ctrl+F6	Cycle between open editors.
Ctrl+F7	Cycle between open views.
Ctrl+F8	Cycle between open perspectives.
Ctrl+E	Activate the editor drop-down.
Ctrl+Shift+E	Open the Switch to Editor dialog.
Esc	Use this key to close a menu. This is the same as clicking the Cancel button on a dialog.
Keyboard arrow keys	Use the arrow keys to navigate through list and tree views in the Workbench. For example, you can navigate through the entire Remote Systems view using just the arrow keys. Use the Up and Down arrow keys to navigate through items that are already showing. Using the Left and Right arrow keys to collapse and expand entries, respectively.
Position by typing	If you are in a table or tree view, and you start typing, the view attempts to position to an entry in the view that matches what you are typing. For example, if you are in the Remote Systems view and you just expanded your library, you can quickly jump to the QRPGLESRC source file by just entering QRPGLESRC. (Chances are, you will only have to enter part of the name.)

TIP

Many of the shortcuts listed in Table 4–2 are standard Windows behavior and will also work in your favorite word processor, spreadsheet, Web browser, or email program.

A mnemonic is a single letter assigned to most control labels (such as buttons, checkboxes, and menus) to assist in choosing an action or a selection. A mnemonic is shown as the underlined character in the action name or label associated with the control. To select the control using its mnemonic, press the Alt key along with the mnemonic letter.

TIP   While working in your favorite editor or view, press **Ctrl+Shift+L** to see a full list of the currently available keyboard shortcuts. The list of keyboard shortcuts is context-sensitive, so it only displays the shortcuts that apply in the current perspective, editor, or view. This is a great way to learn what is available in the user interface and to speed up your productivity by learning keyboard shortcuts. Unfortunately, the Remote Systems LPEX Editor's keyboard shortcuts do not show up in this list. Chapters 6 and 7 describe the various keyboard shortcuts that can be used with the Remote Systems LPEX Editor.

Exiting the Workbench

Each time you exit the Workbench, its state is automatically saved. This state includes all open perspectives, windows, and views, as well as the content and current expansion of some views (like the Remote Systems view). This state is restored the next time the Workbench is reopened, so it appears exactly as it was when it was closed.

To exit the Workbench, select **File > Exit** from the menu bar, click the **X** in the Workbench window's title bar, or press **Alt+F4**. The latter two options prompt if you really wish to exit the Workbench. This dialog includes an option to turn off the prompting. This is the default behavior and can be customized on the General > Startup and Shutdown preference page.

There is a subtle difference between the methods of exiting the Workbench. The File > Exit action closes all Workbench windows, and exits. If you just want to exit the current window (if you are using multiple Workbench windows), use the close button (the X) or Alt+F4. The last Workbench window to close also terminates the application.

The Workspace

The Workspace is the local Windows directory that is used to store local development projects, preferences, and information about the Workbench state. It is an important part of using the Workbench and is accessed and updated frequently.

When you first start the Workbench, the Workspace launcher dialog will come up, asking for a Workspace location. A default location is pre-filled, and is usually somewhere under your My Documents folder. You can change the location by entering a new location or clicking the Browse button.

For performance reasons, it is important that you use a local drive for your Workspace instead of the network drive.

Some users like to create multiple Workspaces to separate their work. This might be useful if you are working on some projects that require Java development and others that require RPG or COBOL development. You could keep a separate Workspace for each, or you could use one Workspace for both. We prefer to keep everything in one Workspace, to avoid losing things! However, we usually create separate Workspaces for playing around and experimenting.

You can also work with multiple Workspaces at the same time. To do this, you need to start the product multiple times, specifying different Workspace locations each time. You will then have a Workbench window for each Workspace.

Normally, you would not have to worry about where your Workspace is located unless you want to switch between Workspaces or back up your Workspace (generally a good idea). To switch between Workspaces, select **Switch Workspace** from the **File** menu.

To show the Workspace location in the Workbench title, add the *-showlocation* command-line parameter to the end of the target field in the Windows shortcut properties for WDSC or Rational Developer for System i, as shown in Figure 4–17. If you use multiple Workspaces, you may find the *-data workspaceLocation* command-line parameter useful.

This parameter tells WDSC or Rational Developer for System i to use the specified Workspace and not prompt for the Workspace location.

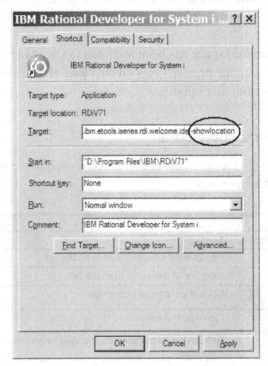

Figure 4–17: Showing the location of the Workspace in the Workbench window.

TIP   Suppose you selected the "Use this as the default and do not ask again" option on the Workspace launcher dialog, but now you really wish it would ask you again. Use the preference on the **General > Startup and Shutdown** preference page to turn this back on.

Workspace Migration

When upgrading to a newer version of the product, pay close attention to the migration guide. Sometimes, the layout of the Workspace or the way information is stored in the Workspace changes between versions of the product.

Your Workspace contains all of your RSE connections, filters, preferences, and other customizations. You will likely want to migrate your old Workspace to work with the new version of the product. Guidance on Workspace migration is provided in the migration guide.

After your Workspace has been migrated to the newer version, it might not work with the previous version anymore. Be sure to back up your Workspace before migrating.

Common Workbench Icons

Table 4–3 lists some of the common icons used in the Workbench and the actions they represent.

Table 4–3 Common Icons Used in the Workbench	
Icon	Meaning
✖	Remove the selected item from the list.
✖	Remove all the items from the list.
▱	Clear the contents of the view.
▨	Link with the editor.
⟳	Refresh the information for the view or for the selected resources.
▭	Minimize the view.
▯	Maximize the view.
⇛	Filter.
⌕	Search.
⇐	Move back to the previous contents of the view or preference page. This works like the Back button on a Web browser.
⇒	Move forward to the next contents of the view or preference page. This works like the Forward button on a Web browser.

Customizations

Many aspects of the appearance and behavior of the Workbench can be customized to suit your individual style. You've already seen how to customize the layout of a perspective, the toolbars, the size, and the position of the views. In addition, you can control several other key aspects of a perspective through the Preferences and the Customize Perspective dialogs.

Preferences

Each tool that plugs into the Workbench defines preferences that can be customized by users, and there are lots of them! The good news is that the preferences are centralized in one place. The Preferences dialog is used to set user preferences for all aspects of the Workbench. Open it from the Workbench window menu under **Window > Preferences**.

You can search the Preferences dialog pages using the filter function, as shown in Figure 4–18. To filter by matching the page title, simply type the name of the page you are seeking. The pages that match will be listed below. The history controls (⇐ ▾ ⇒ ▾) allow you to navigate forward and backward through previously viewed pages. To step back or forward several pages at a time, click the drop-down arrow. A list of the most recently viewed preference pages will appear. You can select from this list the preference page you want to view.

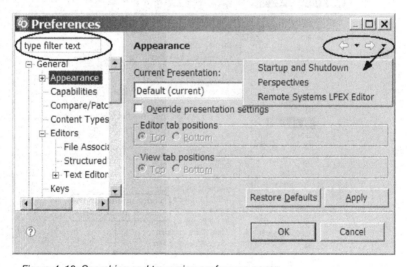

Figure 4–18: Searching and traversing preference pages.

The intent here is not to explain each and every preference pertaining to the Workbench. Relevant preferences are covered in each chapter of this book. Below, we highlight some general Workbench preferences to appreciate the extent to which the Workbench can be customized. Let's start by looking at the General > Perspectives preference page (Figure 4–19). Here you can do the following:

- Choose to open a new Workbench window for each new perspective that is opened. The default is to open in the same window.

- Choose to open new views as fast views. The default is that the view will be opened within the perspective.

- Choose to switch to the appropriate perspective when creating new projects.

- Change the default perspective that is opened when the Workbench starts, by selecting the perspective from the list of available perspectives and clicking the **Make Default** button. You can see here that the default perspective for Rational Developer for System i is the Remote System Explorer. You can also delete user-defined perspectives and reset the perspectives installed with the Workbench to their default settings if they have been modified.

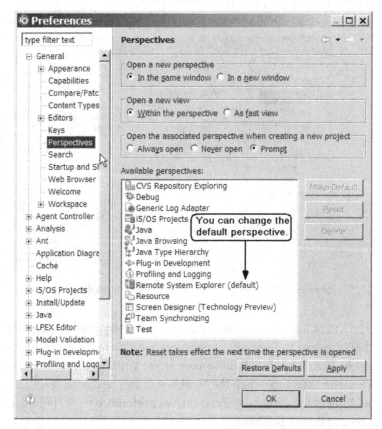

Figure 4–19: Perspective preferences.

To make the preferences take effect, click **Apply** or **OK**. Each preference page has a Restore Defaults button that sets the preferences on the page to the defaults shipped with the Workbench.

If you choose the option to open perspectives in different windows, you can see the list of all open windows from the Window menu, as shown in Figure 4–20. The name of the window is the name of the current active perspective in that window.

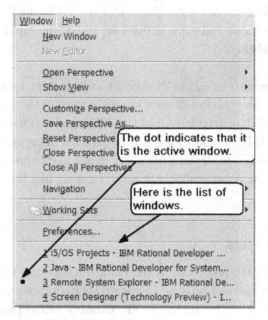

Figure 4–20: A list of open Workbench windows.

TIP   You can have the same perspective open in two different windows. The fastest way to do this is from the perspective itself, going to **Window** > **New Window**. This opens a new Workbench window with the same perspective as the current perspective.

You can customize many other aspects of the Workbench. Go through each of the preference pages on the left-hand pane of the Preferences dialog (Appearance, Editors, and Startup and Shutdown, for example), and use the right-hand pane to customize that preference.

Capabilities

One other preference page worth mentioning is Capabilities. The Workbench is designed to have multiple tools plugged into it, such as tools for i5/OS application development, Java, and XML. Many of these tools provide a capability that can be enabled or disabled. Disabling the capability hides the user interface for the related tools.

By default, a limited set of capabilities are enabled when you start the product, to reduce the clutter that appears in the Workbench. The available views and menu actions depend on the capabilities enabled in the Workbench.

Once you start using the Workbench as your primary development environment, you might want to enable more of the capabilities that are not enabled by default. (All of the i5/OS application development tools are enabled by default.) You can find the list of capabilities on the General > Capabilities preference page. Try to add and remove capabilities and see how the items available in certain menus, like Window > Show view, changes.

Keyboard Shortcuts

Command is a term used by the Workbench to refer to actions such as cut, copy, prompt, or find date. Keyboard shortcuts are predefined for many of the Workbench commands. The General > Keys preference page allows you to view and modify the keyboard shortcuts.

Two pieces of information are required when associating a keyboard shortcut with a command: the key sequence, and when the shortcut is valid. The View tab of the Keys preference page lists all currently defined keyboard shortcuts. Using the Modify tab, shown in Figure 4–21, you can add and remove keyboard shortcuts.

Using the Command section of the preference page, you can select a category and command to see what keyboard shortcuts are currently assigned to the command. Using the Key Sequence area, you can enter a key sequence (by pressing the actual keyboard shortcut) to see what commands the key sequence is currently assigned to.

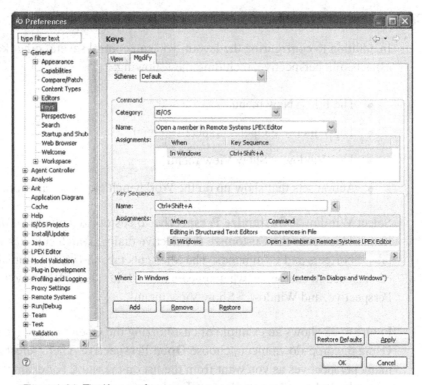

Figure 4–21: The Keys preference page.

To delete a keyboard shortcut, select one of the assignments and click the **Remove** button. To add a new keyboard shortcut, follow these steps:

1. Select the command in the Command area.

2. Enter the key sequence in the Key Sequence area.

3. Select when the keyboard shortcut should be available.

4. Click the **Add** button.

You will quickly learn that most key sequences are already associated to one or more commands. Figure 4–21 shows that the Ctrl+Shift+A key sequence is assigned to the command to open an editor in the Remote Systems LPEX Editor. You can also see that this key sequence is assigned to the Occurrences in File command. This is fine, since the keyboard shortcuts are valid in different contexts (when editing in structured test editors for the "Occurrence in File" command, and when in windows for the "Open a member in Remote Systems LPEX Editor" command).

Customizing the Menus

In addition to configuring the layout, you can control several other key aspects of a perspective, including the following:

- The File > New menu

- The Window > Open Perspective menu

- The Window > Show View menu

- Action sets that show up on the Workbench menu bar and toolbar

Select **Window > Customize Perspective** to customize any one of these items. This opens the Customize Perspective dialog, which contains two tabs: Shortcuts and Commands. The Shortcuts tab, shown in Figure 4–22, can be used to customize what appears in the File > New, Window > Perspective, and Window > Show View menus.

Figure 4–22 shows an example of customizing the Open perspective menu. Using the drop-down menu, choose **Open Perspective**. Then, select as many perspectives as you want from the list on the right. For example, select the **Debug**, **Remote System Explorer**, and **Test** perspectives, as shown in Figure 4–22. Open the **Window > Open Perspective** submenu to see the three perspectives selected, as shown in Figure 4–23.

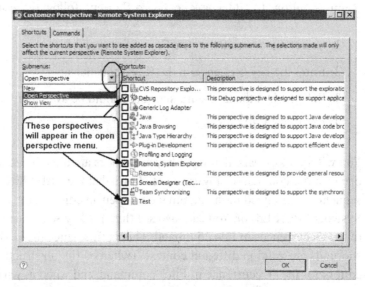

Figure 4–22: Customizing the Open Perspective menu.

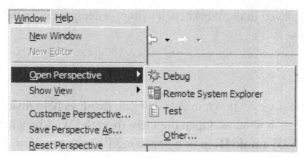

Figure 4–23: The Open Perspective menu.

The Commands tab can be used to customize what actions appear in the menu bar and the toolbar. The leftmost column lists all the available command groups. Selecting a command group shows which actions are added to the menu bar and toolbar if that particular command group is selected. Figure 4–24 shows the menu bar and toolbar details for CVS command group.

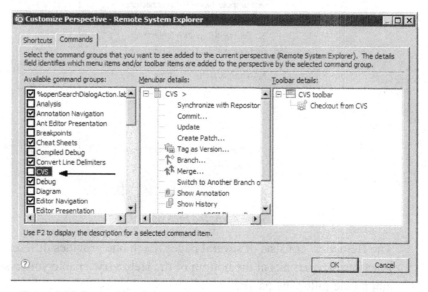

Figure 4–24: Customizing the menu bar and toolbar.

Getting Help

The Workbench help system lets you browse, search, bookmark, and print the documentation shipped with the product. The documentation is grouped into sets of information that are analogous to books. Help can be displayed in the Workbench using the Help view or the separate Help window.

Help View

The Help view, shown in Figure 4–25, displays help inside the main Workbench window. Open the view from the Workbench menu by selecting **Help > Dynamic Help** or by pressing F1 from any Workbench view.

Figure 4–25: The Help view.

The Help view consists of several pages. Each one provides different help functions. Hyperlinks at the bottom of the Help view enable you to switch among the following pages:

- *Related Topics* shows help topics related to the current Workbench context (view or action). The About section shows help specific to your current context, and the Dynamic Help section shows some search results that may (or may not) be related.

- *All Topics* shows the table of contents for the help.

- *Search* allows searching local help, tutorials gallery, IBM developerWorks, Google, Eclipse.org, and the samples gallery. Links to search hits are displayed, along with a summary of topic contents. To add other Internet resources to the search, expand the **Search Scope** section of the search page and click the **Advanced Settings** link.

- *Index* provides an index of keywords that link to specific help pages, similar to an index found at the back of a book. As you type in the text field, the best match will automatically be highlighted in the list of keywords. This page will only appear when index content is available in the Workbench.

- *Bookmarks* displays your list of personal bookmarks in the help.

When on the Related Topics page, the contents of the Help view change automatically as you switch views to show the context-sensitive help for the active view. Figure 4–25 shows the help for the Commands Log view in the Remote System Explorer perspective. This context-sensitive help page includes three hyperlinks into the main help documentation.

Help Window

The Help window, shown in Figure 4–26, also provides access to the documentation, but in a separate window instead of in a view. To open the window from the main menu, select **Help > Help Contents**. The first view shown in the window is the Contents view. It displays the table of contents for the product documentation.

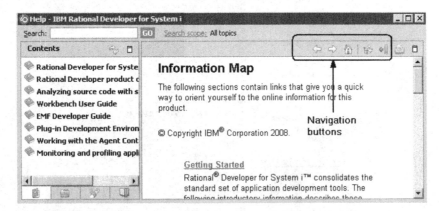

Figure 4–26: The external Help window.

To navigate the Help window, find the topic you want to read in the table of contents by clicking to expand the subtopics. Most help pages provide a list of links to related topics at the bottom. Follow these links to learn more about related features. Use the navigation buttons to go back and forth, get back to the home page, synchronize the topic to the help contents, and bookmark the topic.

TIP

Some users find it difficult to locate the help they are looking for using the Contents view in the main Help window. Instead, try showing the context-sensitive help for the related view (by pressing F1 in the view), and then using the hyperlinks to link into the related documentation page. The Help view includes an icon in its toolbar to open the current page in the external Help window when displaying pages from the product documentation. Once in the external Help window, you can use the icon in the navigation buttons to show the current page in the contents.

Help Preferences

The way help is displayed can be customized on the Help preference page, shown in Figure 4–27. For example, you display help in an external Web browser instead of the Help window.

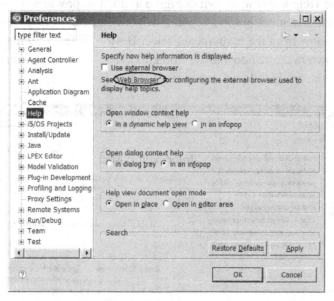

Figure 4–27: Preferences for getting help.

Context Help

If you're working through a task and encounter something you don't understand, you can ask for context help. This opens the Help view, showing information about the view, editor, dialog, or action you are currently using, and possibly some links to topics for further help. Context help can be accessed by pressing the F1 key. Alternatively, in dialogs, you can achieve the same result by pressing the "help" button (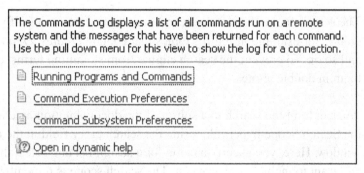) in the dialog's button bar.

You can configure context help to display using *infopops* instead of the Help view on the Help preference page. An infopop is an alternate way of presenting context-sensitive help, where a small window displays the help and links to related online help topics. Figure 4–28 shows the same help as in Figure 4–25, using an infopop instead of the Help view.

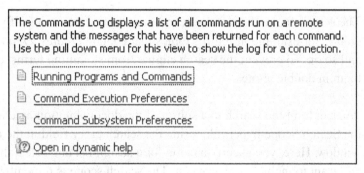

Figure 4–28: Help in an infopop.

TIP   Context-sensitive help is unavailable for toolbar buttons. Instead, let your mouse pointer hover over a toolbar button to view tooltip help for the button.

Searching

The help system includes a search engine that can run simple or complex queries on the documentation to help you find the information you are looking for. To search the help, select **Help > Search** from the Workbench menu, type the word or phrase you want to search for, and press **Enter** or click **Go**. The search results display as hyperlinks below the search entry field. Alternatively, you can search from the Help window using the Search field at the top of the window.

The first time you search the online help, the help system might start an index-generation process. This process of building the indexes for the search engine to use might take several minutes, depending on the amount of documentation and whether pre-built indexes are installed. The results of the search will be available once the indexing process completes. You can continue to use help while the index is being built.

The search expression is case insensitive, meaning it ignores the case of the words. The search expression uses regular expression rules. For example, you can surround your search words with double quotes to search for the exact match. You can also use the asterisk or question mark wildcards, or the Boolean operators (AND, OR, NOT).

The search engine uses fuzzy searches and word stemming. If you enter *create*, for example, it returns topics that contain *creates*, *creating*, *creator*, and so on. To prevent the search engine from stemming terms, enclose them in double quotes.

You can limit the search to a subset of the documentation by clicking on the Search Scope hyperlink beside the search entry field in the main Help window. Here, you specify a name for a search list and select the topics you want to include in the search. The search scope is remembered across Workbench invocations, so always remember to check it before searching.

Bookmarks

Bookmarks are a simple and quick way to navigate to help pages that you frequently use. To bookmark a help page, click the "bookmark document" icon ( ) when the topic you want to bookmark is displayed. This adds the topic to the list of bookmarks. You can access your bookmarks by clicking the bookmark page in the Help view or clicking the "bookmarks" icon ( ) at the bottom left corner of the Help window, as shown in Figure 4–29.

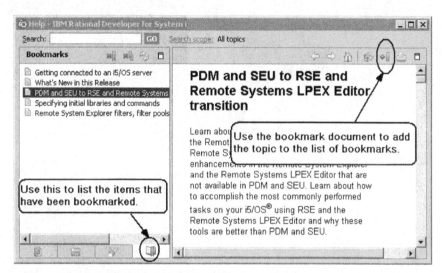

Figure 4–29: A Help window with bookmarks.

You can delete a particular bookmark using the "delete selected topic" icon ( ) in the toolbar for the Bookmarks pane of the Help window. Alternatively, delete all bookmarks using the "delete all topics" icon ( ).

CHAPTER 5

Working with Libraries, Objects, and Members

Editing, compiling, and debugging are important programming tasks, and we have included a separate chapter on each of them. However, underlying all of these is the ability to manage your development environment: to be able to find your libraries, objects, and members; view information about them; and run actions against them.

That is what this chapter is all about. All of the underlying RSE concepts, such as connections, subsystems, and filters are explained, along with information on how to create, manage, and navigate through them.

The Remote Systems View

The RSE is controlled from the Remote Systems view, shown in Figure 5–1. The Remote Systems view provides a central point for defining connections, accessing remote resources (such as libraries, objects, members, jobs, and IFS files), and running actions against those resources.

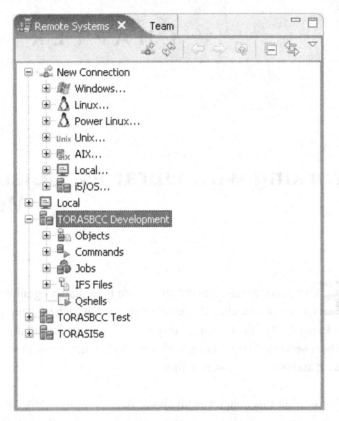

Figure 5–1: The Remote Systems view.

The Remote Systems view is a tree view of your RSE artifacts and remote resources. At the highest level are connections to your systems. The first time you start the Workbench, you only have a connection to your local workstation, named *Local*. Starting from connections, you expand entries in the tree (by clicking on the plus sign) to see contained (*child*) objects. This is commonly referred to as *drilling down*, and is similar to using Microsoft Windows Explorer to access your Desktop, local files, and Control Panel functions.

TIP

You can use the keyboard to navigate the Remote Systems view instead of the mouse. Use the Up and Down arrow keys to move up and down in the tree. Use the Left and Right arrow keys to expand and collapse the currently selected item. Once you have an item selected, use Shift+F10 to show the pop-up menu. Use the keyboard to navigate the actions in the pop-up menu, and press Enter to invoke an action.

Like most Eclipse views, the Remote Systems view has both a toolbar and view menu (accessed through the upside-down triangle). The toolbar contains icons for some common actions such as "create a connection" ( ), "refresh" ( ), and "collapse all" ( ), as well as other advanced actions that are covered later in this chapter. The pull-down menu mainly contains shortcuts to the RSE preference pages and actions related to filter pools. (Filter pools are also covered later in this chapter.)

All resources are shown in the Remote Systems view with an icon and the resources name. In some cases, the icon is *decorated* to reflect the status of the resource. Decorators are extra graphics added on top of the original icon. For example, when an RSE connection is connected to the remote system, its icon is decorated with a green arrow to show this ( ).

Icons are specific to the type of resource; connections, filters, libraries, different i5/OS object types, and members all have different icons. This helps to quickly identify the resource type. Some resources, such as i5/OS objects, also include their type and subtype, appended to the resource name.

TIP A preference on the Remote Systems > i5/OS > Objects Subsystem preference page turns off showing the type and subtype for libraries, objects, and members. Turning this preference off can make the Remote Systems view less cluttered. Existing entries in the view will continue to show the type and subtype until they are refreshed. You can still see type and subtype information in the Properties view and in the status bar at the bottom of the Workbench when you select a resource.

Connections

Each RSE connection represents a remote system. One of your first tasks using the RSE will be to create a connection so you can access the remote system to edit, compile, and debug your programs.

Creating a connection to i5/OS is very similar to defining a new 5250 emulator session. The first time you installed iSeries Navigator (or your 5250 emulator of choice), you had to define a new 5250 emulator session by entering the system's hostname. You also likely saved the emulator definition to a local file, so you could quickly reopen it the next time. Similarly, when you create your RSE connection, you enter the system's hostname and provide a connection name (analogous to the filename), so you can access the connection in the future.

Each RSE connection uses its own i5/OS server job for retrieving lists of libraries, objects, and members, and for compiling and running CL commands. This allows each connection to have its own unique library list for compiling, running, and debugging. Each RSE connection to the same remote system has its own server job and therefore its own library list.

Creating a Connection

There are many ways to launch the new connection action, but here are the most common:

- Expand **New Connection > i5/OS**.

- Click the "new connection" icon in the Remote Systems view's toolbar.

- Right-click a blank area of the Remote Systems view and select **New Connection** . . . .

- Right-click an existing connection and select **New > Connection**.

Each of these actions launches the New Connection wizard. If this is your first time creating a connection in this Workspace, the first page of the wizard will prompt for a profile name, as shown in Figure 5–2. This only happens the first time you create a connection.

This is *not* your i5/OS user profile. The RSE stores all local artifacts (connections, filters, user-defined actions, and customized compile commands) grouped by profile. Profiles, and the artifacts stored in a profile, can then be shared with other members of your team. By default, you will have a Team profile and the profile you name when you create your first connection. The profile name defaults to the hostname of the local workstation. Give the profile a name that uniquely identifies you, and click **Next**. (Profiles are covered in more detail in Chapter 10.)

Figure 5–2: Prompting for a profile name.

The next page of the wizard (or the first page of the wizard, if this is not your first time creating a connection) prompts for the connection information, as shown in Figure 5–3. Depending on how you launched the wizard, there may or may not be an entry field for the system type.

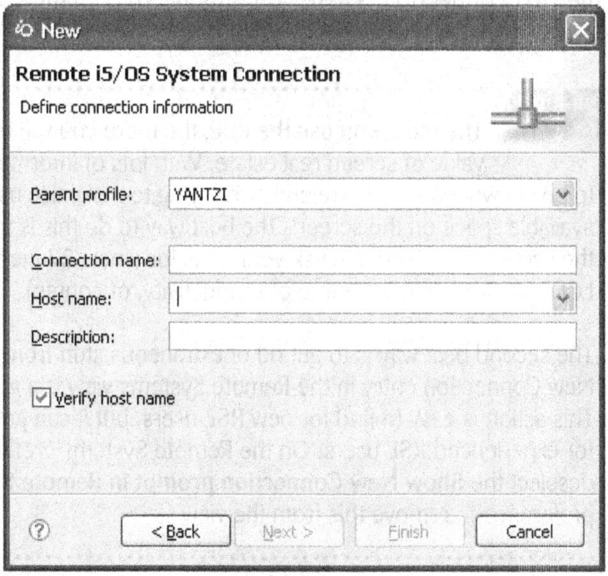

Figure 5–3: The New Connection wizard.

Here is a summary of the fields on this page:

- *Parent profile*: The profile name you entered in the previous page.

- *Connection name*: Any name you want to give your connection. Use a meaningful name that can be associated with your connection. This name will appear for your connection in the Remote Systems view.

- *Host name*: The TCP/IP host name or address of your i5/OS server.

- *Description*: This is an optional field. Any text you put here will appear in the Properties view when the connection is selected.

- *Verify host name*: This checkbox ensures that you have specified a valid TCP/IP hostname. By default, this is checked, and we recommend that you leave it that way. An error message is issued if the host name you specified cannot be resolved to a TCP/IP address.

Click **Finish** to create the connection. Your connection, identified by its connection name, now appears in the Remote Systems view.

If you are creating a second connection to the same system, select the existing connection first, and then select one of the new connection actions. This pre-fills the New Connection wizard with the information from the first connection. Then, you only need to change the connection name and (optionally) the description.

TIP

The more you use the RSE, the more you will realize the value of screen real estate. With lots of information available to be shown, you will be relentlessly trying to maximize usage of all available space on the screen. The best way to do this is to crank up the screen resolution and ask your boss for a new 27-inch widescreen LCD monitor (all in the name of productivity, of course).

The second best way is to get rid of extraneous stuff from the UI. The New Connection entry in the Remote Systems view is a good example. This action is easy to find for new RSE users, but it can get in the way for experienced RSE users. On the Remote Systems preference page, deselect the **Show New Connection prompt in Remote Systems view** preference to remove this from the view.

Connection Properties

There are two ways to view and change properties of connections: use the Properties view shown in Figure 5–4 or use the Properties dialog shown in Figure 5–5. The Properties view always shows the properties of the currently selected resource in the RSE. To open the dialog, right-click a resource and select **Properties**.

Figure 5–4: The Properties view.

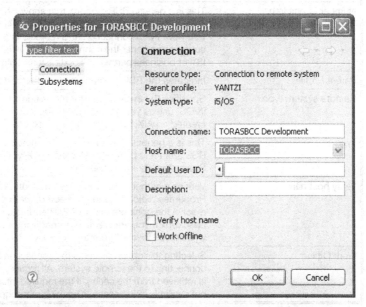

Figure 5–5: The connection's Properties dialog.

The Properties view and the Properties dialog do not always show the same properties. As a rule, the Properties dialog shows all of the editable properties, while the Properties view may only show a subset of them.

Both allow the editing of properties. To edit properties in the Properties view, click in the value field for the property, and enter the new value. If the value field does not change to an editable entry field, the property is not editable. Table 5–1 provides a description for each of the RSE connection properties.

Table 5–1: Connection Properties	
Connection Property	**Description**
Connection status	Indicates whether or not this connection is connected to the remote system.
Default User ID	Specifies the i5/OS user ID used to connect. The value of this property can be explicitly specified here, or it can be inherited from the default user ID specified on the Remote Systems preference page. The "inherit" button (☑) can be used to toggle between inheriting the value (pointing left) and specifying the value (pointing right).
Description	Holds the description you provided for this connection.
Hostname	Provides the TCP/IP hostname or address for the remote system.
Name	Specifies the name that appears in the Remote Systems view. This name is used to refer to this connection throughout the RSE.
Number of children	This is a generic RSE property that shows the number of child items under the selected item in the Remote Systems tree view. For a connection, this represents the number of subsystems under the connection (five, unless you have ISV or business partner RSE extensions installed).
Parent Profile	Indicates the RSE profile that owns this connection.
Remote system type	Specifies the system type for the connection. This will be i5/OS, unless you are using your local connection or have created an AIX, Linux, or Windows connection.
Type	This is a generic RSE property that shows what type of RSE artifact is currently selected, such as Connection, Subsystem, or i5/OS member filter.
Verify host name	Verifies whether or not the hostname entered in the Properties dialog is valid. If selected, the RSE will try to resolve the hostname to a TCP/IP address. De-select this checkbox if you are creating or modifying connections while disconnected from the network.
Work Offline	Selecting this option prevents the connection from connecting to the remote system. All required information is retrieved from the cache. If the required information is not available in the cache, a warning message is displayed.

Subsystems

When you expand an RSE connection, subsystems are shown underneath it. Subsystems represent the various parts of the remote system that can be accessed. RSE subsystems have no relation to i5/OS job subsystems. Five subsystems are provided for i5/OS connections:

- *Objects*: This subsystem is used to access libraries, objects, and members. This is similar to the WRKLIBPDM, WRKOBJPDM, and WRKMBRPDM commands. The Objects subsystem will be the focus for most of this chapter.

- *Commands*: This subsystem is used to run commands and view the resulting messages. By default, it is pre-populated with a set of commonly used commands. This subsystem is covered later in this chapter.

- *Jobs*: This subsystem is used to list and work with jobs. This is similar to the WRKACTJOB command, but only has a subset of the information that WRKACTJOB has. The Jobs subsystem is covered in chapter 10.

- *IFS Files*: This subsystem is used to work with IFS files and folders, similar to the Work with Object Links (WKRLNK) command. The IFS files subsystem is covered in chapter 10.

- *Qshells*: This subsystem starts a Qshell. It is similar to the STRQSH command.

All five of the IBM-supplied subsystems share the same properties. If you change the value of a property for one subsystem, the other four subsystems under that connection will automatically be updated with the new value. Table 5–2 summarizes the subsystem properties shown in the Properties view.

Table 5–2: Subsystem Properties from the Properties View	
Subsystem Property	**Description**
Connected	Indicates whether or not the subsystem is connected to the remote server.
Name	Holds the name of the subsystem.
Number of children	This is a generic RSE property that shows the number of child items under the selected item in the Remote Systems tree view. For a subsystem, this represents the number of filters under the connection.

Table 5–2: Subsystem Properties from the Properties View (Continued)	
Subsystem Property	Description
Port	This property is not used by i5/OS subsystems. i5/OS subsystems use the ports configured on the server for the i5/OS host servers. (See chapter 10 for details on RSE communications.)
Type	This is a generic RSE property that shows what type of RSE artifact is currently selected, such as Connection, Subsystem, or i5/OS member filter.
User ID	Specifies the user ID currently used by this subsystem and whether or not the user ID is being inherited. (The next section in this chapter has more details.)
Version	Specifies the version of i5/OS running on the remote server. This property is only available while the subsystem is connected to the server.

The subsystem's Properties dialog, shown in Figure 5–6, is divided into four pages: Command Execution, Environment Variables, Initial Library List, and Subsystem. The Command Execution page contains properties to override the object library, batch job description, and other compile- and command-related settings for this connection. (This page is covered in more detail in chapter 8.)

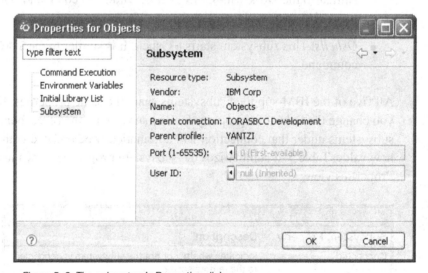

Figure 5–6: The subsystem's Properties dialog.

The Environment Variables page allows you to add environment variables that are set whenever this connection is connected. The Initial Library List page allows you to specify additional library list settings for this connection (discussed later in this chapter). The Subsystem page contains information describing this subsystem.

BACKGROUND As we go through this chapter, you will find that some actions and properties you would think should be on the connection actually appear on subsystems. Here is why.

The RSE was designed to be extended by third-party software providers—and you! There is an Eclipse extension point that allows anyone to add his or her own subsystems to the RSE, based on system type, and have them appear under all connections of that type. This is how a few of the i5/OS change-management providers have integrated their support into the RSE.

Connections from the RSE to the remote system are managed by each subsystem, not the RSE connection that contains the subsystems. The five subsystems provided by IBM all share the same underlying communications connection between the RSE connection and the remote system. Subsystems provided by third parties can use this one, or they may use their own communications.

For example, imagine a database server installed on i5/OS that uses its own user IDs, passwords, and communications server. Someone could create an RSE subsystem that appears under i5/OS connections, and that subsystem would be using a different communications connection, user ID, and password than all the other subsystems under the same RSE connection.

Connecting to the Remote System

You are prompted to sign on to the remote system the first time you try to access resources or run a command, as shown in Figure 5–7. Alternatively, right-click the connection or any of the subsystems and select the **Connect** action. The sign-on prompt requires you to enter a valid i5/OS user ID and password to continue.

Access to the remote system via the RSE is governed by standard i5/OS security. The user profile you use to sign on with will determine which resources and actions you have access to, similar to signing on via a 5250 emulator.

Figure 5–7: The sign-on prompt.

If you have multiple RSE connections to the same host, you can use different user IDs to sign on to each one. Which resources and actions you can run under each connection will be controlled by the user ID used to sign on for that connection.

Saving Your User ID

You might want to save your user ID and possibly your password to avoid having to enter them every time you connect. User IDs can be saved at a global preference, connection, and subsystem level within the RSE. Passwords are saved based on the hostname, system type, and user ID.

At connection time, if the RSE connection has a saved user ID (directly or inherited from the global preference), and there is a matching saved password (based on the user ID, hostname, and system type), then the connection is established without prompting for sign-on. If either the user ID or password is not saved, the sign-on prompt is displayed.

To override the saved user ID and password for the current session, select the **Connect** action from any of the subsystem's pop-up menus. This action always prompts before connecting, even if the user ID and password are saved.

A default user ID can be set for each system type on the Remote Systems preference page, shown in Figure 5–8. Select the **Default User ID** column beside the i5/OS system type, and enter the user ID. This user ID will be used for any i5/OS connections that do not override the value at either the connection or subsystem level.

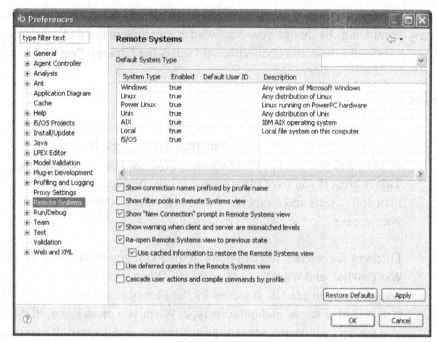

Figure 5–8: The Remote Systems preference page.

Each RSE connection can override the default user ID, if desired. Each connection has a user ID property that can either inherit its value from the global preference setting or override it by providing a value (as described earlier in this chapter, in the section on connection properties).

In the same way that a connection can override the default user ID, a subsystem can override the connection's user ID. (See the "background" sidebar earlier in this chapter for information on why this feature exists.) This is done in exactly the same way, by specifying a value for the subsystem's User ID property via either the Properties view or the Properties dialog.

Managing Your Password

To save your passwords directly form the sign-on prompt, select the **Save Password** checkbox or go to the **Remote Systems > Passwords** preference page. From the preference page, you can also change and remove saved passwords.

If you try to sign onto the remote, system and your password has expired, the RSE will prompt you with a dialog to change your password before continuing. To change your password at any time in the RSE, right-click a subsystem under the connection and select the **Change Password** action.

Filters

When we demo the RSE, we usually start by expanding the Library List filter under the Objects subsystem, then expanding a library to show the objects, and finally expanding a source physical file to show the members. This is great if you have libraries and source physical files that have less than 100 objects and members. In the real world, however, this is usually not the case.

Filters to the rescue! You can think of the PDM commands WRKLIBPDM, WRKOBJPDM, and WRKMBRPDM as filters. When you prompt any of these commands, you can fill in values for the library name, object name, object type, member name, and member type. When you press Enter, PDM shows you the list of libraries, objects, or members you requested. If you used values other than *ALL, this list represents a subset of what actually exists. This is a filter.

Filters in the RSE are very similar. There are library filters that are equivalent to WRKLIBPDM, object filters that are equivalent to WRKOBJPDM, and member filters that are equivalent to WRKMBRPDM. When you expand a filter in the Remote Systems view, the results are shown as children of the filter node in the tree.

There are three main differences between RSE filters and the equivalent PDM Work With commands:

1. *There are generic naming rules.* A generic name is one that contains an asterisk (*), and therefore can match zero or more possible values. PDM allows a single asterisk in any position of the name, or as the first and last characters. RSE names can have up to two asterisks in any positions in the name. For example, *O*N*R* is a valid RSE generic name that would include all names that start with *O*, end with *R*, and have *N* somewhere in between.

2. *Any name can be generic.* In PDM, only the name of what you are filtering can be generic. So, if you are creating a member filter, only the member name can be generic; the library and object fields must have non-generic values. For RSE filters, any of the fields can be generic. For example, you can create a single member filter that shows all ACCT* members, in all Q* source physical files, in all PAYROLL* libraries. Using generic library and object names in member filters can cause performance problems, however. When the filter is resolved, the list of matching libraries is resolved first, then a list of matching source files for each of the libraries is resolved, and finally a list of matching members for each of these is resolve. These types of filters have their place, but be careful when setting them up.

3. *Filters are saved.* Filtering is very important in the RSE. You are likely to spend some time and effort setting up good filters for your projects. You don't want to lose these efforts, so filters are always saved. When you create your filter, the second page of the New Filter wizard prompts you to name it, as shown in Figure 5–9.

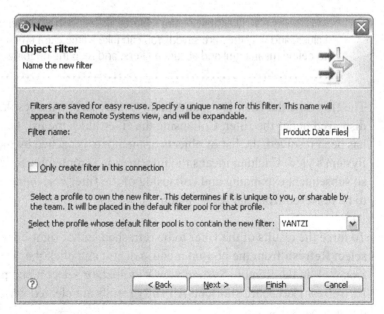

Figure 5–9: Naming a filter.

When you create a new filter, it appears in the Remote Systems view under the Objects subsystem for *all* i5/OS connections. Select the **Only create filter in this connection** checkbox if you would prefer this filter to only appear under the current connection.

TIP

Filters are more important in the RSE than PDM for a couple of reasons. First, network latency affects the RSE, but does not affect PDM. The first time an RSE filter is expanded, the filter is resolved on the remote system and the list is sent down to the workstation (just the names and information, not the actual libraries, objects, or members). The longer the list, the longer it will take to resolve and display.

Second, your own productivity is affected. In most cases, you are interested in working with only a few objects or members at a time. You create a filter to assist in finding those objects or members. Objects or members that you are not interested in, but that show up in the list, just get in the way. The more accurate your lists, the quicker you'll be able to find what you need, and the more productive you will be.

This is why RSE filters have extra features like support for multi-generic values, and why they are saved. You can take a little extra time upfront to define meaningful and accurate filters, and reap the ongoing benefits.

The first time the filter is expanded, it is resolved, and the resulting list is displayed under the filter. Collapsing the filter hides the list. Once a filter has been resolved, the list of objects or members is cached by the Remote System's view. Caching means the information is remembered by the view, so subsequent expanding and collapsing of the filter *does not* cause the list to be retrieved from the server again

To force the results of the filter to be refreshed, either right-click on it and select **Refresh** from the pop-up menu, select it and click the "refresh" icon ( ) in the Remote System view's toolbar, or select it and press the F5 (refresh) keyboard shortcut. All filter results are cleared when the RSE connection is disconnected.

Library Filters

To create a new library filter, right-click the **Objects** subsystem and select **New > Library Filter,** or expand the **Work with libraries** fast path action under the Objects subsystem. Both actions launch the New Library Filter wizard, shown in Figure 5–10.

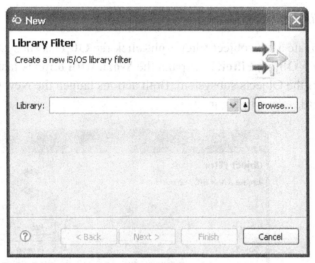

Figure 5–10: The New Library Filter wizard.

TIP
Once you are comfortable using the New > Filter actions from the Objects subsystem's pop-up menu, you can delete the Work with . . . fast path actions under Objects. This frees up more space in the view.

The first page of the New Library Filter wizard prompts for the library name. This can be one of the following:

- A specific library name, such as INVOICEDEV

- A generic name, such as INVOICE*

- One of the predefined special values *ALL, *ALLUSR, *CURLIB, *LIBL, or *USRLIBL

Like most RSE entry fields, the library name prompt includes a drop-down arrow (⌄) to select from previously entered values (the history), a "work with history" option (▲), and the ability to browse the remote system for the library instead of entering a value.

Once you have entered the library name, click **Next** to proceed to the second page of the wizard to enter a name for the filter.

Object Filters

To create a new object filter, right-click the **Objects** subsystem and select **New > Object Filter,** or expand the **Work with objects** fast path action under the Objects subsystem. Both actions launch the New Object Filter wizard, shown in Figure 5–11.

Figure 5–11: The New Object Filter wizard.

The first page of the New Object Filter wizard prompts for the library, object, object type, and object attribute values. The following are allowable values:

- *Library*: The same values allowed for a library filter are allowed here. (See the library filter description in the previous section.)

- *Object*: Use a specific or generic object name. For example, use ORDENTR to show only objects named *ORDENTR*, or ORD* to view all objects whose name starts with *ORD*.

- *Object type*: Specify the type of objects to show. The default is to show all object types, but you can enter a specific object type. Click the **Browse** button to select from a list of common object types. Generic values are not allowed for the object type, but you can click the **More Types** button to enter a list of *object type: object attribute* pairs. The filter will include any object that matches one of the specified entries in the list.

• *Object attribute*: This is the object attribute filter. The default is to allow any object attribute (by using the asterisk). After you enter an object type, the Browse button is enabled for the object attribute, so you can choose an object attribute that is applicable to the specified object type.

TIP
The default is to show all objects when expanding a library in the Remote Systems view. If you only want to see a specific type of object, right-click the library in the Remote Systems view and select an object type from the Expand To menu. For example, to see only the save files in a library, right-click the library and select **Expand To > Save Files.**

Member Filters

To create a new member filter, right-click the **Objects** subsystem and select **New > Member Filter,** or expand the **Work with member** fast path action under the Objects subsystem. Both actions launch the New Member Filter wizard, shown in Figure 5–12.

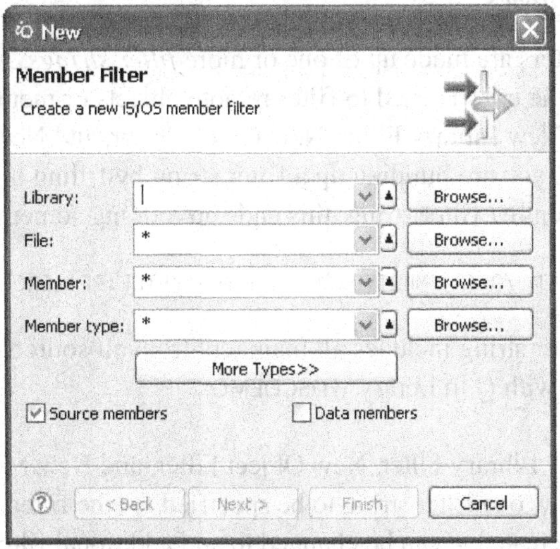

Figure 5–12: The New Member Filter wizard.

The first page of the New Member Filter wizard prompts for the library name, file name, member name, member type, and whether to include source and/or data members. Allowable values are as follows:

- *Library*: The same values allowed for a library filter are allowed here. (See the library filter description earlier in this chapter.)

- *File*: This can be a specific or generic file name.

- *Member*: This can be a specific or generic member name.

- *Member type*: This can be a specific or generic member type. For example, entering *RPG* would include all RPG, RPGLE, SQLRPG, and SQLRPGLE members. Click the **Browse** button to select from a list of common member types. Click the **More Types** button to enter a list of members types. The filter will include any member that matches one of the types in the list.

- *Source or data members*: If you enter a generic file name, you have the option of including source members, data members, or both, by selecting the corresponding checkboxes. The default is to only include source members. This option is disabled if you enter a specific file name, in which case the filter includes all members from the file that match the specified member name.

Changing Filters

RSE filters are made up of one or more *filter strings*. A filter string is simply the criteria used to filter remote objects or members. When you use the New Library Filter, New Object Filter, and New Member Filter wizards, you are building up a filter string by filling in the input fields. For a member filter string, this ends up looking something like this:

```
WDSCDEMO/Q*(*) MBRTYPE(*) OBJTYPE(*FILE:PF*-SRC)
```

This filter string includes all members from all source physical files starting with *Q* in library WDSCDEMO.

The New Library Filter, New Object Filter, and New Member Filter wizards only allow one filter string to be specified for the filter. However, after the filter is created, it can be changed to add additional filter strings. When the filter is expanded, each filter string is resolved, and the results are concatenated into a list under the filter. The results of each filter string are sorted, but the overall results are concatenated and not sorted. If an object or member is resolved by multiple filter strings, the object or member will appear multiple times in the resulting list.

Why would you ever need to do this? Ideally, when you create filters, they should represent a meaningful, related set of objects or members, such as the ten source members required to implement a new feature or fix. You might be able to capture all the required members with a single filter string based on naming patterns, but often this won't be practical. Instead, you can add multiple filter strings that accurately capture the list when combined. In the worst case, this may be ten filter strings that explicitly list each member.

To add additional filter strings to a filter, right-click the filter and select **Change** from the pop-up menu. This opens the Change Filter dialog, shown in Figure 5–13. The left side of the dialog lists each of the filter strings contained in the filter. The right side contains entry fields for modifying the filter strings. These are the same entry fields found on the New Filter wizards.

To add a new filter, follow these steps:

1. Click **New Filter String** in the filter strings list on the left side of the dialog.

2. Enter the filter criteria on the right side of the dialog.

3. Optionally, click the **Test** button to verify the results of this single filter string.

4. Click the **Apply** button to add the filter string.

You can copy and paste filter strings in the Change Filter dialog to quickly create multiple filter strings that share similar filtering criteria. Right-click the filter string in the filter strings list, select **Copy** from the pop-up menu, then right-click again and select **Paste**. This will create a duplicate filter string and will display an error message that duplicates exist. Modify one of the filters so they are unique.

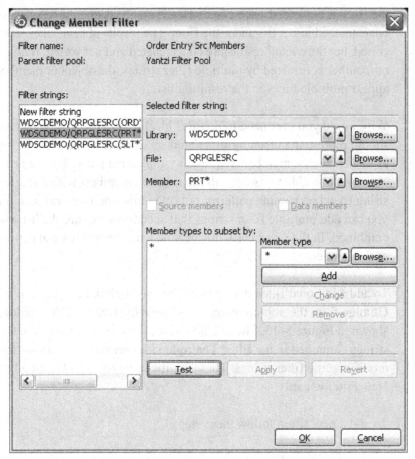

Figure 5–13: The Change Filter dialog.

Actions to delete filter strings as well as move them up or down are available on the same pop-up menu. The order of the filter strings in the Change Filter dialog is the same order in which the results are concatenated.

TIP

The Change Filter dialog does not have buttons to delete, duplicate, move up, or move down the filter strings. Instead, you need to right-click a filter string and access these actions from the pop-up menu. A few other dialogs in the RSE work the same way, such as the Work With User Actions dialog. In general, if you think you should be able to delete or copy something, try to right-click it and look in the pop-up menu.

Deleting Filters

Deleting a filter just deletes the filter from the RSE; it does not delete the objects or members that are shown under the filter. To delete a filter, right-click it and select **Delete** from the pop-up menu, or select the filter and press the **Delete** key. This opens the dialog box shown in Figure 5–14. Double-check that the resource type in the dialog verifies that you are deleting a filter.

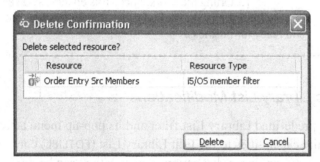

Figure 5–14: A Delete Confirmation dialog.

Managing Your Library List

Before we go any farther, let's take a look at an important topic: setting up your library list in the RSE. Many new users seem to have trouble getting their library lists configured correctly in the RSE, in order to successfully compile and debug. The good news is that configuring your library list in the RSE can be quick and easy. However, there are a couple of "gotchas" to be aware of.

The library list and current library used by your RSE connection default to the library list and current library for the user profile you signed on with (as specified in that user profile's job description). The RSE does not run the initial program specified for the user profile.

RSE connections have a predefined Library List filter under the Objects subsystem that shows the library list for the RSE connection. This filter is refreshed automatically when using any of the library list actions described in the next section.

If you run a command instead of using the library list actions to modify your library list, the Library List filter is not refreshed automatically.

Also, if you have the Library List filter expanded when you shut down the Workbench, the filter is re-expanded when you restart the Workbench, based on cached values from your previous session. These may be incorrect. If in doubt, you can always select the Library List filter and press F5 to refresh it. The result will be the current library list for the RSE connection.

TIP

It's a good idea to refresh the Library List filter when restarting the Workbench. This ensures you see the correct (not cached) library list, and that your RSE connection is connected and ready for business!

Dynamic Library List Modifications

The predefined Library List filter and its pop-up menu actions provide similar capabilities to the Edit Library List (EDTLIBL) command. Table 5–3 lists common library list actions and how they can be done in the RSE. These commands only affect the user portion of the library list.

Table 5–3: Common Library List Actions	
Library List Action	**How to Do This in the RSE**
Add a library (ADDLIBLE)	Right-click the **Library List** filter and select **Add Library** List Entry from the pop-up menu show in Figure 5–15. This opens a prompt for the ADDLIBLE command. Alternatively, right-click a library in the RSE and select **Add to Library List** from its pop-up menu.
Remove a library (RMVLIBLE)	Right-click the library under the Library List filter and select **Remove From Library List** from the pop-up menu shown in Figure 5–16.
Change position of a library within the library list (EDTLIBL)	Right-click the library under the Library List filter and select one of the following: • **Move Up In Library List** moves the library up one position. • **Move Down In Library List** moves the library down one position. • **Move Within Library** List opens a dialog box asking for the new position relative to another library within the library list.
Change the current library (CHGCURLIB)	Right-click the **Library List** filter and select **Change Current Library** from the pop-up menu.

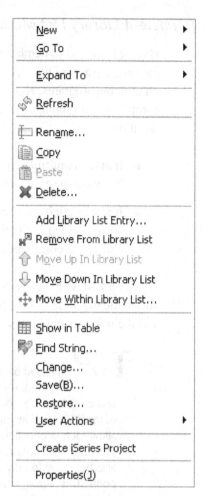

Figure 5–15: The pop-up menu for the Library List filter.

Figure 5–16: The pop-up menu for libraries under the Library List filter.

These actions change the library list for the RSE connection, but only for the current session. If you disconnect and reconnect, the library list defaults back to the values from the user profile, and all dynamic changes from the last session are lost. This is the same behavior as running ADDLIBLE, RMVLIBLE, or EDTLIBL in a 5250 session. The next section describes how to make changes to the library list for each RSE connection that persist between disconnects and reconnects.

Persistent Library List Modifications

Having to always remember to set up your library list after connecting is a pain and a waste of time. At the same time, however, you might be working on multiple programs, and each program requires its own library list for compiling and running. Luckily, the RSE was designed to handle exactly this situation:

- It allows multiple connections to the same system. Each connection has its own server job and therefore its own library list.

- It allows each connection to have a persisted set of libraries that are always added to the library list, as well as a current library setting and initial command.

When an RSE connection is connected, these additional libraries are automatically added to the library list, the current library is updated, and the initial command is run.

TIP Instead of thinking of an RSE connection as a remote system, try thinking of it as an application on that system, and customize it accordingly. This was one of the main design features of the RSE; to allow multiple RSE connections to the same system, and allow each connection to be configured for working with an application that requires a unique library list. Later on, you will see how filters can also be set up to only appear under specific connections using filter pools. This allows you to set up filters under each connection that are also specific to the application.

To modify the persisted library list settings, right-click any of the subsystems under the connection, such as **Objects**, and select **Properties**. This opens the Properties dialog for the subsystem. All of the IBM-supplied subsystems share the same Command Execution, Environment Variables, and Initial Library List properties. So, properties set on any of these pages will show up in the Properties dialog for any of the subsystems under that connection.

To add an entry to the library list for this connection, enter the library name in the Library entry field and click **Add**. (You must click Add, or the entry is not saved, even if you click the Apply or OK buttons shown in Figure 5–17.) The library shows up in the table. By default, it is added to the end of the library list (*LAST). You can modify the library position to add the library to the beginning of the library list (*FIRST).

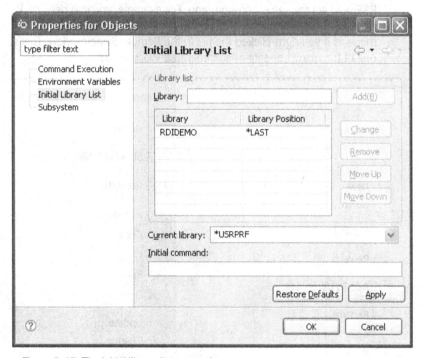

Figure 5–17: The initial library list properties.

Libraries are added to the library list in the order they appear in the table. This has the side effect of causing the libraries to show up in the library list in the reverse order in which they are shown in the table. So, if you wanted libraries A, B, and C to appear at the beginning of the library list in that order, you would need to add them to the table as C, B, and A, and then update their positions to be *FIRST. Select libraries in the table and use the Move Up and Move Down buttons to reorder them.

Working with Libraries, Objects, and Members

You typically work with a library, object, or member in the RSE by first finding it in the RSE, and then right-clicking it and selecting an action from the pop-up menu or expanding it to see contained resources. Example pop-up menus are shown for a library, program object, and source member in Figure 5–18, Figure 5–19, and Figure 5–20, respectively.

TIP ....

We often say to right-click an object or member in the Remote Systems view or Object Table view. However, you can right-click the object or member in most places you see it in the RSE, and get the same pop-up menu. For example, you can right-click a source file in the Remote Search view and see the same pop-up menu as if you right-clicked the file in the Remote Systems view. That's one of the many benefits of an integrated Workbench!

....

Figure 5–18: Library actions.

Figure 5–19: Program object actions.

As you can see from Figure 5–18, Figure 5–19, and Figure 5–20, actions in the pop-up menu are divided into categories. Details on the editing and verifying actions can be found in chapters 6 and 7. Details on the compiling and binding actions can be found in chapter 8. Details on the running and debugging actions can be found in chapter 9. Details on searching and user-defined actions can be found in chapter 10.

"New" Actions

The pop-up menu for libraries and source physical files contains a cascading New menu. On a library, this cascading menu provides actions for creating a new source physical file, message file, data queue, or data area. These are just shortcuts to the underlying CRT . . . commands. The cascading menu also contains an action to create a new object filter. This opens the New Object Filter wizard and pre-fills the wizard with the currently selected library name.

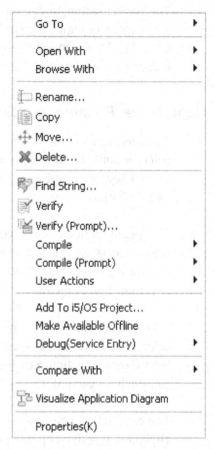

Figure 5–20: Source member actions.

TIP You're probably wondering what's up with the "(F)," "(J)," and "(K)" following some of the actions. Each action in the pop-up menu has a mnemonic associated with it. Mnemonics are the letters that are underscored; pressing the underscored letter is the same as clicking the action. This is an accessibility feature that you can enable in the Windows Control Panel's Accessibility Options. (Select **Show extra keyboard help in programs** in Windows XP.) The RSE assigns these mnemonics automatically, and if all the letters in an action are used by other mnemonics, it adds a letter at the end for the mnemonic. That is what the "(F)," "(J)," and "(K)" are.

The New cascading menu for source physical files contains actions to add a new member (equivalent to F6 in WRKMBRPDM) or create a new member filter. The New > Member Filter action opens the New Member Filter wizard pre-filled with the selected source file and library names.

Copy, Move, Rename, and Delete Actions

All objects and members support the common rename, copy, move, and delete actions. These actions are available from the pop-up menu as well as their keyboard shortcuts (the Delete key for delete, Ctrl+C for copy, and Ctrl+V for paste).

The rename action opens a dialog prompting for the new name, and then runs the RNMOBJ or RNMM command. The Delete action opens a dialog confirming the deletion. The Move action opens a dialog prompting for the target location of the move.

All of the actions allow for multiple selections. In that case, the rename, delete, and move actions handle all the selected objects or members at once. For the rename action, a dialog shows a table and you have to select the new name cell for each of the selections, enter a new name, and click OK.

The copy action does not open a dialog. Instead, it uses the Windows clipboard, just like copying and pasting from any other Windows application. First, select the object or source member. Next, select **Copy** from the pop-up menu. Then, select the target library (for objects) or target source physical file (for source members), and select **Paste** from the pop-up menu.

The paste action is only enabled if the selected target is a valid location for whatever was originally copied. This has to be a library for objects or a source physical file for source members. A very common problem with copy and paste is trying to paste onto an object or member filter instead of the actual library or source physical file. This is very easy to do, especially if you name your filters with the same name as the library or source file. If you do not see the paste action, or it is disabled, double-check that you are selecting a library or source file and not a filter.

TIP •••
The RSE uses the Windows clipboard to store the name of the selected objects or members. You can copy from the RSE and paste into a text editor or email. This pastes the list of names, not the actual objects or members.
•••

Source members can be copied between a source physical file and the IFS using the copy and paste actions. When copying to the IFS, the sequence number and date fields are stripped off, since the compilers cannot compile IFS files that contain them.

Source members can also be copied and pasted between systems. You can copy and paste between the remote system and your local RSE connection, between i5/OS on two physically different machines, or between an i5/OS and Linux LPAR. When copying and pasting between two physically different machines, a network connection between them is not required. The member is first downloaded to the local Workspace and then uploaded to the target machine.

A quick way to perform the copy and paste actions is to use the mouse to simply drag and drop the objects or members. Select the objects or members to be copied, hold down the left mouse button, drag them to the target location, and let go of the mouse button. In the RSE, drag and drop is always a copy action, not a move action.

Save and Restore Actions

The pop-up menus for libraries and objects include save and restore actions that are shortcuts to the CL commands SAVLIB, SAVOBJ, RSTLIB, and RSTOBJ. When selected, the save or restore action prompts the corresponding CL command, pre-filled based on the current selection.

Properties

The Remote Systems view shows the names, types, and attribute information for objects and members. Additional information is available via either the Properties view or the Properties dialog.

The Properties view shows a small subset of the information available from the Properties dialog. The view is automatically updated whenever an object or member is selected in the Remote Systems view or Object Table view, as shown in Figure 5–21.

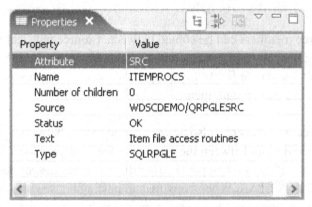

Figure 5–21: The Properties view for a source member.

TIP You might be wondering about the Status field. The i5/OS API used by the RSE to retrieve the information for objects returns this flag to warn if the object has been damaged. Apparently, in much earlier systems, objects did sometimes get damaged, but this rarely happens today. In V7.0, the Status field was removed from the default setting of the Object Table view, but apparently, it was mistakenly left in the Properties view!

To open the Properties dialog, right-click the object or member and select **Properties**. The properties are divided into categories on the left side of the dialog. Select the category to see its related properties, as shown in Figure 5–22. These are the same properties you see when entering 5 (Display) or 8 (Display Description) for members in PDM.

TIP To change the source member type, right-click the member, select Properties, and change the source type in the Properties page.

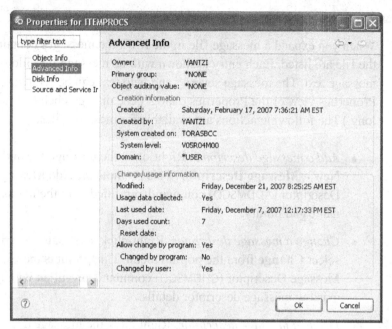

Figure 5–22: The Properties dialog for an object.

Noteworthy Objects

With every release, the RSE development team tries to make the RSE more powerful by enabling more and more details and actions for specific object types. This is often done by enabling them to be expanded in the Remote Systems view to see the additional, lower-level details, and then adding context actions on the lower-level items in the tree. The team has focused in past releases on programs, service programs, message files, and save files, so these deserve special mention here.

Programs and Service Programs

In the RSE, you can expand a program or service program to see a list of the modules bound into it. You can then expand a bound module to see a list of the procedures in the module. By default, all procedures are shown, but you can set a preference on the **Remote Systems > i5/OS > Objects Subsystem** preference page to show only exported procedures for service program objects.

Other than the list of bound modules and procedures, not much additional information is shown yet. However, you can right-click either a bound module or procedure and set a service entry point (for details, see chapter 9).

Message Files

When you expand a message file in the RSE, the messages contained in the file are listed. Each entry is shown with its message ID followed by the message text. The message severity and help text can be seen in either the Properties view or the Properties dialog. (The dialog is better if the text is long.) The following actions are available for message files:

- *Add a message descriptor*: Right-click the message file and select **New > Message Descriptor**. This prompts the Add Message Descriptor (ADDMSGD) command, pre-filled with the message file name and library.

- *Change a message descriptor*: Right-click a message descriptor and select **Change** from the pop-up menu. This prompts the Change Message Descriptor (CHGMSGD) command, pre-filled with the existing message descriptor details.

- *Delete a message descriptor*: Right-click the message descriptor and select **Delete**. This prompts for delete confirmation first, and then runs the Remove Message Descriptor (RMVMSGD) command.

Save Files

As of V7.1 the RSE does not yet support expanding a save file to see its contents (although this is on the list of requirements). You can, however, copy and paste (or drag and drop) save files between systems in the same way you can copy and paste source members. Unlike using FTP, the save file does not have to be created before pasting it. The RSE detects whether or not it exists, and creates it if required.

In addition to being able to transfer save files, the RSE provides special actions on save files. For save files residing in a library, the RSE provides shortcuts to the RSTLIB and RSTOBJ commands on the save file's pop-up menu.

For save files residing on the local workstation, the RSE provides an action to restore the save file directly to an i5/OS connection. Right-click the save file under the Local RSE connection, and select **Restore on i5/OS ...** from the pop-up menu. This opens the Restore i5/OS Save File dialog shown in Figure 5–23.

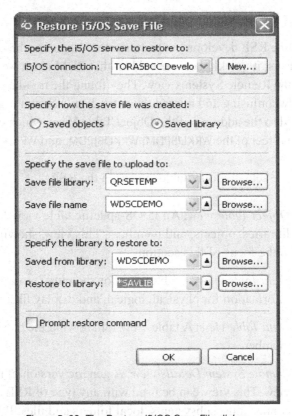

Figure 5–23: The Restore i5/OS Save File dialog.

Specify the following information in the dialog, and then click **OK** to have the save file uploaded and the objects or library restored:

- *i5/OS Connection*: Specify the RSE connection where the save file should be restored.

- *How the save file was created*: Indicate whether the save file was used to save objects (SAVOBJ) or a library (SAVLIB).

- *Where should the save file be uploaded to*: The save file needs to be uploaded to a temporary location on the remote system before it can be restored. QTEMP cannot be used because the job used to upload the save file is a different job than the one used to restore the save file.

- *Where should the save file be restored to*: Specify the name of the library that was originally saved and the name of the library to be restored.

The Object Table View

When the RSE development team started validating the initial RSE designs with users, it quickly became evident that PDM users were not comfortable using the Remote Systems view. They found the tree-based organization initially confusing and missed the extra details shown in the PDM views. This led to the addition of the Object Table View, which closely mimics the look and feel of the WRKLIBPDM, WRKOBJPDM, and WRKMBRPDM screens.

There are actually four "table" views in the RSE:

- *Object Table view*: An i5/OS-specific table view for working with libraries, objects, and members. This view, shown in Figure 5–24, is the focus of this section.

- *Field Table view*: A table view for showing record and field information for physical, logical, and display files.

- *Data Table view*: A table view for showing the contents of a data member.

- *Remote System Details view*: A generic version of the Object Table view. This view can be used with any type of RSE artifact, such as connections, subsystems, local folders and files, IFS folders and files, and i5/OS jobs.

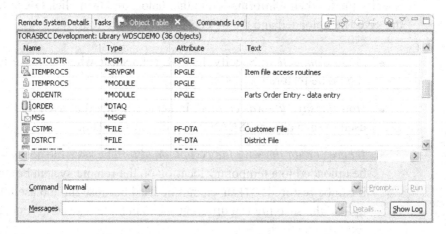

Figure 5–24: The Object Table view.

Populating the Table View

There are two main ways to populate the Object Table view: from the Remote Systems view, or by using the Object Table view menu. To populate the view from the Remote Systems view, right-click any of the following and select **Show in Table** from the pop-up menu:

- Library List filter

- Library filter

- Object filter

- Member filter

- Library

- Source or data physical file (For data physical files you have to select **Show In Table > Members**, since there is also the option of showing fields or data.)

You can also populate the Object Table view using the view menu. Click the view menu (the upside-down triangle in the view's toolbar) and open the **Work With** cascading menu shown in Figure 5–25.

Figure 5–25: The Object Table view's pull-down menu.

There are two main types of options in the cascading Work With menu. The top half of the menu lists the **Libraries . . .**, **Objects. . .**, and **Members . . .** actions, which are similar to creating a filter, except the results are shown in the view and the filter is not saved. (You don't specify a name for the filter.)

The bottom half of the menu shows the recent history of what has been shown in the view. Select one of these entries to repopulate the view.

Using the Table View

Like most Workbench views, the Object Table view has a toolbar that contains actions for navigating the view. Table 5–4 summaries these actions.

Table 5–4: Object Table View Toolbar Actions	
Toolbar Icon	**Action**
	Lock the view. When the lock icon is not selected, the table view updates automatically to show the contents of filters, libraries, source physical files, and data physical files selected in the Remote Systems view. When this icon is selected, the view does not automatically update based on selections; a specific action is required to populate the view. The lock icon is selected by default.
	Refresh the view. This action refreshes the view with the latest information from the remote system.
	Move back or forward through the view's history. These actions work like the Back and Forward buttons in a Web browser.
	Move up one level. This action populates the table view with the parent of the current view's contents. For example, if the view currently shows members, then clicking this button will populate the view with the objects from the library.

Once the table view is populated, you can use the icons in Table 5–4 for navigating around the view. You can also double-click libraries, source physical files, and data physical files to update the view to display the contents of the library or file. The Object Table view menu contains lots of other goodies, such as these:

- *Subset*: Subset the list based on name, type attribute, and text. This is similar to F17 (Subset) in PDM.

- *Show All*: Show all the items in the list again. This action is only enabled if the list is currently a subset.

- *Show Columns*: Choose between showing just the basic information, all information, or a customized selection. This is roughly similar to F14 in PDM, but the RSE has the advantage of having more than 80 columns, so the additional columns are added to the table view, instead of replacing existing columns. Use the **Remote Systems > i5/OS > Table View** preference page to set up your own customized table view columns.

- *Position to*: This action is similar to the "Position to" fields in the top right corner of most PDM screens. The action opens a dialog box that prompts for the name and type to position to.

- *Print*: Print the list of objects or members, along with their information. This is similar to F21 in PDM, except the results are printed to a local workstation printer instead of a spool file.

- *Export to file*: This is the same as Print, except the list is saved to a local workstation file of your choice.

In the top left corner of the view, immediately below the Object Table View tab, is a status bar that shows what the view is currently displaying. Figure 5–24, for example, shows the objects from the library WDSCDEMO, there are 36 objects in total. If you subset the view, the status bar will update to show how many of the total objects are displayed

At the bottom of the Object Table view is the commands area. This is similar to the command line shown at the bottom of a PDM screen. The solid triangle in the top left corner of the commands area can be clicked to toggle between showing and hiding this area.

On the left side of the command area, you select which type of command you want to run. (This is covered later in this chapter.) You can enter the actual command next to this. There are buttons to prompt and run the command, but you can also use the F4 shortcut key for prompting and just press Enter to run the command.

Immediately below the command entry field is the Message field, which displays the messages that resulted from running the command. This is a drop-down list; click the down-arrow button to see a list of the recent messages. You can see the results of the command by clicking the Show Log button. This opens the Commands Log view, containing details of the command execution.

Like most table views, you can click any of the column headings to sort the table by that column. Clicking once sorts the table alphabetically. Clicking again reverses the sort.

TIP
Instead of having to select the pull-down menu, and then the Position To action, just start typing in the table view. The Position To dialog will automatically open. Enter your positioning values, and press Enter. No mouse required!

If the Position To dialog does not open, either the Object Table view is not currently in focus, or you have started to change the name or text for an object or member. If you have accidentally started to change an object or member name or text, press the Esc key to cancel the change, and then start typing again.

PDM Actions

The object and member actions that appear in the pop-up menu in the Remote Systems view are also available in the pop-up menu from the Object Table view.

TIP
The name and text fields in the table are directly editable for objects and members, as well as the type field for members. Entering a value in the field and pressing Enter (or clicking somewhere else in the table) actually changes the name, text, or member type on the remote system.

If you click in one of these fields to select a row of the table, you are automatically put into editing mode. If you then right-click, you will see the editing menu actions (cut, copy, paste, and delete), not the object or member actions. Press Esc to cancel the editing, and then right-click to see the object or member actions. To avoid this, click one of the non-editable fields to select a row of the table.

There is also a PDM Options menu in the pop-up menu for objects and members in the Object Table view, as shown in Figure 5–26. This cascading menu includes the more common PDM options, along with their PDM option number for quick reference. Most of these options are duplicates of actions in the main pop-up menu.

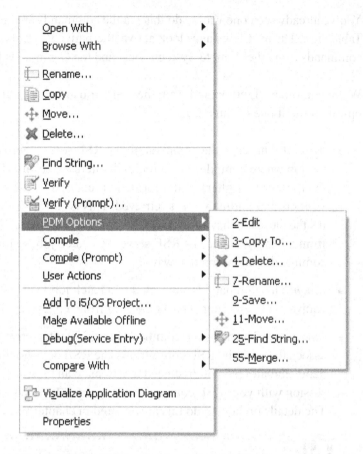

Figure 5–26: The PDM options for a source member.

In PDM, you can enter command parameters on the command line before invoking an option, so that the parameters are included when the corresponding command is prompted or run. You can do the same thing in the Object Table view by first entering the command parameters in the command entry field, and then selecting the action from the pop-up menu. To disable this behavior, use the **Remote Systems > i5/OS > Table View** preference page.

Running CL Commands

CL commands to an i5/OS programmer are like a hammer to a carpenter: an absolutely necessary tool to have in the toolbox. Recognizing this, the RSE has a few ways to run CL commands and view the resulting messages, allowing you to pick the one you find most convenient and easy to use.

You've already seen one way to do this via the commands area in the Object Table view. The next few pages look at two alternative ways to run CL commands using the Remote Systems view and the Commands Log view.

When you run a CL command from the RSE, you are always given the option to run it one of three ways:

- *Normal*: This runs the command in the RSE server job. This is the job where compiles are submitted, filters are resolved (such as the Library List filter), and information required by the program verifiers and outline view is retrieved. This is called *Normal* because it's the closest behavior to how CL commands are normally run from a 5250 session. The RSE server is a batch job, so only batch commands can be run this way.

- *Batch*: The command is submitted to a batch job via SMBJOB. This is equivalent to entering SBMJOB CMD(...) from a 5250 session.

- *Interactive*: This runs the command in a 5250 interactive job that is associated with the RSE connection. The RSE does not include a 5250 emulator, so you first need to associate an existing 5250 telnet session with your RSE connection using the STRRSESVR command. The details on how to do this are covered in chapter 9.

TIP

The RSE has a check that prevents any command that starts with *STR*, *WRK*, *DSP*, or *EDT* from running as either normal or batch. The assumption is these commands always require an interactive job to run. However, this assumption is not always true. For example, the WRKACTJOB command writes its output to a spool file if called from a batch job. Qualify the command with the library name to work around this restriction. For example, use QSYS\WRKACTJOB instead of just WRKACTJOB to run the command as either normal or batch.

The Remote Systems View

Each i5/OS RSE connection has a Commands subsystem, which can be used to run CL commands. Under the Commands subsystem are *command sets*. Each command set representing one or more CL commands. When a command set is expanded, the CL commands contained in the command set are run sequentially.

Some common CL commands are provided under the Commands subsystem out of the box, but chances are you will not need these, since the same actions are available in more convenient places in the user interface. To add your own command sets, expand the **Your Command(s) . . .** entry or right-click the subsystem and select **New > Command Set . . .** This opens the New Command Set wizard, shown in Figure 5–27.

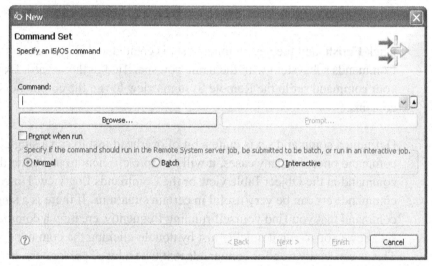

Figure 5–27: The New Command Set wizard.

Enter the CL command you want to run when the command set is executed. You can only enter a single command in the wizard, but you can change the command set after it is created to add additional commands. (This is similar to library, object, and member filters only allowing one filter string to be entered in the new wizard.)

There are two prompt options in the New Command Set wizard. The Prompt button prompts the command immediately, so you can make sure the keywords and parameters are entered correctly. The "Prompt when run" checkbox gives you the option of prompting the command every time before it is run, to allow you to specify additional parameters that might be unique each time.

TIP

If you select the "Prompt when run" checkbox in order to enter an object or member name, consider using a user-defined action instead and having the object or member name automatically filled in based on the current selection. User-defined actions are covered in chapter 10.

Click **Next** when you are finished entering the command. This takes you to the second page of the wizard, where you need to give the command set a name. Like library, object, and member filters, a command set must have a name.

Click **Finish**, and the new command set is created and shown under the Commands subsystem with the name you specified in the wizard. Expand your command set in the Remote Systems view to run the command(s) it contains.

Defining a command set is quite a bit of overhead just to run a single CL command once. In many cases, it will be more efficient to just enter the command in the Object Table view or the Commands Log view. However, command sets can be very useful in certain situations. If there is a single command that you find yourself running frequently, creating a command set allows you to run it quickly just by double-clicking the command set. This is especially true for commands that take a lot of parameters, or for a series of commands.

Although we recommend creating multiple i5/OS connections to handle different development environments (discussed later in this chapter), we have seen some people use commands sets to allow them to set up and switch environments (library list, current library) using a single RSE connection. In 5250, this is often done by writing a CL program that runs the necessary commands. In the RSE, the same CL program could be run, or you could create a command set that has those same commands.

The Commands Log View

You've probably guessed by now that the RSE leverages a lot of CL commands to do the heavy work behind the pretty user interface. All CL commands that are run, either by the RSE or directly by the user, are written to the Commands

Log view. This includes such things as compiles, user-defined actions, library list manipulation, and copying, deleting, or moving objects. So, if you are ever in doubt about whether an RSE action was run or not, check the commands log, shown in Figure 5–28.

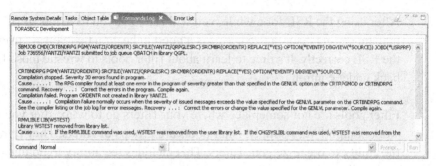

Figure 5–28: The Commands Log view.

The Commands Log view displays a separate tab for each RSE connection that has run a command since the Workbench was started. Your RSE connection will not show if no command has been run by it yet, even if the connection is connected. To force a tab to show for a connection, select **Show Log > *Connection Name*** form the view's pull-down menu.

At the bottom of the commands log is an entry field for entering CL commands similar to the Object Table view. The CL command is run using the RSE connection shown on the current tab in the view. This command entry field contains a history of the commands run since the Workbench was started. Use one of the following to select a previously run command:

- Press F9 to cycle through the previous commands (similar to using F9 in a 5250 session).

- Use the Up and Down arrow keys to cycle forward and backward through the list.

- Click the down-arrow button next to the command entry field, and select the command from the drop-down list.

There is a preference on the Remote Systems > i5/OS > Commands Subsystem preference page to retrieve help for messages displayed in the commands log. This preference is on by default. Turn this preference off if you find that always displaying the message help is confusing or annoying.

However, be warned that the message help cannot be retrieved after the command has completed, like it can in a 5250 session by pressing F1.

Filter Pools

After using the RSE for a while, you will find that you have lots of filters that are getting disorganized. This is a good indication that you are using the RSE correctly. It's time to learn about filter pools to wrestle those filters back under control.

Filter pools are not someplace where your filters go to relax after you leave work at night! Very simply, filter pools are groups of filters. They provide the ability to organize your filters. This includes the ability to do things such as these:

- Provide an extra layer in the Remote Systems view between subsystems and filters to better organize your filters.

- Create filters that only appear under a single connection, or under a subset of your connections.

All filters belong to a filter pool. Filter pools are initially hidden in the RSE to keep things simple for new users. Initially, a default filter pool is created with the name of your profile (your RSE profile, not your i5/OS user profile) followed by *Filter Pool*. All filters you create are added to this filter pool until you enable the preference to show filter pools. This preference is found on the main Remote Systems preference page. Alternatively, use the **Show Filter Pools** action on the Remote Systems view's pull-down menu to enable or disable this preference.

Once you choose to show filter pools, they appear under the subsystems. Figure 5–29 shows three filter pools under the Objects subsystem: Yantzi Filter Pool, Order Entry Filter Pool, and Web Services Filter Pool. Filters are displayed under the owning filter pool. When you choose not to show filter pools, all filters are shown directly under the subsystems.

Figure 5–29: The Show Filter Pools action enabled.

To recap so far: filter pools are just groups of filters that appear under the subsystems, and each filter belongs to a filter group.

Subsystems don't actually *contain* filter pools, they *reference* filter pools. Filter pools are their own entities in the RSE. They can be managed independent of any particular connection.

"So what?," you might ask. This gives a lot of flexibility in how you set up your connections and which filters appear under which connections. It allows you to set up a filter pool with a collection of filters, and then have any of your connections reference the filter pool.

Let's illustrate this with an example. Suppose you have two RSE connections to the same server: one for working on an order-entry application, and another for working on an invoicing application. You will likely want to have at least three filter pools created:

- *Order Entry Filter Pool*: This pool contains filters for the order-entry application and is referenced only by the order-entry connection.

- *Invoicing Filter Pool*: This pool contains filters for the invoicing application and is referenced only by the invoicing connection.

- *Personal Filter Pool*: This pool contains filters for your own personal library, objects, and members and is referenced by both connections.

This way, each connection has the filters for the corresponding development project, as well as your personal filters.

Initially, all subsystems reference the default *Your Profile Filter Pool*. This is why, when you create a filter, it appears under all connections. The option to "Only create filter in this connection" on the second page of the New Filter wizard is implemented using filter pools. If you select this option, a new filter pool is created for your filter, and only the current connection references that filter pool.

TIP One developer on a team can set up the filter pools and filters for a project, and then share them with everyone else. Connections, filter pools, user-defined actions and custom compile commands are grouped into RSE profiles, which can be copied between Workspaces to share these resources. Chapter 10 covers RSE profiles and how to share them.

Creating, Deleting, and Renaming Filter Pools

Filter pools can be created, renamed, and deleted using either pop-up menu actions in the Remote Systems view, or the central Work With Filter Pools dialog. In either case, the Show Filter Pools preference must be enabled in order to access the filter pool actions.

TIP The Show Filter Pools preference only needs to be enabled to create, delete, and rename filter pools, as well as to create and delete filter pool references. Once you have your filter pools set up under each connection, you can turn this preference back off. Then, all the filters from those filter pools appear directly under the subsystem again.

To create a new filter pool, right-click a subsystem and select **New > Filter Pool**. This opens the New Filter Pool dialog, shown in Figure 5–30.

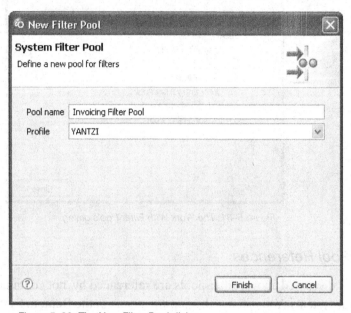

Figure 5–30: The New Filter Pool dialog.

Enter the name for the new filter pool, and click **Finish**. This creates the new filter pool and creates a reference from the subsystem to the new filter pool.

Filter pools can also be renamed or deleted by right-clicking the filter pool and selecting Rename or Delete from the pop-up menu.

The Work With Filter Pools dialog shown in Figure 5–31 provides a central place to work with all filter pools. Right-click the subsystem and select **Work With > Filter Pools** from the pop-up menu to open the dialog. Use the icons in the dialog's toolbar or pop-up menus to create, rename, or delete filter pools. There are also actions to copy and move filter pools between profiles. Profiles are covered in more details in chapter 10.

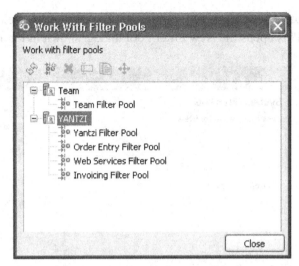

Figure 5–31: The Work With Filter Pools dialog.

Filter Pool References

As discussed above, filter pools are referenced by, not contained in, subsystems. You can use the pop-up menus in the Remote Systems view or the Select Filter Pools dialog to manage which filter pools are referenced by a subsystem.

To add a reference using the pop-up menu approach, right-click the subsystem and select **New** > **Filter Pool Reference** > *Profile Name* > *Filter Pool Name*. To remove a filter pool reference, right-click the filter pool and select **Remove Reference** from the pop-up menu. This only removes the reference to this filter pool from the selected subsystem; it does not delete the filter pool.

If you want to make multiple changes to which filter pools are referenced from a subsystem, it is quicker to use the Select Filter Pool dialog for the subsystem, shown in Figure 5–32. To open the dialog, right-click the subsystem and click **Select Filter Pools** from the pop-up menu.

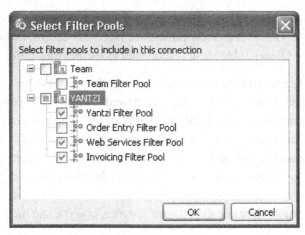

Figure 5–32: The Select Filter Pools dialog.

The dialog shows all filter pools grouped by their owning profiles. Each filter pool has a checkbox that indicates whether or not the subsystem references that filter pool.

The Remote Systems View Revisited

This section covers a few miscellaneous goodies from the Remote Systems view that were not discussed earlier in this chapter to avoid information overload. Hopefully, by now you are a Remote Systems view pro and are ready for some more.

Re-expansion on Startup

When you start the Workbench, the Remote Systems view is re-expanded to the same state it was in when the Workbench was last shut down, with the exception of the Commands and Jobs subsystems. The Object Table view is also repopulated with the same contents.

There are two preferences that affect this behavior, both on the Remote Systems preference page:

- *Re-open Remote Systems view to previous state*: This controls whether or not the view should be re-expanded on startup. If this preference is deselected, the Remote Systems view starts up with all connections collapsed. The default is for this preference to be selected. There is a corresponding preference on the Remote Systems > i5/OS > Table View preference page that controls whether or not the Object Table view is reopened to its previous state.

- *Use cached information to restore the Remote Systems view*: This controls whether the information used to re-expand the view should be retrieved from the local cache or from the remote system. Using cached information allows the Workbench to start up quicker and prevents having to sign on and connect to the remote system. The disadvantage of using the cache is the information shown on re-expansion might be out of date. This is especially pertinent to the library list, which tends to be more dynamic than lists of libraries, objects, and members.

Re-focusing the View

Normally, the Remote Systems view shows your connections at the highest level of the tree, and you drill down from there. However, you can change the input of the Remote Systems view to be a single connection, subsystem, or filter. Right-click the one you are interested in and select **Go Into** from the pop-up menu. This causes the view to show only the children of the selected connection, subsystem, or filter.

After you have gone into something, you can use the back (⇦), forward (⇨), and up (⬆) buttons from the Remote Systems view's toolbar to refocus the view. The back and forward buttons work like those in a Web browser. The up button refocuses the view on the parent of whatever the view is currently focused on. For example, if the view is currently focused on a filter, and you click the up button, the view will refocus on the subsystem (assuming you have Show Filter Pools turned off). These same actions are available in the pop-up menu, under Go To.

In reality, we have never heard of anyone using this feature. Perhaps you will be the first!

Link with Editor

The toolbar of the Remote Systems view has a toggle button that allows you to link the view's selection with the current editor (🔗). When this toggle button is selected, if you select an open editor, the

Remote Systems view tries to find the open member in the tree and automatically select it. We say *tries* because this only works if the member has already been shown in the view at some point and is therefore already in the UI cache.

We find this feature very useful, but also annoying if the option is left selected. If you are frequently switching between open editors, and you have this option selected, the Remote Systems view will keep jumping around to match the selected editor.

We typically leave this option deselected, unless we want to find the member for a specific editor. In this case, we turn the option on, select the editor (which finds and selects the corresponding member in the Remote Systems view), and then turn the option off again.

Recommendations on Setting Up Your Connections

In an earlier tip, we suggested you think about an RSE connection not as a specific server, but as a development project (or environment) on that server. Then, set up and configure a separate RSE connection for each development project on the server. For each connection, you can configure the following:

- A unique library list, as discussed earlier in this chapter

- A unique object library, batch job description, and parameters for compiles

- Application-specific filters that only show under the connection, as discussed in the "Filters" and "Filter Pools" sections of this chapter

This approach to setting up connections is not something that is immediately obvious to new users of the RSE, but it is one of the features that can greatly increase productivity with the RSE.

Green Screen to RSE QuickStart

Table 5–5 describes the mapping between the PDM and RSE functions as they relate to the tasks described in this chapter.

Table 5–5: Mapping Between the PDM and RSE Functions

Green Screen/PDM Action	RSE Action
WRKLIBPM	Create a library filter or use the Object Table view.
WRKOBJPDM	Create an object filter or use the Object Table view.
WRKMBRPDM	Create a member filter or use the Object Table view.
EDTLIBL	Use the pop-up menu actions on the Library List filter and libraries under the filter.
STRSEU	Right-click the Objects subsystem and select **Open Member**, or use the Ctrl+Shift+A keyboard shortcut.
2=Edit (WRKMBRPDM)	Double-click the member to open it in the Remote Systems LPEX Editor (chapters 6 and 7), or use the keyboard shortcut Ctrl+Shift+A.
2=Change (WRKLIBPDM/ WRKOBJPDM)	Right-click the library or object, and select **Change**.
3=Copy	Right-click the object or member and select **Copy**, and then right-click the target location and select **Paste**.
4=Delete	Select the library, object, or member, and press the Delete key.
5=Display	Right-click the member and select **Browse With > Remote Systems** LPEX Editor (chapters 6 and 7), or use keyboard shortcut Ctrl+Shift+A and select the **Browse** radio button.
6=Print (WRKMBRPDM)	Open the member in the Remote Systems LPEX Editor, and then print using the **File > Print** menu action, or use the keyboard shortcut Ctrl+P.
7=Rename	Right click the library, object, or member, and select **Rename**.
8=Display Description	Select the library, object, or member, and look at the Properties view. Alternatively, right-click the library, object, or member, and select Properties.
9=Save	Right-click the library or object, and select **Save**, or use the keyboard shortcut Ctrl+S.
10=Restore	Right-click the library or object, and select **Restore**.
11=Move	Right-click the library, object, or member, and select **Move**.
12=Work With (WRKOBJPDM/WRKLIBPDM)	Click the plus sign to expand the library or object.
13=Change Text	Change the library, object, or member text via either the Properties view or the Properties dialog.
14=Compile	See chapter 8 on compiling.
15=Create Module	

Table 5–5: Mapping Between the PDM and RSE Functions (Continued)	
Green Screen/PDM Action	**RSE Action**
15=Copy file (WRKOBJPDM)	See the entry above for 3=Copy.
17=Change using SDA	Right-click the DDS member and select **Open With > CODE Designer**. (This requires Code Designer to be installed.) Alternatively, select **Open With > Screen Designer**. (This requires the advanced edition if using WDSC.) Details on Screen Designer, which is a Technology Preview, can be found in chapter 13.
25=Find string	Right-click the member and select **Find String**. This is discussed in chapter 10.
26=Create Program	See chapter 8.
27=Create Service Program	
34=Interactive Source Debugger	See chapter 9.
54=Compare	See chapter 6
F6=Create	Right-click a filter, library, or source physical file, and select one of the options from the cascading New menu.
F5=Refresh	Press F5, or click the "refresh" icon in the Remote System view's toolbar.
F16=User actions	See chapter 10 for information on user-defined actions.
F17=Subset	Modify your filter to show only the desired subset, or use the Object Table view's **Subset** action.
F21=Print list	List printing is only available in the Object Table view. Select **Print** from the view's pull-down menu.

Troubleshooting

Below are some common problems related to the topics in this chapter, along with suggestions on diagnosing and fixing the problems:

- *I can't connect to the server.*

  Troubleshooting issues related to communications and signing on are covered in chapter 10.

- *Why do I always get prompted to sign on when starting the Workbench?*

When you start the Workbench, the Remote Systems view is re-expanded to the same state it was when the Workbench was shut down, and the Object Table view is set to its previous contents. This information is retrieved from the cache for library, object, and member lists, if it's available.

If the lists are not available from the cache, or if you previously had IFS folders expanded, then you will be prompted to sign on. If your user ID and password are saved, the RSE will automatically try to connect to the remote system. There are preferences on the Remote Systems and Remote Systems > i5/OS > Table View preference pages to disable Remote Systems and Object Table views from re-expanding and using cached information. See the section "Re-expansion on Startup" in this chapter for additional information.

- *Sometimes I get prompted to sign on to a system I'm not even using. Why?*

This is most likely being caused by the Object Table view refreshing. When the Workbench starts, the Object Table view is set to the same contents it had when the Workbench was shut down. Usually, this information is retrieved from the cache, so the RSE doesn't need to connect to the remote system.

However, as the RSE runs, certain events can force the Object Table view to refresh, even if its current contents are not from the same system you are currently working with. This results in the RSE connecting to the remote system to retrieve the updated list of libraries, objects, or members showing in the view.

- *I've saved my password, but I still get prompted to sign on when connecting to the server.*

Both the user ID and password have to be saved for a connection to have the RSE automatically connect without prompting. Select one of the subsystems under your connection, and check that your user ID is displayed for the User ID property in the Properties view. It's okay if it says *(Inherited)* after the user ID.

Also check that your password is saved for this connection's hostname and user ID on the Remote Systems > Passwords preference page. The hostname for the connection must match the value on the preference page. At connection time, the user ID, system type (i5/OS), and hostname for the connection are used as a key to look up the saved password. See the section "Connecting to the Remote System" for additional information.

- *It takes a really long time when I expand my library or source physical file.*

  Try to keep lists of objects and members to around 100 or less. It will take a while if you expand a library that contains hundreds or thousands of objects. (How long it will take depends greatly on the performance of your workstation, network, and server.) Expanding the library causes the RSE to return the entire list of objects in it. The name and some additional properties need to be sent from the server to the workstation for each object in the list, and then displayed in the user interface. The same is true for source physical files that contain hundreds or thousands of members.

  This is why a lot of effort has gone into making the filtering capabilities of the RSE so powerful. Take the time up front to create filters that capture only the objects/members you are currently working on. Not only do these smaller lists return much quicker, but they also enable you to be more productive by not having to search through large lists to find the objects and members you want.

  That is not to say that all performance problems are the result of large lists of objects or members.

- *Some of my filters take a really long time to resolve.*

  This could be from either the filter results being very large or the filter being too generic. Filters that result in large lists of objects or members will take extra time to send the results back from the server to the workstation. Try to modify your filter so it returns only the objects or members you currently need access to.

  Some of the filtering capabilities provided by the RSE are not directly supported by i5/OS. In these cases, the RSE downloads all the lists and applies the filter on the workstation. You might only see a small list displayed in the RSE, but a much larger list might have been initially returned. Check to see if you are using either of the following filtering capabilities:

» Type and attribute filtering.

» Multi-generic filters. For example, consider an object filter where the library name is generic. The RSE first queries all libraries that match the generic library name, and then queries the objects for each library.

If you are doing this kind of filtering, you might want to modify the filter so it initial returns a smaller list.

If all of your filters take a long time to resolve, however, there is likely some more general performance issue going on.

- *Why is there is always a delay after I click on a filter, library, or source physical file?*

The most likely cause of this is the Object Table view has become unlocked, so every time you select a filter, library, or source physical file, the object table is querying the list of contained objects or members and displaying them. Check that the lock icon in the Object Table view is selected, which means the view is locked and is not updated automatically. See the section "Using the Table View" for additional information.

- *I get an "Empty List" message when I expand my filter.*

Open the **Change Filter** dialog for the filter, and check that the filter is specified correctly and doesn't contain any typos. Use the **Test** button in the Change Filter dialog to test individual filter strings as you modify them. Try testing object and member filter strings without the type and subtypes filters specified, to see if these might be the source of the problem.

- *I get "Expand Failed, Try Again" when I expand my filter.*

Check that your connection is not offline by right-clicking the connection and making sure the **Work Offline** action is not checked. Select the action to toggle back online if there is a checkmark.

- *I'm trying to copy and paste, but I don't see a Paste action when I right- click.*

This is one of the most common questions we get asked during RSE presentations. The most common reason for this is that you are trying to paste onto a filter instead of a library (for object copies) or a source physical file (for member copies). The target of a paste must be the actual target library or source physical file, not a filter.

You might be getting confused because you gave your member filter the same name as the source physical file, so when you look at it in the Remote Systems view, it looks like the source physical file. (After all, it is the parent of the members in the tree.) If in doubt, select the entry and look at the Type property in the Properties view. If the type is i5/OS Member Filter, then you need to find the *FILE object to perform the paste.

The other thing to note here is that you can copy and paste members and source physical files across systems, but you cannot copy and paste libraries or objects across systems.

- *I did a copy and paste (or a move/rename), but the results were not updated in the Remote Systems and/or Object Table views.*

Whenever an action is run in the RSE, the Remote Systems and Object Table views attempt to detect if their contents are affected, and refresh if required. Depending on the type of action and selected target, however, this is not always possible. In these cases, you need to select the parent of the list and press F5 to refresh the list for the Remote Systems view, or just press F5 for the Object Table view.

You should also check the Commands Log view to make sure the CL command for the copy, paste, rename, or move completed with no error messages.

- *The list of libraries/objects/members shown in the Remote Systems view or Object Table view is not correct.*

In most cases, this is caused either by the view being restored from a stale cache, or not being refreshed after an action that modified the list. Refresh lists in the Remote Systems view by selecting the lists' parent and pressing F5. Refresh lists in the Object Table view by making sure the view has focus, and then pressing F5.

Note that collapsing and re-expanding items in the Remote Systems view does not cause the list to be re-queried. The user interface caches these items for performance reasons.

- *I can't find the Remote Systems view or the Object Table view.*

  First, check that you are in the Remote Systems Explorer perspective. The name of the current perspective is shown in the left corner of the title bar for the Workbench window. To switch to the Remote Systems Explorer perspective, select **Window > Open Perspective > Other**, and then select **Remote System Explorer**.

  The Remote Systems and Object Table views are in tabbed notebooks in the Workbench. Check that another view in the notebook has not taken focus over the top of it. For example, the Team view may be showing in the top left corner of the Workbench window, instead of the Remote Systems view.

  The view might also have been accidentally closed. To reopen the view, select **Window > Show View > Other**, and then select **Remote Systems > Remote Systems** or **i5/OS > Object Table view**.

- *I don't see any filters when I expand the Objects subsystem.*

  The most likely cause of this is the connection being created in a profile that is not your default profile, like the Team profile. Connections created in your default profile are automatically set up to reference the default filter pool, and therefore show the default sets of filters under Objects. Connections created in other profiles are set up to reference that profile's default filter pool, but these filter pools do not contain any filters.

  If you want the connection to stay in the profile it's in, you can create filters by following the steps in the "Filters" section of this chapter. Otherwise, you can delete the connection and recreate it under your default profile.

- *I don't see my connection in the Remote Systems view anymore.*

  If you still see the New Connection entry, you have probably made all profiles inactive. Making a profile inactive hides all connections, user-defined actions, and custom compile commands from the profile. Switch to the Team view, right-click the profiles, and select **Make Active** from the pop-up menu.

If you see things at the top level of the Remote Systems view other than connections, you have likely accidentally (or perhaps on purpose while playing around) selected the Go Into action on a connection, subsystem, or filter. Use the up icon in the view's toolbar to refocus the view back to the connections level. (See the section "Re-focusing the View" for details.)

- *The Object Table view keeps changing whenever I click something in the Remote Systems view.*

The Object Table view can be unlocked so the view automatically updates based on a selection in the Remote Systems view. Alternatively, the view can be locked so it only updates based on an explicit action, like selecting the Show In Table action from the RSE. Check that the lock icon in the Object Table view is selected so the view does not change automatically. (See the section "Using the Table View" for additional details.)

- *Whenever I click an editor, the Remote Systems view jumps around.*

Check that the Link With Editor button in the Remote Systems view's toolbar is not selected. When this button is selected, the Remote Systems view is automatically updated to select the file being edited whenever the active editor changes.

- *How do I know if my action or CL command completed?*

If an RSE action is successful, the UI is updated to reflect the result of the action, and no additional messages are displayed. If the action fails, an error message is typically displayed. You can always check the Commands log view to see commands that are run and the resulting i5/OS messages.

- *My initial command or CL command fails to run correctly.*

CL commands run as *normal*, as well as any command that you specify in the Initial Library List property page, run in the RSE server job on i5/OS. They must be able to run as batch. The RSE server job is set up to automatically take the default reply to any exception messages, to prevent the job (and therefore the RSE) from hanging. Check the commands log or the job log for the i5/OS server job to see if any exception messages occurred.

- *I see the property names in the Properties view, but I don't see any property values.*

  Depending on the size of the Properties view, the Values column can sometimes be off to the right and not visible. Try scrolling the view to the right if you don't see the Values column in the view. You can also resize the view or shrink the size of the Property column so everything fits in the view.

- *When I expand my filters, I see more than one copy of the same object in the list.*

  All the filter strings defined for the filter are resolved when expanding the filter. If multiple filter strings contain the same object, it will appear in the filter more than once.

CHAPTER 6

The Remote Systems LPEX Editor: The Best of Both Worlds

Any source-code editor should allow you to enter your source code with ease and flexibility. A good source-code editor should also assist you in entering, navigating, and fixing errors in your source code and should be customizable to suit your style.

In the RSE, the default editor is the Remote Systems Live Parsing Extensible editor, also known as the Remote Systems LPEX Editor (herein referred to as just *LPEX*). LPEX is a powerful language-sensitive editor that can be used for editing many different source types. In addition to basic editing functions, LPEX offers many language-specific editing features that facilitate editing. There are extensive customization capabilities that enable you to adapt LPEX to your editing needs. You can even change the editor to look and feel like you are editing in SEU (green text on a black background). We really hope, however, that you don't do that!

Before proceeding, let's explain a bit about the underlying implementation of LPEX, since it will help you understand the editor and how some things are shown in the user interface. LPEX is designed to serve many different platforms and programming languages. Basic editing features like inserting a line, deleting text, and copying and moving blocks of code are all implemented in the base LPEX.

Base LPEX is intended to be extended to add programming-language and system-specific editing functionality via language parsers. This is how the i5/OS language-specific extensions for RPG, COBOL, CL, and DDS are added to the base LPEX editor. We call this package of base LPEX and the i5/OS language parsers the *Remote Systems LPEX Editor*.

It is important to be aware of this design, so you can understand certain "mysteries" of why the editor behaves the way it does. For example, why are there two places where different editor preferences can be specified? Now you know why: one pertains to base LPEX, and the other is for the i5/OS language-specific preferences. (Preferences are covered later in this chapter.)

We will continue to use just the term *LPEX* to refer to the entire editor, including base LPEX and the i5/OS language parsers. This chapter focuses on the basic editor functionality, including the integration of SEU-like features and the Workbench tools. The next chapter dives into the i5/OS language-specific editor features for RPG, COBOL, DDS, and CL source members.

Opening a Source Member

The RSE is governed by i5/OS user profile authority. Just like SEU, you can only open members that you have access to browse or edit on i5/OS. If the i5/OS user profile used in the RSE to connect to i5/OS does not have the authority to list the member, the member will not show in the Remote Systems or Object Table views.

Double-click a source member, or right-click the member and select the **Open With > Remote Systems LPEX Editor** action, to open the member for editing in LPEX. Before the member is opened in LPEX, your permission to the source file is checked, the member is locked, and the member is downloaded to the RemoteSystemsTempFiles project in the local Workspace. The local copy of the member is then opened in the editor. If you hover the mouse pointer over the editor tab, you will see the location of the local copy of the member, as shown in Figure 6–1.

Before you get concerned about editing a local copy of the member, remember that this is just the way things are implemented internally because originally the Eclipse Workbench could only edit local files. From an outside perspective, it is like you are directly editing the remote member. The member is locked while you are editing the member, and changes made in the editor are saved back to the remote member.

```
CLOUTLINE1.CLP      PAYROLL.RPGLE  X
Line 27      Column 6      Replace
.....  Filename++IH RemoteSystemsTempFiles/TORASBCC/QSYS.LIB/HAJI.LIB/QRPGLESRC.FILE/PAYROLL.RPGLE .....
002200      F*  used are - MSTDSP  - maintenance display file
002300      F*            - EMPMST  - employee master file
002400      F*            - PRJMST  - project master file
002500      F*            - RSNMST  - reason code master file
002600      F******************************************************
002700      FMSTDSP   CF   E              WORKSTN
002800      FEMPMST   UF A E          K DISK
002900      FPRJMST   UF A E          K DISK
003000      FRSNMST   UF A E          K DISK
```

Figure 6–1: The location of the downloaded member on the workstation.

If you try to open a member for editing that you do not have authority to edit, a dialog box indicating this will be displayed, asking if you want to browse the member. If you try to open a member that is already locked, a dialog box will be presented indicating that the member is locked, as shown in Figure 6–2. From this dialog, you have an option to display the job properties of the job that is locking the member. You can then choose to open the member in browse mode, end the job holding the member (if you have sufficient authorities), or cancel opening the member.

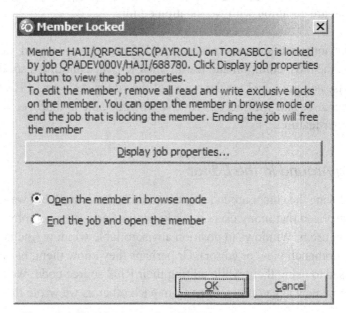

Figure 6–2: The Member Locked dialog.

To purposely open a member in browse (read-only) mode, right-click it, and select the **Browse With > Remote Systems LPEX Editor** action.

The Remote Systems LPEX Editor does not support the editing of source members from QTEMP library.

Using the Editor

In chapter 3, you saw the Remote Systems LPEX Editor's layout (in Figure 3–17) and were introduced to the terminology used for different parts of the editor. We will be using this terminology here when referring to specific areas of the editor, so you might want to go back to chapter 3 and review the section on editing a member.

One of the appealing features of LPEX is that it contains both modern workstation and SEU editing capabilities. This is the reason we call LPEX the best of both worlds. Programmers familiar with SEU can easily to switch to LPEX, while having access to the more advanced editing features that are common with workstation editors.

It's not possible to cover every LPEX feature here. Instead, we concentrate on the most common and useful ones, so you can build a solid knowledge base and get a feel for the power of the editor. As your LPEX experience increases and your needs grow, you will be able to discover and use the other features.

Moving Around in the Editor

Moving the cursor around might sound like basic stuff, but we are continually surprised that many users don't know the various key combinations you can use in Windows to position any scrollable window (including a Workbench view or editor). Or perhaps they know them, but just are not used to using them while editing their RPG source code. We even learned some new key combinations from each other as we wrote this list!

There are several ways to position the cursor in the editor using either the mouse or keyboard. Using the mouse, of course, you can position the pointer and click where you want the text cursor to be. Alternatively, you can use the keyboard navigation as follows:

- Press the Up, Down, Left, or Right arrow to move one line or character in that direction.

- Press Home to move the cursor to the beginning of a line, or End to move it to the end of a line.

- Press Ctrl+Left arrow to move the cursor one word left, or Ctrl+Right arrow to move it one word right.

- Press the Page Up or Page Down key to move the cursor up or down one window at a time.

- Press Ctrl+Up arrow to scroll the editor up one line without changing the cursor position from the current line, or Ctrl+Down arrow to scroll the editor down one line.

- Press Ctrl+Home to move the cursor to the beginning of the document, or Ctrl+End to move it to the end of the document.

- Press Ctrl+J to return the cursor to the place in the editor where you last entered text.

- Press Home and then Shift+Tab to position the cursor in the Prefix area.

TIP If you inadvertently select text, for example by dragging the mouse, deselect it by pressing Alt+U, or right-click and select **Deselect** from the pop-up menu.

Replacing and Inserting Text

The editor's status line indicates the *mode* of the editor. When the editor is in replace mode, the cursor appears as a solid block, one character wide. Text overlaid by this block will be replaced by any new text that you type. When the editor is in insert mode, the cursor appears as a thin vertical line. Any new text that you type is inserted into the source at the cursor position, and existing text after the cursor is shifted. Press the Insert key on your keyboard to toggle back and forth between insert and replace modes.

For column-sensitive languages, you can choose not to shift the entire line in insert mode, only shifting the text in the current column instead.

To configure this, go to the **Remote Systems > Remote Systems LPEX Editor** preference page (**Window > Preferences**), and select the option **Column sensitive editing**.

Deleting Text

There are several ways to delete text:

- Use the Delete or Backspace key to delete a single character.

- Press Ctrl+Delete to delete all text between the cursor and the end of the current line.

- Press Ctrl+Backspace to delete a complete line, or use the *d* prefix command.

- Use the D, D*n*, or DD SEU prefix commands.

If column-sensitive editing is turned on, any required text shifting is done only on that particular column.

Copying Text

To copy and paste text, start by selecting the text using the mouse, then right-click, and select **Copy** from the pop-up menu. Alternatively, use the Ctrl+Insert keyboard shortcut. (The standard Ctrl+C keyboard shortcut also works). You can then position the cursor where you want the text to pasted, right-click, and select **Paste** from the pop-up menu, or use the Ctrl+V keyboard shortcut.

This performs a *stream-based* copy and paste; only the selected text is actually copied. If you want to copy entire lines, make sure all of the text in the lines is selected. Likewise, pasting inserts the text starting at the cursor position. If you are pasting entire lines, make sure the cursor is in column one.

TIP The copy and paste actions use the Windows clipboard, so you can copy from LPEX and paste into any other Windows application. You can also copy from any Windows application and paste into LPEX!

The SEU prefix commands in the Prefix area can also be used to copy lines of text, as shown in Figure 6–3. The SEU prefix commands for copying lines of text only work within a single source editor. If you want to copy and paste from one source member to another then you have to use the copy and paste actions.

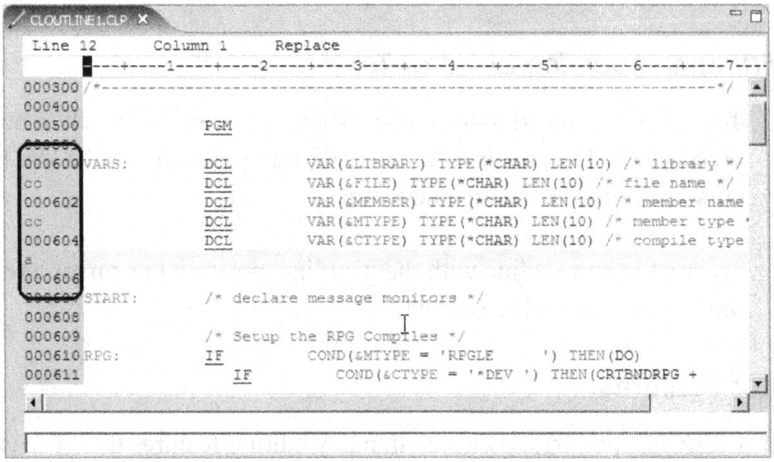

Figure 6–3: The SEU prefix commands.

Inserting a Blank Line

To insert a blank line, do any of the following:

- Position the cursor at any point on a line and press Ctrl+Enter.

- Position the cursor at the end of a line and press Enter.

- Position the cursor in the prefix area and use the I or I*n* SEU prefix commands.

A blank line is created after the current line, and the cursor moves to the first column position of this new line. For RPG source members, the default behavior for the Enter key is to repeat the previous specification type. To change this, go to the **Remote Systems > Remote Systems LPEX Editor > ILE RPG** (or RPG/400) preference page and deselect this option or select one of the other predefined behaviors for the Enter key.

TIP ···

A lot of users struggle with getting the Enter key behavior just the way they want it. The RPG preference pages have options for customizing the Enter key's behavior, but the other languages do not. You can still customize this on the LPEX User Key Actions preference page (discussed later in this chapter).

···

Splitting and Joining Lines of Text

To split a line, position the cursor where you want the break to occur, and press Alt+S. The cursor is left at its current position. All the text after the cursor is moved down to a new line.

To join the current line with the next line, position the cursor anywhere on the current line and press Alt+J.

Editor Features

LPEX is a powerful editor, with many editing features that surpass SEU. The more you learn about these capabilities, the more you will wonder how you ever survived using just SEU. You won't ever want to go back to green screen programming!

The features covered in this section apply to all source member types opened using LPEX. Language-specific features are covered in the next chapter. It is not practical to go through every feature of LPEX here, so we focus on the features you can start using right away. Once you become familiar with this editor, you will know where to look to discover other valuable features to build a rich development environment.

If you are an SEU user, this section will help you realize that most of the editing features you are accustomed to using in your daily tasks are also available in LPEX. Now you have one less excuse for not switching to the RSE!

Sequence Numbers

While editing in LPEX, the sequence numbers are shown on the left, just like in SEU. If you are editing an IFS, local, or i5/OS project source file that does not have sequence numbers, no sequence numbers are shown in the editor.

Start at and *increment by* values can be configured on the Remote Systems > Remote Systems LPEX Editor preference page for resequencing the sequence numbers. When you insert a line, the sequence number is incremented by one, regardless of the increment specified in the preference page. To resequence the source using the preference values, at any time, select **Source > Resequence All Lines** from the Workbench menu bar. This is a different behavior than SEU, where the increment is applied when inserting the next line.

TIP

No decimals are shown in the sequence numbers in LPEX. To achieve the same sequence as in SEU, you need to do some math! For example, an increment of 0.05 in SEU is similar to an increment of five in Remote Systems LPEX Editor.

To have LPEX re-sequence the lines every time the source is saved, select the **Resequence lines at save** checkbox in the preferences, as shown in Figure 6–4. The preferences are used for all members; there isn't a way to specify the re-sequencing for each member. This is again unlike SEU, where you can specify the start and the increment of the sequence number for each member you save, if it is different from the default value.

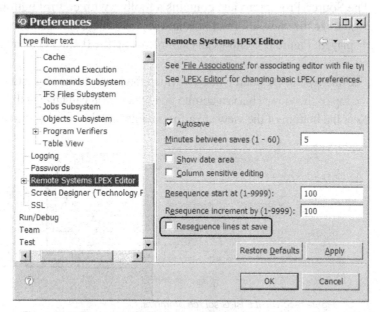

Figure 6–4: Resequencing lines when saving the member.

Prefix Commands

You can use the prefix area to enter SEU-style prefix commands such as I4, DD/DD, and CC/CC. Just type the command in the prefix area and press Enter, as shown in Figure 6–3.

Do you need a refresher on all the SEU prefix commands? Position the cursor in the prefix area, and press F1. Learn SEU prefix commands in a workstation editor! How's that for an oxymoron?

Source Prompting

Just like in SEU, you can invoke the source prompter from anywhere inside the editor. Either press F4 or select **Source > Prompt** from the menu bar.

Prompting for CL is a bit different and will be covered in the next chapter under CL-specific features. For DDS, COBOL, and RPG source members, the Source Prompter view appears in the bottom right corner of the Workbench. The Source Prompter view is not opened as part of the default RSE perspective. The view is first opened when the prompter is invoked. When it is visible, you will see the contents of the prompter updated as you move through the source.

The Source Prompter view contains a toolbar with control buttons to customize the view, a format line, and an area where syntax errors are displayed. Figure 6–5 shows an example using the ILE RPG source prompter.

The *line type* of the source line for which the prompt was requested is shown at the top of the view. This is a combo box, where you can change the line type. Near the bottom of the view are a format line and the current source line.

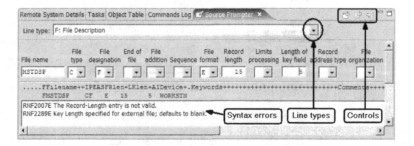

Figure 6–5: The ILE RPG source prompter.

The prompt is laid out according to the columns, just like in SEU. Some entry fields are combo boxes (shown with the down arrow), indicating there a number of choices from which you must choose. You can type the choice in that column, but if the choice is incorrect, it will not be entered in the column. This helps to ensure that only valid choices are entered. The format line is updated as you type in the columns to reflect what the source line looks like. Columns that need to be right-adjusted are automatically adjusted in the format line. F1 language help is enabled in the Source Prompter view.

Changes made in the source prompter are not automatically reflected in the editor. You can select the Revert button to undo the changes. Pressing the Enter key or selecting the Apply button updates the source in the editor. When the source is updated, the syntax checker is invoked, and any syntax errors are shown in the editor and in the prompter.

There are also three control buttons in the Source Prompter's toolbar at the top right corner of the view. The first button (📖) disables the Source Prompter view. If you do not want the prompter to be updated as you move through the source, click this button. The source prompter will be disabled and blanked out. Clicking the button again will enable the Source Prompter view. This allows prompting to be turned off instead of having to close the Source Prompter view.

The second button (📖) disables syntax checking in the prompter. Although no syntax errors will be shown in the prompter, syntax checker is still invoked when the source is updated, and any syntax errors will be shown in the editor (assuming the syntax checking preference is enabled). If syntax checking is disabled through the preferences, the source prompter, regardless of the state of this button, will not perform syntax checking.

The third button (📄) toggles between the insert and replace modes. Insert mode allows new lines to be inserted in the editor through the source prompter.

Date (Timestamp) Fields

In SEU, the date fields are shown at the end of the each line. In LPEX, the date fields are shown next to the sequence numbers at the beginning of the line. The option to show date fields is disabled by default. To enable this option, right-click in the source and select **Source > Show date area**. This shows the date fields for the current member being edited.

To show date fields for all the source members, select the **Show date area** preference on the **Remote Systems > Remote Systems LPEX Editor** preference page. Date fields will then be shown for all members opened in LPEX. Similarly, if you want date fields not to be shown for a member when the preference indicates to show date fields, right-click the member and deselect **Source > Show date area**.

Date Field Manipulation

To filter a source member by the date field, right-click in the editor and select **Filter view > Date**. You can specify the date and comparison criteria for filtering the date in the Filter by Date dialog that opens. Source lines that meet the filtering criteria will be shown in the source with plus signs in the vertical ruler. Clicking on a plus sign expands to show the source lines between the selected line and the next visible line, as shown in Figure 6–6.

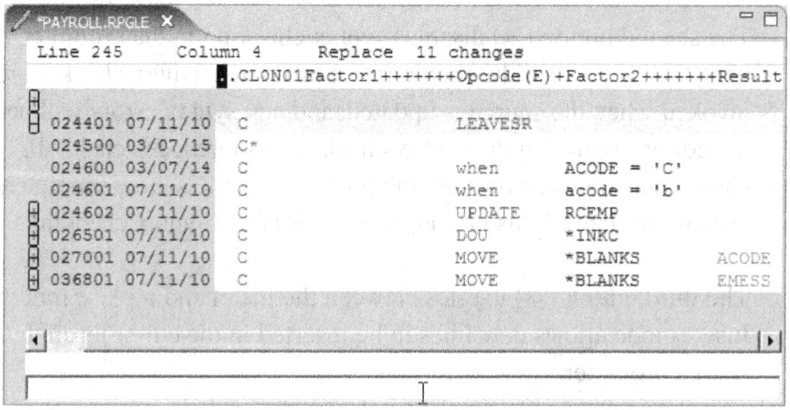

Figure 6–6: Filtering by date.

To show the entire source without the filters, right-click the source and select **Show all**, or use the keyboard shortcut Ctrl+W.

TIP

··

In SEU, you can change all the dates at once to a specified date. This action is not directly available in LPEX, but you can set up a keyboard shortcut that comes close to emulating it with just a few extra keystrokes. LPEX includes a sample "set date" action. On the **LPEX Editor > User Actions** preference page, set this action by selecting **com.ibm.lpex.samples.SetDateAction** from the Class name entry field, enter a name for the action, and select the **Set** button. Then, on the **LPEX Editor > User Key Actions** page, you can associate this name with a keyboard shortcut. (See the section "Configuring Additional Keyboard Shortcuts" later in this chapter for more information).

Now, in the editor, select all lines by first pressing Ctrl+Home, then holding down Shift while pressing Ctrl + End. Press your keyboard shortcut. This prompts to enter the date at the bottom of the editor. Enter the date you want to set, and press Enter.

··

The Format Line

For column-sensitive languages like COBOL, DDS, and RPG, a format line is presented at the top of the editor to assist in entering source. This is automatically updated to reflect the current line specification. You can also type **F** in the prefix area to show the format line of that line, as shown in Figure 6–7.

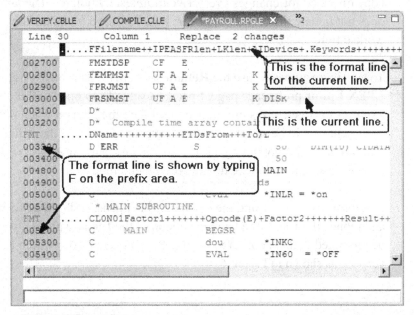

Figure 6–7: Format lines.

Retrieving Contents from Another File

To insert the contents of a remote member into an open member, click **File > Get File**. In the dialog box, browse through your files, select the file you want to insert, and click **OK.** The contents will be inserted starting from the current cursor position. If you had more than one RSE connection, you would have noticed all your RSE connections appearing in the Get Source Member dialog. This means you can "get" a file from another i5/OS server and insert it in your current source.

This get-file feature was implemented in LPEX because the same feature existed in predecessor products. The workstation equivalent of this feature would be to open up the second member in another editor (perhaps for browse only), and just copy and paste the lines from one to the other.

Autosave

If something unexpected were to suddenly happen to your workstation or Workbench while you were editing a file, you would not want to loose an entire day's work! LPEX has an autosave feature that saves a local copy of the editor changes every five minutes, by default. The autosave does not update the remote member; it just stores a local backup on the workstation.

To configure autosave, use the **Remote Systems > Remote Systems LPEX Editor** preference page. Specify a value from one to 60 in the **Minutes between saves** preference to set the time interval when the document should be saved locally on your workstation, if the default of five minutes does not meet your needs. You also have an option to disable the autosave option, but we do not recommend this.

If autosave is enabled, and the unexpected happens, restart the Workbench and reopen the file. If the backup version of the file is available, you will be prompted with an option to open the local backup copy of the last saved version, as shown in Figure 6–8.

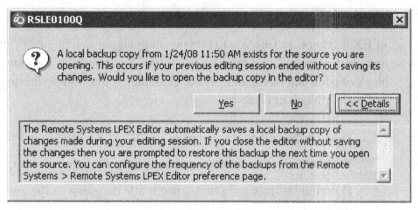

Figure 6–8: The option to open a local backup copy of the source.

In most, if not all, cases, you should select **Yes** in this dialog. This opens the editor with the contents of the autosave. It does not overwrite the remote member, however, so you can always save the autosave off to a temporary member and then compare the autosave with the remote member.

Undo and Redo

Ah, the joys of undo and redo on a workstation source editor! LPEX allows a virtually unlimited number of undo and redo operations. To invoke the undo action, use the **Edit > Undo** menu or the more common Ctrl+Z keyboard shortcut. Once the document is at its original state, the message line will reflect this, and further undo operations will have no effect. To reverse the undo action, invoke redo by choosing **Edit > Redo** or the Ctrl+Y keyboard shortcut.

> **TIP**
>
> You can even undo after saving the source, as long you have not closed the editor. Keep an eye on the editor tab. When you get to the last saved point, the dirty editor flag (an asterisk) will disappear. If you keep undoing past the save point, the asterisk will reappear.

Another way to revert the contents of the source member back to its previously saved version is to use the **File > Revert** menu option. Note, however, that the undo and revert actions do not undo the "resequence all lines" action.

Text Manipulation

LPEX does not confine you to moving, copying, or deleting just entire lines or continuous sequences of characters. You can select a rectangular block of code and manipulate it. For example, if you want to delete a rectangular block of code, follow these steps:

1. Position the cursor at the start of the block you want to delete.

2. Right-click in the source and choose **Select > Select rectangle**.

3. Hold the left mouse button down while dragging to the end of the block.

4. Once the block is selected, right-click, and choose **Selected > Delete selection**.

You can also perform this action without the mouse by using keyboard shortcuts. Press Alt+R at the beginning of the block, and then use the Up, Down, Left, and Right arrow keys to highlight the block. Press Alt+R again to select the block. Once you have the block selected, use Alt+D to delete the block. As you can see from Figure 6–9, many other actions can be performed on the selected text. You can even change it to all-uppercase or all-lowercase!

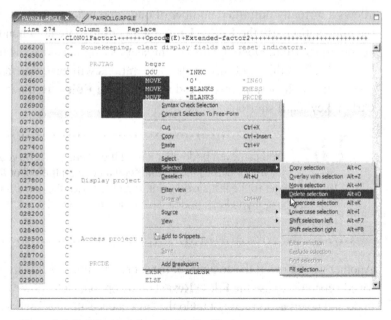

Figure 6–9: Deleting a rectangular block of text.

One block action that is worth mentioning here is "Fill selection." When this action is selected, you will be prompted to enter the characters in the command line, as shown in Figure 6–10. You can fill an area with a single character or a string. The sequence of the fill characters will be repeated to fill the entire block. For example, if the selected text spans 10 columns, and the fill character is only three characters long, then these three characters will be repeated to fill the entire selected block. So, with the fill characters *abc*, the selected block would contain *abcabcabca*.

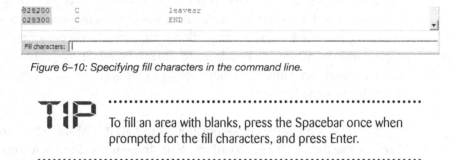

Figure 6–10: Specifying fill characters in the command line.

TIP

To fill an area with blanks, press the Spacebar once when prompted for the fill characters, and press Enter.

Jumping from Here to There

Earlier in this chapter, you learned the basics of moving the text cursor inside the editor. This section takes a look at some other ways for jumping around in the editor, especially getting back to spots where you were previously working.

Location Marks

LPEX provides a way to move around the source using location marks, which are placed in the source and used to easily return to marked locations. Think of location marks like breadcrumbs you drop as you wonder through the forest, in order to find your way home. (Unlike breadcrumbs, the chance of a squirrel eating your location marks is pretty low.)

To create a mark in your source, place the cursor at the position to be marked, and select the **Edit > Mark > Name a Mark** action from the menu bar. In the command line of the editor pane, you will see "Name Mark" followed by the text entry area. Enter the name of the mark and press Enter. To cancel the request, click anywhere in the editor, or press

Esc. You can name as many location marks as you like, and multiple marks can be set for the same location.

To locate a named mark, select the **Edit > Find other > Find Mark** action. In the command line of the editor pane, you will see "Find Mark," followed by the text entry area. Type the name of the mark and press Enter, or use the Up and Down arrow keys to scroll through the existing marks.

You do not have to name a mark. If you want to look at other parts of the source member, but remember the location where you currently are, you can use a *quick mark*. A quick mark allows you to mark one cursor position quickly, without naming it. This is a one-time use only. There is only one quick mark per source member; setting a new quick mark causes the previous one to be removed.

To set a quick mark at the cursor position, select **Edit > Mark > Set Quick Mark**, or use the Ctrl+Q keyboard shortcut. To go back to the quick mark, select **Edit > Find Other > Find Quick Mark**, or use the Alt+Q keyboard shortcut. The cursor will move to the position marked by the quick mark. The quick mark also appears in the list of named marks as @QUICK.

To see how quick marks are used, suppose you are coding a call to a procedure in an ILE RPG source, and you want to see the order of procedure parameters. Press Ctrl+Q to set a quick mark at the current cursor location, move around the source to find the procedure definition, and when you've found it, press Alt+Q to return to coding the call to the procedure.

Marks retain their locations as you add, delete, and modify the source. However, if the line that the location mark is set on is deleted, the location mark is removed. All marks are removed when the source is closed or when the Workbench is closed.

Bookmarks

Bookmarks are another simple way of navigating the source. You can set many bookmarks in the source and easily jump from one to another, either in the same source or between multiple open source members.

To set a bookmark, place the cursor on the desired line, and select **Edit >
Add Bookmark.** A bookmark icon is added in the vertical ruler next to
that line, as shown in Figure 6–11. Alternatively, right-click in the vertical
ruler, and select **Add Bookmark** from the pop-up menu.

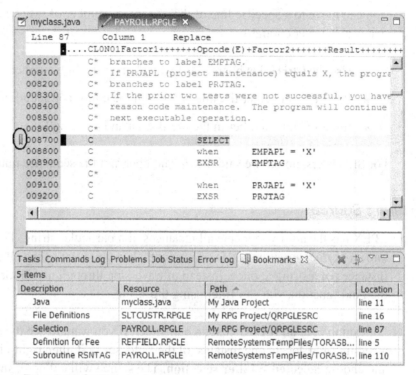

Figure 6–11: Setting a bookmark.

The Bookmarks view displays all bookmarks in the Workspace. By default,
this view is not opened in RSE perspective. To display the Bookmarks view,
select **Window > Show View**, and then select **General > Bookmarks.** The
view opens in the tabbed notebook area in the bottom right corner of the
Workbench, as shown in Figure 6–11. Double-clicking any item in this view
will open the source and position the source at the line where the bookmark
was set. This view can be customized using options from the view menu
(the upside-down triangle in the top right corner of the view).

As explained earlier in this chapter, the local downloaded member is
opened in the LPEX editor. Bookmarks are set on the local member. As
such, these "tags" are placed in the local member. You can see this in the

Bookmarks view under the Path column in Figure 6–11. Keep this in mind when you use bookmarks.

Line Numbers

You can move to a specific line of the editor in a number of ways (because one way is never enough):

- Use the Ctrl+L keyboard shortcut and enter the line number.

- Press Esc and enter the line number in the editor command line.

- Enter the line number in the prefix area and pressing Enter.

For SEU users, notice we said the *line* number, not the sequence number!

Filtering Source

LPEX has the ability to locate all instances of a particular string. This is known as *filtering*. Filtering is convenient when you want to see all the instances of a string at once. Instead of traversing through the editor using the Find function, you can filter using the string.

For example, in an ILE RPG source member, if you want to see the use of a certain field, locate one instance of the field, select it, then right-click and choose **Selected > Filter selection.** The source will collapse, showing only the lines containing the selected string, with a plus sign before the sequence numbers. Sections between two plus signs can be expanded by clicking on the plus sign, as shown in Figure 6–12. When the hidden lines below a line matching the filtering criteria are expanded, the plus sign to a minus sign. Clicking the minus sign collapses the section. This ability to filter and then expand and collapse sections allows you to zoom in and work on a particular section of the source.

In the same way, you can use the filtering capability to exclude lines with the selected string. Select the string to exclude, right-click, and choose **Selected > Exclude selection.** The source will collapse, showing only the lines that do not contain the selected string.

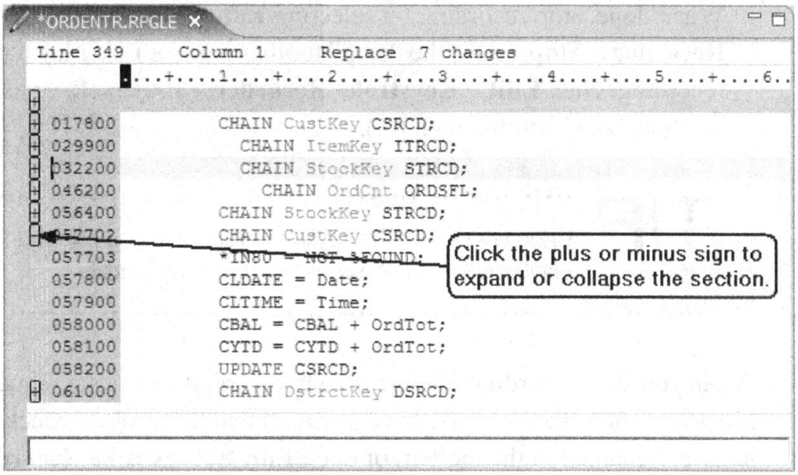

Figure 6–12: Expanding a section after filtering.

When you are done filtering and want to see the entire contents of the source, right-click in the source and select **Show All**, or use the Ctrl+W keyboard shortcut. (Filtering is case-insensitive. If you want to filter on case-sensitive text, use the find feature instead, discussed later in section "Powerful Find and Replace").

Filtering is also available on certain language-specific artifacts, such as comments, procedures, and subroutines. Right-click the source, and select **Filter view**. This opens a cascading menu that lists all the language-specific options you can use to filter the source. These are covered under language-specific actions in the next chapter.

The Keystroke Recorder

The keystroke recorder facilitates recording a set of keystrokes that can be played back later. This is helpful when you have certain keystrokes that you want to repeat a few times. You can record the keystrokes when you first enter them, and play them again and again.

To start recording the keystroke, position the cursor where you want to begin recording. Select **Edit > Keystroke Recorder > Start** from the menu bar, or use the "start" toolbar icon (▣). Record all the keystrokes that you want to be replayed. Mouse moves are not recorded, so use the Home and End keys to position the cursor to the beginning and the end of line, and the Up and Down arrow keys to move up and down the lines.

When done, stop recording by selecting **Edit > Keystroke Recorder > Stop** or use the "stop" toolbar icon ( ). To play back the recording, click **Edit > Keystroke Recorder > Playback**, or use the "playback" toolbar icon ( ).

Undo works with the keystroke recorder. You can undo the playback if you pressed it one too many times!

When you start recording, the previously recorded keystroke sequences are overwritten. To see if you have any recorded keystrokes, check which icons are enabled in the toolbar, or open **Edit > Keystroke Recorder** and check which actions are enabled. If playback is enabled, you already have a recorded set of keystrokes.

Powerful Find and Replace

To invoke the find action, select **Edit > Find/Replace** or using the Ctrl+F keyboard shortcut. This action allows you to search for an expression in the active editor, and optionally replace it with a new one. When this action is invoked, the command line in the editor changes, as shown in Figure 6–13.

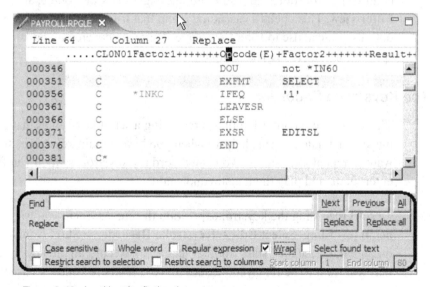

Figure 6–13: Invoking the find action.

Enter the text or expression that you want to search for in the Find text area, or use the Up and Down arrow keys to scroll through previously used search strings. Searching starts from the cursor position when the find action was invoked. If the entered search string is found, the cursor moves to the search string.

Click the **Next** or **Previous** buttons to find the next occurrence of the search string. Alternatively, to show all occurrences of the search string at the same time, click the **All** button. This is similar to filtering the string, but offers an option of entering the search string and choosing to perform a case-sensitive search.

TIP
While the cursor is in the Find field, pressing Enter or Ctrl+N positions the editor on the next occurrence of the search string, similar to clicking the Next button.

To replace the search string with another string, type the new string in the Replace text area, and click the **Replace** button. To selectively replace the search string, click the **Next** button until you locate the search string you want to replace, and then click the **Replace** button. Repeat this step to find and replace multiple occurrences of the search string, or click **Replace All** to replace all occurrences of the search string at once.

TIP
To delete the search string, leave the Replace text area empty, and click the **Replace** button.

When you have completed the find or replace action, click anywhere in the source or press the **Esc** key. This will dispose of the find and replace options and return the command line back to normal. You can still continue searching for the string using the Edit > Find Next menu (Shift+F4) or Edit > Find Previous.

At the bottom of the Find dialog, various options can be selected to control how the search is performed. To select an option, click on its checkbox. A checkmark for the option indicates it is selected.

TIP

You can use Alt+*mnemonic* (the underlined character) instead of the mouse to maneuver in the Find dialog. For example, pressing Alt+C toggles the "Case sensitive" option on and off, and pressing Alt+O toggles the "Whole word" option on and off.

Let's go through the options in the Find dialog, since some of them are not self-explanatory:

- *Case sensitive:* This indicates whether the find feature should respect or ignore the capitalization in the search string.

- *Whole word:* This restricts the search to match the exact word and its length. For example, you would select this option if you wanted the search string *subr* not to locate the word *subroutine.*

- *Regular expression:* The search string will be treated as a regular expression pattern. For example, if you want to search for either *EXSR* or *BEGSR* in a source member, specify *EXSR/BEGSR* and select this option.

- *Wrap:* This causes a search of the entire document, including parts that precede the cursor position. If this option is selected, the search will continue in a loop, and you will see the word *Wrapped* in the message line after the top or the bottom of the document is reached, depending on the direction of the search.

- *Select found text:* This automatically selects the search string found in the source. This option is useful if you want to perform editor actions that require the string to be selected first.

- *Restrict search to selection:* This limits the scope of the search to the selected text in the editor.

- *Column restricted search:* This limits the scope of the search to the range of columns specified in the "Start column" and "End column" fields. This is useful when you want to perform a column-sensitive search.

The selected options are remembered as long as the source member is not closed. Each open member can have different options selected. Defaults for all of these options can be configured on the LPEX Editor > Find Text preference page. The preference page has the following options, in addition to those already discussed:

- *Emphasize found text:* This highlights the search string found in the editor, making it easier to see in the source. If this option is not selected, the line in which the search string is found will be shown as the current line in the editor.

- *Incremental find dialog*: This incrementally finds matches in the editor as you enter the search string. This is very helpful, since you can find a match without having to type the entire search string first.

The Compare Function

To compare your current member to another, select **Edit > Compare to file,** or select the "compare" icon (△) in the toolbar. This opens up the Compare File dialog, where you select the other member. You can even select a source member residing on a different server!

Once the compare function completes, the source member where the compare was invoked from will show lines highlighted in pink and yellow. These lines indicate the differences in the two source members, as shown in Figure 6–14. Lines containing differences in the opened member are highlighted yellow, while the lines in the member being compared to are highlighted pink.

The source is positioned to the first mismatch. To navigate to the next one, right-click in the source and select **Compare > Next Mismatch,** use the Ctrl+ Shift+N keyboard shortcut, or select the "next mismatch" toolbar icon ( ). Similarly, to navigate to the previous mismatch, select **Compare > Previous Mismatch**, use the Ctrl+Shift+P keyboard shortcut, or select the "previous mismatch" toolbar icon ( ).

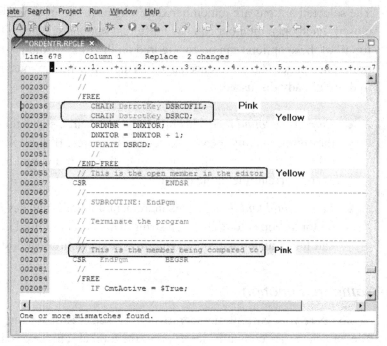

Figure 6–14: Comparing source members.

LPEX is aware of sequence numbers. It will not mismatch lines just because the sequence numbers are different.

While in compare mode, you can continue to modify the member that was originally open. If you modify the source, right-click and select **Compare** > **Refresh** to refresh the compare, or use the Ctrl+Shift+R keyboard shortcut. When done, right-click and select **Compare** > **Clear** to end the comparison.

When you right-click and choose **Compare**, you might notice that there are other options, as well. These options customize the compare function. You select an option by clicking it. If it was already selected, clicking it will deselect it. The options are as follows:

- *Ignore leading blanks:* White space at the start of a line is ignored during comparison.

- *Ignore trailing blanks:* White space at the end of a line is ignored during comparison.

- *Ignore all blanks:* All white space in a line is ignored during comparison.

- *Ignore case:* Differences in character case (uppercase/lowercase) are ignored during comparison.

- *Ignore comments:* Comments are ignored during comparison. All white space is also ignored when this option is selected. Use this option cautiously.

- *Ignore sequence numbers:* Sequence numbers are ignored during comparison.

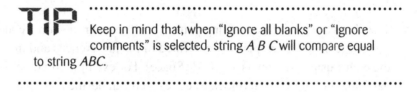

Keep in mind that, when "Ignore all blanks" or "Ignore comments" is selected, string *A B C* will compare equal to string *ABC.*

Like the find function, these options are remembered for the current editor as long as the editor is not closed. Each editor has its own settings. Defaults for these options can be changed on the LPEX Editor > Compare preference page. The preference page has an additional setting:

- *Column restricted comparison:* The scope of a compare operation is limited to the range of columns specified in the "Start column" and "End column" fields.

Uppercase/Lowercase

To change a block of selected text to all-uppercase or all-lowercase, right-click the block of text and select **Selected > Uppercase selection** or **Selected > Lowercase selection.** Alternatively, or use their respective keyboard shortcuts, Alt+K or Alt+I.

Display Hex Value

To edit the current line in hexadecimal (if you really want to), right-click it and select **Source > Hex Edit line.** This shows the hex values for Unicode, the native workstation codepage encoding, and the server codepage encoding.

Content Assist and Templates

In SEU, the only function to actually help you enter code is the source prompter. LPEX, on the other hand, has several functions to help you quickly enter code, including content assist and templates.

The purpose of content assist is save you typing. It provides you with a list of suggested completions based on the context (column) of the cursor position and any partially entered strings. To invoke content assist, select **Edit > Content assist,** or use the much more common Ctrl+Space keyboard shortcut. Content assist is available for ILE COBOL and ILE RPG (free-form RPG and free-form SQL) source, and is covered in more detail in the next chapter.

Templates are predefined coding patterns that reoccur in source code. Language-specific templates are defined in the preferences and inserted in the editor using content assist (Ctrl+Space). For example, if you often use a particular coding pattern (block of code), you can define a template instead of having to enter the code every time or copy it from another member. To insert a template, invoke content assist and select the template by name. This inserts the template code into the editor and places the cursor at the specified position in the template, so you can edit the details.

Template support is available for ILE RPG, ILE COBOL, and C++ source members. The RSE provides some predefined templates (which you can modify), or you can create your own templates. To view the templates, go to the **Remote Systems > Remote Systems LPEX Editor > i5/OS Parsers** preference page, and expand one of the languages that support templates on the left. Then, select **Templates**. You will see the templates on the right, as shown in Figure 6–15.

Use the buttons on the right of the page to work with the templates. For example, to create a new template, click the **New** button. This opens the New Template dialog box, where you can type the name of the template, select a language from the Context drop-down list, and enter the source code you want content assist to insert in the Content field. To insert the template in the editor, type the template name (full or partial) in your code, and press Ctrl+Space.

When you press Ctrl+Space in the editor, you are presented with the list of options for the completion of the statement and the templates. The templates appear at the bottom of the list. The icon beside the template is different from the rest of the completions. For example, when "i" is typed in an ILE COBOL source and Ctrl+Space is pressed, the list of completions is shown in Figure 6–16. The first four show the language constructs that are possible in this source member, and the last one is the template.

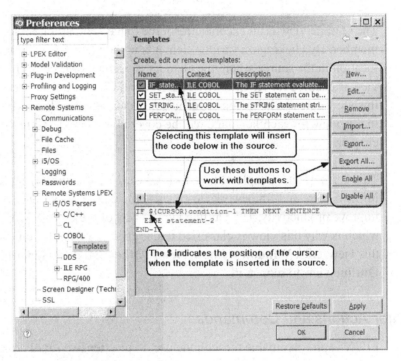

Figure 6–15: Viewing the templates.

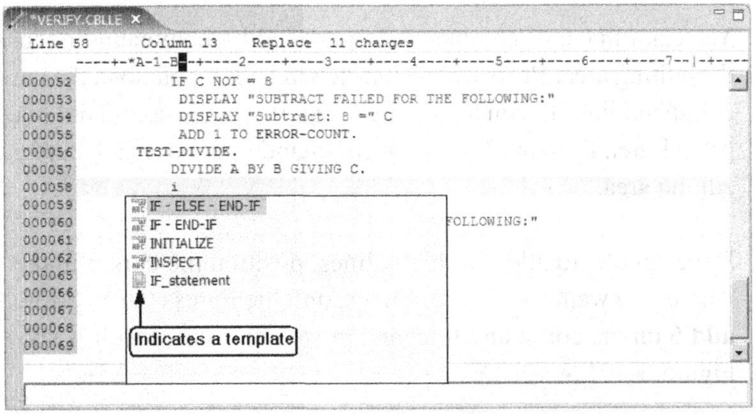

Figure 6–16: The list of options presented by content assist.

Outline View

The Outline view displays a high-level outline of the source member currently open in the editor. It shows the lists of structural elements and is specific to the source member. By default, the Outline view appears at the top right corner of the RSE perspective.

The Outline view is an excellent resource to navigate around a source member. By clicking on various elements in the view, you can jump to the location in the source where the element is defined or used. In LPEX, the view is enabled for RPG, COBOL, DDS, and CL source members. Since this view portrays language-specific constructs, the details of what appears in this view for each language will be covered in more detail in the next chapter.

This is a perfect example of how LPEX leverages the underlying Eclipse infrastructure and frameworks to enhance the editing experience and improve productivity. The Outline view is part of the Eclipse Workbench, which is why this view is classified under general views. If you ever close this view, click **Window > Show View > Other** and then **General > Outline view** to reopen it.

Editor Actions and Commands

LPEX is programmable through the use of an extensive set of commands and actions. Editor commands and actions can be used to customize the editing environment and perform many editor functions.

You can run editor commands from the editor command line located below the editing area. Pressing the Esc key in LPEX positions the cursor on the command line. To run a command, enter it on the command line, and then press Enter. Pressing Esc in the command line moves the cursor back to the editing area.

For example, to add five blank lines, position the cursor in the source where you want to add these lines, and then press the Esc key. Type **add 5** on the command line, and press Enter. The result is shown in Figure 6–17.

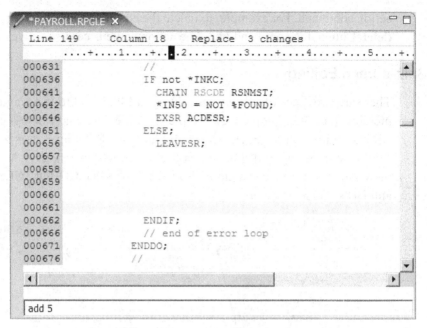

Figure 6–17: Adding five blank lines using an editor command.

You can scroll through previously used commands using the Up and Down arrow keys while on the command line. (This is similar to pressing F9 at a 5250 CL prompt.) Once you get to the one you want, you can (optionally) modify it, and then press Enter to rerun the command.

We are not going to list all the editor commands and their parameters here, but we will tell you how to find them. On the command line, type **help**, and press Enter. This brings up the external help window with links to locating the editor commands and actions.

> **TIP** You can customize LPEX to not show the command line. (See the "Customizations" section later in this chapter for more on customizing the editor.) If the command line is not visible, pressing the Esc key will make it visible and give it focus. The command line stays visible until focus is returned to the editor area.

Editor actions are a bit different from editor commands, in that they are usually assigned to menu items, toolbar buttons, keyboard shortcuts, and mouse events. You can issue actions through the command line using the action command. For example, to delete the current line, run **action deleteLine** in the command line. The action name is case-sensitive.

Split-screen Editing

There are two types of split-screen editing in LPEX: splitting a single member to create multiple views of the same member, and side-by-side editing of different members, shown in Figure 6–18. Tiling editors to have side-by-side editing of different members is covered in chapter 4. Multiple view support of the same member is enabled for RPG, COBOL, CL, C, and DDS source members.

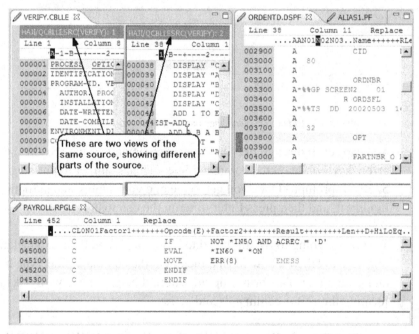

Figure 6–18: Multiple views and tiled editors.

Multiple Views

To open multiple views of the same source member, do one of the following:

- Right-click in the editor and select **View > Open new view**.

- Right-click the editor tab and select **New Editor**.

- Use the Ctrl+2 keyboard shortcut.

A maximum of five views of the same source member can be opened at a time. Chances are, however, that you'll run out of screen space before that. (Time to ask for that new 30-inch flat-screen monitor, so you can be more productive!)

To navigate among the editor views, right-click in the editor and select **View > Next view** or **View > Previous view**, or use the Alt+Shift+Right arrow or Alt+Shift+Left arrow keyboard shortcuts.

There is one copy of the source, but it is presented in the multiple editor views simultaneously. Each of the open editor views has full editor capabilities. This allows editing of different parts of the source in each view, which can be very useful. For example, in an ILE RPG source member, you can see the parameters of a procedure while coding the call to the procedure. If a syntax error occurs while you are typing, it appears in all open views.

Views are split vertically by default. To switch to a horizontal split for a particular source member, right-click in the editor and select **View > Horizontal split**. To change the default so that splitting happens horizontally all the time for all source members, change the preference on the **LPEX Editor > Controls** preference page.

To close an editor view, right-click in it and select **View > Close view**. Alternatively, use the keyboard shortcut or using the Ctrl+0. (That's a zero—we are running out of letters!) When you create multiple views, they are numbered as shown in Figure 6–19. The first view is the primary one, and the rest are secondary. The primary view cannot be closed while secondary views are open. However, you can still close the entire editor by selecting File > Close from the menu bar, using the Ctrl+F4 keyboard shortcut, or clicking the "X" in the editor tab.

Looking closely, you will see that there are no vertical rulers in secondary views. For that reason, if you perform actions in secondary views that provide the results in the vertical ruler, the results might be added in the primary view. For example, right-click in a secondary view and select **Add breakpoint**. The breakpoint will appear in the vertical ruler of the primary view.

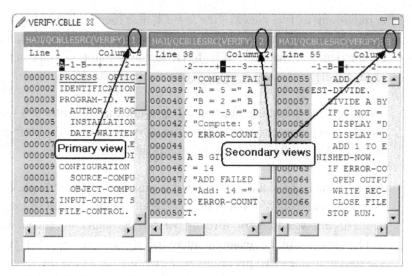

Figure 6–19: Primary and secondary views.

Switching Between Open Members

Usually, the easiest way to switch between open editors is to use Ctrl+F6.
Pressing Ctrl+F6 switches back the most recently used editor. Holding down
the Ctrl key while pressing and releasing F6 displays a list of all open members.
Continue pressing F6 until you get to the member you want to edit, and then
release the Ctrl key. The editor for the selected member will get focus.
(Remember that you can tell from the color of the editor tabs which editor
has focus.)

To switch between open members, click the editor tab for the source member
that you want to edit. If all the open editor tabs are not visible, you can get
the list of open members by clicking the ⁘ symbol or using the Ctrl+E
keyboard shortcut. This opens the Quick Switch Editor pop-up, which lists
all open editors. Use the Up and Down arrow keys to select the source
member you want to edit, and press Enter. In the Quick Switch Editor dialog,
you can also start typing the name of the source, and the list presented will
be filtered by the characters typed (including wildcard strings like *ord*).

If you have multiple views of the same member, only one will show in the
list. As explained earlier, there is really one copy of the source presented
in multiple views. To move between the multiple views, use the navigation
explained in the previous section.

Printing

To print source members from LPEX, either select **File > Print**, use the "print" icon in the toolbar, or use the Ctrl+P keyboard shortcut. Printing in LPEX prints to your local Windows printer, not the i5/OS printer.

For print-related preferences, go to the **LPEX Editor > Print** preference page. This page includes preferences to print line numbers, sequence numbers, margins, and color-tokenized source (one advantage of printing from LPEX over SEU). A page header and footer can also be specified. The header/footer text can contain the following substitution variables:

- *%p*: Page number

- *%n*: Source name

- *%f*: Full path of the source name

- *%d*: Date

- *%t*: Time

You can use the printing prefix commands that you use in SEU here, too. For example, LP in the prefix command prints the line. Similarly, the LP*n* prefix command, where *n* is an integer, prints the current line and the next *n*-1 lines. LLP prints all lines between the boundaries formed by the two LLPs.

You can also set printer preferences from the Page Range section of the Print Page dialog, shown in Figure 6–20. If you selected some text before selecting the print action, you could check the Selection radio button and only print the selected lines.

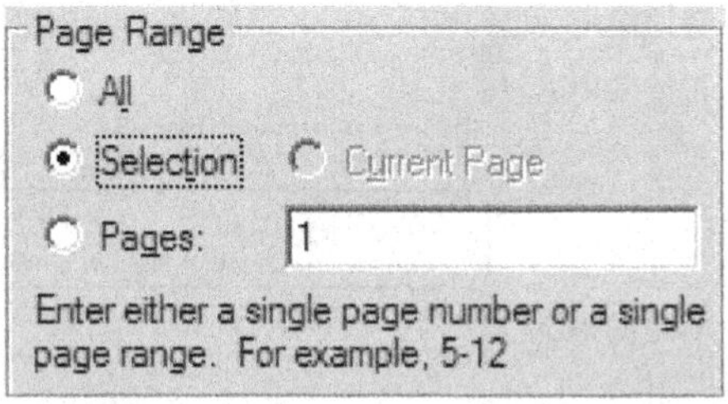

Figure 6–20: Setting printing options.

If that's not enough, you can also print using the LPEX print command in the command line! For example, select some text, and issue **print block** on the command line to print what you have selected. The print command has various options. To review them, enter **? print** on the command line.

The print command even works when File > Print is disabled, such as in the RPG Indentation view.

Saving and Closing

To save the active editor, either use the **File > Save** menu, click the "save" icon in the toolbar, or use the Ctrl+S keyboard shortcut. This saves the editor back to the remote member on i5/OS (or to the local project if you are using i5/OS projects). If multiple members have changed, you can save them all at once by either selecting **File > Save All** or using the Ctrl+Shift+S keyboard shortcut. This uploads one member at a time to the i5/OS server.

The options to save the source are enabled only if you have at least one dirty editor (an editor with unsaved changes).

Let's look at the how the save really happens and the options you have. When you save from LPEX, the contents of the editor are first written to a local Workspace file in the RemoteSystemsTempFiles project. Then, the file is uploaded back to the original host member. The Remote Systems > i5/OS > Objects Subsystem preference page contains two options related to saving a member, shown in Figure 6–21.

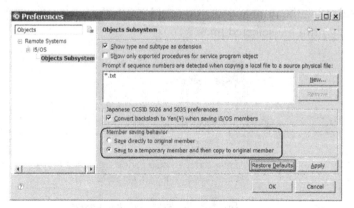

Figure 6–21: Options related to saving

When LPEX saves the member back to the server with the first option, "Save directly to original member," it first clears the existing member by running the CLRPFM CL command. Then, it writes back all the records with any changes you made. In rare circumstances, problems can occur if the network connection is dropped right after CLRPFM runs, but before or while the records are written back to the member. This causes the host member to be cleared but not updated, resulting in an empty member! The locally saved copy in the RemoteSystemsTempFiles project still exists, so you can recover the changes.

The second option, "Save to a temporary member and then copy to original member," was added in Rational Developer for System i 7.1 and made the default behavior to avoid the problem described above. In this case, the updated file contents are first written to a temporary member in the same library and source file as the original member, and editor contents are saved to it. (The ADDPFM CL command is used to create the member.) Once this is successful, the contents of this temporary member are copied to the original member (using the CPYSRCF CL command) and the temporary member is deleted (using the RMVM CL command).

This approach requires more steps than the first one, but it safeguards against the possibility of the original member being accidentally cleared. The downside of this method is that the user profile needs to have the authority to add members to the source physical file and run these CL commands.

TIP •••
If something goes wrong after saving the contents into the temporary member, the temporary member is not deleted. You can try to save the editor again, or if you closed the editor, recover the changes by locating the temporary member in the same library and source physical file as the original member. Temporary members have a name starting with *RSE*, followed by a random number.

•••

When saving a member, you can also choose the Save As option. There are two choices with this option: save to a new source member, or save to an existing member. You can even save to a different server!

To close LPEX, select **File > Close**, or use the Ctrl+F4 keyboard short-cut. If the editor has unsaved changes, you will be presented with the dialog, where you can choose to save the changes, not save (lose) the changes, or cancel the close and return to the editor. To close all open files at once, select **File > Close All**, or use the Ctrl+Shift+W keyboard shortcut.

Customizations

You can customize many aspects of LPEX. For example, you can customize whether the editor tabs appear at the bottom or the top using the general Workbench preferences. You can also change the color of the tokens in the source member, change and add keyboard shortcuts, and much more.

Editor Preferences

Like most of the Workbench, LPEX has preference pages where you can customize its default look and behavior. There are two places where you can change LPEX preferences. Well, maybe we should say there are three places, since there is a generic Workbench control of the editor pane. We touched on this in chapter 4. For example, on the General > Appearance preference page, you can change where the editor tabs appear. Changing the preferences here affects all Workbench editors, including LPEX.

The second preference, found under LPEX Editor in the preferences, contains general LPEX editing preference. Most of the settings found here are global in scope, meaning they apply to any member type opened in LPEX. The preferences found here are not i5/OS-specific.

As you can see in Figure 6–22, quite a few preferences can be customized. By clicking on a preference category on the left, the preferences appear on the right. We will go through a few, so you can get a feel for the different types of customizations.

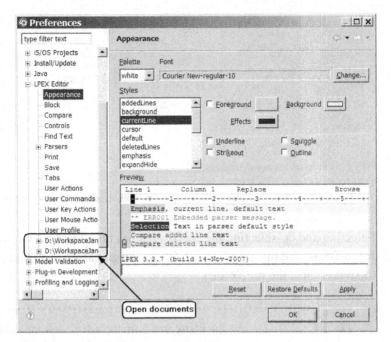

Figure 6–22: The Appearance preference page.

Go to the **LPEX Editor > Appearance** page to change the look of the editor by changing the color and style for different entities. The Preview area shows a preview of the current settings. Go to the **LPEX Editor > Controls** page, shown in Figure 6–23, to specify which controls and information areas are displayed in the editor.

Figure 3–17 in chapter 3 shows the editor with all of the controls. You can choose here which controls you want to appear in the editor view. Figure 6–24 shows what the editor would look like if the status line, format line, message line, and command line were de-selected.

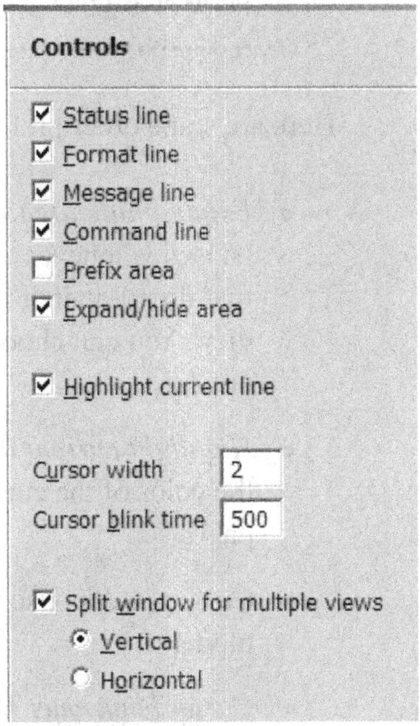

Figure 6–23: The Controls preference page.

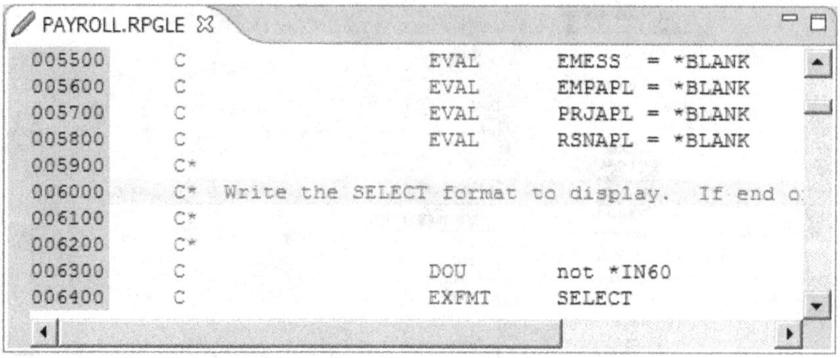

```
/ PAYROLL.RPGLE ⊠                                                        ─ ⊟
  005500      C                    EVAL       EMESS  = *BLANK          ▲
  005600      C                    EVAL       EMPAPL = *BLANK
  005700      C                    EVAL       PRJAPL = *BLANK          ─
  005800      C                    EVAL       RSNAPL = *BLANK
  005900      C*
  006000      C*  Write the SELECT format to display.  If end o
  006100      C*
  006200      C*
  006300      C                    DOU        not *IN60
  006400      C                    EXFMT      SELECT                   ▼
  ◄                                                                   ►
```

Figure 6–24: The editor view with no status, format, message, or command line.

Selecting and de-selecting the prefix area has no effect on the editor view for i5/OS source members. The i5/OS language parsers override this option to always show the prefix area.

TIP ··
To remove the prefix area from the editor view for a single source members, go to the command line and enter **set prefixArea off**. (Note that this command is case-sensitive.) To show the prefix area, enter **set prefixArea on**.
···

Here are some other preferences on this page:

- *Expand/hide area:* Earlier in this chapter, you saw that a plus sign is used whenever a filter or find operation causes a group of lines that do not match the filter or find criteria to be hidden from the view. You can choose not to show the plus sign by deselecting this option.

- *Highlight current line:* This option highlights the current line. To set the color of the current line, use the **LPEX Editor > Appearance** page.

- *Cursor width:* Use this to set the pixel width of the cursor in insert mode.

- *Cursor blink time:* This is the time interval, in milliseconds, at which the cursor blinks. A value of zero stops the cursor from blinking.

- *Split windows for multiple views:* This indicates whether to use a horizontal or vertical split when opening multiple views of the same source member.

For each open document (source member), you will also see a preference node added to the LPEX Editor preference page. In Figure 6–22, you can see two open documents nodes. Expanding an open document node shows preferences that can be changed while editing the source member, such as disabling the parsing of the source member.

TIP

The LPEX Editor customizations covered so far, the ones under the main LPEX Editor preference page, can be exported and imported between Workspaces. To do this, on the editor command line, type **profile export prompt**. This prompts for the location of the export file to save the preferences. Alternatively, instead of entering *prompt*, you can directly specify the filename. To load these preferences in another Workspace, replace *export* with *import*.

The third group of editor preferences is found under Remote Systems > Remote System LPEX Editor. These preferences, which apply to i5/OS-specific source types, are discussed in the next chapter.

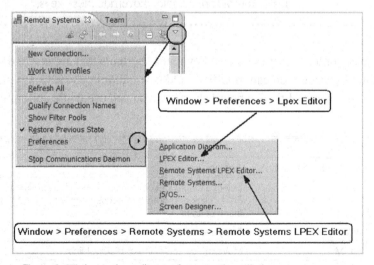

Figure 6–25: Accessing editor preferences through the Remote Systems view.

The editor preferences shown in Figure 6–25 are quickly accessible from the Remote Systems view, using the "view menu" button (). This avoids having to go through the Window > Preferences menu and then find the preference category.

Throughout this chapter, instructions and screen shots have been shown using the Window > Preferences menu and the full preference dialog. The next chapter uses the preference-page shortcuts from the Remote System view's menu to get to the editor preference pages. The dialog that opens up only shows the preferences for the selected shortcut, making the dialog easier to read.

Keyboard Shortcuts

Many keys have default actions already defined by the editor. The Workbench also defines some keys with actions. These Workbench actions are classified into categories and the context in which the keyboard shortcuts are applicable. To find this list of shortcut keys, go to the **General > Keys** preference page. This is covered in chapter 4.

TIP The operating system or editor reserves certain keys, such as F1. You will not be able to override these keys.

The editor also defines its own keyboard shortcuts that are active during an editing session. You can modify or add new editor keyboard shortcuts. Table 6–1 lists some of the keyboard shortcuts you can use while editing in LPEX.

Table 6–1: Editing Keyboard Shortcuts	
Keyboard Shortcut	**Action**
Alt+L	Select a single line or block of lines. After pressing Alt+L, click and drag the mouse pointer to select the block of lines.
Alt+C	Copy the selected line or block of lines.
Alt+M	Move the selected line or block of lines.
Alt+D	Delete the selected line or block of lines.
F1	Invoke language-sensitive help.

Table 6–1: Editing Keyboard Shortcuts (Continued)	
Keyboard Shortcut	**Action**
F3	Position the cursor to an ILE RPG subroutine or procedure declaration.
F4	Invoke source prompting.
Ctrl+Shift+C	Invoke the compiler for the source member.
Ctrl+Shift+V	Invoke the program verifier for the source member.
Ctrl+,	After verifying or compiling, go to the previous problem.
Ctrl+.	After verifying or compiling, go to the next problem.
Ctrl+Backspace	Delete the current line.
Ctrl+Shift+O	Show the block nesting.
Ctrl+F4	Close the current source member from the editor.
Ctrl+Shift+W	Close all open files from the editor.
Ctrl+F5	Remove error messages, any pending actions, and filtering.
Ctrl+Shift+F5	Refresh the Outline view.
Ctrl+Shift+M	Jump to the other end of a structured block.
Ctrl+M	Select the structured block.
Ctrl+Shift+E	Open the Switch to Editor dialog.
Ctrl+Delete or Ctrl+Shift+Delete	Delete to the end of the line (Field Exit).

You can use the command line to request help for the keyboard shortcuts and see the full list of predefined shortcuts. For example, type **help seu** in the editor's command line. (The i5/OS language parsers use the SEU editor profile by default.) The help window opens, listing all the commands with their default key assignments. Try it; you might learn some shortcut keys you didn't even know existed!

Configuring Additional Keyboard Shortcuts

To reassign keys or assign actions to new keys, use the **LPEX Editor > User Key Actions** preference page. (Remember the shortcut of selecting Preferences > LPEX Editor from the Remote System view's view menu.)

In Figure 6–26, the table on the right shows all the user-defined keys. To add a new one, enter the key sequence you want to assign and the action to be associated with that key sequence. You can use the drop-down menu in the Action box to select one of the defined actions. In the Key field, specify *c* for Ctrl, *s* for Shift, and *a* for Alt. To enter the keyboard shortcut Ctrl+Shift+Z, for example, you would type *c-s-z*.

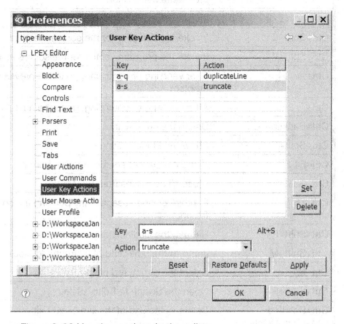

Figure 6–26 User key actions in the editor.

TIP   Key and action names are case-sensitive. Make sure you use the correct mixed-case character sequence when defining both the key definition and the action name!

To modify an action for a predefined keyboard shortcut, type the key and the new action. For example, Alt+S is predefined in the editor to split the line. If you wanted this key action to truncate the line instead, you would need to override the default, by entering *a-s* in the key area and selecting *truncate* from the Action list, as shown in Figure 6–26. Don't forget to press the Set button on the right, or the change you made will not be saved! The changes made here are activated immediately, even for currently open members.

You can also customize the keyboard from the editor command line with the "set keyAction" command. These settings are only active in the current view during the current edit session. For example, make the Ctrl+T keyboard shortcut scroll the text in the editor up one page at a time by typing **set keyAction.c-t pageUp** on the editor command line. To learn more about the keyAction command, type **help keyAction** on the editor command line.

7

The Remote Systems LPEX Editor: RPG, COBOL, DDS, and CL Editing Features

The focus of this chapter is on using the Remote Systems LPEX Editor (herein referred to as just *LPEX*) for editing RPG, COBOL, CL, and DDS source members. This editor has many exciting language-editing features specific to RPG, COBOL, CL, and DDS. When we refer to *i5/OS languages* in this chapter, we are referring to these four languages.

The language features in the RSE and LPEX editor are always at the latest i5/OS release level when they were shipped. The RSE in WDSC 7.0 supports the languages at i5/OS V5R4 level. The RSE in Rational Developer for System i 7.1 supports the languages at i5/OS V6R1 level. Rational Developer for System i supports i5/OS V5R3, V5R4, and V6R1 (until they go out of service). If you use Rational Developer for System i with a V5R4 system, the syntax checkers and program verifiers will allow you to enter V6R1 language features. You won't discover the errors until you try to compile.

In this chapter, instructions and screen shots for preference pages go through the preference shortcuts in the Remote Systems view's menu (the upside-down triangle), as described in chapter 6. When instructions in this chapter refer to the preferences, they mean the preferences from the Remote System view's menu.

Common Language Features

As you might expect, some editor features apply to all, or almost all, of the i5/OS languages. These common features are covered in this section. Language-specific features are covered later in this chapter. As we go through each of the features, we will state if a particular feature is not available or applicable to a particular language.

Help!

Help is literally at your fingertips in the RSE. While editing the source, you can press F1 at any time to open the context-sensitive help. *Context-sensitive* means that the RSE looks to see where the cursor is positioned in the editor and opens the page of the related language's help documentation that most closely reflects the cursor position. For example, if your cursor is on a keyword, and you press F1, the help for the keyword (or list of keywords) is opened in the help window.

The "Programmer's Guide," "Language Reference," and "Concept" manuals for each language are shipped in the help. To quickly open one of these manuals from the editor, select **Source > *Language* Help > *manual***, where *Language* is the name of the source language being edited and *manual* is the name of the manual you want to open.

For example, when editing ILE RPG source, select **Source > ILE RPG HELP** to see a menu with five options that provide quick access to the "ILE RPG Reference," "Programmer's Guide," "What's New" in the release, operation codes, and built-in functions.

Automatic Uppercasing

LPEX can automatically convert your source code from lowercase to uppercase while you are editing. To control this, use the **Remote Systems > Remote Systems LPEX Editor > i5/OS Parsers** preference pages. In the preferences window, on the left side, there are entries for each of the i5/OS languages. Clicking either CL, COBOL, DDS, ILE RPG, or RPG/400 displays the preferences on the left pane for the selected language. Each one has an automatic uppercasing preference. For RPG/400 source members, automatic uppercasing is enabled by default. It is disabled or all other languages by default.

Automatic Indenting

LPEX can also automatically indent your source while you are editing. With automatic indenting enabled, when you enter an opcode that starts a block of code (such as a loop or if statement), the editor automatically indents the next line. When you enter the opcode that ends the block of code, the editor automatically stops indenting.

Indentation only makes sense when you are not editing column-sensitive parts of a language. Thus, this feature only applies to CL and ILE RPG, which support free-form editing. To configure automatic indenting, go to the **Remote Systems > Remote Systems LPEX Editor > i5/OS Parsers > CL (or ILE RPG)** preference page. Specify whether or not to enable automatic indenting and how many spaces (blanks) you want the source to be indented when you press the Enter key.

Column-sensitive Editing

Normally, in a Windows application, inserting and deleting text shifts the remaining text left or right. With column-sensitive languages, this results in syntax errors. Column-sensitive editing limits text inserts and deletes to the current column. As you type in one column, text in the other columns does not move.

Column-sensitive editing is available for RPG and DDS source members. By default, this option is not enabled. To enable it, open the **Remote Systems > Remote Systems LPEX Editor** and select **Column sensitive editing**.

Change Signature

Programmers often use the first five columns of an RPG or DDS source line to specify a change flag (signature) for the line. LPEX can be configured to automatically add a signature, up to five characters, to all new or changed lines. Configure this by choosing the **Add signature to changes lines** preference on the **Remote Systems > Remote Systems LPEX Editor > i5/OS Parsers** preference page, as shown in Figure 7–1. The signature is only supported for RPG/400, ILE RPG, and DDS source members and is not enabled by default.

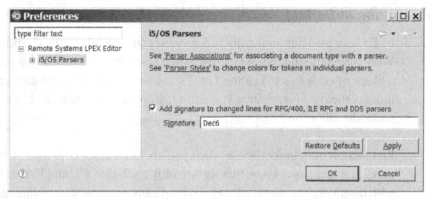

Figure 7–1: Enabling a signature from the preference page.

Suppose you have enabled the signature "Dec6," as shown in Figure 7–1. If you edit a DDS source member, this signature will be inserted in the source, as shown in Figure 7–2.

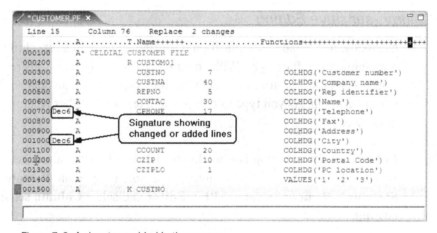

Figure 7–2: A signature added in the source.

User-defined Tab Stops

Each source member type has a set of tab stops defined per line type that are set as defaults. The tab stops help you move to the desired column by pressing the Tab key. You can customize the tab stops to suit your needs. This customization is available for CL, COBOL, ILE RPG, and RPG/400 source members.

Go to **Remote Systems > Remote Systems LPEX Editor > i5/OS Parsers to** find this preference. Expand **i5/OS Parsers** in the preference window and select the language you want to customize tab stops for. Select the **User defined tabs** preference to override the default tab stops. For ILE RPG and RPG/400, you can then select the line type for which you want to configure tab stops by using the drop-down box, as shown in Figure 7–3.

A tab is shown in the tabbing area as a caret symbol (^). To add or remove a tab, position the mouse in the tabbing area where you want to add or remove the tab, and double-click. If the tab exists at the position where you double-clicked, the tab will be removed; otherwise, one will be added. In the "And every" field, you can specify how often you would like to have tabs after the last tab.

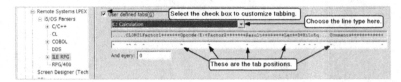

Figure 7–3: Customizing the tabs.

Defining your own tabs can help reduce the number of keystrokes to get to the correct column in the source. For example, in an ILE RPG source member, if you rarely use the conditional or control level indicators, you might want to remove these tabs from the calculation specification.

Syntax Checking

The purpose of the syntax checker is to check the syntax of the code as it is entered or changed in the editor. The syntax checker cannot detect semantic errors, such as an undefined variable or an incorrect use of the variable. This is the same as syntax checking in SEU. One difference between LPEX and SEU, however, is in the way the errors are presented in the editor.

In SEU, the first error is visible at the bottom of the screen with a plus sign on the bottom right corner. You position the cursor to the first error and then scroll through the rest of the errors. This can be a bit cumbersome if you are unfortunate enough to have multiple errors. In LPEX, all the errors are embedded into the editor view, making them all visible at the same time. This makes fixing errors easier, since you can see all the syntax errors in the source at the same time, next to the lines with the errors.

Figure 7–4 shows how syntax errors are all shown in the editor at once. As you fix an error and move your cursor away from the line, or press the Enter key, the statement is syntax checked again. Old errors are removed, and new errors, if any, are inserted into the editor.

```
*PAYROLL.RPGLE ×                                                    ▭ ▢
  Line 24      Column 25      Replace  6 changes
       .........1....+....2....▐....3....+....4....+....5....+....6....+...
002400      F*             - PRJMST  - project master file            ▲
002500      F*             - RSNMST  - reason code master file
002600      F*****************************************************************
002700      FMSTDSP    CF   E                WORKSTN
002800      FEMPMST    F               K DISK
       RNF2003E The File Type is not I, O, U, or C; defaults to O if File
       RNF2006E The File-Format entry is not F or E; defaults to F.
       RNF2007E The Record-Length entry is not valid.
       RNF2290E Record-Address-Type entry only valid for an externally-de
002900      FPRJMST    UF A E          K DISK
003000      FRSNMST    UF A E          K DISK
003100      D*
003200      D* Compile time array containing error descriptions.
003300      D ERR         S             50    DIM(10) CTDATA PERRCD(1
003400      D EMESS       s             50                            ▼
  ◄                                                                  ►
```

Figure 7–4: LPEX showing syntax errors all at once.

TIP Don't forget that you can position the cursor on an error message and press F1 to see the help text for the error.

Syntax checking is enabled for DDS, COBOL, RPG, and CL source members. For DDS, COBOL, and RPG, syntax-checking is done locally on the workstation, meaning that communication between the workstation and i5/OS server is not required. Syntax checking of embedded SQL in COBOL and ILE RPG is supported, but a connection to the server is required, because the syntax checking of SQL statements is performed on the server.

For CL source members, the syntax checking is all done on the server the first time. The CL syntax checker stores information locally and is available when disconnected. This is discussed in detail later in this chapter.

Go to the **Remote Systems > Remote Systems LPEX Editor > i5/OS Parsers** preference pages to see the preferences for syntax checking. Click each of the languages under **i5/OS Parsers**. You will see the preferences for that language. For example, click on **COBOL** to display the syntax checking preferences for COBOL source members, shown in Figure 7–5.

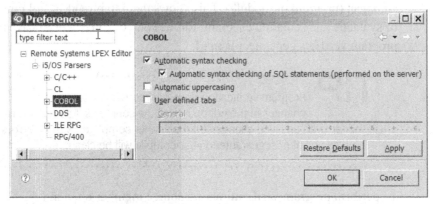

Figure 7–5: COBOL preferences for syntax checking.

To turn off the option to syntax-check SQL statements for COBOL source members, deselect the preference **Automatic syntax checking of SQL statements (performed on the server)**. You might want to do this if you are working disconnected. To choose not to invoke syntax checking for any lines in the source, deselect the **Automatic syntax checking** preference.

Regardless of your preference for automatic syntax checking, you can always invoke the syntax checker manually. To syntax-check the entire source member, select **Source > Syntax Check All** from the menu bar. To syntax-check parts of the source member, first select the part of the source, and then right-click in the editor and select **Syntax Check Selection**. To syntax-check a single line or statement, position the cursor on the line, right-click, and select **Syntax Check Line.**

To remove the errors from the source, select **Source > Remove Messages** from the Workbench menu. You can also use **Source > Refresh**. or the Ctrl+F5 keyboard shortcut.

Program Verification

The RSE includes program verifiers for ILE RPG, COBOL, and DDS. The program verifiers provide a middle option between syntax checking and compiling for detecting errors in your source. They perform the same checks as the compilers, but they run on the workstation and do not generate an object (program or module). This allows them to provide a full range of syntactic and semantic checking for the source. You can even have the program verifiers generate a listing!

TIP Program verification does not require you to save the changes in the editor. It uses the source as it appears in the editor (with unsaved changes)! If the verifier completes with no errors, you can be almost guaranteed your compile will be clean, too.

To perform program verification of a source member open in LPEX, either select **Source > Verify** from the menu bar, use the "verify" button in the Workbench toolbar (▤), or use the Ctrl+Shift+V keyboard shortcut. This launches the program verifier with the options specified in the preferences for that source type.

TIP If the Source menu is missing, or if the actions in the Source member are disabled, the editor does not have focus. Click anywhere inside the editor area to ensure that the editor has focus, and the actions will be enabled.

You can control the behavior of the program verifiers through their preference pages. Program verification preferences provide many of the same options as the corresponding compilers. For example, in the program verifier preferences, you can specify to generate a listing for your source during verification. To override the options from the preferences when verifying a member, select **Source > Verify (Prompt)**. This opens the Program Verification Options dialog, where you can modify the options before running the verifier.

The general rule with preferences is that, if you want a preference to apply all the time, you need to change it through **Window > Preferences**.

This rule applies for program verification as well. The options you specify on the Verify (Prompt) action apply to that particular program verification. If you bring up the verify options again, the preferences specified in the previous verification will not be there. If you want options to apply to all the program verifications, change them on the **Remote Systems > i5/OS > Program Verifiers** preference pages.

Once the program verification is completed, the editor message line displays a message indicating whether or not there were errors. If the program verification reports errors, they are displayed in the Error List view. This view opens automatically and contains the informational, warning, and error messages. By default, this view is positioned at the bottom right corner of the Workbench, in the tabbed notebook view.

Double-clicking an error in the Error List view inserts the error in the source where the error occurs. By default, all the errors are inserted in the source. You can easily navigate from error to error in the editor by using the "next problem" and "previous problem" buttons ( ) on the Work-bench toolbar, or by using the keyboard shortcuts Ctrl +. (period) to go to the next problem and Ctrl+, (comma) to go to the previous problem.

The same Error List view is used for displaying compiler errors. After all, the program verifiers do exactly what the compilers do, except they don't generate an object. Using and customizing the Error List view is covered in more detail in chapter 8.

To remove errors from the source, select **Source > Remove Messages** from the Workbench menu. You can also use **Source > Refresh** or the Ctrl+F5 keyboard shortcut.

TIP
The difference between the Source > Remove Messages and Source > Refresh actions is that, in addition to removing messages, the Refresh action also clears the prefix area (removing all the pending actions), and displays all the lines of the source (removing any filtering of the source).

For COBOL and ILE RPG, one of the options when you verify the source is to generate a listing. (The program verifier options for each language are covered later in this chapter, in the individual language sections.) When a listing is requested, it is created by the program verifier and stored locally on the workstation. Once the program verification completes, the Listings view is opened, but it will not get focus because the Error List view has focus. Click the Listing view's tab to see the program verifier listing, shown in Figure 7–6.

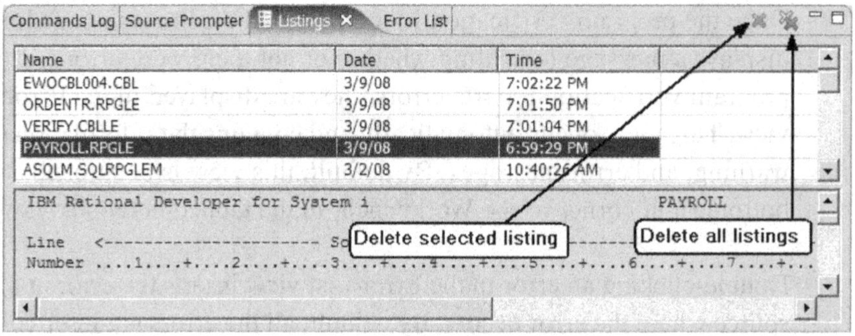

Figure 7–6: The Listings view.

All program verifier listings are shown in this view. Select an entry in the table at the top of the view, and the listing appears in the lower pane. Double-click the Listing view tab to maximize the view, to see more lines in the listing (or use the Ctrl+M keyboard shortcut). You can also drag the separator between the table and listing to add more space to the listing area. All listings remain in the Workspace until they are explicitly deleted.

TIP   The listings are stored in your Workspace under the directory *workspace\.metadata\.plugins\com.ibm.etools. iseries.core\listings*. The file names are the same as the source member, concatenated with the source member type and an *.lst* extension. One side effect of this naming convention is that if you have source members with the same name and type, only one listing can be stored. The source member verified last with the listing option wins.

Program verification can be invoked without having to open the source member in LPEX. In the Remote Systems view or Object Table view, right-click the member, and select **Verify** or **Verify (Prompt)**. Verification errors are displayed in the Error List view. Double-clicking an error opens the source member in LPEX and positions to the line with the error.

TIP ·
You can invoke the program verifier for multiple members
at the same time from the Remote Systems or Object Table
view. They don't have to all be the same source member type, as long
as all of the selected source members have a program verifier.

· ·

You might be wondering how the program verifier obtains external descriptions, like externally described files and copybooks, if it runs locally. It is time we explain this in a little more detail. For external information that resides on the server, the program verifier does make a call to the server to obtain the information. However, once it is obtained, it is cached locally and used for subsequent verifies. This increases performance, since the communication trip to the server is costly in terms of time. Therefore, information from the cache is used the next time the information is needed, instead of making a call to the server. The other advantage of the cached information is that you can verify your source even when disconnected from the server.

Why do you need to know about the cache? As a programmer, you will need to decide when to update the information in the cache. A common question we hear is, "Why is the program verifier not picking up the changes I made in the externally described file?" If you know the answer, you have mastered the understanding of the cache. If not, it's okay; we will explain. During program verification, if information about an externally described file is available in the cache, it will be used, to avoid going to the server to get the information.

After you change the external description and re-create the file object, the cache still has the old external description. To tell the program verifier to retrieve the new external description from the server and update the old cached values, invoke the program verifier with a prompt and select the **Refresh the cache** option. Figure 7–7 shows this option for the COBOL program verifier.

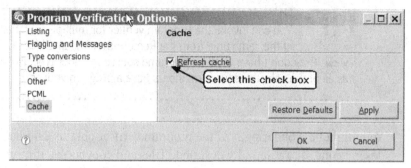

Figure 7–7: The cache option for the COBOL program verifier.

Alternatively, select the updated file object in the RSE, right-click, and select **Cache File Descriptions**, as shown in Figure 7–8 . This creates the required cached information for the file if it does not exist, or updates the existing information if it already existed in the cache. The Cache File Descriptions action is also useful to prepare for working offline. If you know you will be adding code to access a new file from your RPG or COBOL application while offline, you can cache the file descriptions for that file before disconnecting.

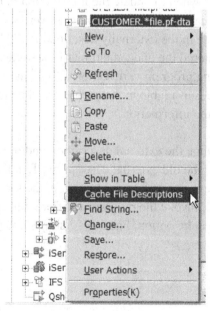

*Figure 7-8: Creating cached file
descriptions.*

TIP ··

If you are making many modifications to externally described files, it is a good practice to enable the refresh cache option from the preferences. Go to the **Remote Systems > > i5/OS > Program Verifiers** preference page, and select the option **Refresh cache**. Don't forget to deselect this option after you complete the modifications of the external descriptions. Otherwise, you will see performance degradation, as each call to retrieve the external description for that file will make calls to the server.

··

Program verification can be performed on i5/OS Project source members as well. To "link" i5/OS projects so they can reference members from each other, right-click the i5/OS project and select **Properties**. In the Properties dialog, check the projects that the selected i5/OS project needs to reference.

These project references only affect the program verifiers and how they resolve copy books. For example, you might have an ILE RPG source member belonging to the "Order Entry Project," while the /copy member is in another project, say, "Inventory Project." As shown in Figure 7–9, you can add the Inventory Project as a reference project to the Order Entry Project. When you verify source members from the Order Entry Project, if the copy member is not found in the current project, the search continues in the referenced projects. i5/OS projects are covered in more detail in chapter 11.

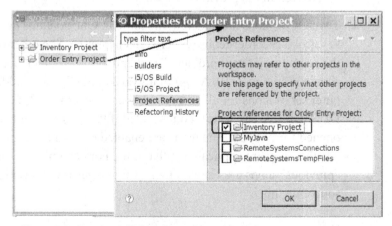

Figure 7–9: Creating i5/OS Project references.

Language-specific Actions

This section covers actions that are specific to a particular language. The languages covered here are ILE RPG, COBOL (both COBOL/400 and ILE COBOL), DDS, CL, and RPG/400. For all these languages, when a source member is opened in the Remote Systems LPEX Editor, the following are added to the Workbench:

- A compile menu is added to the menu bar, and the "compile" icon ( ) is added to the toolbar. This allows compiles to be launched from the editor without having to find the member in the Remote Systems or Object Table view. This menu is only added for source opened from i5/OS. For details on compiling i5/OS members, see chapter 8.

- The following actions are added to the Source menu:

  » *Prompt (F4)*: This is similar to prompting in SEU using F4. Source prompting is covered in chapter 6.

  » *Syntax Check All*: This action syntax-checks the entire source. Any errors are inserted into the source as described in the earlier section on syntax checking.

  » *Resequence All Lines*: This action is covered in chapter 6.

  » *Remove Messages* and *Refresh (Ctrl+F5)*: These actions are covered in the previous section.

- Two sets of icons are added to the toolbar. One contains the keystroke-recorder icons (covered in chapter 6). The other contains the "compare," "next problem," and "previous problem" icons shown in Figure 7–10. A "program verification" icon is added to the latter set of icons for all source members except CL, RPG/400, and DDS ICFF. A "compile" icon is added if the source member was opened from i5/OS. The icons are enabled or disabled depending on whether they are applicable at that time. For example, the "next" and "previous" icons are enabled if error messages are inserted into the source member.

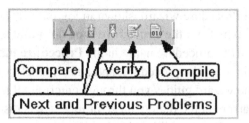

Figure 7–10: The toolbar for i5/OS source members.

A few of the actions available on the Workbench Source menu are also available by right-clicking in the editor. It doesn't matter which one you use, since the same underlying action is run. The right-click actions covered in subsequent sections are language-specific. The generic actions have already been covered in earlier sections of this chapter or in chapter 6.

ILE RPG

This section walks through the editor actions available for ILE RPG source members. When we talk about the ILE RPG source members, we are referring to source members of types RPGLE and SQLRPGLE. If you use a different source member type for ILE RPG source, refer to the section on LPEX parsers later in this chapter.

The New Procedure and D-Spec Wizards

In addition to prompting, content assist, and templates to help in entering code, LPEX includes wizards to guide you through entering complicated language definitions, reducing the need to refer to manuals for additional help (or copying and pasting existing code to modify). Three wizards are available for ILE RPG source members: the Procedure wizard, the D-Specification wizard, and the Java Method Call wizard. To access a wizard, use the **Source > New** menu from the menu bar or right-click in the editor and select **New**, and then choose the wizard.

A wizard builds up the entire structure, validating as it is built, and then inserts the generated source code into the editor. For example, you can construct an entire data structure through the D-Specification wizard before it is inserted in the source at the location you specified.

To use the Procedure wizard, shown in Figure 7–11, begin by selecting the procedure type from the **Procedure type** drop-down menu. Then, enter a valid ILE RPG procedure name in the **Procedure name** field. Select any of the options for the procedure, and add parameters by clicking the **Add** button. The wizard guides you through entering all required information. If there are errors in the dialog, an error message is displayed near the bottom of the dialog. To get additional help, press F1 anywhere in the wizard, or click the "help" icon (⑦) in the bottom left corner.

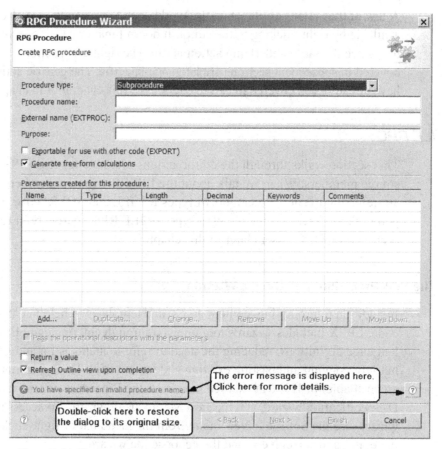

Figure 7–11: The Procedure wizard.

Once you complete this wizard page without errors, the Next or Finish button will be enabled. If the Next button is enabled, additional information is required. Another wizard page will be presented, where you can enter this information. For example, select the **Return a value** option, and you will need to specify the details of the return value.

The Finish button is enabled when all required information is specified. Click this button. You will be delighted to see that the information from the wizard is constructed into RPG statements and inserted into the source member. For the Procedure wizard, the procedure prototype and procedure interface information are generated in the appropriate places.

TIP
You can resize a wizard dialog by dragging its edges or sides. To restore the dialog to its original size, double-click the blank space at the bottom of the dialog, near the dialog's buttons.

In the D-Specification wizard, shown in Figure 7–12, you enter the field name and purpose (a comment), and select the type of the D-specification, using the drop-down menu. You can also select where you want the new definition to be inserted in the source member.

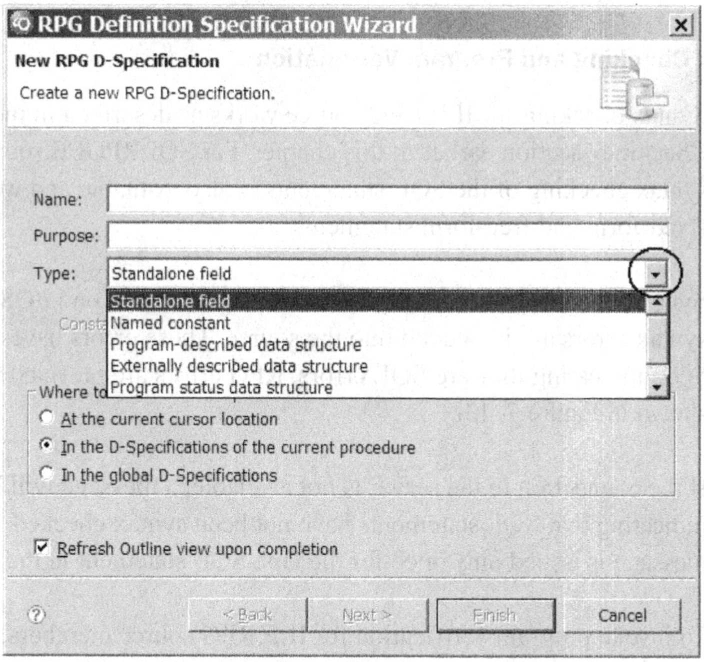

Figure 7–12: The D-Specification wizard.

Depending on the type of definition selected, clicking the Next button will present a page prompting for information needed to construct that particular type. When all the needed information is gathered through the wizard pages, the Finish button is enabled. Click this button to insert the code into the source member.

You can call Java methods from ILE RPG programs using the RPG Java method call. The Java Method Call wizard assists in creating the ILE RPG code to call a Java method from your RPG program. Have you ever tried to code this manually, and got it right the first time? Okay, you don't have to answer this question.

In the Java Method Call wizard, you start by specifying the Java package and class name you want to use for the method call. Use the **Browse workspace**, **Browse local**, or **Browse remote** button to search for the class, even within Java archive (JAR) files. Once you complete the wizard and press Finish, you will not only have the prototype for the Java method call, but the call itself will be entered in the source on a calculation specification. How cool is that?!

Syntax Checking and Program Verification

Syntax checking for ILE RPG source works as described in the "Syntax Checking" section earlier in this chapter. For SQLRPGLE source members, syntax checking of the SQL statements is also available and works with fixed-form and free-form statements.

Syntax checking of the SQL statements is performed on i5/OS, and any syntax errors are imbedded into the source. These errors have a prefix of *SQL*, indicating they are SQL errors. RPG errors are prefixed with *RNF*, as shown in Figure 7–13.

If the connection to the server is not available, a message will be issued, indicating that SQL statements have not been syntax checked. This message is issued only once for the first SQL statement in the source.

To invoke program verification for ILE RPG source members, use either **Source > Verify**, the "verifier" icon in the toolbar, or the Ctrl+Shift+V keyboard shortcut. This invokes the program verifier described earlier in this chapter.

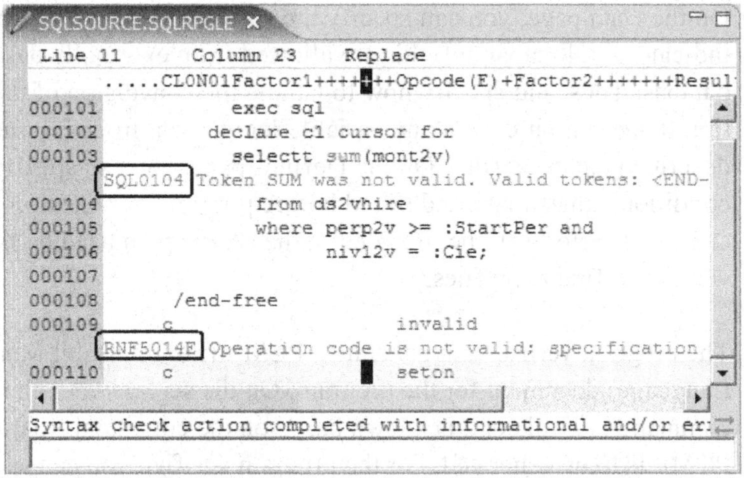

Figure 7–13: SQL and RPG errors in the source.

Invoking the program verifier through Source > Verify (Prompt) first opens up the Options dialog for the program verifier, shown in Figure 7–14. The options provided here are similar to the ones you saw when compiling the source member. There are five pages listed on the left side, and the details for the pages are listed on the right side. For example, click the **Listing** page, and you can select the listing to be created with the options you want. By default, the listing option is unchecked, meaning a listing is not created.

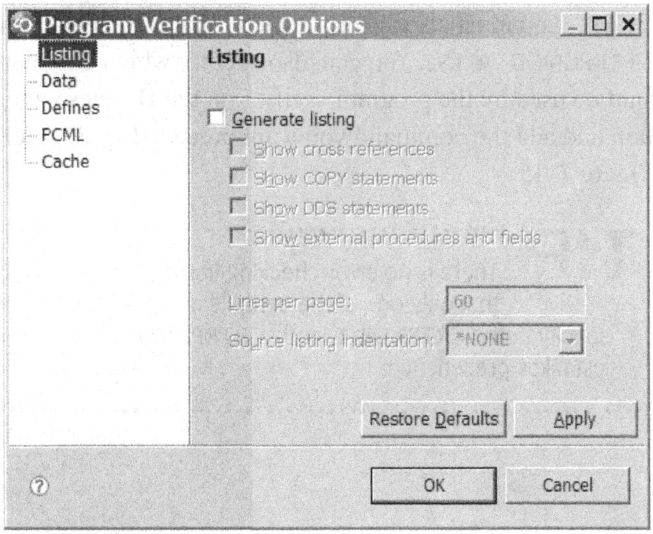

Figure 7–14: ILE RPG program verifier options.

On the Data page, you can specify the sort sequence table to be used, indicate if null-capable fields are allowed from externally described database files, and specify how to handle the conversion of date, time, timestamp, graphic data, and variable-length data from externally described database files. On the Defines page, you can specify the condition names that are defined before program verification begins, and the directories to be included in the search path used by the program verifier to find copy files.

The program verifier can generate a PCML (Program Call Markup Language) document for the program. On the server, when the compile command is invoked, it is known based on the command what type of PCML is to be generated. For the program verifier, you can specify whether you want the program verification to be done for program creation (CRTBNDRPG) or for module creation (CRTRPGMOD) on the PCML page. This ensures that correct PCML is generated. If you have changed any externally described data, select the **Refresh cache** option on the Cache page. See the section "Program Verifier" earlier in this chapter for details on caching.

By default, the ILE RPG program verifier behaves like CRTRPGMOD. This can be changed to CRTBNDRPG either by using the PCML option or by defining the command on the Defines page. If you specify the generation of PCML, you must also specify which command behavior (CRTBDNRPG or CRTRPGMOD) to use. You can also specify which command behavior should be used by the program verifier on the Defines page. Click the **New** button and add the command you want preceded by an asterisk, as shown in Figure 7–15.

TIP There is no error checking in the Defines dialog to ensure that only one of the compile commands is specified. If you specify both *CRTBNDRPG and *CRTRPGMOD, the one that appears last takes precedence.

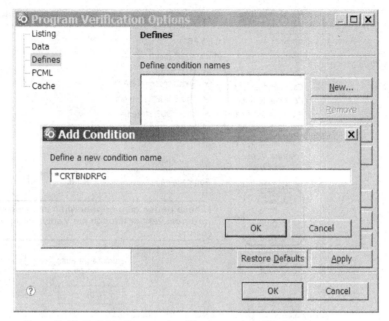

Figure 7–15: Defining the command for program verification.

If you want changes to the program verifier preferences to apply to all program verifications, use the **Remote Systems > i5/OS > Program Verifiers > ILE RPG** preference pages. These preferences apply to program verifications invoked without prompting, as well. For example, if you want a listing with all listing options to always be generated by the ILE RPG program verifier, go to the preference page shown in Figure 7–16, select all the options, and click **OK**. The next time you invoke the program verifier, a listing will be generated. You can still override these preferences using the Verify (Prompt) action. When you invoke the verifier this way, the options in the Prompt dialog take their default values from the preferences.

TIP

During compilation, you can specify the control-specification in a data area instead of including it in your source; you can do the same for program verification. However, instead of a data area, you create a file named *RPGLEHSPEC.RPGLE* in the *.metadata* directory in your Workspace. This is used as the H-spec's data area during program verification.

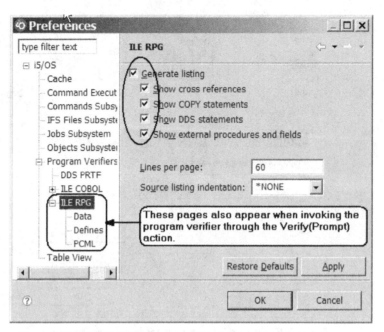

Figure 7–16: The ILE RPG program verifier preference pages.

Converting to Free-form

LPEX includes a tool to convert fixed-form ILE RPG calculation specifications into free-form. Free-form code can be formatted and indented, making it easier to read and work with, since it is not restricted tocolumns.

To convert an entire source member, select **Source > Convert All To Free-Form** in the editor. To convert only a subset of the source, first select the lines to be converted, then right-click, and select **Convert Selection to Free-Form**. The conversion goes through the source and converts each line, one by one. It does not convert MOVE statements. It also does not perform any code improvements, like switching from using indicators to using built-in functions.

When you convert the source to free format, the default preferences for automatic indentation will determine how your source is indented. To see how this is controlled, go to the **Remote Systems > Remote Systems LPEX Editor > i5/OS Parsers > ILE RPG** preference page. By default, the "Automatic indent" option is selected, and the number of blanks to use for indentation is set to two.

The conversion process does not create a new source member. In fact, it overwrites the current member by replacing the fixed-form statements with free-form statements. A message appears in the editor message line when conversion completes. If the source had statements that were converted, the "dirty" flag is set for the editor, indicating that it contains unsaved changes. Either save the converted source, or undo the conversion by selecting **Edit > Undo**.

TIP
You can still undo changes after saving the source member by using Edit > Undo, as long as you have not closed the source member.

Working with Nested Structures

The ILE RPG language contains common structured programming structures and operations like subroutines, procedures, loops, if statements, and select statements. When a source member contains these nested controlled structures, and you happen to miss an "end" statement, it can be difficult to determine where it should be added. This is especially true when using fixed-form instead of free-form statements, since you need to code in the correct columns, and indenting is not possible.

How many times have you had to create a listing and struggle to locate the missing "end"? Well, no more. LPEX can save you time and frustration! You can display an indented view of the source and quickly locate the problematic area. This works for fixed-form and free-form RPG statements.

To display the indented view of the source, select **Source > Show Indentation** from the Workbench menu bar. This opens the RPG Indentation view with the indented source in browse mode. By default, this view opens in the tabbed notebook at the bottom right of the Remote System Explorer perspective. You cannot edit in this view. The intent of this view is to display the flow of the controlled structures and to ensure that the beginning and ending of blocks are correctly matched. You can print the indented source using the view's pull-down menu, as shown in Figure 7–17.

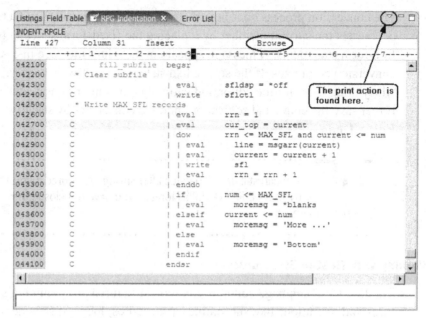

Figure 7–17: The indented view of the source, showing flow.

There is another useful feature that shows you the block closure within the editor. Unlike the RPG Indentation view, which shows indentation of the entire source, here you can select the block of code you are interested in and show the block nesting, select the block, or even jump to the end of the block.

To do this, position the cursor on the line containing the beginning or ending opcode for the block you want to match. Right-click in the editor, and select **Source > Show Block Nesting**, or use the Ctrl+Shift+O keyboard shortcut. This displays an arrow matching the beginning and end of the code block. All nested control structures will also contain arrows indicating their beginning and ending lines, up to five levels deep, as shown in Figure 7–18.

You can only show one set of controlled structures this way. When you show another set, the arrows are removed from the previous one. To remove the arrows showing the block nesting yourself, select **Source > Refresh** from the Workbench menu bar, or use the Ctrl+F5 keyboard shortcut.

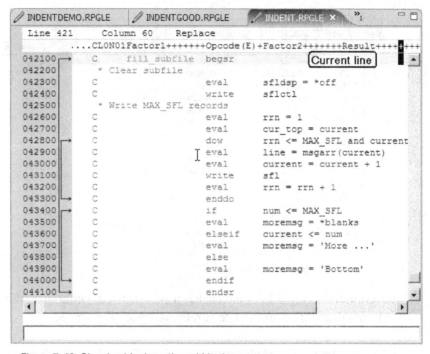

Figure 7–18: Showing block nesting within the source.

To select a block structure, position the cursor on the beginning or ending line and select **Source > Select Block**, or use the Ctrl+M keyboard short-cut. To jump to the beginning or end of the block, select **Source > Jump To Block End**, or use the Ctrl+Shift+M keyboard shortcut. If you are at the beginning of the block, this action positions the cursor at the end, and vice versa.

Viewing Fields from an Externally Described File

If you have an externally described file in your source, you can easily display the list of fields for this file in the Field Table view. Position your cursor anywhere on the file specification line for the externally described file, and select **Source > Show fields** from the Workbench menu bar. Alternatively, right-click inside the editor and select **Show fields**. The Field Table view opens and displays the fields from the externally described file, as shown in Figure 7–19.

This action is enabled only when the cursor is positioned on the file specification that defines an externally described file. If the external

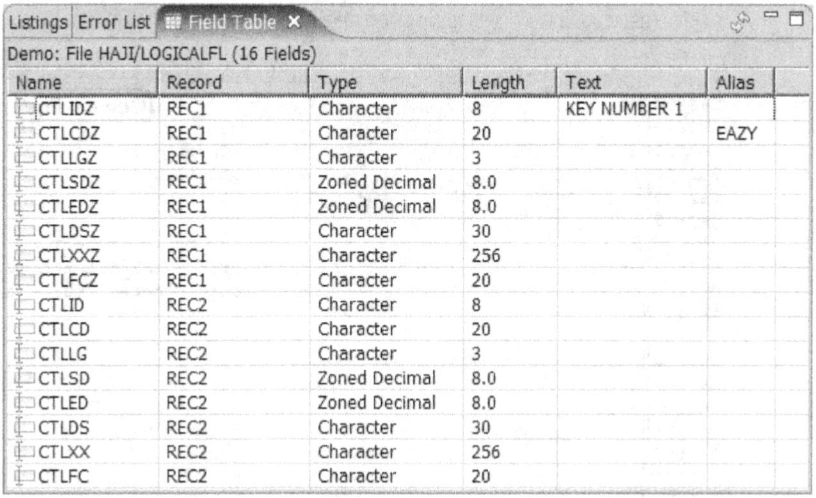

Name	Record	Type	Length	Text	Alias
CTLIDZ	REC1	Character	8	KEY NUMBER 1	
CTLCDZ	REC1	Character	20		EAZY
CTLLGZ	REC1	Character	3		
CTLSDZ	REC1	Zoned Decimal	8.0		
CTLEDZ	REC1	Zoned Decimal	8.0		
CTLDSZ	REC1	Character	30		
CTLXXZ	REC1	Character	256		
CTLFCZ	REC1	Character	20		
CTLID	REC2	Character	8		
CTLCD	REC2	Character	20		
CTLLG	REC2	Character	3		
CTLSD	REC2	Zoned Decimal	8.0		
CTLED	REC2	Zoned Decimal	8.0		
CTLDS	REC2	Character	30		
CTLXX	REC2	Character	256		
CTLFC	REC2	Character	20		

Figure 7–19: The Field Table view.

description is available in the cache, it will be used. Otherwise, the external description of the file is retrieved from the server.

The Field Table view shows the name of the file and the number of fields in the file at the top. The fields are listed in the table. You can sort the view by clicking on any of the column headings.

The "Show fields" action uses the library list of the RSE connection to resolve external files, just like the compiler and program verifier. If the library list does not contain the file, a message to that effect is displayed in the message line.

TIP

You can also display the list of fields in a display file, data physical file, or logical file from the Remote Systems view or the Object Table view. Right-click the file and select **Show in Table** for display files and logical files, or **Show in Table > Fields** for data physical files.

Opening Copy Members

If the cursor is positioned on a copy or include directive, and you right-click in the editor, actions to edit or browse the copy member are added to the pop-up menu, as shown in Figure 7–20.In this case, *copy member* means the member specified in either copy or include directives.

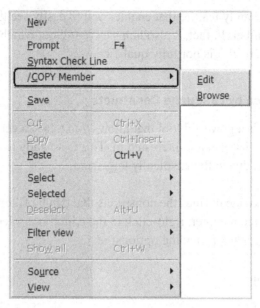

Figure 7–20: The option to open the copy member.

TIP

When using the "Show fields" and "COPY Member" edit or browse actions, make sure you position the cursor on the line, but don't select anything. If you select part of the line (like the file name or member name), and then right-click, the pop-up menu contains only selection related actions, not the line- or editor-related actions.

These actions are also added to the menu bar under Source > /COPY Member. The source menu actions are always displayed, regardless of whether or not the cursor is positioned on a copy or include directive. However, the edit and browse actions are enabled only if the cursor is positioned on a line containing one of these directives.

This action resolves the copy member the same way the compiler or the program verifier resolves the copy member when it is not fully qualified. If the copy member is not found, a message appears in the editor message line; otherwise, the copy member will be opened in a new editor, as requested.

This is a handy feature that enables you to easily see the contents of the copy member. In fact, it also helps to figure out which copy member will be "chosen" if it is not fully qualified.

Filtering Source by Language Constructs

Filtering is a powerful tool that allows you to see a certain type of language construct that you are interested in. This is a handy tool for i5/OS source members, due to their typically large size.

Each language defines the constructs that can be filtered on. For an ILE RPG source member, right-click in the editor and select **Filter View**, and you will see the following options:

- Date
- Code
- Comments
- Control
- Procedures
- Subroutines
- Errors

If the source member is of type SQLRPGLE, you will also see an option to filter on SQL statements.

This allows you to filter the source to see only the lines containing the selected language constructs. For example, select **Filter View > Subroutines**. You will only see the lines containing BEGSR and ENDSR. You can use the plus and minus signs on the editor's vertical ruler to expand and collapse the sections of the source that are filtered out. (Filtering is described in more details in chapter 6.)

Unfortunately, you can only choose one of the items from the list to filter the source. For example, you cannot filter to see all the subroutines and procedures in one filter.

Outline View

The Outline view provides a high-level overview of the source member currently being edited. It is very helpful in understanding the source and navigating around the source member. The Outline view is consistently rated one of the favorite RSE features by users!

The Outline view is not automatically refreshed while editing an ILE RPG source member. The first time you open an ILE RPG source member, the view contains the text "Press Refresh to update view."

The Outline view for an ILE RPG source member does an extensive analysis of the source, retrieving all the externally described data, including copy members. This can sometimes take a long time, depending on the number of external descriptions required from the server. For this reason, the Outline view is not created when opening the member.

Internally, the program verifier is invoked, and the information about the source is displayed in the Outline view. As such, all the program verifier options specified in the preferences are used during the creation of the Outline view. The preferences that you specify to control the behavior of the program verifier also influence the contents of the Outline view. (When we refer to the source member in the rest of this section, we are referring to the source member being edited as, well as the external descriptions and copy members.)

To create the Outline view for an ILE RPG source member, click the "refresh" button ( ) in the view's toolbar. This displays up to three high-level nodes in the outline:

- *Global Definitions:* This contains the global files, data structures, indicators, constants, fields, prototypes, and key lists for the source member. A node appears for each of these, if there are corresponding definitions. For example, if there are no prototypes defined in the source member, there will not be a Prototypes node.

- *Main Procedure*: This contains information related to the main procedure (entry point) for the source member. This node contains at most two children: Parameters and Subroutines. If there are program parameters, they will be listed under the Parameter node.

If there are any global subroutines in the source, they are shown under the Subroutines node.

- *Subprocedures*: This contains a list of all procedures defined in the source. Each procedure has up to three child nodes: Parameter, Local Definitions, and Subroutines. The Local Definitions node cascades into entries like the Global Definitions node.

Click any item in the Outline view to position the editor to the corresponding line in the source. Let's look at a simple example in Figure 7–21. "Fld2" is defined as one of the subfields of the "ds1" data structure. The data structure is not qualified, so the subfield's name appears under the Fields node with its type and size, as well as in the Data Structures node.

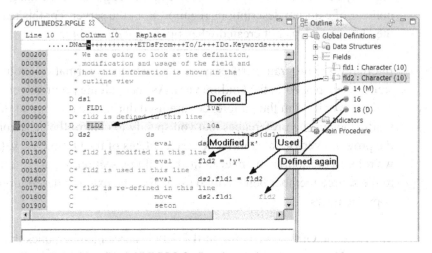

Figure 7–21: Mapping the ILE RPG Outline view to the source.

The fld2 entry under the Fields node indicates the field's definition. Clicking it positions the editor to where this field is first defined. The vertical ruler area also has a bar indicating the line of the definition, line 10, in this case. There is a plus sign next to fld2 in the Outline view, indicating this field is referenced (used, modified, or redefined) in the source member. Expanding fld2 displays the line numbers where the field is referenced. In this example, you see *14 (M)*, *16*, and *18 (D)*. This means that on line 14, fld2 was modified; on line 16, it was used; and on line 18, it was redefined. Clicking the line number positions the editor to that line number.

TIP   You can tell if an entity was defined and never referenced in
the source, since you will not see a plus sign beside it.

The numbers that you see under the entity are line numbers, *not*
sequence numbers.

If any of the definitions are in a copy member, clicking the item in the
Outline view will position the cursor to the copy statement in the source
member, indication that the definition or usage is in the copy file. You can
quickly open the copy member for editing or browsing as discussed earlier
in this chapter.

It is also worth mentioning that the Outline view preserves the case
of names. If an entity appears with a case other than uppercase in
the source, this will be used in the Outline view. However, there are
situations where fields retrieved from an external description may be
shown in uppercase only.

Different icons are used by the Outline view to convey information about
an entry. For example, under the Files nodes, different icons are used to
represent "externally described files" (⬛) and "program described files"
(⬛).

While editing an ILE RPG source member, you will need to periodically
refresh the Outline view to reflect the current contents of the source. This is
done by clicking on the "refresh" button at the top of the view or using the
Ctrl+Shift+F5 keyboard shortcut. The Outline view runs asynchronously
so you can continue working, even editing the source member, while the
view is being refreshed. The Outline view is updated as soon as the refresh
completes.

Content Assist

The content assist feature available in ILE RPG has three parts: static
content, dynamic content, and templates. Templates are covered in chapter
6. Static content assist is information that does not depend in any other
factors. For example, if you are on a calculation specification in fixed-form
RPG, and the cursor is anywhere in position 26 to 35 (the opcode column),

pressing Ctrl+Space will display the list of opcodes. Details about the currently selected opcode are shown beside it.

You can choose an opcode from the content assist list, or simply start typing. As you type, the list is filtered to reflect the correct possibilities. Figure 7–22 shows that by typing the letters *rea*, the list of opcodes narrows down to show the possible completions. By selecting the readp opcode in the list (using the arrow keys), the details of that opcode are shown.

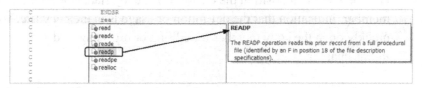

Figure 7–22: Content assist for opcodes.

In this example, if you select readp, and tab to factor two, and press Ctrl+Space, the readp opcode information is repeated. Wouldn't it be nice if you could get a list of files and record formats defined in the source? Well, you can, but you need to refresh the Outline view first. This is what we refer to as *dynamic content*: the information changes depending on what is defined in the source. This is what makes content assist in ILE RPG such a powerful tool in providing code assistance.

Content assist uses the information from the Outline view to populate the dynamic content possibilities. Therefore, if you create an Outline view and then use content assist, you will be amazed by the amount of assistance that is provided to help you while coding. To continue the example from Figure 7–22, pressing Ctrl+Space in factor two displays the list of files and record formats in Figure 7–23.

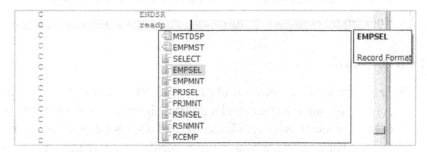

Figure 7–23: Content assist to provide a list of files and record formats.

Content assist, combined with Outline view, provides a powerful tool to enhance your editing experience and improve productivity in your application development cycle.

Locating Subroutines and Procedures

You can quickly jump to the definition of the subroutine or the procedure from any source line that contains a call to it. To do this, position the cursor on the name of the subroutine or procedure, right-click, and select **Source > Open Declaration**, or use the F3 keyboard shortcut. (Be careful not to switch back to SEU, position the cursor on a subroutine call, and press F3!)

This only works for subroutines and procedures defined in the same source member as the call. (It does not resolve calls or definitions in copy members.) If the definition is found, the cursor position changes to the start of the definition of the subroutine or the procedure. A quick mark is also set, to allow you switch between the line containing the call and the definition using the Alt+Q keyboard shortcut.

If the definition of the subroutine or the procedure is not found within the source, a message is displayed in the editor's message line.

TIP
If the current line has an opcode of EXSR or CASXX, the search looks for a subroutine. Otherwise, the search looks for a procedure, by default.

Preferences

To see the editing preferences specific to ILE RPG source members, go to the **Remote Systems > Remote Systems LPEX Editor > i5/OS Parsers > ILE RPG** preference page. The tabbing and syntax-checking preferences are covered earlier in this chapter. The ILE RPG preference page allows you can control the behavior of the Enter key as well, as shown in Figure 7–24.

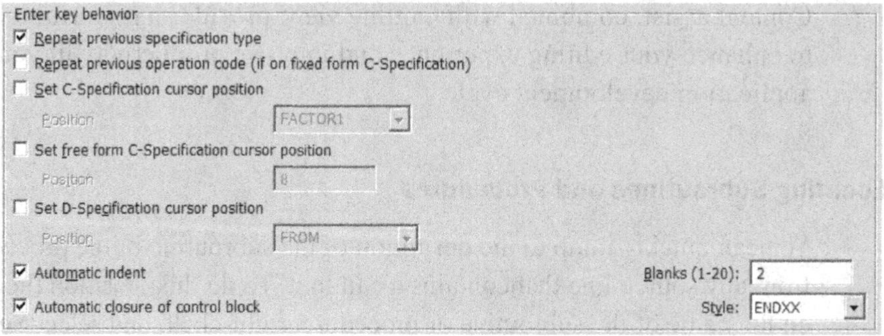

Figure 7–24: Customizing the Enter key for ILE RPG source members.

In LPEX, the default action of the Enter key is to create a new line. However, this default behavior can be overridden. For ILE RPG source members, the behavior of the Enter key is set to repeat the specification from the previous line. In addition to this, you can choose to repeat the previous operation code and specify where the cursor should be positioned.

Two other options are available to customize behavior of the Enter key:

- *Automatic indent*: This preference applies only to free-form RPG, and controls whether or not you the next line is automatically indented if the previous line contains the start of a control structure, such as loop or if statement. You can also specify how many blanks it should be indented. (The default is two.)

- *Automatic closure of control block:* This preference controls whether or not you want the corresponding end of a control block inserted into the editor when you press Enter on the starting line. For example, if you type the SELECT opcode and press the Enter key, the ENDSL is inserted in the new line. This preference applies to fixed and free-from specifications. You can also choose the character case (style) for the closure line.

You can also choose not to have the Enter key customized for ILE RPG source members by deselecting the "Repeat previous specification type" preference. This disables all the other options pertaining to the Enter key. The Enter key behavior reverts to using the base LPEX editor behavior. This can be useful if you want to set up the same behavior for the Enter key across all languages using the LPEX > User Key Actions preference page, as discussed in chapter 6.

TIP

If you press the Enter key one too many times in the editor, you can always use Ctrl+Backspace to delete the current line, or Ctrl+Z to undo. You will love these keys when your fingers start working a bit faster than your brain!

If you drill down under the ILE RPG preference page, you will see two more preference pages, shown in Figure 7–25: Free-form SQL Formatting and Templates. The SQL formatting preferences apply to SQL statements in free-form in source members of type SQLRPGLE. Here you can control the indentation and formatting of SQL statements, uppercasing of keywords, built-in functions and identifiers, and the placement of comments within the source. Templates are covered in chapter 6.

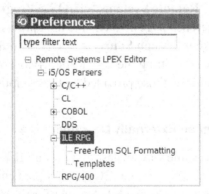

Figure 7–25: ILE RPG preferences.

COBOL

This section walks through the editor actions available for COBOL source members. When we refer to COBOL members, we include source member of types CBLLE, SQLCBLLE, CICSCBLLE, CBL, SQLCBL, CICSCBL, and CICSSQLCBL. Refer to the section on LPEX parsers, later in this chapter, if you use a different source member type for COBOL source.

Syntax Checking and Program Verification

COBOL/400 and ILE COBOL source members use the same syntax checker and program verifier. Therefore, when we say *COBOL*, we include both COBOL/400 and ILE COBOL. These two versions of COBOL are similar, except for the new language features added to ILE COBOL. If you try to use these new language features in COBOL/400, LPEX will not flag them as errors.

Syntax checking for COBOL source members work as described earlier in this chapter. There is one difference in the way SQL statements are handled for syntax checking. With ILE RPG, syntax checking for SQL statements is performed only for source members of type SQLRPGLE. This is different for COBOL, where SQL statements in any COBOL source member will be syntax checked if the SQL syntax checking preference is enabled. This includes source members of type CBL, CBLLE, CBLLEINC, CICSCBL, and so on. This is different behavior than SEU.

To invoke the program verifier without prompting, use the preferences defined on the **Remote Systems > i5/OS > Program Verifiers > ILE COBOL** preference pages. To change the options for the member being verified, invoke it through **Source > Verify (Prompt)**, and change the options before submitting the verification. Most of the options you see here are the same as those provided by the compiler.

Viewing Fields from an Externally Described File

This works the same way as described for an ILE RPG source member earlier in this chapter. For COBOL source, the cursor needs to be on a COPY DDS statement in the File Section for the action.

Opening Copybooks

This feature works the same way as described for ILE RPG. The only difference is that instead of seeing "/COPY Member" in the menu, you will see "Copy Book," to reflect the COBOL language's terminology.

Filtering Source by Language Constructs

Filtering works the same way as described for ILE RPG. In a COBOL source member, right-click and select **Filter view** to see the following options:

- Date

- Divisions

- Comments

- Outline

- Embedded SQL/CICS/DLI

- Errors

- Tasks

There is a keyboard shortcut for filtering the divisions: Ctrl+G.

Outline View

The Outline view for COBOL members is populated as soon as a member is opened. However, any changes made to the source member are not automatically shown in the Outline view. You have to press the "refresh" button in the Outline view's toolbar to synchronize the Outline view with the source.

The Outline view displays up to four top-level nodes that represent the four divisions in the COBOL source: Identification Division, Environment Division, Data Division, and Procedure Division. Each division entry includes nodes to represent the sections in the division.

For example, the Data Division is divided into four sections. For each of the sections defined in the source, a node appears in the Outline view. Figure 7–26 shows a Data Division with a File Section and Working-Storage Section. The Outline view shows these two sections as entries under the Data Division node. Selecting an entry in the Outline view positions the editor to the corresponding location in the source.

The Outline view for COBOL members uses only the information from the source member. It does not scan any externally described data, nor does it include information from the copybooks.

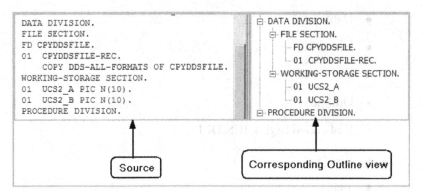

Figure 7-26: COBOL's Outline view.

Content Assist

Content assist in a COBOL source member uses the information from the editor to provide a list of possible suggestions. The advantage of this is, as soon as the type information appears in the source, it is available to content assist. This is unlike Outline view, where you need to refresh the view to show the changes in the member.

In Figure 7-27, the Outline view is created when the source member is opened. Now, edit the source and add this line:

```
77 callee3 pic x(1) value 'CALLG5A3'.
```

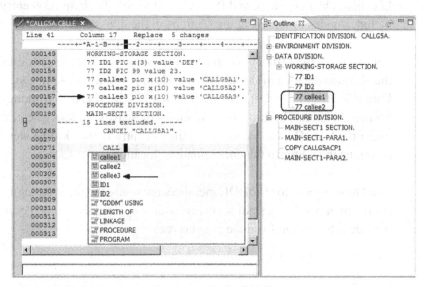

Figure 7-27: Outline view and content assist for COBOL.

The Outline view does not show callee3 because it has not been refreshed. However, the content assist on a CALL statement does include callee3.

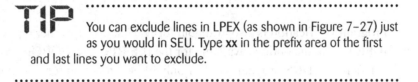

TIP You can exclude lines in LPEX (as shown in Figure 7–27) just as you would in SEU. Type **xx** in the prefix area of the first and last lines you want to exclude.

Commenting-out Source Lines

To comment-out a line of source, place the cursor on the line, right-click, and select **Source > Comment**, or using the Ctrl+/ (forward slash) keyboard shortcut. This adds an asterisk in column 7, changing the line to a comment. To uncomment a line, right-click it and select **Source > Uncomment**, or using the Ctrl+\ (backslash) shortcut. These actions can be performed on multiple lines at the same time by first selecting all the lines.

In most cases, when new editor functions are added for i5/OS languages, you might have noticed they are usually added for ILE RPG first, and then COBOL. This is not true for this commenting feature. RPG programmers have been asking for it for a long time!

Preferences

To see the COBOL editing preferences, go to **Remote Systems > Remote Systems LPEX Editor > i5/OS Parsers > COBOL**. Here you can configure automatic syntax checking, automatic uppercasing, user-defined tabs, and COBOL templates.

DDS

This section walks through the editor actions available for DDS source members. When we refer to *DDS*, we mean source member types of ICFF, PF, LF, PRTF, DSPF, and MNUDDS. In addition to using LPEX for editing DDS source, you can visually edit DPSF DDS source using the Screen Designer, covered in chapter 13.

Syntax Checking and Program Verification

Syntax checking is available for all DDS source member types. It works as described earlier in this chapter.

Program verification is also available for DDS source member types, except ICFF. Unlike the options available for the ILE RPG and COBOL program verifiers, the DDS program verifier only offers an option for refreshing the cache. The exception is printer files. As shown in Figure 7–28, they have their own options to specify the printer device type and page dimensions.

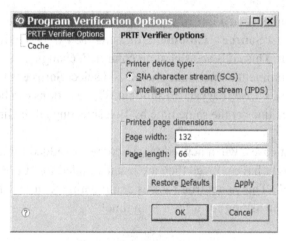

Figure 7–28: The program verification options for printer files.

Filtering Source by Language Constructs

Filtering for DDS source members works the same way as described for ILE RPG and COBOL. The filtering options depend on the DDS source type being edited. The following options are available for all DDS source types when you right-click in the editor and select **Filter view**:

- Date
- Code
- Record specifications
- Record and field specifications
- Field-level keywords

- Record-level keywords

- File-level keywords

- Comments

- Errors

In addition, source members of types DSPF and MNUDDS allow filtering on help specifications. Source members of type PF allow filtering on key fields, and source members of type LF allow filtering on join specifications, select-omit specifications, and key fields.

Outline View

The Outline view for DDS members displays the hierarchy of file, records, fields, help specifications, and keywords in the DDS source member. The DDS Outline view is used by both LPEX and the Screen Designer. Additional details on the content of this view are covered in chapter 13.

The Outline view for DDS works differently than other source types. There is no "refresh" button; the view is automatically populated when the source member is opened. As you modify the source, the Outline view is automatically updated to reflect the current contents of the source, without moving the cursor away from the line or even pressing the Enter key! An outline is not available for ICFF member types.

There is a two-way linkage between the editor and the Outline view for DDS source members. By clicking an item in the Outline view, the editor is positioned to the corresponding line the item is defined on (just like in ILE RPG and COBOL source members). Also, by moving the cursor in the editor, you will see the Outline view updated to show the same record or field selected in the editor.

Content assist is not available for any of the DDS source members.

Preferences

To see the DDS editing preferences, go to **Remote Systems > Remote Systems LPEX Editor > i5/OS Parsers > DDS**. Here you can configure automatic syntax checking and automatic uppercasing.

CL

This section walks through the editor actions available for CL source members. When we refer to *CL*, we are referring to source members of types BND, CL, CLLE, CLP, and CMD. Refer to the section in this chapter on LPEX parsers if you use a different source member type for CL source.

Prompt, Indent, and Format

You can prompt CL statements the same way as the other languages: use **Source > Prompt** from the menu bar or the F4 keyboard shortcut. However, prompting is implemented differently for CL than the other languages.

The prompt information for CL is not installed locally on your workstation. Instead, it is constructed dynamically from the server, and therefore requires a connection to the server. This has two benefits:

- You can always get the correct prompt and the help for the prompt based on the version of i5/OS you are running on the server.

- You can prompt and get help for non-IBM commands.

After a command has been prompted once, the information obtained from the server is cached locally. This improves the response time of subsequent prompts and allows the command to be prompted when working offline.

The Remote Systems > i5/OS > Cache preference page provides preferences to control the granularity of caching for CL prompts and help, as shown in Figure 7–29. The default option is to cache the CL command prompts and help using the server name. This method ensures accuracy, since you might have different versions of commands on different servers of the same i5/OS release. One downside of this approach is the extra disk space required (not that much). Another downside is there is less chance that a command prompt or help will be available in the cache if you are working with multiple servers. (This increases the time it takes to prompt the command or display the help.)

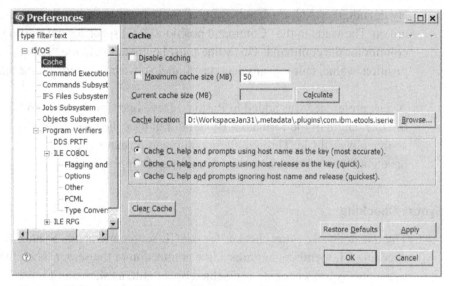

Figure 7–29: Caching for CL command prompts and help.

Once you complete the prompt and the command is updated in the source, the formatting preferences come into play. Similarly, when you manually enter source into the editor, the text is automatically formatted when you go to a new line or move your cursor away from the current line. You can customize this formatting to suit your preferences or your shop's coding standards. To see the formatting preferences, go to the **Remote Systems > Remote Systems LPEX Editor > i5/OS parsers > CL** preference page, shown in Figure 7–30.

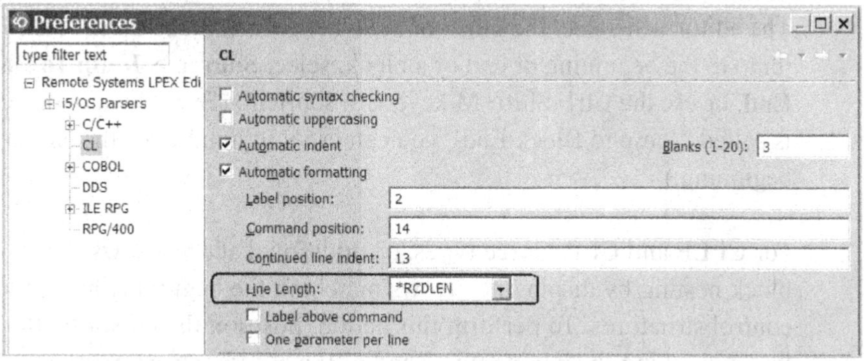

Figure 7–30: Indenting and formatting options for CL commands.

By default, the "Automatic indent" and "Automatic formatting preferences" are on. The value in the "Command position" field specifies the starting column for the command. This value must be greater than the "Label position" value, unless you select the "Label above command" check box.

A new preference was added in Rational Developer for System i to limit the line length of the formatter. By default, it uses the record length of the source physical file. Through these command formatting preferences, you have good control over how the CL commands appear in the source.

Syntax Checking

There is no local syntax checker for the CL source members. Syntax checking CL members requires a live connection to the server. Therefore, automatic syntax checking is disabled by default, as shown in Figure 7–30.

Working with Nested Structures

CL source members can contain controlled structures, like subroutines, if statements, and loops. You can use the formatting and indenting options to help ensure that control blocks are ended correctly, but it is still sometimes difficult to match the beginning and end of control blocks.

The same editor functions that exist for ILE RPG to show block nesting and jump to a block's beginning or end are available for CL. For example, position the cursor on SUBR, right-click, and select **Source > Select Block**. The editor will select the block of code between SUBR and ENDSUBR. To jump to the beginning or end of a block, select **Source > Jump To Block End**, or use the Ctrl+Shift+M keyboard shortcut. (Even though the action is called "Jump to Block End," you can use it to jump from the end to the beginning.)

For CLLE and CLP source types, an additional action shows the block nesting by displaying arrows matching the beginning and end of control structures. To perform this action, position the cursor on the line containing the beginning or end of the control structure, then right-click in the source and select **Source > Show Block Nesting** or use the Ctrl+Shift+O keyboard shortcut. This displays an arrow connecting the beginning and end of the block. All nested controlled structures (up to five levels deep) will also contain arrows indicating their beginnings and ends, as shown in Figure 7–31.

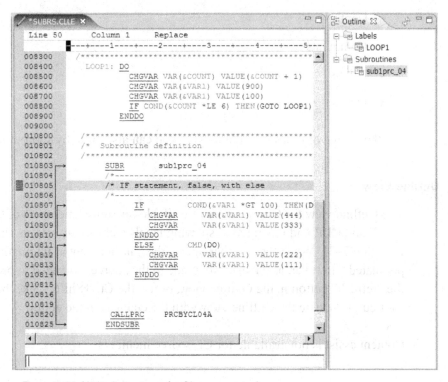

Figure 7–31: Nested structures for CL source members.

The Include Member

With the introduction of the new INCLUDE statement in CL for V6R1, you can open CL include members for editing or browsing in the same way as ILE RPG copy members and COBOL copybooks. Right-click the line with the include statement, and select **INCLUDE > Edit** or **INCLUDE > Browse** from the pop-up menu.

Filtering Source by Language Constructs

Filtering for CL works the same way as described for other source types. Right-click in the editor and select **Filter view**. The following options are available for all CL source types:

- Date

- Code

- Control

- Comments

- Labels

- Errors

For the source of types CLLE and CLP, you can also filter by subroutines.

Outline View

The Outline view for CL members is available for source members of types CLLE and CLP, and is limited to showing labels and subroutines, as shown in Figure 7–31. When the member opens, the Outline view is automatically populated. However, as changes are made to the source, you need to press the "refresh" button in the Outline view, or use the Ctrl+Shift+F5 keyboard shortcut, to update the Outline view with the changes in the editor.

Content assist is not available for CL source members.

Preferences

To see the CL editing preferences, go to the **Remote Systems > Remote Systems LPEX Editor > i5/OS Parsers > CL** preference page. Here you can configure automatic syntax checking, uppercasing, indenting, formatting options (described earlier in this chapter), and user tabs (as shown in Figure 7–30).

RPG/400

This section walks through the editor actions that are available for RPG/400 source members. The term *RPG/400* here includes source members of type RPG, RPG/36, RPG/38 and SQLRPG. Refer to the section on LPEX parsers if you use a different source member type for RPG/400 source.

As you might expect, some of the language-specific features available for
ILE RPG source members are also available for RPG/400 source members.
If the feature works the same way, we will refer back to the discussion
about the ILE RPG source member's feature, instead of repeating the same
thing here. If there are differences, we will cover them in here.

Syntax Checking

Syntax checking for RPG/400 source members works the same way
as described earlier in this chapter for general syntax checking. One
difference in syntax checking between ILE RPG and RPG/400 source
members is that for ILE RPG, you have an option to syntax check SQL
statements. For RPG/400 source members, SQL statements are ignored
and never syntax checked.

Program verification is not available for RPG/400 source members.

Working with Nested Structures

You can display an indented view of RPG/400 source members the same
way as for ILE RPG source members. To display the indented view of the
source, select **Source > Show Indentation** from the menu bar. This opens
the RPG Indentation view, with the indented source in browse mode. See
the section "Working with Nested Structures" earlier in this chapter for
additional details.

Viewing Fields from an Externally Described File

Viewing fields works the same way as it does for ILE RPG source
members. To view the fields of an externally described file, position the
cursor on the file specification, right-click, and select **Show fields** from
the pop-up menu. Refer to the section "Viewing Fields from an Externally
Described File" earlier in this chapter for details.

Opening Copy Members

Opening a copy member works the same way as for ILE RPG source
members. To open a copy member, position the cursor on the /COPY line,
right-click, and select **/COPY Member > Edit** or **/COPY Member >**

Browse. Refer to the section "Opening Copy Members" earlier in this chapter for details.

Filtering Source by Language Constructs

Filtering works the same way as described earlier in this chapter for ILE RPG source members: right-click in the editor and select **Filter view**. The following options are available for all RPG/400 source types:

- Date

- Code

- Comments

- Control

- SQL statements

- Subroutines

- Errors

Outline View

There is a limited Outline view for RPG/400 source members. Only information from the source member is used to build the contents of the Outline view. Information from external descriptions and copy members is not used.

The Outline view for RPG/400 is not created when a source member is opened; you need to press the "refresh" button in the Outline view's toolbar to create it. This displays only one high-level node, *Global Definitions*. If there are any subroutines defined in the source, an entry called *Subroutines* is created under Global Definitions, listing all the subroutines. Clicking a subroutine's name positions the editor to the definition of the subroutine in the source (the BEGSR line). Usage lines for subroutines are not shown in the Outline view as they are for ILE RPG source members.

There is no content assist for RPG/400 source members.

Preferences

To see the RPG/400 editing preferences, go to the **Remote Systems >
Remote Systems LPEX Editor > i5/OS Parsers > RPG/400** preference
page. By default, the preferences for automatic syntax checking and automatic uppercasing are enabled, and the Enter key behavior is set to repeat
the previous specification type. You can change these options, as well as
changing user tabbing, from the preference page.

LPEX Parsers

The LPEX editor is used in many different development environments, like
i5/OS, z/OS, and the Transaction Processing Facility (TPF) toolkit. The
editor is divided into two main parts:

- A base editor that provides all the non–language-specific functions
  and is used in all development environments

- Parsers, which provide the programming language-specific features

A parser determines the language syntax, the colors used to highlight the
fields, keywords and constants, content assist, Outline view, and other
language-specific actions. All of the features described in this chapter are
added to LPEX by the corresponding language parser.

All along in this chapter, we have talked about the source type and how
actions are tied to the source member type. This was to keep things
simple. In reality, the source member type does not determine the editor
features. It is actually the document parser associated with the source type
that determines the editor features. If you use the standard IBM source
member types, you shouldn't have to worry about the parsers.

Just like in PDM, type **14** next to the source member, and the source
member type determines what compile command to invoke. The RSE
associates all of the common RPG, COBOL, CL, and DDS source types
with their corresponding parsers. When you open a source member, LPEX
checks if the source type is associated with a parser.

If you are using non-standard source types, you will want to associate them
with the corresponding language parsers so you can use all of the language-

specific editing features described in this chapter. For example, if you use a source member type of SQLRPGLEM, you will want it to be treated like an SQLRPGLE source member, so that all the options, menu, and actions are available while editing. You can achieve this by associating the SQLRPGLEM source type with the ILErpgSql parser.

TIP

To determine what parser is associated with the source member you have open, type **query parser** in the editor's command line (or simply type **parser**). The parser's name will appear in the message line.

Parser Associations

To see a list of document type and document parser associations, go to the **LPEX Editor > Parsers > Parser Associations** preference page, shown in Figure 7–32. To add a new association, enter the document type, select one of the existing document parsers, and click the **Set** button. Table 7–1 shows the LPEX parsers that you can use for the i5/OS languages.

Table 7–1: LPEX Parsers for Languages	
Language	**LPEX Parsers**
ILE COBOL	ILEcobolSqlCics
OPM COBOL	cobol400SqlCics
	cobolSqlCics
ILE RPG	ILErpg
	ILErpgSql
RPG/400, RPG/36, RPG/38	rpg
DDS	dds
CL	cl

To modify the document parser for an existing document type, select the current association in the parser associations list. The current values of the entry are placed in the "Document type" and "Document parser" fields, where you can edit them. Click the **Set** button to update the association.

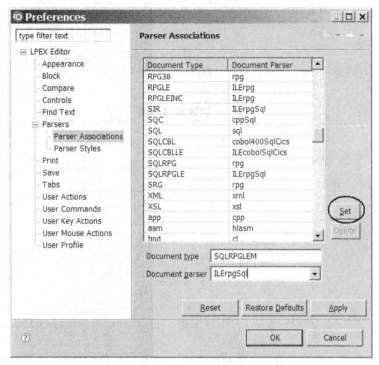

Figure 7–32: The LPEX Parser Associations table showing the new document type SQLRPGLEM being associated with the ILErpgSql parser.

TIP
....
After you change the document type or parser in the Parser Association table, it is important to click the Set button. If you do not click this button and instead click Apply or OK, the new or modified association will not be added in the table.
....

If you scroll down in this table, you will see that both lowercase and uppercase document types are associated with the same parser. This is not required for i5/OS source members and source member types, but it is required for i5/OS projects, where the file type may be uppercase or lowercase. As a general rule, it is good to associate both cases with a parser.

Each document parser has a customizable style. To configure it, go to the **LPEX Editor > Parsers > Parser Styles** preference page, shown in Figure 7–33. Choose the parser you want view or modify. In the example in Figure 7–33, the ILEcobol parser is selected. Choose a style from

Figure 7–33: LPEX parser styles

the Styles list, and use the buttons on the right to customize that style. Changes are reflected in the Preview area.

You can use the Reset button to undo the changes while you are editing the styles. The Restore Defaults button changes all the styles to the defaults shipped with the product.

Editors and File Types

This section applies only to editing IFS files, local files, and files inside of Workspace projects. It does not apply to editing i5/OS source members. In the RSE, the Remote Systems LPEX Editor and the Screen Designer are the only editors that appear in the Open With menu for source members. They always appear for source members, regardless of the source type.

File type is a workstation terminology that is similar to source type in i5/OS. On the workstation, file types are determined based on the file name's extension. For example, the file name *getitem.rpgle* has a file type of *rpgle*. As such, when we talk about the file extension for a workstation file, it has the same meaning as the source type for an i5/OS member.

Workstation and IFS files are associated with editors based on the file type. The default editor is the one that is opened when you double-click a file. The Remote Systems LPEX Editor is registered as the default editor for the common RPG, COBOL, CL, and DDS file types. If you want a different editor to be used when opening a file, associate the type of the file with the editor using the **General > Editors > File Associations** preference page, as shown in Figure 7–34.

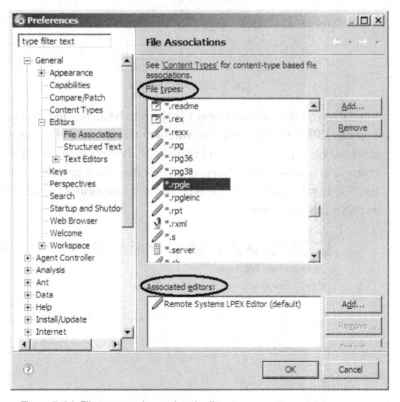

Figure 7–34: File types and associated editors.

To associate a different editor with a file type, select the file type in the "File types" list, go to the Associated Editors list, and click the **Add** button.

You can then choose from the list of internal editors (editors integrated into the Workbench) or external programs to be associated with the file type, as shown in Figure 7–35.

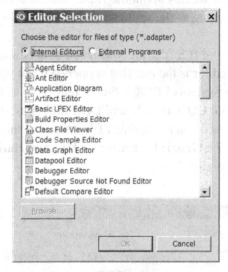

Figure 7–35: Editor selection.

Similarly, you can add additional file types to be associated with the Remote Systems LPEX Editor. Click the **Add** button next to the "File types" list, and enter the file type, as shown in Figure 7–36. For example, to add the file type myrpgle you would enter *.*myrpgle*. The extension type will be added to the list. You can then select the file type and add editors to be associated with it, as previously described.

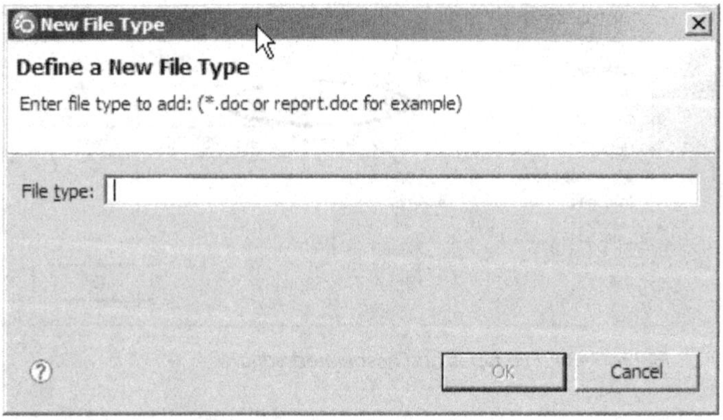

Figure 7–36: Adding a new file type.

Editing IFS Files

You can edit files from the Integrated File System (IFS) in LPEX the same way you do for the native (QSYS) file system. This ease of editing IFS files, and the ability to verify and compile them, makes the RSE more appealing than the SEU and PDM.

You can open IFS files by expanding the IFS Files subsystem and drilling down to the file you want to work on. Once you have located the file, double-clicking will open it using the default editor associated with it, as discussed in the previous section. Once the file is open in this editor, there is no difference in the way LPEX handles the IFS file versus a native source member. All the actions and features discussed in this chapter are also available when editing IFS files.

TIP
The Save preferences covered in chapter 6 do not apply to IFS files. When saving a file back to the IFS, it directly overwrites the original file.

Troubleshooting

General communications troubleshooting is covered in chapter 10. The troubleshooting tips below are related to editing.

- *My source member opens in LPEX, but I don't see any color highlighting or any of the features described in this chapter.*

  If you are using a non-standard source member type, make sure you have associated it with the appropriate LPEX parser, as described in the section "LPEX Parsers" earlier in this chapter.

- *Actions in the Source or Compile menu don't show or are disabled.*

  Ensure the editor is in focus. Actions are added and/or enabled depending on the part that is in focus.

- *When verifying a source member, the external descriptions are not found.*

a. Ensure that the library list for the connection is correct. Sometimes, the library list that appears in the Remote Systems view for the connection is the cached library list. Refresh the library list filter by right-clicking on the filter and selecting **Refresh** (or use the F5 keyboard shortcut).

b. If you added libraries to the Initial Library List page, you will need to disconnect and reconnect for these libraries to be added in the library list.

- *When verifying an ILE RPG source member, I get an RNF0401 error, "error communicating with the host."*

a. Ensure that you can still communicate with the server in the RSE by expanding (or refreshing) a filter.

b. Try clearing the cache. To see cache preferences, go to **Preferences > Remote Systems > i5/OS > cache**.

- *When verifying a source member, I get the message "The RSE communications daemon could not be started."*

a. From the Remote Systems view menu, select **Preferences > Remote Systems**, and select the **Communications** preference page shown in Figure 7–37. Ensure that the port number specified is not in use. (Port 4300 is the default.) If you are running two Workbenches at the same time, the first Workbench will be using this port. You should change the port number for the second Workbench.

b. You can start and stop the communications daemon from the Remote Systems view menu. If the daemon is already started, you will see the menu option "Stop Communications Daemon." If it has not been started, you will see the option "Start Communications Daemon."

c. By default, the RSE communications daemon starts when the Workbench starts. Uncheck the **Start RSE communications daemon on Workbench startup** preference if you want to start the daemon when needed.

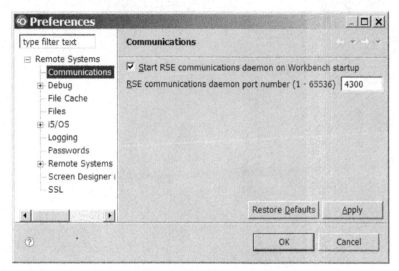

Figure 7–37 Communications daemon preferences.

CHAPTER 8

Compiling and Binding

You've run your source code through the syntax checker and program verifier, fixed all the errors they identified, and are now ready to compile. As you would expect, you can run compiles directly from the RSE. In most cases, you can also have the RSE automatically display the resulting compiler messages.

In this chapter, you will learn how to compile members using the RSE, how the results of the compile are communicated back to RSE and displayed, and how to customize the compile commands to meet your project's requirements.

Compile Actions

Compiles can be launched from either the Remote Systems view, the Object Table view, or the Remote Systems LPEX Editor. When you right-click on a source member in the Remote Systems or Object Table view, the pop-up menu contains two choices: Compile and Compile(Prompt). Each of these cascades to show a submenu with all the compile commands currently associated with that member type in the RSE.

Selecting a compile command from the Compile submenu runs the command without prompting first. This is the equivalent of entering option 14 in PDM and pressing Enter. Selecting a compile command from the Compile(Prompt) submenu first prompts the command before running it. This is equivalent to entering option 14 in PDM and then pressing F4.

Any command defaults set on i5/OS for the compile command
will also be picked up when compiling from the RSE.

When a source member is opened in the Remote Systems LPEX Editor, a
compile menu is added to the Workbench menu bar, as shown in Figure 8–1.
This menu contains the same Compile and Compile(Prompt) submenus that
appear in the pop-up menu of the Remote System and Object Table views.
These compile actions were added to the Remote Systems LPEX Editor as
a convenience, since you will probably want to compile your source after
making some changes.

Figure 8–1: Compiling from the Workbench menu.

The last-used compile command for the source type is shown in the
compile menu with a checkmark next to it. The RSE stores the last-used
compile command per source type, not per member. Figure 8–1 shows
that CRTBNDRPG was the last-used compile command for RPGLE source
members. In this case, if CRTRPGMOD were invoked, the next time you look
at this submenu, CRTRPGMOD would be checked.

In addition to the Compile menu in the Workbench menu bar, a "compile"
icon is added to the toolbar, as shown in Figure 8–2. Clicking this icon, or
using the Ctrl+Shift+C keyboard shortcut, invokes the last-used compile
command for the member type.

Figure 8–2: The toolbar icon for the Compile command.

TIP

The primary shortcoming of relying on the "last command used" is that it might not be applicable for the next compile of the same source member type. Therefore, use the toolbar icon and the keyboard shortcut with care.

Now that your compile has completed, don't go looking for that spool file just yet! The compiler messages are automatically downloaded and displayed in the Error List view. Double-clicking an error in the Error List view positions the editor to the line that caused the error and inserts the compiler message into the source member.

It's this integration and ease of jumping back and forth between the editor and compiler messages in RSE that really sets it apart from PDM. No more looking at the spool file, finding the error, going back to the source member, and manually finding the line number! Later in this chapter, you will learn more about this in the discussion of the Error List view.

When compiling from the editor, you can only submit compiles for one member at a time. From the Remote Systems or Object Table view, you can submit compiles for multiple members at a time. First, select all the members you want to compile by holding down the Ctrl key and clicking the members. Then, right-click. You should see a single Compile action in the pop-up menu, as shown in Figure 8–3. If you don't see this action, at least one of the members does not have an associated compile command. When submitting compiles for multiple members, the option to compile with prompt is not available.

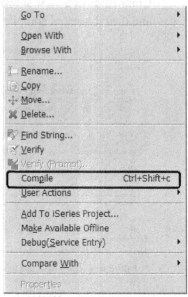

Figure 8–3: The compile option for multiple members.

Clicking the Compile option submits the last-used compile command for each member type, one at a time. The order in which the members are compiled is controlled through a preference. For example, you would probably want to compile a DDS physical file members first, then DDS logical file members, and then RPGLE source members. Preferences are discussed in detail later in this chapter.

TIP Compile menu actions behave a bit differently than other menus, in that when the Compile option is not applicable to the selected resource, it does not even appear. Other options, like Verify, are still included, but disabled (grayed out) if not applicable.

Compile Command Execution

By default, the compile commands are submitted to batch. You can switch to running compiles in the RSE server job or configure the job description and SBMJOB parameters for batch compiles through preferences, which are covered in later in this chapter.

You can check the compile command and parameters that were submitted from the RSE by looking at the Commands Log view. For batch compiles, the Commands Log view shows two entries: first, the SBMJOB command in the log, and then the actual compile command when it finishes running (Figure 8–4).

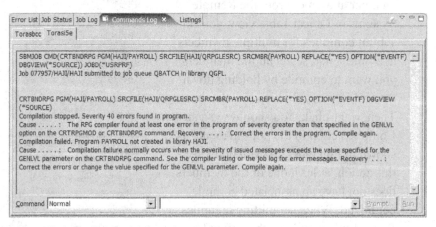

Figure 8–4: The Commands Log view.

TIP It is a good idea to look at the Commands Log view to check the status of the submitted command. It might contain useful information, especially when you do not see the compiler messages in the Error List view.

If the Commands Log view does not appear, open it by right-clicking the **Objects** subsystem and selecting **Show Log**, or by selecting **Window > Show view > Commands Log** from the Workbench menu bar.

The Library List and File Overrides

The library list used for compiles, both batch and non-batch, is the library list currently set for the RSE connection. Expand the Library List filter under your RSE connection to check the library list. If you have run commands that modified the library list, you might need to refresh the filter (by pressing F5 or right-clicking and selecting Refresh).

If you require different library lists for compiling different applications, instead of always having to change the library lists before submitting a compile, you can create multiple RSE connections to the same server with different library lists and compile from each connection. Each RSE connection you create has a separate server job associated with it, and hence, a different library list.

If your source member requires file overrides in order to compile, you will need to set up the overrides in RSE before using the program verifier or compiling. You can run the override command from the Commands Log view or Commands subsystem, just like you would run any other command. However, you must specify OVRSCOPE(*JOB).

Compiler Command Messages

When compiling DDS source members, it is good practice to delete the compiled file first, if it exists, because the corresponding compile commands do not have a REPLACE parameter. For example, consider a DDS physical file source member. If you use CHGPF and specify a file that does not exist, you will not see any results in the Error List view. It might seem that the command never completed, but if you check in the Commands Log view, you will see a return message that the object to change was not found.

If you use CRTPF, and specify a file that already exists, the Error List view will indicate that there are no messages in the events file (assuming you don't have errors in your source). You might be tempted to think that the command completed successfully, but if you check that Commands Log view, shown in Figure 8–5, you will see that the file object was not created.

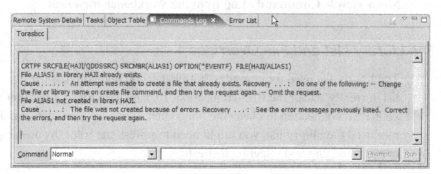

Figure 8–5: The Commands Log view with the details of CRTPF.

In PDM, in this situation, you would be prompted to replace the object. Currently, there is no mechanism in the RSE to prompt to replace.

This situation stresses the importance of checking the results in the Commands Log view if there are no messages in the Error List view, to ensure that the command did indeed run to completion. If the command results in errors, the details of the cause and recovery of the error will be logged in the Commands Log view.

The Error List View: Look Ma, No Spool File

One of the big advantages of compiling from the RSE is the ability to easily and quickly locate and fix errors in your source. Gone are the days of having to jump back and forth between spool files and SEU! The integration of live source editing and compile messages allows you to quickly fix the errors.

When compiling from the RSE, the compiles still run on i5/OS. After a compile completes, the RSE retrieves the resulting compiler messages and displays them in the Error List view. These are exactly the same as the compiler messages written to the spool file.

By default, the Error List view is located at the bottom right corner of the RSE perspective. When a compile completes, the Error List view is automatically opened. All the compiler messages (informational, warnings, and errors) are automatically displayed in this view. We refer to all these messages as errors, even though some might only be informational (severity 0).

The program verifier uses the same Error List view to display errors from a program verification. So, details about the Error List view apply to both errors resulting from a compile and program verification.

The Error List view displays errors in a table format. For each error, the view displays the following:

- An icon that identifies the severity of the error, as shown in Figure 8–6
- The message identifier (ID) of the error
- The text of the error message
- The numerical severity of the error
- The line number in the source that caused the error
- The fully qualified name of the source where the error occurred (which could be a copy member or an include)
- The corresponding RSE connection name

To jump to the location of an error in the source member, double-click the error. This opens the source member in the Remote Systems LPEX Editor, positions it to the corresponding line, and highlights the text that caused the error. The error message is also inserted into the source member below the line that caused the error, as shown in Figure 8–7. Another advantage of the Error List view is that, if the error occurs in a copy member, the copy member is opened, and the error will be inserted into the copy member!

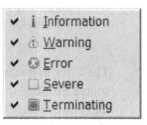

Figure 8–6: Icons identifying the severity of the error.

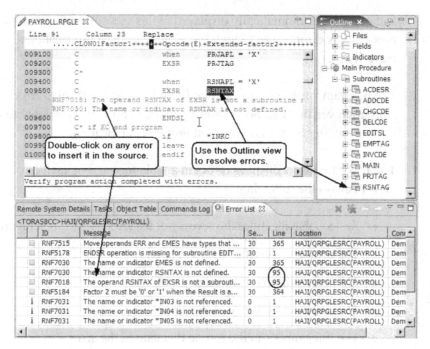

Figure 8–7: Errors inserted in the source from the Error List view.

TIP   After double-clicking an error in the Error List view and jumping to the editor, you might be able to use the Outline view or content assist to correct the problem. For example, if the error is a misspelled opcode, built-in function, or field name, then Outline view and content assist might show close matches.

The Error List view can be used as a to-do list. As you fix errors in the source member, the Error List view is updated to indicate the status of the error messages. If you change the line where the error is reported, a checkmark appears next to the error in the Error List view. If you delete the line on which an error is reported, an *X* appears next to the error. A blank indicates that the error has not been fixed yet, as shown in Figure 8–8. The Error List view can't guarantee you've *fixed* an error; the icons just indicate that it was addressed.

TIP   After the Error List view is updated with a checkmark or a cross, performing an undo in the source member does not update the Error List view to remove the corresponding mark.

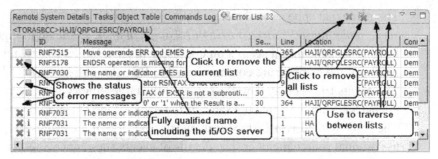

Figure 8–8: Manipulating the Error List view.

The results of compiles and verifies are added as additional pages to the Error List view. Each results page has a qualified name, including the RSE connection name where the source resides. To move between different pages in the Error List view, use the Back and Forward buttons located in the view's toolbar, near the top right corner of the view. If you launch multiple compiles at the same time, the results for each compile are also shown as separate pages.

Each page remains in the Error List view as long as the Workbench is running. You can remove pages that you do not need, or remove all of them at once, as shown in Figure 8–8.

The name that appears in the error list after a program verification is of the form *<servername>sourcelibrary/sourcephycicalfile(sourcemember)*, as shown in Figure 8–9 . This is straightforward; it shows the location of the source member.

	ID	Message	Se...	Line	Location	Con
	RNF7515	Move operands ERR and EMES have types that ...	30	365	HAJI/QRPGLESRC(PAYROLL)	Dem
	RNF5178	ENDSR operation is missing for subroutine EDIT...	30	1	HAJI/QRPGLESRC(PAYROLL)	Dem
	RNF7030	The name or indicator EMES is not defined.	30	365	HAJI/QRPGLESRC(PAYROLL)	Dem
	RNF7030	The name or indicator RSNTAX is not defined.	30	95	HAJI/QRPGLESRC(PAYROLL)	Dem
	RNF7018	The operand RSNTAX of EXSR is not a subrouti...	30	95	HAJI/QRPGLESRC(PAYROLL)	Dem
	RNF5184	Factor 2 must be '0' or '1' when the Result is a...	30	364	HAJI/QRPGLESRC(PAYROLL)	Dem
i	RNF7031	The name or indicator *IN03 is not referenced.	0	1	HAJI/QRPGLESRC(PAYROLL)	Dem
i	RNF7031	The name or indicator *IN04 is not referenced.	0	1	HAJI/QRPGLESRC(PAYROLL)	Dem
i	RNF7031	The name or indicator *IN05 is not referenced.	0	1	HAJI/QRPGLESRC(PAYROLL)	Dem

Remote System Details | Tasks | Object Table | Commands Log | Error List

<TORASBCC>HAJI/QRPGLESRC(PAYROLL) — Name after program verification

Figure 8–9: A name in the error list after program verification.

The name that appears in the error list after a compile is of the form *servername:targetlibrary/EVFEEVENT(objectname)*, as shown in Figure 8–10. The name might seem a bit confusing at first, but let us explain. The results of the compile are communicated to RSE through an events file. The events file is created on the server in the target library in a file called EVFEVENT, with the name the same as the name of the object to be created. The name in the Error List view shows the location of the events file, not the original source member. The details of events files are covered in the next section.

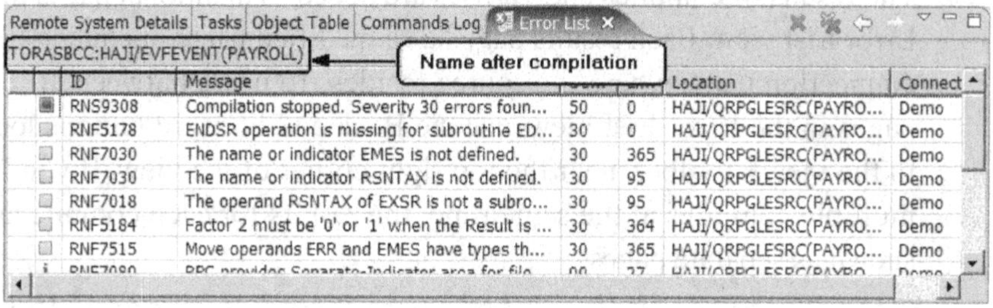

Figure 8–10: A name in the error list after compilation.

Entries in the Error List view can be sorted by clicking the column headings. For example, if you want the messages to be sorted by ID, click the ID heading. This sorts the list in ascending order. Clicking again on the ID heading sorts in descending order.

Right-clicking an error message in the Error List view gives you the following options:

- *Open*: Open the Remote Systems LPEX Editor and position it to the error. This is the same as double-clicking the error.

- *Copy*: Allow copying the message ID and the message text to the clipboard.

- *Show Help*: Display the second-level help for the message, as shown in Figure 8–11.

- *Remove*: Delete the message from the Error List view.

Selecting multiple messages and right-clicking them gives options to copy or remove the selected messages.

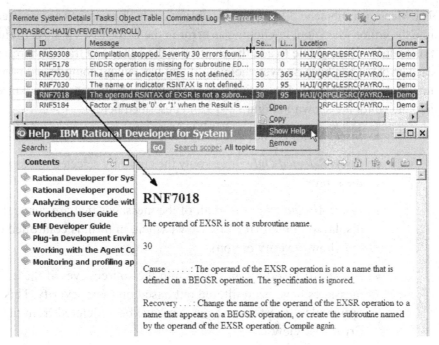

Figure 8–11: Obtaining message help from the Error List view.

One of the menus that is often overlooked is the view menu, accessed through the upside-down triangle shown in Figure 8–12. If you click this menu, you will see four submenus: Show Severity, Messages, Automatically Remove, and Automatically Insert.

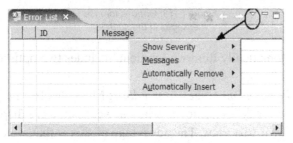

Figure 8–12: The Error List view menu.

The Show Severity submenu allows you to customize what types of errors you want to see in the Error List view. The different types of errors, as you saw in Figure 8–6, are Information, Warning, Error, Severe, and Terminating. Each type has a checkmark next to it, indicating that these types of errors will be shown in the Error List view. Clicking an error type removes the checkmark, causing the Error List view to filter out this type of errors.

The Messages submenu allows you to configure which messages are inserted into the editor when double-clicking an error in the Error List view. As useful as this feature is (being able to add the errors into the editor and traverse through each error), it can become overwhelming if you have many compile errors or informational messages. The options for controlling which messages are inserted into the editor are shown in Figure 8–13 and described here:

- *Insert None*: Do not insert any of the messages in the source.

- *Insert Selected Only*: Insert only the currently selected message into the source.

- *Insert All Showing*: Insert all of the messages that are currently displayed in the Error List view (which, in turn, is controlled by the Show Severity option).

- *Insert All*: Insert all messages into the source, even if the messages have been filtered out based on their severity. This option also inserts messages that have been deleted from the Error List view.

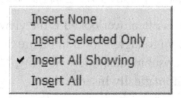

Figure 8–13: Options for inserting
messages in the source.

The Automatically Remove submenu includes two options:

- *Previous messages from editor*: Messages from a previous compile or verify are removed when newer results are displayed in the Error List view. The advantage of this is that, when the source is verified or compiled again, the previous errors (which ideally are already fixed) do not linger in the editor. This option is selected by default.

- *Addressed messages*: Messages are removed from the editor when the corresponding line is modified. One word of caution here: you might not have necessarily fixed the problem! The fact that you modified the line with the error is taken as an indication that the error is handled. In addition to removing the error from the Remote Systems LPEX Editor, the error is also filtered out of the Error List view, so it will no longer appear in the view. This option is not selected by default.

These two options are not mutually exclusive. You can have one, both, or neither selected.

The Automatically Insert submenu allows errors from the Error List view to be automatically inserted into the corresponding source members, without having to first double-click an error in the view. Options from the Automatically Insert submenu are only applicable (and therefore only enabled) when either the Insert All or Insert All Showing option is selected from the Messages submenu. There are two options for automatically inserting messages:

- *Into open members and files*: Automatically insert messages into any applicable source members that are currently open in the Remote Systems LPEX Editor. For example, suppose you verify an ILE RPG source member that contains a copy member, and there is an error in the copy member. If this option is selected, and the copy member is open in the editor, then the errors will be inserted in the copy member. If the copy member was not already open, then this option will *not* open the member.

- *Into members and files*: Automatically open any members that contain errors and insert the errors into the members.

Automatically opening the member is the only difference between the two options. Therefore, you can only have only one, or none, of the options selected. Neither option is selected by default; which means to insert the errors in the source, you need to double-click an error in the Error List view.

Once errors have been inserted in the source, you can easily navigate among them using the icons in the toolbar, as shown in Figure 8–14.

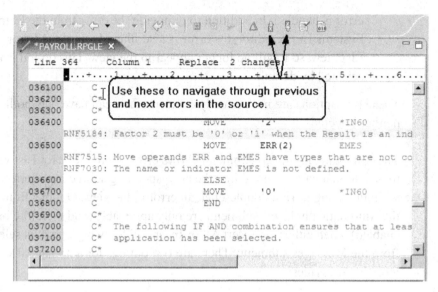

Figure 8–14: Navigating through errors in the source.

The Events File

What are events files, and why are they required? Events files are temporary files created by the compilers and program verifiers. An events file contains results from these operations, in particular, the compile errors and their locations in the source code. This allows the editor to locate an error in the source member and identify the line, or part of a line, that caused the error.

The events files are not meant to be read by mere mortals (i.e., humans). Events files have a common format, which allows tools such as the RSE to process them and present the information in an easily readable layout. The events file's format is documented in the product help.

The program verifiers create events files locally in the Workspace, in the RemoteSystemsTempFiles project with the same name as the source member, and with the extension *.sourcetype*.EVT.

Removing the results of a program verify from the Error List view, as shown in Figure 8–8, will delete the temporary events file from the Workspace. All events files created by the program verifiers are deleted when the Workbench is closed.

When a source member is compiled, the events file is created on the server (where the compile command runs) as a member in the EVFEVENT file, in the library where the created module or program object is to be stored. If the physical data file EVFEVENT does not exist, it is created in the target library. The events file member name is the same as the name of the object being created with the source type of *mbr*. For example, if the source member DEVLIB/QRPGLESRC(PAYROLL) is compiled to generate an object PAYDAY in library EMPLOYEE, the events file EMPLOYEE/EVFEVENT(PAYDAY) is created to hold the compile results.

When a compile or verify completes, the events file is automatically downloaded (for compiles), and the results are loaded into the Error List view. A message is displayed in the Workbench status bar (at the bottom of the Workbench window) indicating that the events file is being retrieved after a compile completes, as shown in Figure 8–15.

Figure 8–15: Retrieving the events file after compilation.

TIP The members in EVFEVENT physical file created by the compilers are not deleted by the RSE. Over time, this file might grow to the point where you want to delete it. Right-click a member in the EVFEVENT file, and you will see the action Show in Error List view. This action will download and display the events file in the Error List view.

Most of the compile commands supplied by IBM for the ILE languages have an option to generate an events file. This option is used by the RSE to download and display the results of the compile. When you look at the compile commands used by the RSE, you will see an OPTION(*EVENTF) parameter. The following is the default RSE command for compiling ILE COBOL members (with the parameter bolded):

```
CRTBNDCBL PGM(&O/&N) SRCFILE(&L/&F) SRCMBR(&N) OPTION(*EVENTF)
DBGVIEW(*SOURCE) REPLACE(*YES).
```

Compile commands for the OPM languages do not have this OPTION(*EVENTF) parameter, but can still generate events files. Instead of OPTION(*EVENTF), they use OPTION(*SRCDBG) or OPTION(*LSTDBG) to instruct the compiler to generate an events file.

The following is the default RSE command for compiling OPM COBOL members:

```
CRTCB1PGM PGM(&O/&N) SRCFILE(&L/&F) SRCMBR(&N) OPTION(*SRCDBG)
REPLACE(*YES).
```

OPM SQL source members use the OPTION(*LSTDBG) parameter instead of OPTION(*SRCDBG).

It is great to have the RSE use the events file to populate the errors from the compile command. This only works, however, if the compile command runs successfully! There are various reasons why the compile command might not run, or might not complete successfully. Refer to the troubleshooting section at the end of this chapter to see examples of these situations. Don't forget to check the Commands Log view to see the details of the command and the causes for failure.

One twist to compiling in batch from the RSE is that you need write access to your IFS home directory, as specified in your i5/OS user profile (which defaults to */home/userprofile*). What does the IFS have anything to do with compiling? Let us explain. When you submit a compile command in batch, the RSE actually submits a call to the program QDEVTOOLS/QRSEEXEC to batch. This program, in turn, runs the compile and processes the resulting events file. The RSE needs to retrieve the return messages from running the compile command, as well as the events file. This is done using the IFS directory. Information such as the command that gets run and the results of the command are logged in *%homedir%/.eclipse/RSE/SBM0000x.log*, where *x* is a number that guarantees uniqueness when multiple compiles are run simultaneously. When the batch compile completes, the information from this log file is read by the RSE and logged in the Commands Log view. If the compile command did produce the events file, the compiler errors will also be displayed in the Error List view.

Customizing the Compile Commands

Many aspects of the RSE can be customized. Compile commands are no different! You can add your own compile commands to the Compile menu

or modify the ones predefined by the RSE. This is done from the Work
With Compile Commands dialog, shown in Figure 8–16.

To invoke this dialog, right-click the **Objects** subsystem and select
Work With > Compile Commands, or select the **Work With Compile
Commands** action in the Compile menu, as shown in Figure 8–1.

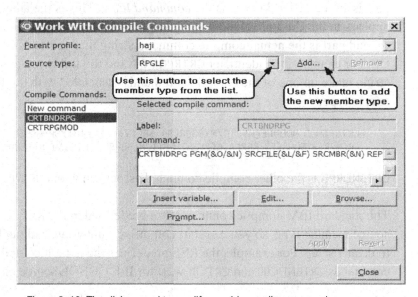

Figure 8–16: The dialog used to modify or add compile commands.

Each RSE profile can contain unique compile commands. The Compile
menu shown in the RSE includes all applicable commands from all active
RSE profiles. The top of the Work With Compile Commands dialog lets
you select which RSE profile you want to customize compile commands
for. The predefined compile commands are only supplied for your private
profile; use this one unless you are planning to share your customizations
with other team members.

 You can create customized compile commands in the Team
profile to share them with other developers on your team.

In the RSE, compile commands are grouped by source member type.
So, when you right-click a source member, only the compile commands
applicable to the selected source member's type are shown in the Compile

menu. At the top of the Work With Compile Commands dialog, you can select the source type you want to customize compile commands for. Additional source member types can be added if you use a non-standard source type that is not in the drop-down list.

Compile commands are defined in the RSE with two parts. The first part is an identifier, known as the *command label*. This is the label that appears in the Compile menu when you right-click a source member. The second part is the actual compile command string that gets runs on i5/OS. For example, the identifier CRTRPGMOD and the following command string make up one of the compile commands associated with the RPGLE source type:

```
CRTRPGMOD MODULE(MYLIB/MYSOURCE) SRCFILE(MYLIBI/QRPGLESRC)
SRCMBR(MYSOURCE) REPLACE(*YES) OPTION(*EVENTF) DBGVIEW(*SOURCE)
```

CRTBNDRPG is the other compile command associated with this type.

The standard IBM compile commands are predefined in the RSE for each source member type, so you can start compiling right away, without having to do any setup. For example, the RSE predefines the default compile commands CRTBNDCBL and CRTCBLMOD for ILE COBOL source member types.

The list on the left of the dialog in Figure 8–16 shows the existing compile commands for the selected source type, and an option to create a new command. Selecting one of the existing commands on the left shows the corresponding command string on the right.

Changing the Predefined Compile Commands

The compile commands that are predefined by the RSE are treated a bit differently than user-defined compile commands. Predefined RSE compile commands have these restrictions:

- They cannot be deleted.

- They cannot have their label changed.

- If the actual command is the same, and you are just changing the parameters, you will not be able to remove the SRCMBR(&N) or

OPTION(*EVENTF). If you try to remove these parameters, they will be reinserted when you save the command.

- To restore the compile command string to its original predefined value, right-click the command in the left pane and select **Restore defaults** from the pop-up menu shown in Figure 8–17. This action is only enabled if the command has been changed.

After reading these restrictions, you are probably wondering if you can change anything for the predefined RSE compile commands! Of course you can. You can change the parameters for the compile command, or you can even change the command itself. To edit an existing compile command, select the command in the list, update the information in the edit pane on the right, and click the **Apply** button.

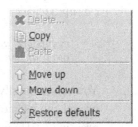

Figure 8–17: The pop-up menu for the compile commands.

Creating Your Own Compile Commands

You can add your own compile commands using the Work With Compile Commands dialog, shown in Figure 8–16. First, select the profile and the source member type for which the compile command is to be created. Then, click the **New command** link on the left side of the dialog.

On the right side of the dialog, enter the label that you want to appear in the Compile menu. Enter the compile command in the Command area. The Browse and Prompt buttons provide help in selecting and entering the command. The Edit button opens up a separate dialog that can be used for entering the command (which is not really that useful).

Compile command strings are defined using the substitution variables that are given values at compile time based on the selected member (or the current editor, in the case of compiling from the Remote Systems LPEX Editor). The valid substitution variables are as follows:

- *&F*: The name of the file containing the selected member.

- *&L*: The object or member library name.

- *&N*: The name of the selected resource.

- *&O*: The object library. This defaults to the source library, but it can be set globally in the preferences and overridden for each RSE connection.

- *&R*: The replace object when compiling. This can also be set in the preferences and overridden for each RSE connection.

For example, here is the compile command string for the predefined CRTRPGMOD:

```
CRTRPGMOD MODULE(&O/&N) SRCFILE(&L/&F) SRCMBR(&N) REPLACE(&R)
OPTION(*EVENTF) DBGVIEW(*SOURCE)
```

You can manually enter the substitution variables (if you remember them), or you can use content assist by selecting the Insert Variable button or pressing Ctrl+Space. This pops up a list of the substitution variables for you to choose from, as shown in Figure 8–18.

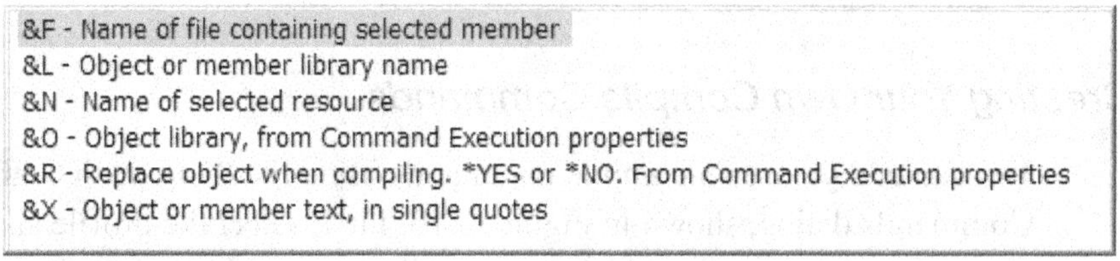

&F - Name of file containing selected member
&L - Object or member library name
&N - Name of selected resource
&O - Object library, from Command Execution properties
&R - Replace object when compiling. *YES or *NO. From Command Execution properties
&X - Object or member text, in single quotes

Figure 8–18: Substitution parameters for the compile commands.

TIP

When entering your compile command string, you can use the standard copy (Ctrl+C), paste (Ctrl+V) and undo (Ctrl+Z) actions. This includes copying a compile command from some other application (say, an email) and pasting it into the text area. Don't forget, this is a full workstation application, not a 5250 emulator!

The command label that you entered will appear in the Compile menu for the source member type. Suppose you entered *MyCompile* as the label for your compile command for ILE RPG source members (source type RPGLE). The Compile and Compile (Prompt) menus for ILE RPG source members will now contain a MyCompile action that runs your compile command. After you run the compile, there will be a checkmark next to it as shown in Figure 8–19, indicating that it is the last used compile command. A mnemonic is also added for the command.

There are a few things to consider
when adding your own compile
commands. Your custom compile
commands can have compile errors
automatically downloaded and
displayed in the Error List view, but
two things have to occur for this to happen:

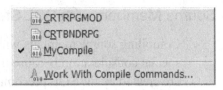

Figure 8–19: A new compile command.

- The compiler has to generate an events file. This is done by passing
  OPTION(*EVENTF) to the ILE compilers, or OPTION(*SRCDBG) or
  OPTION(*LSTDBG) for the OPM compilers. This could be directly
  from the RSE or via your own command that runs first, and in turn
  calls the compilers.

- The RSE has to know that the compiler is going to generate an
  events file, and where to find it. The RSE does this be scanning
  the compile command string for the keywords *EVENTF and
  SRCMBR(*member_name*). If you are calling your own command
  (which in turn calls the IBM compiler commands), then you need
  to pass these keywords as parameters to your command. If your
  command doesn't take these parameters, you can specify them as
  comments to your command string, for example:

```
MYCOMPCMD MODULE(&O/&N) SRCFILE(&L/&F) /* *EVENTF
SRCMBR(&N) */
```

If your command does not issue an IBM compile command explicitly, but
instead uses QCMDEXC to execute an IBM compile command, there is an
extra set of steps to go through, in addition to the two requirements just
mentioned. The RSE needs to know the location of the events file in order
to retrieve it. Therefore, you will need to write the location of the events
file in the local data area, *LDA, the library name in the first 10 bytes,
and the member name in the next 10 bytes. Both names should be padded
with blanks if they are less than 10 bytes. The library is the target library
where the compiled object will be created. The member is the name of the
member being compiled.

Modifications and additions to compile commands affect all
i5/OS RSE connections

Source Members with SQL Statements

Compiling source members with embedded SQL statements requires special consideration because of the intermediate source members that are created by the SQL precompiler. There are different scenarios where limitations are encountered. We will go through these scenarios and explain how RSE handles them.

When invoking any of the SQL compile commands, like CRTSQLRPGI and CRTSQLCBL, the SQL precompiler gets control first. If there any SQL errors, the SQL precompiler fails, and no further compilation happens. In certain situations, errors reported in the RSE might not be pointing to the correct line numbers.

Figure 8–20 shows an RPG source member with SQL statements. The expansion of the copy member by the SQL precompiler causes the line numbers in the events file to not match the line numbers in the original source member. When you try to insert the errors in the source by double-clicking in the Error List view, an error message comes up, since the line number does not exist in the source. In this scenario, the errors will be inserted after the last line.

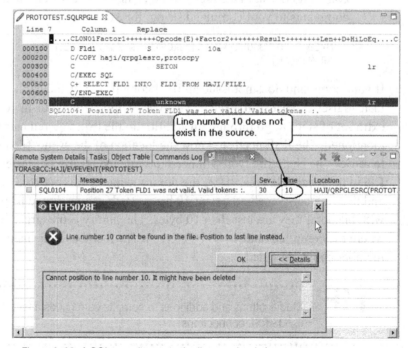

Figure 8–20: A SQL error because the line number is incorrect.

Continuing this scenario, you fix the error in the SQL statement and compile again. Now, the SQL precompiler completes successfully and creates a temporary member in QTEMP/QSQLTEMP1 with the SQL statements resolved to database calls. This temporary source member is then read by the RPG or COBOL compiler. Because of the SQL expansion, the line numbers in the temporary member are different from the original source member. This results in the same limitation described above.

Double-clicking an error in the Error List view surfaces two limitations that currently exists in RSE:

- The errors in the Error List view reference the temporary member created by the SQL precompiler, not the original source member. This defaults to a source file in QTEMP, as shown in Figure 8–21.

- Members from QTEMP cannot be edited with the RSE.

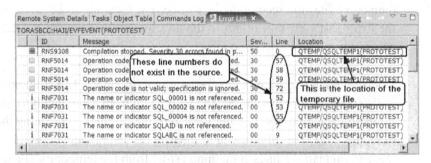

Figure 8–21: A temporary file in QTEMP.

Since the location of the errors points to the temporary file in QTEMP, you will see the error message shown in Figure 8–22.

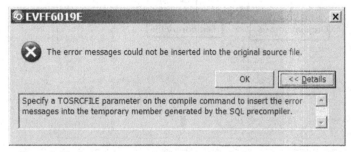

Figure 8–22: An error because editing members in QTEMP is not allowed.

To avoid this error, you can override the TOSRCFILE parameter for the SQL precompiler compile command (CRTSQLRPGI, in this example) to create the temporary file in a library other than QTEMP. This allows the intermediate file to be downloaded and opened with the errors embedded into the source. The TOSRCFILE parameter can be specified in a few ways:

- Prompt the command every time in RSE, and change the TOSRCFILE parameter.

- Change the IBM-supplied command to override the TOSRCFILE parameter. This will allow you to issue the command without prompting.

- Create your own compile command, specifying the TOSRCFILE parameter.

Continuing this scenario further, you now specify the location of the temporary file, and recompile the source. The location of the errors in the Error List view now points to the location specified in the TOSRCFILE parameter. All looks good, so far!

Double-clicking an error opens the temporary member. The temporary file is also opened in browse mode, to prevent you from accidentally fixing the errors in the temporary member instead of the original member, as shown in Figure 8–23. This allows you to identify the errors, but you will need to manually remap the lines containing errors from the temporary file to the original file (perhaps using side–by-side editing).

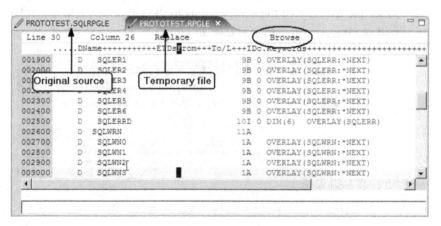

Figure 8–23: A temporary file opened in browse mode.

Binding Programs and Service Programs

The RSE provides actions for binding modules into new programs and service programs, as well as updating existing programs and service programs. To bind one ore more modules into a new program or service program, right-click one of the modules, and select **Create > Program** or **Create > Service Program** from the pop-up menu. This prompts the corresponding CRTPGM or CRTSRVPGM command, where you can enter the required parameters.

Unfortunately, you can't multi-select all the modules first, and then select Create or Update commands. If you do this, the RSE runs the corresponding command on each module individually.

To update an existing program or service program, right-click it and select **Update** from the pop-up menu.

The i5/OS binders (CRTPGM, CRTSRVPGM, UPDPGM, and UPDSRVPGM) do not generate events files. Instead, you will have to look at the Commands Log view to see any errors returned from the binders, as shown in Figure 8–24. This didn't work in prior versions of the RSE because the Commands Log only showed the messages from the command completion. Starting in WDSC 6.0.1, the RSE was updated to download and display all messages that resulted during the execution of the command, so binding errors could be displayed.

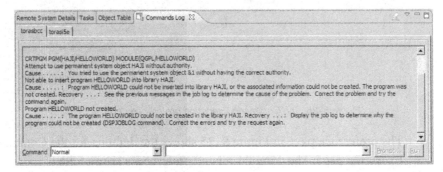

Figure 8–24: The Commands Log view, with details of the command run.

Compile Preferences

The Remote Systems > i5/OS > Command Execution preference page contains preferences that affect compiles. Settings made on this page are global and apply to all RSE connections. This preference page can also be accessed through the Remote Systems view menu by clicking the view menu (the upside-down triangle) and selecting Preferences > i5/OS to open the preferences dialog, then selecting i5/OS > Command Execution, as shown in Figure 8–25. This preference page is used for compile commands and other commands, too.

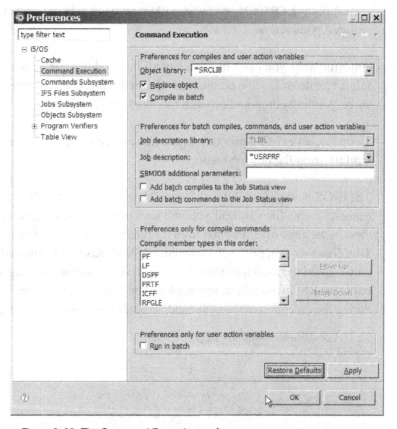

Figure 8–25: The Command Execution preference page.

The preference page in Figure 8–25 shows the defaults for the Command Execution page. The compile-related preferences are as follows:

- *Object library*: Specify a value for the object library substitution variable (&O). The default is to use the source library.

- *Replace Object*: Indicate whether or not to replace existing compiled objects (the value for the &R substitution variable).

- *Compile in batch*: Indicate whether compiles should be submitted to a batch job or run in the RSE server job. The RSE server job is a batch-immediate job type. (No interactive cycles are required.) While the compile is running in the RSE server job, no other communication requests can be processed by the RSE.

- *Job description*: This is the job description used for batch compiles, commands, and user actions.

- *SBMJOB additional parameters*: Specify additional parameters added to the SBMJOB command when submitting batch compiles, commands, or user actions. For example, you can pass additional parameters to the SBMJOB command, like INLLIBL(*JOBD).

- *Add batch compiles to the Job Status view*: Adding batch compile jobs to the Job Status view allows you to monitor the status of the job. If you have this checked, the Job Status view will be opened with the job details when a batch compile is submitted.

- *Compile member types in this order*: Control the order that member types should be compiled when multiple members are selected for compile.

The Job Status view allows you to monitor the ongoing status of any i5/OS job, as shown in Figure 8–26. Batch compile jobs can be added to this view automatically using the preference described above. To add other jobs manually to the view, right-click a job in the RSE, and select the **Add to Job Status View** action.

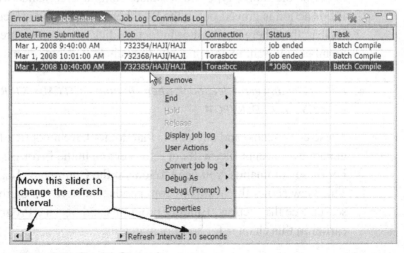

Figure 8–26: The Job Status view.

You can work with jobs in the Job Status view by right-clicking the job and selecting an action from the pop-up menu. (This is the same menu shown for jobs in the Remote Systems view.) Additional details on the Job Status view are provided in chapter 11.

Most of these global compile preferences can be set for each RSE connection. To set the value for an RSE connection, right-click the **Objects** subsystem and select **Properties**. Select the **Commands Execution** page in the dialog, and you will see preferences similar to those shown in Figure 8–25.

The global preferences apply to all connections. Properties set at the RSE connection level take precedence over global preferences. For example, if the global preference specifies to use *SRCLIB for the object library, but an RSE connection property specifies ORDENTR as the object library, then compiles submitted from that RSE connection will use ORDENTR as the object library.

Troubleshooting

- *I don't see any predefined compile commands under the Compile menu.*

  If the source member type does not have any predefined RSE compile commands associated with it, you will only see the Work With Compile Commands action. One reason for this is that you are using a nonstandard member source type, in which case you will need to define the source type and associate compile commands with it. If this action is grayed-out in the Workbench menu or disabled in the toolbar, then there is no editor in focus. Click in the editor area for the member you want to compile, and then click the Compile menu.

- *I don't see any error feedback when running CRTPGM, CRTSRVPGM, UPDPGM, or UPDSRVPGM.*

  These commands, and any others that do not have an option to generate an events file, will not return errors in the Error List view. For these commands, you need to look at the Commands Log view. This view shows the details of commands that were run on the server. See the section "Binding Programs and Service Programs" earlier in this chapter for additional details.

- *I am trying to compile a few members at the same time by selecting the members and right-clicking, but I don't see the Compile action.*

  When you select multiple members, the actions available by right-clicking are those applicable to all the members selected. Mathematically speaking, it is the lowest common denominator of actions! In this case, you might have selected a member for which compiling is not applicable action. (See the first problem in this section, about compile commands not being associated with a source member type.)

- *In the Error List view menu, I have selected the option to remove addressed messages, which removes messages from the source and the Error List view as I handle them. However, I want to see error messages again, without having to recompile to reverify the source. Is there a way to do this?*

  The automatically removed messages are not deleted from the generated events file. The messages are only filtered out from the source and the Error List view. Reload the events file by right-clicking it and selecting **Show in Error List**. The section earlier in this chapter on the events file provides details on where to find this file.

- *I don't get any error list back. In fact, I see no response.*

  a. If you compiled interactively, check that you have write access to the target library. Even if the compiled object (*MODULE or *PGM) is not created because the source member contained errors, the target library is where the events file is also created. If your i5/OS user profile does not have authority to create or change the events file, the command will fail. The Error List view will not contain anything, since there is no events file. However, the Commands Log view will contain some information on why the command failed.

  b. If you compiled in batch, you might want to check the status of your batch queue, to make sure the job isn't being held. If the job has completed, and you did not receive any feedback, check if there is anything in the log file in the IFS directory. (See section earlier in this chapter on the events file for more information.)

- *I changed the library list, but when I submit a compile, it ignores my library list, and my compile fails.*

  a. Refresh the library list for the RSE connection to ensure that the library list is correct. To do this, right-click the Library List filter under the Objects subsystem, and select **Refresh**.

  b. If you added the libraries through the preference page, these libraries are only added after you disconnect and reconnect to the server. Disconnect and reconnect, and ensure the libraries do appear in the library list.

  c. If you are compiling in batch, check whether you changed the library list to be used, by overriding the INLLIBL parameter for the SBMJOB command.

- *The Error List view is empty.*

  First, check the Commands Log to ensure that the command completed successfully. Then, check whether you have filtered out the messages to be displayed in the view.

- *When I try to compile, I get the message "Host PTF is missing. The requested function is not available."*

  Ensure that all the required PTFs are available on the server. To do this, right-click the **Objects** subsystem and select **Verify Connection**.

- *I have associated the source member type SQLRPGLEM with the ILErpgSql LPEX parser, as explained in chapter 7. However, I do not get any compile options, even though I get the program verification and syntax checking actions.*

  The compile actions do not use the LPEX parser associations to determine the compile commands. The compile commands are determined using the source member type. This is similar in behavior to what you see in SEU/PDM. If you typed PDM option 14 on the source member of type SQLRPGLEM, you would get a message indicating that the compile command was not allowed. However, you can define the compile command for the new source member type, as explained in the section "Customizing the Compile Commands" earlier in this chapter. These compile commands can be the same as the predefined RSE ones.

CHAPTER

9

Running and Debugging Programs

A good debugger is, without a doubt, one of the must-have tools in any developer's toolbox. Luckily, the Integrated i5/OS Debugger is one of the best features of WDSC and Rational Developer for System i. It makes debugging i5/OS applications a snap.

There are at least four i5/OS debuggers that we are aware of. Here is a list of them, and a brief summary of each:

- *Integrated i5/OS Debugger*: This is the debugger that is integrated into WDSC and Rational Developer for System i.

- *System debugger*: This is the traditional, 5250 debugger (STRDBG).

- *Distributed debugger*: This is the old debugger shipped with the CODE workstation tools. The Integrated i5/OS Debugger is the replacement for the distributed debugger.

- *Toolbox debugger*: The IBM Toolbox for Java includes a standalone graphical user interface to the system debugger.

This chapter covers the integrated debugger. When describing the debugging capabilities of the integrated debugger, we often say that it's the same debugger, regardless of whether you're debugging RPG, COBOL, Java, JavaServer Pages, or eXtensible Stylesheet Language (XSL) Transformations. Technically, this is not correct; it is the same debugging user interface, which is provided by Eclipse, but separate teams add their own debugging engines under the covers, to provide debugging support for specific languages. Actually, then, it's the same debugger controls and look-and-feel, regardless of what you are debugging.

So what can the Integrated i5/OS Debugger debug? The short answer is pretty much anything that runs on i5/OS. The long answer is the following list:

- RPG, COBOL, C, C++, and CL
- Both Original Program Model (OPM) and Integrated Language Environment (ILE) versions of the above languages
- Batch applications
- Interactive applications
- Stored procedures (invoked either locally or from Java via JDBC or .NET via ODBC)
- WebFacing and HATS applications
- CGI Web applications
- Web services
- Java

Given all the ways the debugger can be used, we find it makes the most sense to break down discussions about the debugger into two main topics: how to start the debugger and how to use the debugger. The debugger can be started differently depending on whether the program being debugged is batch, interactive, a stored procedure, or invoked via the Web. However, using the debugger is the same, once it is started and attached to the i5/OS job.

Starting the Debug Server

The Integrated i5/OS Debugger communicates with the debug server running on i5/OS. There is one debug server that handles requests from all workstations. Normally, the debug server is already running, but if you happen to be the first person to debug after a re-IPL, you might need to start the debug server (or have someone else start it, if you are not authorized to do so).

The debug server can be started with the Start Debug Server (STRDBGSVR) command and ended with the End Debug Server (ENDDBGSVR) command. The RSE also provides actions to start and stop the debug server from the pop-up menu for the Objects subsystem, shown in Figure 9–1. You need to be connected to the remote system for the actions to be enabled. You can tell whether the debug server is started or stopped based on which action is enabled.

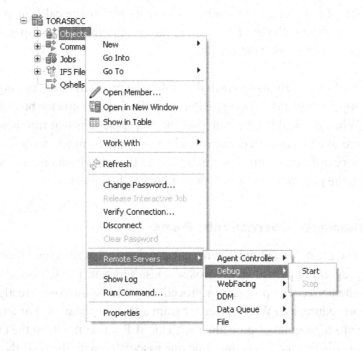

Figure 9–1: Starting the debug server.

Launching the Debugger

The integrated nature of WDSC and Rational Developer for System i allow the debugger to be launched from within the RSE perspective, even though the debugging is done from a different perspective. There are four main ways to launch the debugger:

- Service entry points

- "Single-click" actions

- Launch configurations

- Attaching to an existing job

Service Entry Points

The ability to start the debugger using service entry points (SEPs) was added to WDSC in version 6.0. This is by far the easiest way to start the debugger. Think of an SEP as a breakpoint that is set on a program or procedure, but which is not specific to an i5/OS job. Instead, the breakpoint is set system-wide for any job running under the user profile specified on the SEP. When a job running under that user profile calls the program or procedure with the SEP set on it, the job automatically suspends, and the debugger connects to the job.

SEPs were originally created to solve the problem of debugging Web applications that leverage RPG or COBOL programs for business logic. When invoked from a Web user interface, the jobs that run these programs are often created dynamically. The programs complete so quickly that it is very difficult to attach the debugger to the job without adding special code to the programs that cause them to wait when invoked.

The Advantages of Service Entry Points

The great thing about service entry points is that the type of job or how the program or procedure is invoked doesn't matter. The job could be batch or interactive. The program or procedure could be invoked directly, as a stored procedure, as a Web service, or from a Web application. For any job that calls a program or procedure with an SEP set on it, where the current user profile for that job is the same one associated with the SEP, the job suspends and connects to the debugger.

Service entry points allow you to start using the debugger in the most unobtrusive way. Simply set the SEP on the program or procedure you need to debug, and then go and run the application as you normally would have if you were not debugging. This is not to say that the other methods of starting the debugger don't have their advantages, just that using SEPs is the easiest.

Now, having praised the virtues of service entry points, let's provide a word of caution: remember to remove them as soon as you are done debugging. We typically use the same library whenever doing user demos. During a live demo of WebFacing, we were having problems getting the WebFaced application to start the RPG program. The program seemed to hang every time it was launched. When we got back to the lab, there on a desktop PC was a debug session open for every time the program was launched because it had an SEP set on it!

Setting a Service Entry Point

Service entry points can only be used with the ILE languages, and only one SEP can be set on a procedure at a time. To set an SEP, first right-click a program, service program, bound module, or procedure in the RSE. From the pop-up menu, select **Debug (Service Entry) > Set Service Entry Point**, as shown in Figure 9–2. Bound modules are the modules you see when you expand a program or service program in the RSE, not the standalone *MODULE objects inside a library.

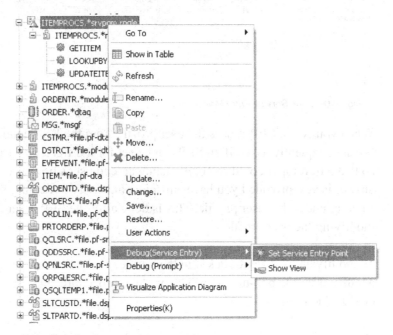

Figure 9–2: Setting a service entry point.

TIP By default, all procedures are shown when you expand a module in a service program. To only show exported procedures, set a preference in the **Remote Systems > i5/OS > Objects Subsystem** preference page.

Internally, SEPs are always set on procedures. Setting an SEP on a program or service program in the RSE actually sets it on all procedures in all modules bound into the program or service program. In the case of a program, this includes the procedure that represents the main-line code of the program. So, even if you don't use procedures, you can still use SEPs.

Once set, the SEP will show up in the i5/OS Service Entry Points view, as shown in Figure 9–3. Using the view's toolbar icons or pop-up menu, you can modify, remove, disable, enable, and refresh SEPs. You can also set SEPs from here, by keying in the program or service program name instead of selecting the object in the RSE.

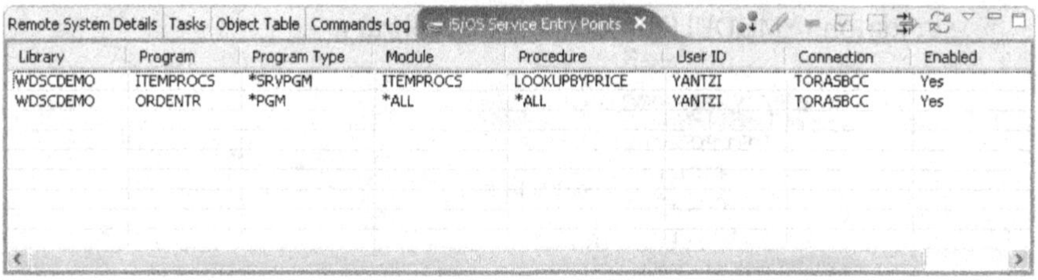
Remote System Details
Tasks
Object Table
Commands Log
i5/OS Service Entry Points
Library
Program
Program Type
Module
Procedure
User ID
Connection
Enabled
WDSCDEMO ITEMPROCS *SRVPGM ITEMPROCS LOOKUPBYPRICE YANTZI TORASBCC Yes
WDSCDEMO ORDENTR *PGM *ALL *ALL YANTZI TORASBCC Yes

Figure 9–3: The Service Entry Points view.

When you set an SEP, it uses the user profile from the RSE connection. We are frequently asked if an SEP can be set for a different user profile, so that a developer could remotely debug an end user's problem. The answer is yes, provided you have sufficient authority to debug jobs running under that user profile. This is done after the SEP is set, by modifying the user profile.

To modify an SEP, right-click it in the Service Entry Points view, and select **Modify** from the pop-up menu. The module, procedure, and user ID are all changeable fields.

Once a program or service program is in debug, any SEPs set on it are no longer active. Calls to procedures inside of the program or service program will not cause the job to suspend. Use regular line breakpoints to stop at the desired location.

If you recompile a program or service program, you need to refresh any SEPs associated with it. Recompiling creates a new program or service program object, but the existing SEP still references the old object. Refreshing the SEP updates the reference to the new object.

"Single-click" Debug Actions

When you right-click a program in the RSE, the pop-up menu has two cascading debug menus in addition to the SEP menu discussed in the previous section. The Debug As menu, shown in Figure 9–4, provides the single-click actions covered in this section. The Debug (Prompt) menu provides access to the launch configurations, discussed in the next section.

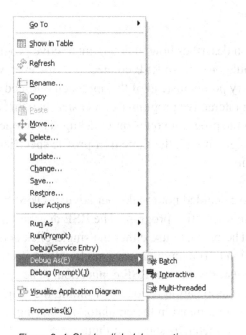

Figure 9–4: Single-click debug actions.

These are called "single-click" actions because they call the selected program, suspend the job, and connect the debugger to the job without prompting for any additional information.

The Debug As and Debug (Prompt) menus both cascade into three options: batch, interactive, and multi-threaded. Select the action that corresponds to the type of program you are running:

- *Batch*: Choose this action if your program should run in a regular batch job (type BCH).

- *Interactive*: Choose this action if your program requires a 5250 emulator. This requires you to associate a 5250 emulator with the RSE connection, covered in more detail in the next section.

- *Multi-threaded*: Choose this action if your program creates multiple threads (typical of C and C++ programs) and needs to run in a batch immediate job (type BCI).

For the batch and multi-threaded actions, a new job is created to run the program. This new job inherits the library list from the RSE connection.

This section describes how to debug interactive programs by associating a 5250 emulator with an RSE connection. However, we recommend using service entry points instead of the approach outlined here. SEPs have made debugging interactive programs a lot easier than this approach. Simply set an SEP on the program you want to debug. Then, open your 5250 emulator, sign on with the same user profile specified on the SEP, and call the program.

So, you have decided not to take our advice! Okay, here is the harder way to debug an interactive program. The RSE does not include a 5250 emulator. Therefore, to use either the single-click action or launch configuration to run an interactive application, you have to first associate a 5250 emulator with your RSE connection. (The type of emulator doesn't matter.) This association is done by running the Start RSE Server (STRRSESVR) command in the emulator, specifying the RSE connection name as a parameter, as shown in Figure 9–5.

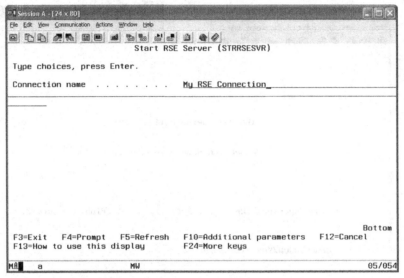

Figure 9–5: The STRRSESVR command.

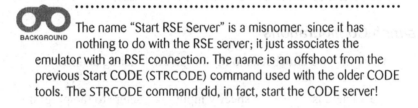
The name "Start RSE Server" is a misnomer, since it has nothing to do with the RSE server; it just associates the emulator with an RSE connection. The name is an offshoot from the previous Start CODE (STRCODE) command used with the older CODE tools. The STRCODE command did, in fact, start the CODE server!

Once the STRRSESVR command has successfully associated the emulator with the RSE connection, it displays a 5250 screen saying "IBM RSE Communications Server," along with the RSE connection and job name, as shown in Figure 9–6. The emulator is now blocked for exclusive use by the RSE connection.

When you run or debug a 5250 program or command from the RSE, it will appear in this emulator. To un-associate the emulator and RSE connection, right-click **Objects** and select the **Release Interactive Job** action.

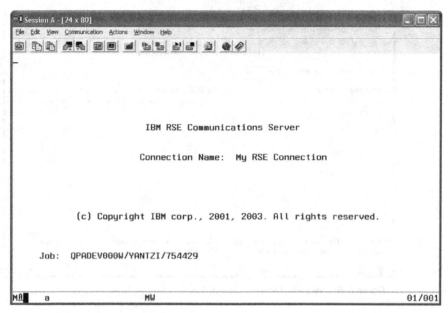

Figure 9–6: The emulator associated with the RSE connection.

Launch Configurations

There are two drawbacks to the single-click debug actions:

- There is no way to specify input parameters to the program.
- The program that is selected is both the program used in starting the overall application and the one being debugged.

Launch configurations address both of these drawbacks. Launch configurations provide the same options for debugging your program as the single-click actions (batch, interactive and multi-threaded), and also allow you to enter additional information to control the debugger and your program.

Creating a launch configuration is comparable to the system debugger's Start Debug (STRDBG) command. Both allow you to specify which programs and service programs to debug and whether updates to production files should be allowed.

Launch configurations are saved so they can be rerun without having to enter the information again. To create a new launch configuration, select

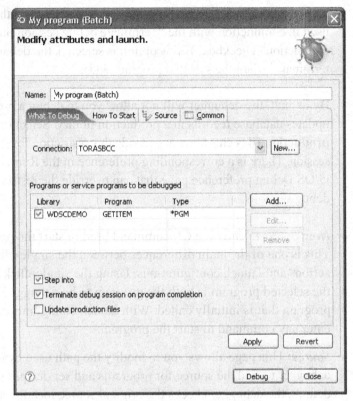

Figure 9–7: The Debug Batch launch configuration.

one of the actions from the Debug (Prompt) menu on a program or service program in the RSE. This opens a new launch configuration dialog, as shown in Figure 9–7.

At the top of the dialog, you give the launch configuration a name, which is used to save the launch configuration. Each tab prompts for different types of information:

- *What To Debug*: Enter which programs or service programs you need to debug. If you specify the "Step into" option, the debugger stops at the first executable line for any of the programs or service programs in the list. If this option is not specified, the debugger stops at the first breakpoint it hits. (The breakpoint could be saved from a previous debug session or set in the Remote Systems LPEX Editor.)

The checkbox next to each program/service program in the list is used in conjunction with the "Terminate debug session on program completion" checkbox. If this option is selected, the debug session terminates when the selected program ends.

By default, the debugger will not allow you to debug a program that updates database records in a production library. Select the **Update production files** checkbox to override this restriction for this debug session. There is a corresponding preference in the Run/Debug > i5/OS Debug preference page that can override the restriction for all debug sessions.

- *How To Start*: Enter the CL command used to start the program. This is one of the main differences between the single-click debug actions and launch configurations. Using the single-click actions, the selected program is both the program to be debugged and the program that is initially called. With launch configurations, you can enter any command to start the program.

- *Source*: This page allows you to modify the path used by the debugger to find the source for programs and service programs. By default, the debugger checks the original source location set in the program or service program. You need to specify where the debugger can find the source for any programs and service programs executing on a different system than the one on which they were compiled. You also need to specify if the source was moved after compiling. You can add any of the following to the source lookup path:

  » A local directory

  » An IFS folder ("Remote Folder")

  » An i5/OS source file

  » The local Workspace

  » A project within the local Workspace (more granular than the Workspace)

  » A folder within the local Workspace (more granular than a project)

- *Common*: By default, launch configurations are private to the workstation where they are created. However, you can save them to a Workspace project, and then share the launch configurations with the other members of your team. To save the launch configuration to a Workspace project, change the type of launch configuration from "Local" to "Shared," and enter a Workspace project or folder in the "location entry" field. This saves the launch configuration into the project or folder with a *.launch* extension. The launch configuration file can now be shared with other team members.

When you are done entering information about the launch configuration, click the **Debug** button to start debugging, or click the **Close** button to save the launch configuration without starting the debugger.

To rerun an existing launch configuration, use the Workbench's **Run > Debug** . . . menu. This brings up a dialog similar to the one shown in Figure 9–7, but with an additional column on the left side listing all the types of launch configurations that can be created. In this list, you will find the four i5/OS launch configuration types: Debug Batch Application, Debug Interactive Application, Debug Multi-Threaded Application, and Debug Job. Previous launch configuration instances are listed under their corresponding type. Select an instance and click the **Debug** button to re-launch it.

SHORTCUT The last-used launch configuration can be quickly re-launched by clicking the "debug" icon (🐞 ▾) in the toolbar or using the F11 shortcut key. Clicking the drop-down menu next to the icon provides a list of the most recently used launch configurations and access to the main launch configuration dialog.

Attaching to an Existing Job

A single-click action and launch configuration can also be used to attach the debugger to an existing job. To use the single-click action, find your job under the Jobs subsystem, right-click it, and select **Debug As > i5/OS Job**. This is comparable to using the Start Service Job (STRSRVJOB) command to attach the green-screen system debugger to a different job.

One of two things happens once the debugger attaches to the job. If there is no program with debug information on the top of the call stack, the debugger attaches to the job and displays a message prompting you to start your program in the job. Once your program starts, the debugger suspends the job, and you are debugging.

If there is a program with debug information on the top of the call stack, the debugger will attach to the job and suspend the program or service program that is currently running. Version 7.0 of WDSC added support to allow the debugger to attach to a job where a program is waiting on an inquiry message.

The Debug Job launch configuration is similar to the ones described above, with two exceptions. First, there is no How To Start tab. Second, the What To Debug tab contains entry fields for specifying the job to debug, in addition to the table where you can specify which programs and service programs should be debugged, as shown in Figure 9–8.

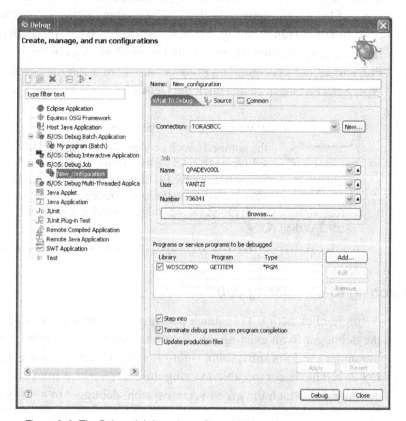

Figure 9–8: The Debug Job launch configuration.

Using the Debugger

The Workbench switches to the Debug perspective when a new debug session is started. The Debug perspective is made up of menus, actions, and views specific to debugging. Figure 9–9 shows the default layout for this perspective. The top left corner contains the Debug view used for controlling the debugger. The top right corner contains various views for examining fields and working with breakpoints.

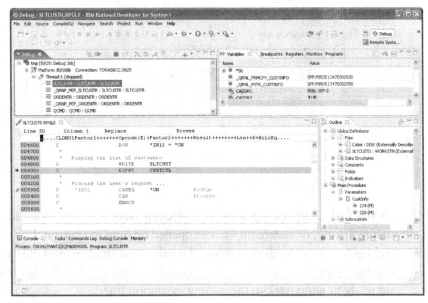

Figure 9–9: The Debug perspective.

The editor area is in the middle of the perspective, where editors will appear when required for stepping through your source code. Perspectives do not control which editors are shown, so an editor opened in one perspective will show in all other perspectives within the same Workbench window. You may already have one or more editors showing in the editor area if you opened members in the RSE before switching to the Debug perspective.

Remember that the Debug perspective is used for debugging Java, XSL transformations, JavaScript, and more, as well as for RPG, COBOL, and CL. Because of that, you are likely to come across actions and views, such as the Debug Console and Registers views, that are not used when debugging RPG, COBOL, and CL. Feel free to close views you are not using, so they don't clutter up the Workbench.

Controlling the Debugger

The Debug view provides the main controls for the debugger, shown in Figure 9–10. Each job you are debugging shows up as an entry in this view. Yes, that's right—you can debug multiple jobs at the same time! Under the job entry is a list of threads for the job. Under each thread is the call stack for that thread. Interactive and batch jobs on i5/OS are single-threaded, so you will only see one thread under the job.

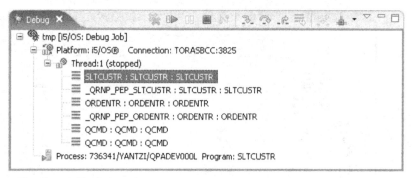

Figure 9–10: The Debug view.

As you select call stack entries in the Debug view, the corresponding source, listing, or statement view is opened up, and the current line is highlighted. You can then examine the values for fields within the caller. Use the "show stopping thread" keyboard shortcut (Ctrl+F9) when you are ready to jump back to the current execution line.

The debugger is controlled using actions from the Debug view. These actions, along with their icons and shortcut keys, are described in Table 9–1.

Table 9–1: Actions for Controlling Debug Execution			
Name	Icon	Keyboard Shortcut	Description
Resume		F8	Resume execution of a suspended program.
Suspend		N/A	Suspend execution of a running program.
Terminate		N/A	Stop the debug session. This does not end the program or job being debugged. If the job was currently suspended, it will be resumed.

Table 9–1: Actions for Controlling Debug Execution (Continued)			
Name	Icon	Keyboard Shortcut	Description
Step Into		F5	If the current executable line is a program or procedure call, selecting the Step Into action will start debugging the first debuggable line of code within the program or procedure.
Step Over		F6	Execute the current line and stop at the next executable line. If the current line is a program or procedure call, the program or procedure is executed without stepping through it.
Step Return		F7	Resume program execution until the current program or procedure call returns.

The debugger stays attached to the job until one of two things happens: either the initial program being debugged ends, or you terminate the debug session. Terminating the debug session just releases the job; it does not end the current program or the job.

TIP While using the debugger, you can switch back to other perspectives without affecting your current debug sessions. For example, you might want to switch back to the RSE to make changes to some other members, recompile, or view some data. All your current debug sessions stay open while you are in the RSE perspective. When you're ready, you can switch back to the Debug perspective and continue debugging. Ctrl+F8 can be used to quickly switch between open perspectives.

The Debug Editor Area

As you select call stack entries in the Debug view, an editor is opened up and positioned to the current line of that call stack entry. Typically, you would select the top-most entry to view the current execution line and control the debugger execution. However, you can select other call stack entries to examine the line performing the call as well as field values within the caller.

The debugger provides the ability to use a source, listing, or statement view of the program while debugging. (The views available depend on which

Debug view option was specified when the source was compiled.) To switch between views, right-click anywhere in the editor, and select one of the options from the cascading Switch View menu, shown in Figure 9–11.

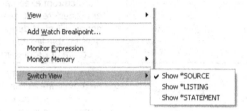

Figure 9–11: Switching views in the debugger.

In earlier releases, the debugger used its own editor to display source code while stepping through programs. However, this debug editor didn't color-tokenize the language statements and didn't populate the Outline view. So, support was added to use the Remote Systems LPEX Editor while debugging.

There is a preference on the Run/Debug > Compile Debug preference page to use the debug editor instead of the Remote Systems LPEX Editor. *Always use the debug editor while debugging.* When using the Remote Systems LPEX Editor, it is possible to have unsaved changes in the editor that cause the editor line numbers to not match the line numbers from the debugger. This, in turn, causes the debugger to highlight the incorrect current line in the editor. If you often find yourself in this situation, change this preference to use the debug editor instead.

Viewing and Modifying Field Values

One of the most important features of any debugger is the ability to examine the values of fields in the running program. The Integrated i5/OS Debugger provides three specialized views for this purpose: Variables, Monitors, and Memory.

TIP Hovering the mouse over a field in the editor causes a window to pop up and display the current value of the field. Moving the mouse causes the window to disappear again.

The displayed value for fields in any of the three views is updated automatically as you step through your program. The field name is highlighted in red and decorated with a blue triangle ( ) when the value of a field changes. All three views allow you to change the value of a field. In the Variables and Monitors views, you can change the value of a field by right-clicking the field and selecting Change Value from the pop-up menu. In the Variables view, you can also edit the value of a field directly in the table.

Data structures and arrays show up in the Variables and Monitors views as expandable entries. Initially, only the name of the data structure or array appears, with a plus sign next to it. Clicking the plus sign expands the entry to show the subfields or array elements.

The Variables View

The Variables view displays all variables (fields) defined in the currently selected call stack frame, as shown in Figure 9–12. If the mainline code of an RPG IV program is selected, this view shows all global fields defined for the program. If an RPG subprocedure is selected, the view shows the fields defined inside of the subprocedure.

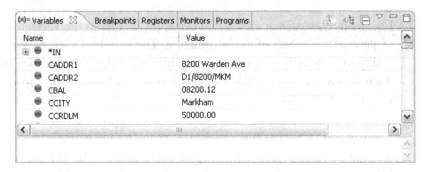

Figure 9–12: The Variables view.

It is common for an RPG program to contain many global fields. The Variables view has a handy "find" function for quickly finding and positioning to the field you are interested in. Within the view, press Ctrl+F, and a Find dialog appears, as shown in Figure 9–13. As you enter the name of the field in the dialog, the list of fields is filtered based on what you have typed. Once the field you are interested in is selected, click **OK** (or press Enter), and the Variables view is positioned to that field. The Find dialog supports generic search strings. For example, enter ***ID*** to see all fields that contain the string *ID*.

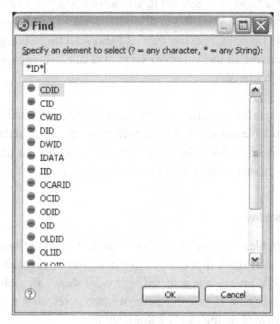

Figure 9-13: Searching the Variables view.

Like many Workbench views, you can apply a filter to the Variables view to show only a subset of the information. The Variables view provides the ability to show only user-defined variables or predefined variables (such as the indicators) using the Filter Locals action, available on the pop-up menu within the Variables view.

The Variables view has two restrictions. First, it only works when debugging i5/OS V5R3 or later and is only populated for ILE RPG and ILE COBOL source. Second, it does not support RPG's *INZSR, or mainline subroutines. It does support the mainline code, subprocedures, and subroutines defined within a subprocedure.

The Monitors View

The Monitors view allows you to view and change the values of specific fields you are interested in by explicitly adding them to the view, as shown in Figure 9–14. To add a field to the Monitors view, select it in the debug editor, right-click, and select **Monitor Expression** from the pop-up menu. Alternatively, the Monitors view provides an "add" action in the toolbar (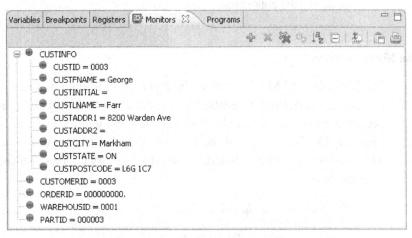) that allows you to type in the name of the field you wish to monitor.

Figure 9–14: The Monitors view.

Most of the other icons in the Monitors view's toolbar are common Workbench actions, such as "remove selected" and "remove all." The following actions are specific to the Monitors view:

- Disable/Enable Monitored Expression ( ): Use this action to temporarily disable the automatic updating the of a field's value in the view. If you have a lot of fields added to the Monitors view and are noticing a delay while stepping through your program, you might want to disable or remove the fields that are not of interest.

- Show Type Names ( ): This action is not applicable to debugging native i5/OS applications.

You can also right-click a field in the Monitors view to access additional actions, such as changing the value of the field (Change Value) or changing how the value is displayed (Change Representation). Using the Change Representation action, you can toggle between showing the value as hexadecimal or the system default for the field's data type.

TIP

One advantage of using the "add" action from the Monitor view is you can enter an array name with an array index. Suppose you are only interested in monitoring the tenth element of the orders array. You could enter ORDERS[10] as the expression, instead of adding the entire array.

The Memory View

The Variables and Monitors views both show fields along with a visual representation of their contents. The Memory view allows you to dig deeper and look at the actual layout of a field in memory, as shown in Figure 9–15. The left side of the Memory view holds a list of the fields added to the view. The right side shows the memory contents for the selected field.

```
Console  Tasks  iSeries Commands Log  Debug Console  [] Memory 
Monitors        Renderings
   CUSTOMERID    CustInfo : 0xD847F67F5B002930 <Hex>
   PARTID
   CustInfo       Address        0 - 3       4 - 7      8 - B       C - F
                  D847F67F5B002930  F0F0F0F3  C7859699  87854040  40404040
                  D847F67F5B002940  40404040  4040C681  99994040  40404040
                  D847F67F5B002950  40404040  4040F8F2  F0F040E6  81998485
                  D847F67F5B002960  9540C1A5  85404040  40404040  40404040
                  D847F67F5B002970  40404040  40404040  40404040  4040D481
                  D847F67F5B002980  99928881  94404040  40404040  40404040
                  D847F67F5B002990  4040D6D5  D3F6C740  F1C3F740  40400000
                  D847F67F5B0029A0  C6819999  6B40C785  96998785  40404040
```

Figure 9–15: The Memory view.

To add a field to the Memory view, right-click it in the editor, and select **Monitor Memory** from the pop-up menu. This action cascades into a list of options for how the contents of each memory location should be displayed. Select the correct option based on the field's data type, or select **HEX** to see the raw data in memory.

Once a field has been added to the Memory view, you can add and remove additional renderings using the view's toolbar actions. Additional rendering shows up as tabs on the right side of the view.

Setting Breakpoints

Most people think of a breakpoint being set on a specific line of code in the debugger, so that the debugger stops just before the line is executed.

We refer to this as a *line breakpoint*. The debugger also allows breakpoints to be set in the Remote Systems LPEX Editor before the debugger is even started. We refer to these as *source breakpoints*, since they are set in the source editor. There are also w*atch breakpoints* that can be set on a field to cause the debugger to suspend the program if the value of that field changes.

All breakpoints show up in the debugger's Breakpoints view, which provides a central place to work with them. A blue dot is the Workbench's universal symbol for a breakpoint. In Figure 9–16, some of the breakpoints have a checkmark over the blue dot. Those breakpoints are active in the current debug session. The section on source breakpoints, later in this chapter, covers why a breakpoint might not be active and how to activate it.

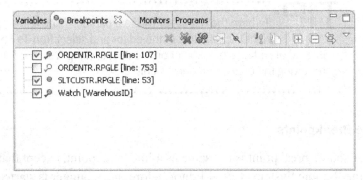

Figure 9–16: The Breakpoints view.

From the Breakpoints view, you can do the following:

- Enable and disable breakpoints by toggling the checkbox beside the breakpoint.

- Remove breakpoints using the "remove selected" and "remove all" icons in the view's toolbar.

- Add breakpoints by right-clicking in the view and selecting **Add Breakpoint > Line** . . . or **Watch** . . . from the pop-up menu.

- Edit breakpoints to make them conditional. (Conditional breakpoints are discussed in more detail later in this chapter.)

- Use the pull-down menu to change how breakpoints are grouped. For example, to have all breakpoints grouped by their corresponding file (member), select **Group By > Files**.

Line Breakpoints

A line breakpoint can be set in the editor after the debugger is running. The most common way to set a line breakpoint is to double-click in the vertical ruler on the left side of the editor (to the left of the sequence numbers). Alternatively, right-click any executable line and select **Add Breakpoint** from the pop-up menu. Both actions set a line breakpoint on the selected line and add a blue breakpoint dot to the margin of the editor.

Double-clicking the blue dot removes the breakpoint. If you attempt to set a breakpoint on a non-executable line, the breakpoint will be set on the first executable line after the selected line.

TIP

To have the debugger run to a particular line and stop, right-click the line in the editor and select **Run To Location**, instead of setting a breakpoint on the line, clicking "resume," and then removing the breakpoint once it's hit.

Source Breakpoints

A source breakpoint is the same as a line breakpoint, except that it is set in the Remote Systems LPEX Editor before the debugger is started. This is useful if you know you want to step through an exceptionally tricky section of code. This is a great example of integration within the Workbench. You can seamlessly flow back and forth between editing and debugging, by setting breakpoints in the editor before debugging, and continuing to use the same editor while stepping through the code.

To set a source breakpoint, double-click in the vertical ruler of the editor. Alternatively, right-click any executable line and select **Add Breakpoint** from the pop-up menu. In either case, a blue dot should appear in the left margin, indicating the source breakpoint has been set. Unless you are already debugging, the blue dot will probably not have a checkmark on it. This means the breakpoint has not been added to a debug session yet.

One of the technical differences between line breakpoints and source breakpoints is that the debugger knows the program or service program object when a line breakpoint is set. A source breakpoint, however, is set in a source member that might not even be compiled yet. Internally, the debug engine associates all breakpoints with a program or service program object, not the source member. With source breakpoints, the breakpoint needs to be mapped from the member to the object. Whether this mapping is done by you or the debugger depends on which version of WDSC you are using.

In earlier versions of WDSC, this mapping was done manually, by prompting the user for the name of the object when the source breakpoint was set. In WDSC 6.0, this was improved by having the debugger automatically add source breakpoints to any program or service program object that was compiled from the member. However, the program or service program had to be manually added to the debugger via the Programs view before the source breakpoints were activated.

In version 7.0, a preference was added to have the debugger automatically add service programs bound to your application to the debug session, and therefore have any related source breakpoints activated, as shown in Figure 9–17. This is the "Include bound service programs when installing source breakpoints" preference on the Run/Debug > i5/OS Debug preference page. The default value is off (unchecked), so if you want this behavior, you have to click the checkbox for the preference.

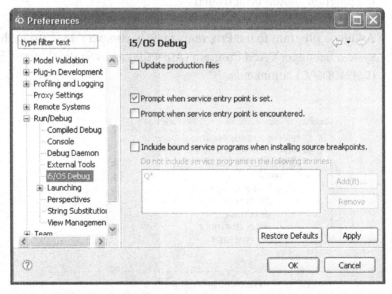

Figure 9–17: The i5/OS Debug preference page.

The same preference page also allows you to specify a list of libraries (including generic names) to exclude from being automatically installed. Service programs from these libraries will not be added automatically by the debugger. This was primarily added to exclude the IBM runtime service programs (libraries starting Q*), but can be used to exclude service programs from libraries you are not interested in debugging.

Source entry points set in called programs (as opposed to bound service programs) still need to have the called program manually added to debug. Once the debugger is attached to the i5/OS job, you can add a program or service program to debug using the following steps:

1. Make sure the job is suspended, either at a breakpoint or by selecting the job and clicking the Suspend button.

2. Switch to the Programs view. By default, this appears in the tabbed notebook in the top right corner of the Debug perspective, as shown in Figure 9–18.

3. Click the "add" icon in the view's toolbar.

4. Enter the program name when prompted.

The program is now added to debug, and all source breakpoints related to the program should be activated.

Adding a program to the Programs view is comparable to using the system debugger's Add Program (ADDPGM) and Display Module Source (DSPMODSRC) commands.

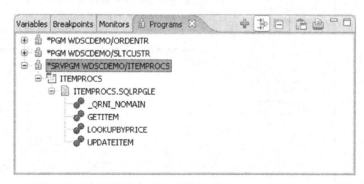

Figure 9–18: The Programs view.

TIP

The Programs view is actually called the Modules view. The name of the view is automatically changed when you are using the Integrated i5/OS Debugger. If you are looking for this view in the Show View menu, you will need to look for the Modules view.

Watch Breakpoints

We often come across situations where the value of a field is being unexpectedly modified, and we want to track down when in the program execution this occurs. This can be done using a *watch* breakpoint. Watch breakpoints are set on a field instead of a line of code. When the value of the field changes, the debugger displays a message box stating that the field has changed, and suspends program execution. The current line in the debug editor will be the first executable line immediately following the line that caused the field to change.

To set a watch breakpoint, select the field in the debug editor, right-click, and select **Watch** . . . from the pop-up menu. Alternatively, right-click in the Breakpoints view and select **Add Breakpoint** > **Watch** . . . . This opens the Add a Watch Breakpoint dialog, shown in Figure 9–19. Enter the field name and number of bytes to watch, and click **Finish**. A value of zero for the number of bytes to watch means all bytes in the field are monitored for changes. A value of one or higher means only that number of bytes of the field are monitored for changes.

Figure 9–19: Adding a watch breakpoint.

TIP
You can enter an expression in the Add Watch Breakpoint dialog instead of a field name. For example, if you are only interested in knowing when location 89 of the PARTS array is modified, enter **PARTS(89)** for the expression.

Conditional Breakpoints

Bugs have a nasty way of waiting until the last iteration of a loop until they appear. If you're like us, you repeatedly press F6 as fast as possible to keep stepping through until that last iteration, only to accidentally press it a few too many times and miss the bug completely. (It's amazing that our F6 keys still work!)

Conditional breakpoints to the rescue! After a line or source breakpoint has been set, you can edit the breakpoint to make it conditional. To change how often (the frequency) a line breakpoint suspends the debugger, follow these steps:

1. Right-click the line breakpoint in the Breakpoints view and select **Edit Breakpoint** . . . . This opens the Edit a Line Breakpoint dialog, shown in Figure 9–20.

2. Click **Next** to proceed to the Optional parameters page.

3. Change the frequency fields to adjust how often the breakpoint causes the debugger to suspend the job.

Figure 9–20: Editing a line breakpoint.

In addition to the frequency, you can enter a Boolean expression using fields from your program. When the breakpoint is hit, the debugger evaluates the expression to determine if the job should continue or suspend. If the expression evaluates to true, the debugger suspends the job; otherwise, the job continues. For RPG, this can only be a simple Boolean expression, not a compound expression.

Conditions on watch breakpoints have to be set when the breakpoint is added; they cannot be modified afterward. When setting the watch breakpoint, click **Next** on the first page to proceed to the Optional parameters page. Watch breakpoints allow the frequency to be set, but do not support expressions.

Running a Program

The actions to run or debug a program are very similar in the Workbench. Earlier in this chapter, you saw how to launch the debugger. With the exception of service entry points and attaching to an existing job (which are specific to debugging), this entire section also applies to running programs.

Follow the same instructions for debugging, except use the Run As or Run (Prompt) actions in the RSE, instead of the Debug actions. Even the launch configurations are the same for running and debugging. In fact, run and debug share the same launch configurations, so if you create a launch configuration for debugging a program, you can reuse it for running the same program.

The Debug Perspective

The Debug perspective contains many different views to display information about the program being debugged and to assist in controlling debug execution. Table 9–2 provides a summary of the commonly used views in this perspective.

Table 9–2: Commonly Used Debug Views	
View	**Description**
i5/OS Service Entry Points	The i5/OS Service Entry Points view lists all service entry points and provides actions to set, modify, remove, enable/disable, and refresh them.
Debug	The Debug view is the central control point for the debugger. All debug jobs and their call stacks show up here.
Variables	The Variables view shows all local variables for a procedure, or the global variables for main-line code.
Monitors	You can add fields to the Monitors view to watch and change their values.
Memory	The Memory view shows the contents of memory for a field.
Breakpoints	The Breakpoints view provides a central list of all breakpoints and provides actions for enabling, disabling, and removing them.
Programs	The Programs view (also referred to as the Modules view) lists all programs and service programs current under debug. You can add additional programs and service programs to debug from this view.

Debug Preferences

All debug-related preferences can be found under the Run/Debug preference category. The two main subcategories are Compiled Debug and i5/OS Debug. (The i5/OS debug support leverages the compiled languages debug engine provided by another IBM team.)

On the Compiled Debug preference page, the most relevant preference is this one:

- *Always use Debug Editor while debugging*: This preference switches between using the debug editor or the Remote Systems LPEX Editor for displaying source code while debugging. This preference is covered in the section "The Debug Editor Area" earlier in this chapter.

On the i5/OS Debug preference page, the most relevant preferences are these:

- *Update production files*: By default, the debugger will prevent you from debugging a program that opens a file in a production library for update. This can be overridden on a case-by-case basis in the launch configurations, or globally by selecting this preference.

- *Include bound service programs when installing source breakpoints:* This preference is covered in the section on source breakpoints earlier in this chapter.

Green Screen to RSE Quick Start

Table 9–3 describes the mapping between the green screen debugger's commands and the Integrated i5/OS Debugger commands.

Table 9–3: System Debugger to Integrated i5/OS Debugger Command Mappings	
System Debugger	**Integrated i5/OS Debugger**
STRSRVJOB	Right-click the job in the RSE and select **Debug As > i5/OS Job** from the pop-up menu. Alternatively, set a service entry point on the program and call the program in the desired job.
STRDBG	Right-click a program in the RSE, and select one of the debug options from either the Debug As or Debug (Prompt) cascading menu. Alternatively, set a service entry point on the program and call the program in the desired job.
ADDPGM, DSPMODSRC	Use the Programs view to add additional OPM and ILE programs to debug. This view is named Modules if the debugger is not running or you are opening the view from the Window > Show View menu.
ADDBKP	Double-click in the vertical ruler at the left side of the editor. Alternatively, right-click in the Breakpoints view and select **Add > Breakpoint > Line** . . . .
F5: Refresh	Using the system debugger, pressing F5 will position to the current execution line within a single member. Ctrl+F9 ("show stopping thread") is the equivalent action in the Integrated i5/OS Debugger. As a bonus, Ctrl+F9 works anywhere in the Debug perspective.
F10: Step	Click the "step" icon in the Debug view, or use the F6 keyboard shortcut.
F11: Display variable	Hover the mouse over the variable or add the variable to the Monitors view.
F12: Resume	Click the "resume" icon in the Debug view.
F13: Work with module breakpoints	Use the Breakpoints view.
F14: Work with module list	Use the Programs view.
F15: Select view	Right-click in the editor and select one of the options from the Switch View cascading menu.
F17: Watch variable	Right-click the variable and select **Watch** from the pop-up menu.

Table 9–3: System Debugger to Integrated i5/OS Debugger Command Mappings (Continued)	
System Debugger	Integrated i5/OS Debugger
F18: Work with watch	Use the Breakpoints view.
F21: Command entry	Switch to the RSE perspective and run commands.
F22: Step into	Click the "step into" icon in the Debug view, or use the F5 keyboard shortcut.

Troubleshooting

In the past, the debugger had a reputation as being difficult to start. This was largely due to the underlying communications layer not handling firewalls and Network Address Translation (NAT). These communication problems were fixed in WDSC 6.0.1. Service entry points have also made starting the debugger a lot easier.

Below are some common problems with debugging, along with suggestions on diagnosing and fixing the problems:

- *The RSE's Start and Stop Debug Server actions are both disabled.*

  The RSE connection has to be connected to check the current status of the debug server. If the connection is not connected, both actions are disabled.

- *I don't see the debug or run actions when I right-click a program in the RSE.*

  Make sure the i5/OS Debug capability is enabled. From the Workbench Preferences dialog, select the **General > Capabilities** preference page. Ensure that **i5/OS Application Developer** capability is checked . If it does not have a checkmark, or has a solid box, click it until the checkmark appears.

- *I set a breakpoint, but the debugger doesn't stop on it.*

  The first thing to check is that your breakpoint is enabled. Switch to the Breakpoints view and make sure the breakpoint is checked.

Next, make sure the breakpoint has been activated in the current debug session. If the blue dot beside the breakpoint is not checked, the breakpoint has not been activated in the debugger yet.

The main reason for a breakpoint not being activated in the debugger is the program or service program for the breakpoint has not been added to debug yet. Switch to the Programs view, and add your program or service program to debug. This will cause the debugger to activate all related breakpoints.

- *The debugger does not stop on my service entry point.*

The most common reason for this is the program or service program was recompiled after the SEP was set. You must refresh the SEP after recompiling the program or service program. This can be done from the i5/OS Service Entry Points view; right-click the corresponding entry and select **Refresh** from the pop-up menu.

- *The STRRSESVR command fails to connect to my workstation.*

When the STRSRESVR command is run, it creates a TCP/IP socket connection from the server to your workstation. If this connection fails, you receive the message "Error connecting to Remote Systems Explorer (RSE2001)." There are a number of situations where this can occur. That's why we usually recommend using SEPs to debug 5250 applications instead of using the STRRSESVR command.

Below are the most common reasons why the STRRSESVR command is not connecting to the workstation:

a. Your physical network configuration does not allow socket connections to be created from the server to your workstation. For example, your workstation and the server are on different subnets separated by Network Address Translation (NAT). This is a restriction of the STRRSESVR command. You will have to attach to the job or use SEPs to debug 5250 programs in this network environment.

b. There is a firewall blocking the connection. The firewall could be on the server, your workstation, or the network in between. In most cases, we find that the firewall is installed on the workstation (such as the firewall included in Windows XP SP2 or the Symantec Client Firewall). The TCP/IP port used on the workstation to accept the incoming socket connection is 4300. You need to configure a rule in the firewall software to allow this incoming connection. (You might want to configure the rule so only connections from your server are allowed.)

c. The port number can be changed on the Remote Systems > Communications preference page. If you change the port, you will need to specify the new port number on the STRRSESVR command's TCP/IP port parameter.

d. By default, the STRRSESVR command attempts to determine the IP address of your workstation based on the 5250 session. If the command fails to correctly resolve the workstation IP address, the connection attempt fails. Press F1 on the RSE2001 message to see which IP address the command used. If the IP address is incorrect, prompt the command and manually specify the remote location name using either the workstation's IP address or the TCP/IP hostname.

e. The RSE communications daemon is not started. By default, this daemon starts when the workbench is started and listens on port 4300. The daemon can be started and stopped manually via the "[Start | Stop] Communications Daemon" action in the Remote Systems view's pull-down menu.

10

Additional Functions

So far, you have learned about many of the important tools that exist in the Remote System Explorer. You should now be able to navigate with ease within the Workbench, and perform the routine tasks of editing, compiling, and debugging without going to the green screen. If you're not there yet, though, don't give up! Like mastering anything else, education gets you started; experience using the tools gets you a lot farther.

In this chapter, you'll explore some additional goodies that exist in RSE. These features are not covered in other chapters, as they did not really "fit" under any of their topics. Nonetheless, they are important and useful functions. We would be remiss if we didn't at least mention them, so you are aware of their existence.

RSE Profiles

We have referred to profiles in different places. It's now time to explain a bit more about them. First, the profile in RSE should not be confused with the i5/OS profile. They are unrelated. An RSE profile is a unique name that identifies you within the group and allows you to share RSE configurations with your team, if you wish to do so.

Even though the RSE is built on top of Eclipse technology, which is project-based, the RSE is designed for direct access to remote resources and is not project-based. However, the RSE uses an Eclipse project to manage non-remote resources. This project is called *RemoteSystemsConnections.*

When you create connections, filter pools, filters, user-defined actions, and customized compile commands, they are all stored in an RSE profile. This is the reason you need to specify the profile name when creating these artifacts. Subsystem properties, like the initial library list, current library, and initial command are also stored with the subsystem in the connection's RSE profile.

The RSE creates a unique profile per team member, referred to as your *private* profile, plus a common profile called *Team*. The first time you create a connection in a new Workspace, the RSE prompts you to rename your private profile. (It guesses the name based on the hostname of your workstation.)

Working with Profiles

To work with your RSE profiles, click the View menu (⌄) from the Remote Systems view, and select **Work With Profiles**. This opens the Team view. (Alternatively, you can just click the Team view tab next to the Remote Systems view tab.) The Team view is used to view and manage RSE profiles.

To create a new profile, right-click the **RemoteSystemsConnections** project in the Team view, and select **New Profile**, as shown in Figure 10–1. This opens the New Remote System Profile dialog, where you specify the name for the profile.

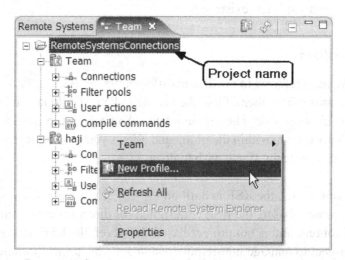

Figure 10–1: Creating a new profile from the Team view.

Profiles appear under the RemoteSystemsConnections project. Profiles can be active or inactive. The RSE shows all connections, filters, user-defined actions, and compile commands from all active profiles. In other words, resources in inactive profiles is hidden. By default, only your private profile and Team profile are active. To make a profile active or inactive, right-click it and select the **Make Active** or **Make Inactive** action.

> **TIP** You might be wondering why you would ever create additional profiles. Perhaps there is an application in your shop that you only work on for a few weeks every year. You could create a separate profile just for that application and add all related connections, filters, and compile commands for that application to this profile. Make the profile active when you need to work on the application. Make the profile inactive when you aren't working on it, so the related connections, filters, and compile commands don't clutter up the RSE views.

Profiles map to a folder under the RemoteSystemsConnections project. You can share profiles with coworkers or copy them from one Workspace to another by copying the profile folder (and all subfolders and files) from the RemoteSystemsConnections project in one Workspace to another. This can be done using either Window Explorer, or the Workbench's export and import wizards. You might need to right-click the RemoteSystemsConnections project and select **Refresh All**, and then right-click and select **Reload Remote System Explorer** for the new profile to appear.

Don't copy a profile from one project to another if it already exists in the target project!

Remote Searches

"Now where did that go?"

Searching in the RSE is similar to using PDM option 25, the Find String Using PDM (FNDSTRPDM) command. The RSE is flexible in terms of the search patterns you can use and the wide mixture of ways to select the members to be searched.

To run a remote search from the RSE, select the libraries, physical files, or members you want to search, then right-click, and select the **Find String**

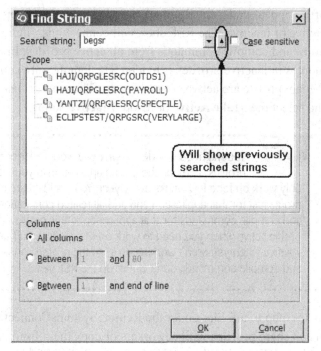

Figure 10–2: The Find String dialog.

action. This opens the Find String dialog, shown in Figure 10–2. This is actually a graphical interface to FNDSTRPDM.

You can specify the search string as character or hexadecimal. The scope lists all of the libraries, physical files, and members you initially selected. Figure 10–2 shows a selection of a few source members from different libraries and source physical files.

The Find String dialog is customized depending on the selected resources. For example, if libraries are selected, an option to search source members, data members, or both is given. To perform a case-sensitive search, check the **Case sensitive** box. You can also restrict the search to specific columns, by selecting the appropriate radio button, and specifying the range.

Click the **OK** button, and the remote search (which is performed on i5/OS) begins. Depending on the initial selection, FNDSTRPDM might be run multiple times on the server. The Commands Log view logs the commands as they complete.

TIP
You can invoke the Find String dialog on a filter, as well.
This allows you to search flexible patterns using generic
filter strings. This is not possible to do in one operation using PDM or
FNDSTRPDM.

Search Results

An events file is created in the current library that contains the results
of the search. Once the search completes, the results are displayed in the
Remote Search view, shown in Figure 10–3. A summary of the results is
displayed at the top of the view, showing the search string, total number of
occurrences of the string, and the number of members searched.

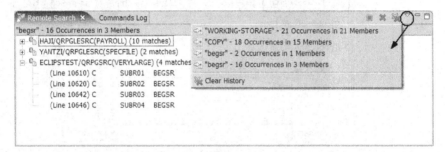

Figure 10–3: The results of the Find String action in Remote Search view.

You can expand and collapse the matched members to quickly locate the
match you want. The entire line where the match is found is shown in
the list.

Double-clicking any of the lines containing the search string will open
the source member and position the cursor to the matching line. Individual
results can be removed from the list by selecting them and clicking the
"remove selected matches" button ( ) on the view's toolbar. All results
can be removed by clicking the "remove all matches" button ( ).

TIP
You can sometimes use the Remote Search view as a to-do
list. If you need to rename a field, search for the field to view
all matches in the Remote Search view. Then, remove the matches as
you modify the source.

If you run another search, your previous results are not lost. You can switch between your searches using the View drop-down menu, as shown in Figure 10–3. To clear the previous searches, select the **Clear History** option from the menu.

Another Way to Search

Another way to search is to use the i5/OS Search dialog. Open the dialog through the **Search > i5/OS** Workbench menu. The dialog will have i5/OS tab highlighted, as shown in Figure 10–4.

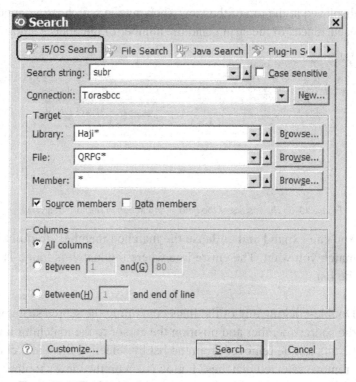

Figure 10–4: The Search dialog.

This dialog allows generic names for the library, physical file, and member fields. Clicking the "history" button (▼), you can select from the list of previously used strings. Clicking the "work with history" button (▲), you can remove or reorder the items stored in the history. The search results are consolidated in the Remote Search view to provide a single view of the results, just as they were for the Find String action.

As you can see from the Search dialog, you can perform many different kinds of searches in the Workbench. The tabs at the top take you to customized pages for each specific search type. If you are not interested in other kinds of searches, tailor this dialog to show only the i5/OS Search tab by clicking the **Customize** button at the bottom of the dialog.

TIP

You can use the keyboard shortcut Ctrl+H to open the Search dialog. This might not give focus to the i5/OS Search tab, but you can use the "previous" and "next" buttons (◄ | ►) to locate it.

User-defined Actions

User-defined actions in the RSE are actions that you define in the Workbench against objects, such as libraries, programs, data queues, source physical files, and source members. User-defined actions (also called just *user actions*) appear in the pop-up menu for the objects. When selected, a user action runs as a command on i5/OS.

This is similar to F16 in PDM, where you can define user options. The difference is that user actions are more flexible and can be scoped to a group of object or member types. These details will be covered shortly.

Creating User-defined Actions

Let's start by taking a look at how to create a new action. In the Remote Systems view, right-click the Objects subsystem and select **Work With > User Actions**. This opens the Work With User Actions dialog, shown in Figure 10–5. This dialog is used to create, change, and delete user-defined actions.

RSE user actions are grouped into two categories: object actions and member actions. To create a new action, select its type ("Object action" or "Member action") under the New category on the left. You can then define the user action on the right. The following information is required:

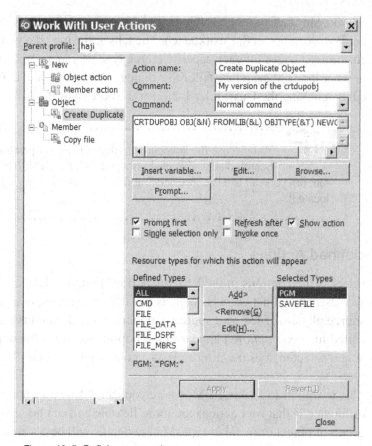

Figure 10–5: Defining user actions.

- *Action name*: This is a brief label for the action (not quite as brief as the two characters used in PDM).

- *Command*: This specifies where the command is run. The options are as follows:

  » *Normal*: Run the command in the RSE server job (discussed later in this chapter).

  » *Batch*: Run the command in a new batch job via the SBMJOB command. This uses the preferences specified for SBMJOB parameters on the Remote Systems > i5/OS > Command Execution preference page.

  » *Interactive*: Run the command in an interactive job. This requires you have an emulator associated with the RSE connection, using the STRRSESVR command invoked in the emulator. (For more on this, see chapter 9.)

You can then type the actual command to run when this action is invoked. Use the **Insert variable** button (or Ctrl+Space) to view and select valid substitution variables. PDM-like substitution variables are available here. Values for the substitution variables are plugged in at runtime based on the current selection.

Click the **Edit** button to edit the command in a separate edit window (which is actually not so useful). Click the **Browse** button to browse for the command on i5/OS. Use the **Prompt** button to prompt the command currently entered in the Command area, to assist in entering parameters.

The following options can be used to customize when your command appears and how it is run:

- *Comment:* This appears as a tooltip for your action when you hover the mouse pointer over the action.

- *Prompt first*: This indicates whether the command should be prompted before it is run.

- *Refresh after:* Use this if you want the RSE to refresh the selected artifacts in the Remote Systems view or the Object Table view after the command completes. This is useful if the action changes attributes of the selected resource, say for example, the action changes the name of the selected member.

- *Show action:* This shows the action in the pop-up menu when it applies as defined for the selected types. If you want to temporarily disable the action to show, you do not have to delete the action; just deselect this checkbox.

- *Single selection only:* This shows the action only when a single object or member is selected.

- *Invoke once*: This collects the full names of all selected resources into a temporary member, named by substitution variables: ML, MF, and MM. These hold the full name of each object, delimited by blanks. The action will be invoked once for all selected objects, instead of once for each selected object.

The RSE allows you to define collections of object and member types and refer to them by a group name. These collections are referred to as *named types*. Named types facilitate the scoping of user actions to one or more resource types. For example, the predefined named type "RPG" consists of all members types RPG*, RPT*, SQLRPG, and SQLRPGLE. If you define a member action to apply to the RPG named type, it will appear in the pop-up menu for members of these member types.

Select the resource types that an action applies to by selecting the names from the Defined Types and adding them to the Selected Types. To edit the defined named type, click the **Edit** button. This opens the Work With Named Types dialog, where you can create and delete named types and modify which resource are associated with existing named types.

Once the user-defined action is created, if you right-click an object that matches one of the actions selected types, the action will appear on the cascading User Actions menu. For example, Figure 10–5 shows that an object action named "Create Duplicate Object" will apply to the object types PGM and SAVFILE. When you right-click an object of one of these types, the action will be listed in the pop-up menu, as shown in Figure 10–6.

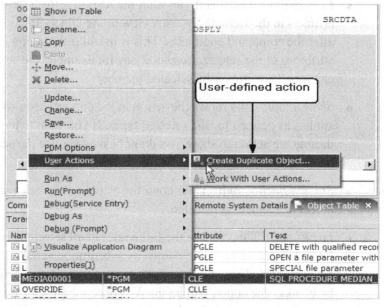

Figure 10–6: The user-defined action "Create Duplicate Object."

The Data Table

The RSE can display the contents of data physical file members in the Data Table view. Right-click the physical file and select **Show in Table > Data** to display the view, as shown in Figure 10–7.

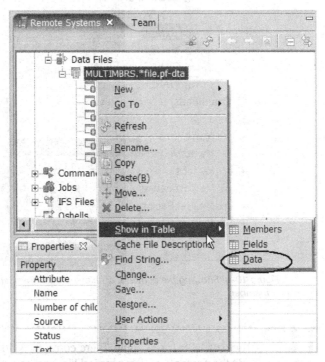

Figure 10–7: Showing the contents of the first data physical file member.

You can also right-click a specific data physical file member and select the **Show in Table** action (Figure 10–8) to display the contents of the selected member in the view. Notice here that there is no Show in Table submenu like there is for physical files. Data physical files have three types of information that can be shown in a table view: member list, fields, and data. Only the data option is applicable to an individual data member.

The Data Table view is read-only. Records in the member are displayed as rows in a table, with columns representing the fields in the record format. The column heading contains the name of the field. Field values are formatted according to the field data types.

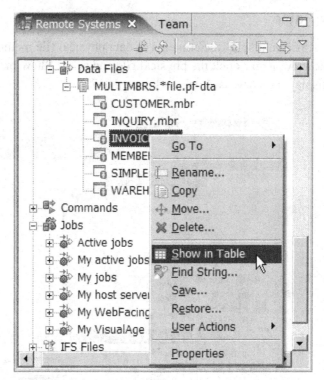

Figure 10–8: Showing the contents of selected data physical file member.

TIP The data table is read-only. There currently is no support to edit the contents of data physical file members in the RSE.

If the data physical file is keyed, the key field(s) will display the "key" icon () in the column heading, as shown in Figure 10–9. If the data physical file is sequential, there will be a special column "*RCDNBR" to represent the record number, as shown in Figure 10–10.

PARTNO	PARTSHIP	BRANCH	TIME_T	QTY	DESTINATN	COUNTRY
00002	1999-09-02	20322	14.15.30	2,012...	CHICAGO AIRPORT	USA
00003	1999-09-13	20333	13.15.30	33,33...	LAS VEGAS AIRPORT	USA
00005	1999-09-09	12345	11.12.16	1,234...	BUTTONVILLE AIRPORT	CANADA
00010	1999-09-10	10010	10.30.15	4,001...	VANCOUVER AIRPORT	CANADA
00011	2000-01-11	12345	11.11.11	110.00	FUN WORLD	ARGENTINA

Figure 10–9: Key fields in the Data Table view.

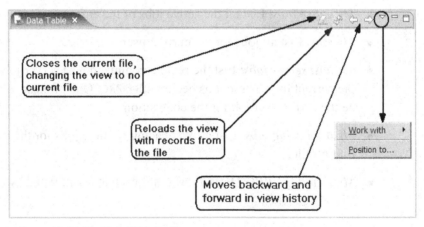

Figure 10–10: A sequential file in the Data Table view.

Null-capable fields that are null will be shown in the Data Table with the "null" icon (⬚⊘) followed by the word "*NULL."

Working with the Data Table view

You can control the Data Table view using the view toolbar, as shown in Figure 10–11 .

Figure 10–11: The Data Table toolbar.

The view menu contains two actions: "Work with" and "Position to." The "Work with" action is enabled only when there are items in the view history. It lists the items in the view history for easy switching to a previous data member. A maximum of ten items is shown in the list.

The "Position to" action opens a Position To dialog that prompts for the relative record number for non-keyed files or key values for keyed files. Partial key values are allowed in the dialog. The view is positioned to the search value indicated or the next available record if the specified record is not present in the file.

TIP

Instead of selecting "Position to," just start typing when the Data Table view has focus. The Position To dialog automatically opens up.

Working with i5/OS Jobs

You can monitor and perform actions on i5/OS jobs using the Jobs subsystem. The Jobs subsystem, like all other RSE subsystems, uses filters to display only a subset of all the jobs running on i5/OS.

If you expand the Jobs subsystems, you will see that it predefines six filters:

- *Active jobs*: List all the currently active jobs on the i5/OS server.

- *My active jobs*: List all the active jobs of the current user.

- *My jobs*: List all jobs for the current user.

- *My host server jobs*: List the remote command host server jobs for the current user. These jobs begin with QZRC. One of these jobs will be the RSE server job for the connection.

- *My WebFacing jobs*: List all WebFacing runtime jobs for the current user profile.

- *My VisualAge RPG DDM Jobs*: List jobs that are initiated by VisualAge RPG.

By expanding any one of these job filters, you will see the corresponding jobs, grouped by i5/OS job subsystems. (Not to be confused with the RSE Object, Commands, Jobs, IFS Files, and Qshells subsystems!) There is a preference on the Remote Systems > i5/OS > Jobs Subsystem preference page to hide the job subsystems, so filters immediately show the list of jobs.

For example, expand the **My active jobs** filter to list all of your active jobs, grouped by i5/OS job subsystems, as shown in Figure 10–12.

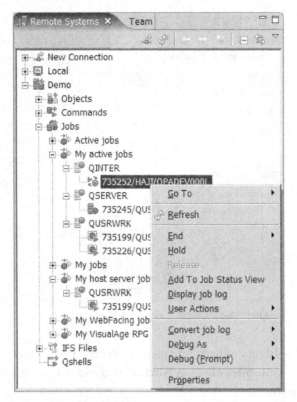

Figure 10–12: Job actions.

Job Filters

Library, object, and member filters are discussed in chapter 5. You can also create job filters, which are similar to using the Work with Active Jobs (WRKACTJOB) 5250 command.

To create a job filter, right-click the **Jobs** subsystem and select **New > Job Filter**. This opens the New Job filter dialog, shown in Figure 10–13, where you can specify the filtering criteria.

You can filter based on a generic job name. For example, specify **HA*** as the job name to see all jobs whose names begin with *HA*. If you know the exact number of the job you want, you can specify it in the "Job number" field. Otherwise, leave this field as an asterisk to search all the jobs. For active jobs, you can specify a current user profile and the i5/OS job subsystem to include jobs from.

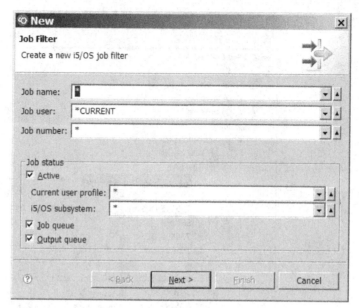

Figure 10–13: Creating a new job filter.

Just like library, object, and member filters, you have to give your job filter a name after clicking **Next.** This name will appear under the Jobs subsystem.

Managing Jobs

To display the attributes of a job, right-click the job and select **Properties**. The Properties dialog contains four pages for displaying different types of attributes: Status, Definition, International, and Run. These correspond to options 1, 2, and 3 on the 5250 Work with Job menu.

Actions are performed on a job by right-clicking the job in the Remote Systems view, Job Status view, or Remote System Details view. This includes actions such as holding or releasing the job, ending the job, displaying the job log, and debugging the job.

Another action, called "Add To Job Status View," opens the Job Status view and adds the job to the view. The Job Status view, shown in Figure 10–14, allows you to monitor a collection of jobs. This view displays the following:

- The date and time a job was submitted

- The name of the job

- The name of the RSE connection associated with the job

- The status of the job

- The type of task being performed by the job:

  » *Batch Compile:* Batch compile jobs submitted by the RSE

  » *Batch Program*: Batch programs running and submitted by the RSE

  » *Batch Command*: Batch commands submitted by the RSE

  » *Project_build_name Build:* Jobs submitted as the result of an i5/OS project build

  » *Blank:* Regular jobs that are explicitly added to the Job Status view

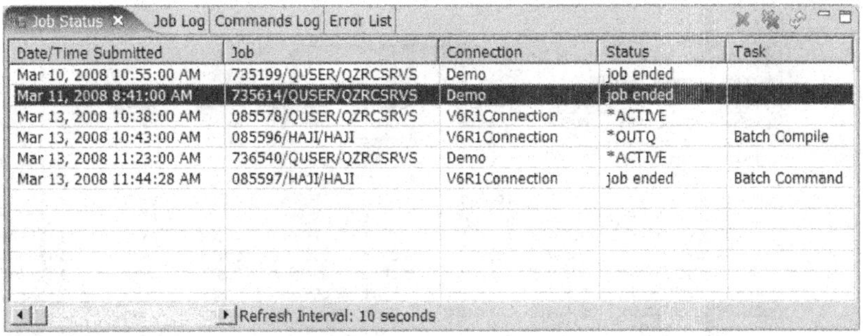

Figure 10–14: The Job Status view.

Jobs remain in the Job Status view until they are explicitly removed. To remove one or more jobs, select the job(s), then click the "remove" icon ( ) in the view's toolbar. To remove all jobs in the view, click the "remove all" icon ( ).

There are preferences on the Remote Systems > i5/OS > Command Execution preference page to automatically add jobs for batch compiles and batch commands to the Job Status view.

User-defined Actions

Just as you can create user action for members and objects, you can create user actions for jobs. Right-click the **Jobs** subsystem and select **Work With > User Actions**. This opens the Work With User Actions dialog, which is similar to the one you saw in the section "Creating User-defined Actions" earlier in this chapter. Fill out the details, and give your action a name. The substitution variables here pertain to the selected job when your action is invoked. Once the user action is created, it appears in the cascading User Actions menu in the pop-up menu for jobs.

The Table View for Jobs

If you right-click the Jobs subsystem, a job filter, or an i5/OS job subsystem, you will see an action to "Show in Table." Selecting this action displays the contents of the selection in the Remote System Details view. This view shows different details, depending on what was selected. Figure 10–15 shows the contents of the Remote System Details view when an i5/OS job subsystem, in this case QSERVER, is selected when Show in Table is invoked.

Name	User	Number	Status	Subsystem	Curr...	Job type	Entered system
085566/QUSER/QPWFS...	QUSER	085566	*ACTIVE	QSERVER	HAJI	Batch	3/13/08 10:31 AM
085172/QPGMR/QSERVER	QPGMR	085172	*ACTIVE	QSERVER	QPGMR	Autostart	3/13/08 10:03 AM
085494/QPGMR/QZLSSE...	QPGMR	085494	*ACTIVE	QSERVER	QPGMR	Batch	3/13/08 10:04 AM
085533/QUSER/QPWFS...	QUSER	085533	*ACTIVE	QSERVER	QSECOFR	Batch	3/13/08 10:12 AM
085148/QUSER/QZDAINIT	QUSER	085148	*ACTIVE	QSERVER	QUSER	Batch	3/13/08 10:03 AM
085153/QUSER/QPWFS...	QUSER	085153	*ACTIVE	QSERVER	QUSER	Batch	3/13/08 10:03 AM
085156/QUSER/QPWFS...	QUSER	085156	*ACTIVE	QSERVER	QUSER	Batch	3/13/08 10:03 AM
085158/QUSER/QPWFS...	QUSER	085158	*ACTIVE	QSERVER	QUSER	Batch	3/13/08 10:03 AM
085159/QUSER/QPWFS...	QUSER	085159	*ACTIVE	QSERVER	QUSER	Batch	3/13/08 10:03 AM
085162/QUSER/QPWFS...	QUSER	085162	*ACTIVE	QSERVER	QUSER	Batch	3/13/08 10:03 AM
085165/QUSER/QZLSFILE	QUSER	085165	*ACTIVE	QSERVER	QUSER	Batch	3/13/08 10:03 AM

Figure 10–15: The Remote System Details view.

The Integrated File System

Yes, you can access the Integrated File System using the RSE. This is similar to Work with Object Links (WRKLNK) command, but it's much easier to access and work with the IFS in the RSE than from a 5250 emulator! This section will get you started accessing the IFS using the RSE.

Access to the IFS is through the IFS Files RSE subsystem. Expanding the IFS Files subsystem displays three predefined IFS filters:

- *File systems:* This lists most of the file systems available on i5/OS. There are quite a few! For example, there is the root files system (/), QSYS.LIB (native file system), and QDLS (Document Library Services file system).

- *Root file system:* This lists all folders and files under the IFS root (/).

- *Home:* This lists the contents of the */home* IFS directory.

Creating Filters

By now, you've probably realized that filters in the RSE are powerful tools that can display subsets of i5/OS artifacts, so you only see what you need. To create filters for IFS files and folders, right-click the IFS Files subsystem and select **New > Filter**. Alternatively, right-click an IFS folder and select **New > Filter**, as shown in Figure 10–16.

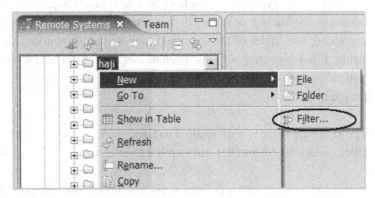

Figure 10–16: Creating filters.

This opens the New File Filter dialog, shown in Figure 10–17. If you selected New > Filter on an IFS folder, the folder name is pre-filled with the selection.

The folder field specifies which IFS folder to use for the filter. You can subset by file name or by file types. The default is the asterisk wildcard, which subsets by file name and includes all files. You can specify a simple file name or a generic name containing up to two wildcard characters, such as *ab*cd**.

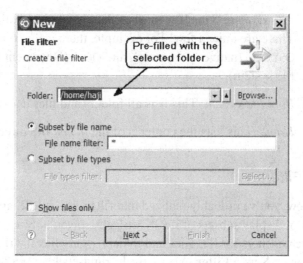

Figure 10–17: The New File Filter dialog.

To filter by file types, select **Subset by file types**. Then, click the **Select** button to choose one or more file types to be included when the filter is expanded. Only files of the selected types will be shown for this filter string. File types are really just filename extensions. The list shown in the Select Types dialog comes from the General > Editors > File Associations preference page.

The filename filter is only applied to files; folders always appear for the filter. Select the **Show files only** option to exclude all folders from the filter.

Filters can contain multiple filter strings, although this wizard only prompts for one. To add more filter strings, right-click the filter name in the Remote Systems view, and select **Change**.

The Table View for IFS Files

The Object Table view is used when working with the QSYS file system. This is discussed in detail in chapter 5. However, the "Show in Table" action is also available for IFS folders and files. When this action is invoked, the files and folders are shown in the Remote System Details view. This is a generic version of the Object Table view and is used for RSE resources other than libraries, objects, and members. Earlier in this chapter, the section on using the table view for jobs describes how this view can be used to show i5/OS jobs.

Working with IFS Files

You can create new files and folders in the IFS by right-clicking an IFS filter or folder. The pop-up menu contains a New menu, which contain two submenu actions: "File" and "Folder." Selecting a filter creates the new folder or file in the folder specified for the filter.

Right-click an IFS file, and you will see that all of the typical options, like verify and compile, are available here. Working with IFS files and folders is easier and more intuitive in the RSE compared to the green screen, where you need to use WRKLNK command to locate files and folders. (Then, even after locating a file, there is no quick way of compiling!)

TIP ....
You can copy source members from a source physical file and paste them into an IFS folder to copy the source member to the IFS. This strips the sequence number and date fields from the source member, since the RPG and COBOL compilers cannot compile IFS files with these fields.
....

Once you have mastered using the RSE with the QSYS file system, it's easy to start working with the Integrated File System using the RSE.

Editing IFS Files

Just like native source members, IFS files can be edited using the Remote Systems LPEX Editor. Once an IFS file is open in the Remote Systems LPEX Editor, almost all of the actions discussed in chapters 6 and 7 are available. So, you can edit IFS files the same way you edit source members from the QSYS file system.

Unlike source members, the Remote Systems LPEX Editor and Screen Designer are not the only editor options available for IFS files. While the Remote Systems LPEX Editor is the default editor for RPG, COBOL, CL, and DDS files, you can use other editors like the Text Editor or System Editor. Be aware that if you edit an RPG, COBOL, CL, or DDS source member with a different editor, you will not have the Remote Systems LPEX Editor and language-specific editing features.

An example of when you might want to use a different editor is for non-RPG, COBOL, CL, and DDS source files. When editing an XML file in the IFS, for example, you can use the Workbench XML Editor. To open an IFS file with a non-default editor, right-click the file, click the cascading **Open With** menu, and select one of the editors. IFS files use the editor associations specified on the General > Editors > File Associations preference page.

Remote Search

You can also search IFS files and folders, right from the RSE. There are two ways of invoking the search: right-click a folder or file and select the **Search** action, or using the Workbench **Search > Remote** menu. Both actions open the Remote Search dialog, shown in Figure 10–18.

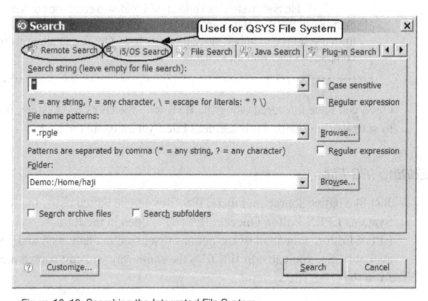

Figure 10–18: Searching the Integrated File System.

This dialog allows regular expressions for the search string and filename patterns to search for. To specify to recursively search subfolders within the selected folder, check the **Search subfolders** checkbox.

The results of the search are populated in the Remote Search view. Working with the IFS search results is the same as working with search results from the QSYS file system, discussed earlier in this chapter.

User-defined Actions

To create user-defined actions for IFS files and folders, right-click the file or folder and select **User Actions > Work With User Actions**. This opens the Work With User Actions dialog, similar to the one shown earlier in this chapter for the QSYS file system. For the QSYS file system, user-defined actions are grouped into member and object actions. For the IFS, user-defined actions are grouped into file or folder actions. Some common folder and file actions are predefined. To define your own action, click either **File action** or **Folder action** on the left side, then fill out the action details on the right side, as shown in Figure 10–19.

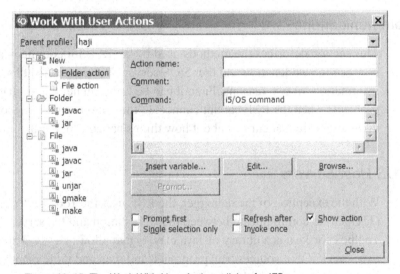

Figure 10–19: The Work With User Actions dialog for IFS.

The Command field has four options. The first three, "i5/OS command," "i5/OS bath command," and "i5/OS interactive command" are the same as the "Normal," "Batch," and "Interactive" options described in the section "Creating User-defined Actions" earlier in this chapter. The fourth option, "Qshell command," runs the command in a Qshell.

The rest of the options are also the same as those described in the section on user-defined actions. The substitution variables change depending on the command type, to accommodate the Qshell and QSYS commands.

Preferences

The RPG and COBOL compilers do not support IFS files with sequence number and date fields, so the RSE automatically strips these off each line when they are detected during the copy of a local file to an IFS file. Files that do not have sequence numbers and date fields, but that still have numeric data in the first 12 bytes, might confuse this automatic detection.

On the Remote Systems > i5/OS > IFS Files Subsystem preference page, you can specify a list of file types to prompt first, before automatically removing sequence numbers and date fields when copying local files to the IFS.

Communications

This section describes the methods used by the RSE for communicating between the workstation and the i5/OS server. We've included this information for two reasons. First, it can be useful in helping to diagnose problems when the RSE cannot connect to the remote system. Second, many users are just curious about how things happen "under the hood."

i5/OS Host Servers

With the exception of the debugger, the RSE uses the Toolbox for Java (JTOpen) to communicate between the workstation and the server. The Toolbox for Java is a library of Java classes that allows any Java application to access i5/OS resources, run programs, and read and write members. JTOpen was originally developed in the Rochester lab, but is now an open-source project on SourceForge.net (*http://jt400.sourceforge.net*).

In most cases, the JTOpen library provides direct Java APIs to access everything needed by the RSE. In the cases where it doesn't, the RSE accesses the required information by calling i5/OS APIs using JTOpen's program call support.

JTOpen communicates with the host servers that are included with i5/OS. This means there is no RSE server that needs to be installed and configured on i5/OS, and in most cases, the RSE is able to connect to i5/OS without having to do any setup other than starting the required host servers, if they are not running.

Table 10–1 lists all of the host servers required by the RSE, along with the port number each server listens on, the command used to start the server, and the part of the RSE that requires the server.

Table 10–1: Required Host Servers		
Host Server (Port)	**Command to Start**	**Related RSE Function**
Sign-on (8476)	STRHOSTSVR SERVER(*SIGNON)	Authentication
Remote command (8475)	STRHOSTSVR SERVER(*RMTCMD)	Everything
Distributed Data Manager (DDM) (446)	STRTCPSVR SERVER(*DDM)	Reading and writing source members
File (8473)	STRHOSTSVR SERVER(*FILE)	Batch compiles, batch i5/OS project builds, and Integrated File System access
Data queue (8472)	STRHOSTSVR SERVER(*DTAQ)	Interactive job support (STRRSESVR command)
Server mapper (449)	STRHOSTSVR SERVER(*SVRMAP)	Required by JTOpen
Central (8470)	STRHOSTSVR SERVER(*CENTRAL)	Required by JTOpen

The remote command and DDM host servers are key to RSE communications. The remote command host server is used for everything except IFS file access and reading and writing source members. This includes resolving library, object, member, and job filters, running commands, running user-defined actions, compiling, and verifying. Each RSE connection has its own remote command host server job allocated to it. This is considered the *RSE server job*. When you expand the library list filter in the RSE, it is the library list of this job that is shown.

Remote command host server jobs are named QZRCSRVS and run in the QUSRWRK subsystem, by default. The job user is QUSER, but the current user profile for the job is the user profile used with the RSE connection.

The DDM host server is used by the RSE for displaying data members in the Data Table view and for downloading and uploading source members (editing, adding to an i5/OS project, and copy and pasting to the local connection). Each RSE connection has its own DDM host server job associated with it. These jobs have the same properties as the remote command host server jobs, except they are named QRWTSRVR.

The sign-on, server mapper, and central host servers are required by the Toolbox for Java. The file host server needs to be started if you want to run batch compiles or access the Integrated File Subsystem. The data queue host server only needs to be started if you plan to use the STRRSESVR command on i5/OS to associate a 5250 emulator with an RSE connection (as described in chapter 9).

The Integrated i5/OS Debugger uses its own debug server for communications. This server can be started with the STRDBGSVR command on i5/OS. The debug server listens on port 3825 on i5/OS.

Actions to start and stop the host servers are included in the RSE under Remote Servers in the Objects subsystem's pop-up menu. Each of the host servers is listed, along with start and stop actions, as shown in Figure 10–20. The start and stop actions are enabled based on the current status of the server. Both actions are disabled if the RSE connection is not connected.

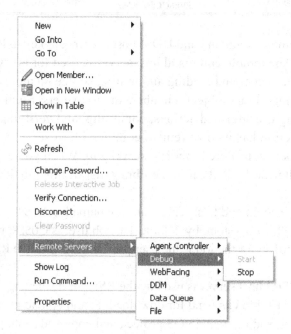

Figure 10–20: Host server actions.

Other Server Requirements

The i5/OS host servers described above are the only hard requirement for connecting to i5/OS. However, parts of WebSphere Development Studio are required for certain RSE functions. WebSphere Development Studio is the i5/OS product that includes the RPG, COBOL, C, and C++ compilers, and ADTS (5722-WDS for V5R4 and earlier; 5761-WDS for V6R1). WebSphere Development Studio option 60 installs a library called QDEVTOOLS that includes programs and service programs required by the RSE.

The RSE functions that require option 60 are remote text searching, batch compiles, i5/OS project builds, debugging, and remote Qshells. You can connect to a machine that doesn't have option 60 installed (such as a production machine), but you won't be able to perform any of the RSE functions that require this option.

Verifying the Connection

The first time you create a connection to a remote system, check that all required host servers are started and all required PTFs are applied. This can easily be done. Right-click any of the subsystems under the connection, and select **Verify Connection** from the pop-up menu. This checks that the host servers are started, required PTFs are applied, and the server can callback to the workstation. The results of these checks are shown in the Verify Connection dialog, shown in Figure 10–21.

The top section of the dialog shows each of the required host servers and whether or not the server is started. This actually shows whether the RSE could connect to the host server. The most common cause of a failed connection is the host server not being started; however, the host server might be started, and a firewall could be blocking the connection.

The middle section of the dialog shows the results of checking required PTFs. When the "verify connection" action is invoked, it first checks the IBM Web site for an updated list of required PTFs. If you have an Internet connection, and the HTTP connection is not blocked by a firewall, the latest list is retrieved and used for checking. Otherwise, the locally stored list is used. The list of required PTFs is always shipped with the product and updated on the IBM Web site as new PTFS become available.

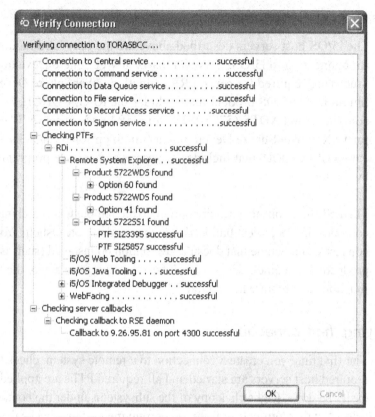

Figure 10–21: The Verify Connection dialog.

The bottom section of the dialog tests whether or not the server can callback to the workstation. This is only required if you use the STRRSESVR command to associate a 5250 emulator with an RSE connection. It is quite common for this check to fail because of workstation firewall software and network address translation. (See the troubleshooting section at the end of chapter 9 for additional details.) It is not required for regular use of the RSE, so don't be too worried if it fails.

TIP

To copy entries from the Verify Connection dialog, select them, right-click, and select **Copy Resources**. This can be useful if you need to email a list of PTFs to your system administrators for them to install

See the troubleshooting section at the end of this chapter for a list of common reasons why an RSE connection might fail to connect to a remote system.

Caching

The RSE caches information on the workstation for two reasons: to improve performance and to allow disconnected development. This section describes what types of information are cached and when the information is used by the RSE.

The Library, Object, and Member List Cache

Lists of libraries, objects, and members are cached by the RSE to allow the RSE tree to be quickly restored to its previous state when the Workbench is restarted. Details on this behavior, and the preference page for controlling it, are covered in chapter 5.

The cache is stored by the hostname, as specified for the RSE connection. Multiple connections can share a cache if they specify the same hostname. If you create two connections to the same server, but one uses a short hostname (such as *torasbcc*), and the other uses a fully qualified hostname (such as *torasbcc.ibm.com*), they will use different caches.

The maximum cache size and location are configurable on the Remote Systems > i5/OS > Cache preference page, shown in Figure 10–22. The cache location defaults to the .metadata area of the workspace.

Click the **Clear Cache** button on the preference page to clear all cached information from disk (except for cached files, as discussed later in this chapter). Any information that has already been loaded into memory is not cleared. We recommend that you shut down and restart the Workbench after clearing the cache, to ensure that in-memory information is not written back to disk. Alternatively, you can shut down the Workbench and delete the directory specified in the cache location.

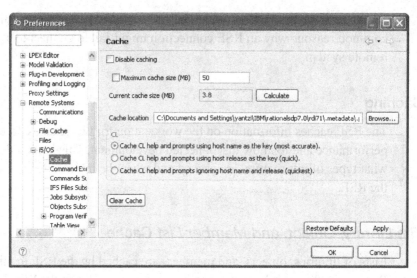

Figure 10–22: The caching preference page.

The Program Verifier Cache

The program verifiers share the same cache location, behavior, and preferences as described above. The program verifiers cache quite a bit more information than just lists of libraries, objects, and members. For example, they cache descriptions for externally described files, sort sequence tables, file overrides, and environment variables. Chapter 7 contains information on the program verifiers and details about using, and refreshing, cached information with them.

The CL Cache

The RSE does not ship the help for CL commands or the CL command definitions that are required for prompting CL commands on the workstation. Instead, the help and command definitions are downloaded from the server as required, and cached locally.

The CL cache uses the same preferences for cache size and location as described above. It also includes preferences for controlling how the CL help and command definitions are grouped in the cache. This grouping results in a trade-off among accuracy, speed, and cache size. You can select to cache CL help and prompts based on the host name from which they were retrieved. This gives the most accurate information because different hosts might have different versions of non-IBM commands and different command defaults. This option might be slower, however, if you are actively using multiple hosts because cached information from one host is not reused by other hosts.

You can select to have CL help and prompts cached by i5/OS version, so all servers running the same version of i5/OS will share cached CL information. This is less accurate than caching by hostname, since the command version and command defaults stored in the cache will reflect the server from which the command information was downloaded.

The third option is to cache all CL help together, ignoring the hostname and i5/OS version altogether. This is the fastest because there is a higher probability that information will be available from the cache if you are using multiple machines. However, it is less accurate for the command defaults problem previously described and because it won't reflect differences in command parameters that may occur between i5/OS versions.

Some cached CL command definitions are only used when working offline; new command definitions are always retrieved when working online. This includes commands that use proxy chains, such as the compiler commands.

The Member and File Cache

Source members, and their last modified timestamps, are cached in a Workspace project called RemoteSystemsTempFiles. Before a member is downloaded, a check is made to see if the member exists in the project and if the last modified timestamp of the cached copy equals the last modified timestamp of the remote copy. The local cached member is used instead of re-downloading the member if the cached copy exists and the timestamps are equal. The remote member is still locked while the member is open in the editor.

A maximum size (in megabytes) can be set for the file cache on the Remote Systems > File Cache preference page. There is also a button on this preference page that will clear all cached files and members. You should close all editors before clearing the cached files.

Troubleshooting

Below are some common problems related to the topics in this chapter, along with suggestions on diagnosing and fixing the problems:

- *I can't connect to the remote i5/OS server.*

  First, run the "verify connection" action described in the section "Verifying the Connection" earlier in this chapter. This will tell you whether or not the RSE can connect to the i5/OS host servers. A failed connection reported to one or more of the host servers could mean either the host server is not started, or a firewall is blocking the connection.

  Start the host servers that failed through the RSE host server actions, the IBM Systems Director Navigator for i5/OS Web interface, or in a 5250 emulator. If the verify connection action still reports some of the host server connections failing, the problem is likely related to a firewall. If you have workstation firewall software installed on your PC, you might need to configure a rule to allow connections from your PC to the server on the ports used by the host servers.

  If the "verify connection" action reports that connections to all host servers are successful, your user profile might not be authorized to use the host servers, or an exit program might be preventing you from connecting to the host server.

- *I can connect to the i5/OS server but I can't edit.*

  This is a fairly frequent problem reported by users. It is almost always caused by one of the following:

  - » The DDM host server is not started.

  - » Workstation firewall software is blocking the request.

  - » A DDM exit program is blocking the connection or member-open request.

  - » Your user profile is associated with a job description that no longer exists.

First, check that your workstation can connect to the DDM host server using the "verify connection" action. (This shows up as the record access service in the verify connection results.) If the connection fails, either the host server is not started, or a firewall is blocking the connection.

We have found that many workstation firewalls are configured to allow connections to all host servers except the DDM host server. We suspect this has to do with the DDM port being in a lower range than the ports used by other host servers.

If the "verify connection" action reports a successful connection to the record access service, have your systems administrator check if there is an exit program on the DDM host server that is blocking your requests.

Finally, check that the job description associated with your i5/OS user profile exists. The remote command host server allows connections with user profiles that are associated to job descriptions that don't exist, but the DDM host server won't allow the connection. So, you would be able to connect with the RSE, but not be able to edit any source members.

- *The connection to my server drops after about 15 minutes of inactivity.*

  » The default Windows setting for sending "keep alive" packets over a socket connection is two hours. You can lower this setting so "keep alive" packets are sent more frequently, to avoid the connection being dropped. See the KeepAliveTime setting documented in the Microsoft knowledgebase article at *http://support.microsoft.com/default.aspx?kbid=314053*

- *Everything seems to be hosed! Should I re-install?*

  There are two main components to using the product: the Workbench and the Workspace. The Workbench is composed of the plug-ins you have installed into a package group. The Workspace is where all your RSE connections, filters, preferences, customized layouts, and local projects are stored.

In the rare case that something seems to be wrong, chances are that it's the Workspace, and not the product install. The simplest way to determine this is to start the Workbench with a clean Workspace, and see if everything is working fine in the new Workspace. If so, the problem is with the old Workspace. You can copy the RemoteSystemsConnections project from the old Workspace to the new one, to copy over your RSE-related resources.

We do not recommend that you delete the old Workspace. Instead, contact IBM support to track down the cause of the problem.

- *Where are the log files stored?*

The main Workbench log file is stored in *[workspace location]/. metadata/.log* (where *[workspace location]* is the directory you specified for your Workspace). This is where all Workbench tools write their log messages.

A separate log file is used by the RSE communications layer. This file is written to *C:\Documents and Settings\[windows userID] \.eclipse\RSE\rsecomm.log.*

Another log of events would be the job log for the RSE server job. This is the QZRCSRVS job used by the RSE connection. (See the section "i5/OS Host Servers" earlier in this chapter for additional details.)

- *Why do I get a message that the server is not responding or the current communication request is taking a long time?*

If a communication request takes longer than 60 seconds, a separate thread is created to perform some diagnostics. A dialog reports that the request is taking a long time and asks if you want to cancel the request or continue. The original request continues to process while the diagnostics and dialog are displayed. To change the default of 60 seconds, go to the **Remote Systems > i5/OS** preference page.

- *Why do I see duplicate compile actions?*

Compile actions are stored in RSE profiles. When a new Workspace is created, your private profile is populated with the predefined RSE compile actions. The team profile is not populated with any compile actions. If you load someone else's private RSE profile into your Workspace and make it active, you will see the compile actions from both your private profile and the other person's. This is what causes the duplicate compile actions.

Create a new RSE profile if you want to share connections, filters, user-defined actions and custom compile commands. This new profile is not pre-populated with the default compile commands, so you and your teammates can load this profile without having duplicate compile commands show up.

11

i5/OS Projects: The Other Way to Manage Your Source

When the Rational Developer for System i development team originally designed the Workbench-based tools for RPG and COBOL, it was faced with a fundamental question on where the source code should reside. RPG and COBOL developers are accustomed to having the source code stored in i5/OS source members and remotely accessing the members on the server, using SEU/PDM via a 5250 telnet session.

In this environment, team support often consists of setting up a single development library containing the source for an application, with the library being shared by a group of developers. Source members are locked while they are opened in SEU to prevent others from making changes at the same time.

This mode of development is quite different from the project-based approach used by the other Workbench tools, like the Java and Web tools. In the project-based approach, all source files are stored locally on the workstation in projects in the Workspace. When working in a team, each developer has a copy of the projects on his or her own workstation. Changes are managed using a software configuration-management system like Subversion or Rational ClearCase.

There are advantages to both approaches, which is why the development team ended up supporting both. The RSE supports the traditional approach of keeping the source in source members on the server. i5/OS projects provide the alternative approach, where source code is organized and stored in local Workspace projects.

Using i5/OS projects does not mean you have to give up all the great features of the RSE. You still use the Remote Systems LPEX Editor when editing members from i5/OS projects. You still have tokenizing, syntax checking, prompting, the outline view, content assist, the indent view, program verifiers, and integrated help. Compile errors are still downloaded and displayed in the Error List view when compiling from i5/OS projects.

If you use i5/OS projects for working with your source code, you still need to use the RSE to manage your libraries and objects and to run and debug your programs. As you will see throughout this chapter, the RSE and its features are tightly integrated with i5/OS projects.

What Exactly Are i5/OS Projects?

Before we look at why you might want to use i5/OS projects, let's start with a deeper look at what they are and how they work.

Projects are the highest level of organization inside of the Eclipse Workspace; all files and folders must be in a project. Projects have a type that defines properties for the project, what types of files the project contains, and what actions are available on the project and files inside the project.

i5/OS projects are Eclipse projects that understand i5/OS libraries, source files, and members. Each project is associated with a server (an RSE connection) and a single library via project properties. Folders within the project map to source physical files in the associated library, and files within those folders map to source members. i5/OS projects provide actions for the following:

- Import remote members into the project.

- Push changed members from the project to the associated library.

- Launch compiles directly from the project.

- Push changes and build the project.

When it comes time to compile changes from your i5/OS project, you have two choices: compile each member individually, or set up a build for the project. Compiling from an i5/OS project is covered later in this chapter. Project builds are intended to compile (and bind if required) all members from the project via a single action. This is done by configuring a *build style* for the project. Configuring and using project builds is also covered later in this chapter.

The following is a high-level overview of using i5/OS projects to work with your application:

1. Create an i5/OS project and populate it with source members.

2. Make changes to the source members.

3. Push changed source members from the local project to the associated library on i5/OS.

4. Compile each member or run a project wide build.

5. Repeat steps 2 through 4 until changes are completed.

6. (Optional) Delete the project.

How many projects you create and when a project should be deleted will largely depend on how you decide to set up your projects. You might decide to create a new project for each change you make to an application, and only populate the project with the members required for that change. In this case, you will be creating and deleting projects quite frequently.

Alternatively, you might decide to create a single project and store all the source members for the application in it. In this case, you will be creating only a few projects and never deleting them.

Why Use i5/OS Projects?

The RSE makes it easy to start using the modern RPG and COBOL development tools without having to change the way you currently manage source code. This makes it a lot easier for SEU and PDM users to start using the new tools. It also allows some developers in a shop to start using the new tools, while others continue to use SEU and PDM. (Those poor people!)

When IBM first came out with i5/OS projects, it touted disconnected development and more structured development as the primary reasons to use them. With i5/OS projects, the source code is stored locally on the workstation, so you don't need a network connection to the i5/OS server in order to edit your source code. You can work on the plane, in the car (as long as you're not driving), or at home on the weekend (sorry).

Using i5/OS projects, you can set up a more structured development environment by doing the following:

- Break up an application into multiple projects, with each project representing a well-defined component of the overall application.

- Create a build script that can be used to build the overall project, instead of manually compiling individual members.

- Use i5/OS projects in conjunction with a software configuration-management system to manage versions and releases, and to track changes made to source members. Because i5/OS projects are normal Workspace projects, they can be managed using any change-management system that provides Eclipse support, such as the open-source offerings CVS and Subversion, or a commercial offering like IBM Rational ClearCase.

As it turned out, i5/OS projects were not widely used for the first few years they existed for a few reasons. First, Virtual Private Networks (VPNs), along with increasingly ubiquitous Internet access, reduced the need for disconnected development. Second, it's not a trivial task to break up an existing application into smaller components and set up an intelligent project-level build.

However, there has been an increase in the adoption of i5/OS projects recently, for a reason that was not originally envisioned: developers want a way to manage and track their own software changes. Before making a change to an application, the developer creates an i5/OS project and adds the members needing modification to the project. They make the changes locally in the project, and then push and build/compile the changes on the server as required. This provides two main benefits:

- The developer has a single project that stores all members that have been modified for the new feature or bug fix.

- Using the Workspace's local history support (discussed later in this chapter), developers can track modifications made to those members over a short period of time.

Some developers have even gone so far as to set up their own CVS or Subversion server to track their personal changes, as well as those made by the rest of the team. These are developers who recognize the benefits of using a change-management system, but who work in organizations that have not yet seen the light! A section at the end of this chapter covers using i5/OS projects in a team environment, whether or not the rest of the team also uses i5/OS projects.

The i5/OS Projects Perspective

The Workbench includes an i5/OS Projects perspective that has some of the standard Workbench views such as Navigator, Properties, Tasks, Problems, and Outline, as shown in Figure 11–1. It also includes the following i5/OS-specific views:

- *i5/OS Project Navigator*: This is the main view for working with your i5/OS projects and their contained source files and members. From this view, you can right-click a project, source file, or member to access all the local and remote actions that can be performed on it.

- *Job Status*: When you run a batch compile or build from i5/OS projects, the batch job is added to the Job Status view. (See the section on the Job Status view later in this chapter for additional details.)

- *Remote Systems*: This is the Remote Systems view from the RSE perspective. You still need to work with your remote objects, so the Remote Systems view is included in the i5/OS perspective for convenience.

- *Commands Log*: i5/OS projects use RSE connections for running remote commands and compiles. All of these commands are written to this log, along with their completion messages. This is the Commands Log view from the RSE perspective. (See chapter 5 for additional information.)

- *Error List*: The Error List view is not included in the i5/OS Projects perspective by default. It is added to the perspective the first time you retrieve compiler errors from a compile or build. This is the same Error List view used by the RSE.

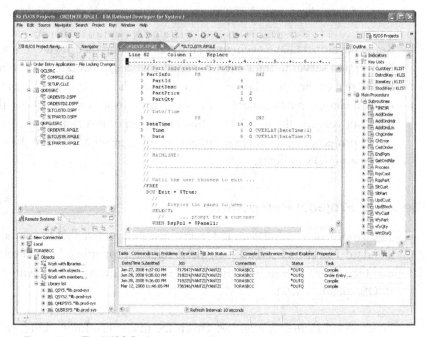

Figure 11-1: The i5/OS Projects perspective.

i5/OS projects are decorated with an *i* decorator on the project icon (⊞). This signifies an i5/OS project. A project generally has a letter or graphic decorator to signify its type. Web projects, for example, have a globe decorator icon.

Setting Up an i5/OS Project

The first step in using i5/OS projects is to set up a new project and add source files and members to it. This is done using either wizards in the Workbench or actions from the RSE. The wizards are useful for creating projects when disconnected or for adding source files and members that do not exist yet.

The RSE actions are useful for creating a new project, or adding a source file or member to an existing project, while connected to the remote system. The RSE actions require less user input than the wizards because most, if not all, required information is inferred based on the context.

Creating a New Project, Source File, or Member

To create a new i5/OS project using the New wizard, right-click in the i5/OS Project Navigator and select **New > i5/OS Project** from the pop-up menu. This opens up the New i5/OS Project wizard dialog, shown in Figure 11–2. Enter a name for the project that represents the contents and/or usage of the project.

Figure 11–2: The New i5/OS Project wizard.

The second page of the New i5/OS Project wizard prompts for the RSE connection and associated library properties for the project, as shown in Figure 11–3. The RSE connection is used by the project for downloading and uploading members, as well as for running remote compiles and builds. The associated library is the library to which all members are uploaded (*pushed*) whenever a push, compile, or build action is invoked.

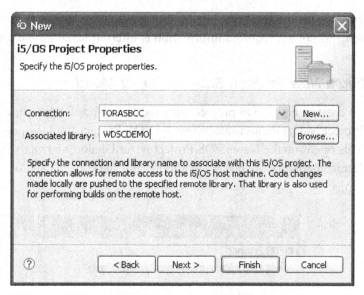

Figure 11–3: The second page of the New i5/OS Project wizard.

A third page in the wizard prompts for the build style to be used with the new project. Build styles are covered later in the chapter. For now, select *NONE.

You can bypass using the wizard to create a new project via a shortcut action in the RSE. Right-click the library you want the project associated with, and select **Create i5/OS Project**. This creates a new i5/OS project associated with the selected library and opens the i5/OS Projects perspective. The name of the project is set to the *RSEConnectionName_ LibraryName*. Change this to a more meaningful name by right-clicking the project and selecting **Rename**.

Just like the New i5/OS Project wizard, there is a New i/5OS Source Physical File wizard that can create a new source physical file in an i5/OS project. If the source file does not exist in the associated library, it is created the first time a member is pushed to the server. If the source file already exists, the information entered in the wizard is ignored.

The first page of the New i/5OS Source Physical File wizard prompts for the name of the source physical file and the i5/OS project in which to create it. The second page of the wizard prompts for additional information required for the Create Source Physical File (CRTSRCPF) command, if the file needs to be created. This information includes the following:

- The CCSID for the file (defaults to *JOB)

- The record length for the file (defaults to 112)

- Whether or not the file contains DBCS data (IGC Data, defaults to false)

- A text description for the file

For adding new members to a source physical file in a project, there is the New i5/OS Member wizard. The New i5/OS Member wizard creates an empty member in an i5/OS project that can later be pushed up to the associated library. This wizard is very simple. It just prompts for the member name, source type, and text description, as well as the local source physical file in which to create the member.

Adding Existing Source Files and Members to a Project

In most cases, you will probably create a new i5/OS project and then add existing members from the server to it, instead of using the wizards. When you add an existing member to a project, the related source physical file is also automatically created, if required.

Adding Versus Importing

You can add a member from the associated library or you can import a member from a different library to the project. There is a very important difference between the two! Remember that members are always pushed from the project to the library associated with the project.

When you add a member from the associated library to the project, make changes to the member, and then push it back, the original member is over-written with the changes. This is the behavior that most users expect.

When you import a member into a project from a library that is not the associated library and later push the member, the member is uploaded to the associated library. The original member is not overwritten. This might seem obvious, but we have found that some users expect the original member to be overwritten, since that is where the member came from. If this is the desired behavior, you should create a new i/5OS project associated with the library where the original member is located.

Using the RSE Actions

You can add or import existing members into an i5/OS project using actions from the Remote Systems view or the Object Table view. In either view, right-click a source member and select one of the following actions:

- **Add To i5/OS Project**: If you only have one i5/OS project in your Workspace, this action will add the selected RSE member to the project. If you have no i5/OS projects, the action will create a project called *RSEConnectionName_LibraryName* and add the member to it. The new project is associated with the RSE connection and library where the member was selected. If multiple i5/OS projects exist in the Workspace, the action prompts for the project to which the member should be added.

- **Make Available Offline**: The original intent of this action was to quickly enable a developer to work offline with the selected members. The action always adds the members to a project that is associated with the same RSE connection and library from which the selected RSE members came. If one such project exists, the members are added to it. If multiple matching projects are found, the RSE prompts you to select the project to add the members to. If no such project exists, the action creates one with the name *RSEConnectionName_LibraryName*.

Both of the above actions are also available on source physical files. In this case, all members in the source physical file are added to the project.

TIP

We use the Make Available Offline action almost exclusively to set up our i5/OS projects, regardless of what we are using the project for. Simply multi-select the members you are interested in, right-click, and select **Make Available Offline**. This one action creates the project, associates it to the required library, and adds all the members to it. You can then rename the project from the default to something more meaningful.

Using the i5/OS Project Actions

You can also add or import existing members into an i5/OS project using actions from the i5/OS Project Navigator view. Right-click the project you want to import into, and select **Import Remote Objects**. This opens the

Import Remote Objects dialog, where you drill down via RSE connections and select one or more source physical files or members to import.

There is an Add to Project action available on remote source physical files and members in the i5/OS Project Navigator. This is only available in a special mode of the i5/OS Project Navigator and is covered in the next section.

If your libraries and source physical files contains hundreds of objects and members, you might want to avoid using the i5/OS project actions for adding and importing, and only use the RSE actions. The Import Remote Objects dialog and the ability to show remote objects in a project do not support filtering, so all objects/members are shown. This can cause a performance delay. It would be better to use filters in the RSE to list only the source files and members you are interested in, and then use the RSE actions to add the required resources to the project.

Viewing Local and Remote Resources in a Project

Normally, the i5/OS Project Navigator only shows source files and members that are local. However, it can also show the remote objects and members from the associated library. To see them, right-click the project and select **Show Remote Objects**. The result of this action is shown in Figure 11–4.

In the "show remote objects" mode, the i5/OS project shows both local and remote resources. The icon for each resource is decorated with an arrow

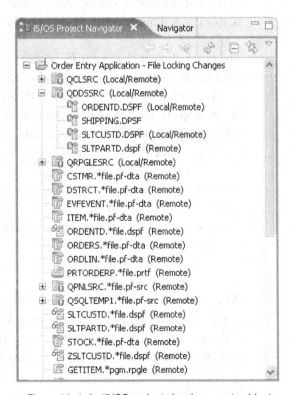

Figure 11–4: An i5/OS project showing remote objects.

to show the resource's status. Table 11–1 outlines the meaning of each icon decorator. In addition to the icon decorator, the label for the resource is decorated with text appended to the resource name to indicate the local and/or remote status of the resource.

Table 11–1: i5/OS Project Icon Decorators	
Icon Decoration	**Meaning**
Double-headed green arrow	The member is local and remote, and both copies are *in sync*, meaning the remote copy has not been modified since it was added to the project. However, the local copy might or might not have been modified.
Double-headed red arrow	The member is local and remote, and they are out of sync. The remote copy of the member has been modified since it was added to the project.
Single-headed green arrow pointing right or left	If the arrow points right, the resource only exists locally. If the arrow points left, the resource only exists remotely.

A source physical file is shown with a decorator that represents the collective status of its members. For example, if one of the members is out of sync, the source file and member will both show double-headed red arrows.

The i5/OS Project Navigator view's menu contains two actions that affect what is shown in the view when show remote objects is enabled. First, an action called "Show Local/Remote Decorators" can be used to hide the i5/OS project's local or remote decorators. This is a shortcut to enabling or disabling the decorator on the General > Appearance > Label Decorators preference page (where all Workbench decorators can be controlled).

The second action toggles whether or not you want to show only local, only remote, or both local and remote objects. This is available via the Show menu, which cascades into two selection items, one for local objects and the other for remote objects. Both are selected by default, which causes the view to show both local and remote objects.

While showing remote objects, you can right-click source files and members that are only remote, and add them to the local project by selecting the Add to Project action. You can refresh local members that also exist remotely, using the Replace from Associated Library action.

TIP
··

You might be wondering why you would select Show Remote Objects and then turn off the showing of remote objects. Icon and label decorators are only available when Show Remote Objects is enabled. This is very useful information, since it shows the whether each member is in or out of sync with its remote counterpart. However, showing all remote objects can cause the view to become very confusing. So, first deselect **Show > Remote Objects** in the view's menu, and then select **Show Remote Objects** for the project. Only the local members will be shown, along with decorators to indicate their status.

··

Tracking Local Changes

The Workspace maintains a local history for each file in it. Every time a file is saved, the Workspace stores a copy of the changes. To compare the current file with any of the previously saved copies from the local history, right-click the file and select **Compare With > Local History**. This opens the Compare with Local History dialog, shown in Figure 11–5.

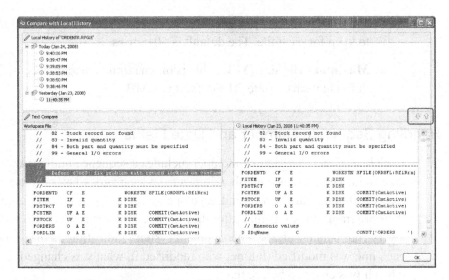

Figure 11–5: The Compare with Local History dialog.

The top panel of the dialog shows the timestamp for each save. The bottom panel of the dialog is divided to show the current Workspace file on the left side and the copy from the local history on the right side. Select one of the timestamps from the top panel to compare the current file against the contents of the file at that point in time.

The bottom right margin of the dialog shows an overview of where the two files differ. Each box represents a difference between the two files. Clicking on a box will position the editors to the location of the difference. You can cycle through the differences using the up (⬆) and down (⬇) arrows in the toolbar above the editors.

There is a corresponding action to replace a Workspace file with a copy from the local history, if you want to revert to a previously saved copy of the file. Right-click the file and select **Replace With > Local History**.

The size of the local history can be configured via the General > Workspace > Local History preference page. Here you can configure the following:

- **Number of days to keep files**: This is the number of days to keep local history before it is deleted. The default is 7 days.

- **Maximum entries per file**: This is the maximum number of entries to keep for each file. The default is 50 entries.

- **Maximum file size (MB)**: This is the maximum size of each individual saved state. The default is 1 MB.

Handling Sequence Number and Date Fields

Each line of an i5/OS source member includes a sequence number and date field. The sequence number comes from long ago, when programs were written on punch cards and developers needed some way of putting their programs back together after they dropped the cards. The date acts as a very rudimentary change-management system, indicating the last time each line was modified (but not who modified it, what was changed, or when it was changed before that).

Despite their historic good intentions, these fields can be a nuisance with stream-file based change-management systems like CVS, Subversion and Rational ClearCase. These systems are designed to track each change made to a file, every time the file is checked in. If someone re-sequences the sequence numbers, the change-management system flags every line in the file as being changed.

i5/OS projects have a preference to automatically remove the sequence number and date fields when members are downloaded to the project. The default values are added back when members are uploaded to the associated library. This capability is enabled by selecting the "Remove sequence number and date fields on download" preference on the i5/OS Projects preference page.

Selecting the preference does not modify the members that are already inside of a project. Two other preferences on the i5/OS Projects preference page can help with this: "Generate sequence number warnings" and "Enable add and remove sequence number actions."

The "Generate sequence number warnings" preference triggers i5/OS projects to scan each of the existing members (and any new members added to a project) and log a warning message in the Problems view for each line that violates the current preference. Figure 11–6 shows the Problems view. If you have the "Remove sequence number and date fields on download" preference selected, but you have a member in a project that has sequence number and date fields, a warning messages will be issued for each line.

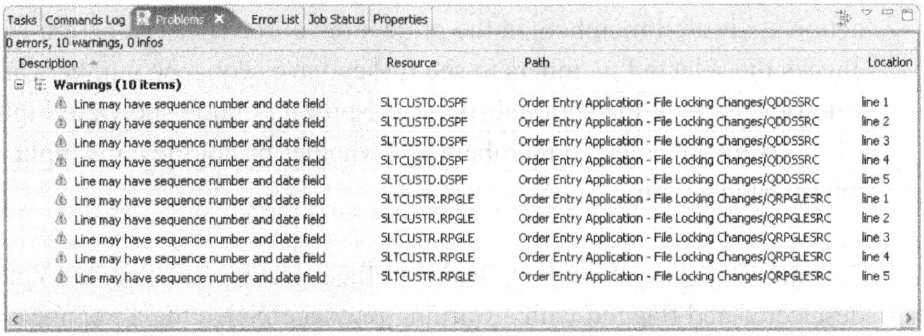

Figure 11–6: The Problems view with sequence number and date field warnings.

A related preference, "Limit sequence number warnings," controls how many warnings are issued for each member. (A warning is issued for each line that violates the sequence number and date field preference.) The default is ten warning messages per member, so that the Problems view doesn't fill up when it hits the first 32,000-line member!

You can manually add and remove sequence numbers and date fields from members in a project by selecting the "Enable add and remove sequence number actions" preference. When selected, actions to add or remove the sequence number and date fields are added to the pop-up menu for i5/OS projects, source files, and members, as shown in Figure 11–7.

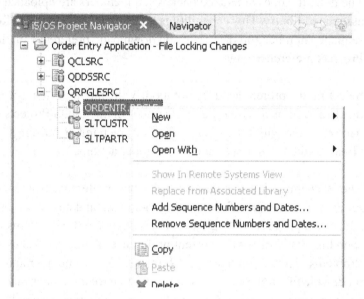

Figure 11–7: Adding or removing sequence number and date field actions.

Selecting either of these actions on a project or source file will run the action against all members in the project or source file. The action first checks the selected members to see if they have sequence numbers and date fields. Then, the action displays the prompt dialog shown in Figure 11–8, listing all selected members and whether or not they are applicable to the selected action.

Any members that are not applicable to the selected action are automatically deselected and flagged with a warning message. Selecting a member in the top pane of the dialog displays a preview of the source in the bottom pane. This allows you to visually check whether the member has sequence numbers and date fields.

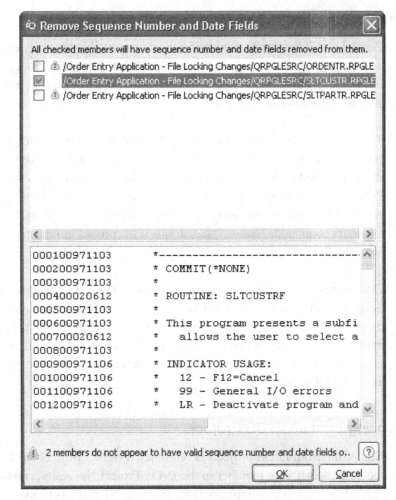

Figure 11–8: The prompt dialog for removing sequence numbers and date fields.

Non-source Objects and i5/OS Projects

i5/OS projects were designed to store and manage source members. However, you might also want to store other i5/OS objects (such as programs, data physical files, or data queues) in the project, in order to version them in a change-management system or upload them onto a different system.

The only way to copy these objects off i5/OS is to use a save file. (i5/OS does not support directly copying them off the system.) WDSC 7.0 Advanced Edition added the ability to transfer save files between an i5/OS project and the associated library using the same actions that are available for source files and members. This capability is also included in Rational Developer for System i.

Pushing (Uploading) Members

Compiles still have to be run on i5/OS, so eventually, you will need to upload (push) your source members from the project to the associated library. Members are automatically pushed to the associated library when you invoke a compile or build.

There are actions you can invoke to push members without having to compile or build. The trick is that these actions don't appear if you set the build style to *NONE for the project. You have to specify either the CL Program or Command build style. (Build styles are discussed later in this chapter.) You can start by using the Command build style and entering a dummy command. That way, it just fails if the project build action is accidentally invoked.

Once you have a build style set for the project, the Push Changes and Push Selected actions appear under Remote Actions in the pop-up menu for projects, source files, and members. The Push Changes action pushes all members in the project that have been modified since the last time they were pushed. The Push Selected action pushes all selected members to the associated library.

Compiling from an i5/OS Project

Compiling from i5/OS projects is not much different from compiling from the RSE. Select your member in the i5/OS Project Navigator, right-click, and select one of the compile actions from the **Remote Actions > Compile** cascading menu, as shown in Figure 11–9. Any custom compile commands that you configure in the RSE will also appear in the Compile menus for i5/OS projects, and vice versa. More information on customizing compile commands can be found in chapter 8.

After selecting the compile command, an i5/OS project first pushes all changed members in the project, then submits the compile command to batch and adds the batch job to the Job Status view.

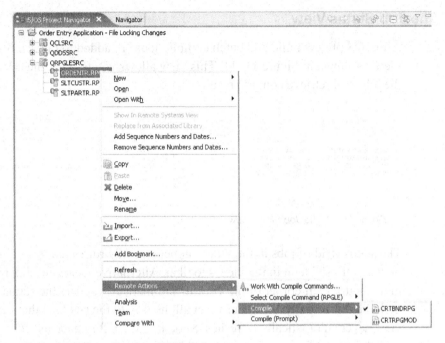

Figure 11–9: Compiling from i5/OS projects.

There is a preference on the i5/OS Projects > Build and Compile preference page that can change the push behavior on member compiles, so that only selected resources are pushed, instead of all changed resources. This preference is shown in Figure 11–10.

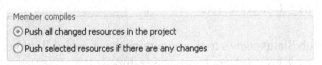

Figure 11–10: The preference to push resources.

When batch compiles are launched from an i5/OS project, the compile results are not automatically populated into the Error List view. Instead, the batch job is added to the Job Status view. You need to invoke an action from the Job Status view to show the compile results (discussed in the next section). Batch compiles can be turned off on the i5/OS Projects > Build and Compile preference page. When turned off, compiles are run immediately in the RSE server job, and the compile results are automatically displayed in the Error List view.

The Job Status View

All i5/OS project build and batch compile jobs are added to the Job Status view, as shown in Figure 11–11. This view allows you to track the status of the jobs and retrieve compile results.

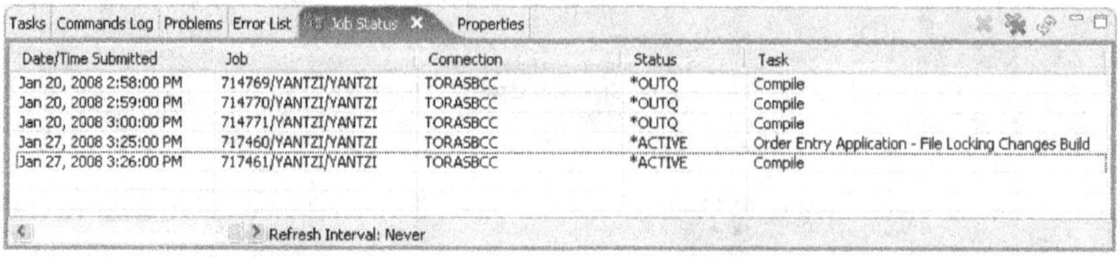
Tasks
Commands Log
Problems
Error List
Job Status
Properties
Date/Time Submitted
Job
Connection
Status
Task
Jan 20, 2008 2:58:00 PM
714769/YANTZI/YANTZI
TORASBCC
*OUTQ
Compile
Jan 20, 2008 2:59:00 PM
714770/YANTZI/YANTZI
TORASBCC
*OUTQ
Compile
Jan 20, 2008 3:00:00 PM
714771/YANTZI/YANTZI
TORASBCC
*OUTQ
Compile
Jan 27, 2008 3:25:00 PM
717460/YANTZI/YANTZI
TORASBCC
*ACTIVE
Order Entry Application - File Locking Changes Build
Jan 27, 2008 3:26:00 PM
717461/YANTZI/YANTZI
TORASBCC
*ACTIVE
Compile
Refresh Interval: Never

Figure 11–11: The Job Status view.

The status field of jobs in the view can be manually refreshed by clicking on the "refresh" icon in the view's toolbar. Alternatively, use the slider in the bottom left corner of the view to automatically update the status periodically. Initially, the slider is set all the way to the right, so that the view never automatically refreshes. Slide it to the left to decrease the refresh interval from a maximum of five hours down to ten seconds.

Compile results can be retrieved once a job has ended (when its status is *job ended* or *OUTQ). Right-click the job and select **Task Actions > Retrieve Errors**. This downloads the compile results and displays them in the Error List view. To cancel active build and compile jobs, use the **Task Actions > Cancel** action.

The Job Status view's toolbar contains the standard Workbench toolbar icons to remove selected entries or remove all entries from the table. Old entries can also be removed by selecting them in the table, right-clicking, and selecting Remove.

TIP

You can add any job to the Job Status view; it doesn't have to be an i5/OS Project build or compile job. In the RSE, right-click a job under the Jobs subsystem and select **Add To Job Status View**. The same pop-up menu actions are available on jobs in the Job Status view as jobs under the Jobs subsystem.

Project-level Builds

The alternative to compiling each individual member in a project is to set up a build for the project. When invoked, the project build uploads all members modified since the last build and runs a build program that compiles (and optionally binds) all members into programs and service programs.

This makes it easy to compile source changes in the project without having to keep track of which members were modified or which compile options are used for each member. It also sets up a repeatable build process, so others can easily build the project if it is shared via a change-management system.

The downside of the current build support for i5/OS projects is that it is designed to rebuild all members in the project, whether or not they were modified. It does not support a *delta build* (detecting which members have changed since the last build and only building those members). This might result in long build times if the project contains a large number of members. This might be okay for periodic *integration builds* (builds that integrate changes from multiple developers), but unacceptable for individual developers.

Whether or not setting up a build for a project will be useful depends on the following:

- How many members are in the project?
- How often will each member be changed?
- How long is the project going to be used?
- Will the project be shared among developers on a team?
- How is the build and integration environment set up on the i5/OS side?

For example, if you have a project for a new program that has only a few members, and you will be working on the program for a couple of weeks, you might gain productivity from taking the time to set up a build. Project builds can be used in conjunction with member-level compiles. When a change involves only one member, you can compile just that member. For changes that involve multiple members, a project build can be used.

Project builds are set up by selecting and configuring a build style for the project. i5/OS projects include two builds styles: CL Program and Command. The build style for a project can be configured on the New i5/OS Project wizard or the i5/OS Build page in the properties for the project, as shown in Figure 11–12.

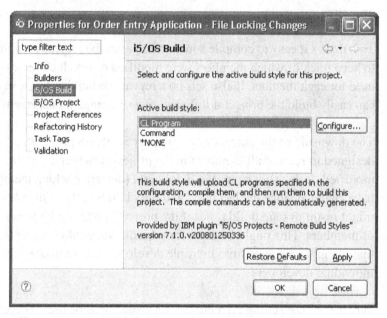

Figure 11–12: The i5/OS Build page of the project's properties.

The CL Program Build Style

The CL Program build style uses two CL programs to build the project: COMPILE and BIND. The role of the COMPILE program is to compile members into programs or modules. The role of the BIND program is to bind modules into programs and service programs.

The source for both programs is kept inside the project, in the QCLSRC source file. This source file location can be changed on the CL Program build style configuration dialog shown in Figure 11–13. Open this dialog by clicking the **Configure** button on the i5/OS Build properties page.

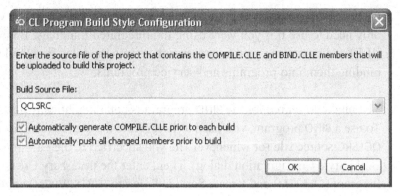

Figure 11–13: The CL Program Build Style Configuration dialog.

By default, the compile.clle source member is regenerated every time a build is submitted. A compile command is added to this source member for each of the other members in the project, using the default compile command associated with the member's source type.

Automatically regenerating the compile.clle source member can be turned off if the generated commands need to be customized. This is done on the CL Program build style configuration dialog. If you turn automatic generation off, you need to manually add the compile command to the compile.clle source member every time a new member is added to the project.

To change which compile command is associated with each source type, right-click any member of that source type, and select one of the compile commands from the **Remote Actions > Select Compile Command** (*SourceType*) menu, as shown in Figure 11–14. To change the order in which compile commands are added to the compile.clle source member, use the **Remote Systems > i5/OS > Command Execution** preference page. The default ordering is physical files first, followed by logical files, display files, printer files, RPG, CL, and so on. This should be sufficient in most cases.

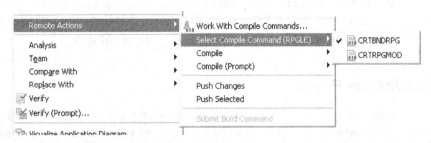

Figure 11–14: The Select Compile Command menu.

Using a BIND program as part of the project build is optional. You would only need to use it if you were using the Integrated Language Environment (ILE) and compiling your source members into modules first, and then binding them into programs and service programs.

The bind.clle source for the BIND program is not automatically generated. To use a BIND program, you need to first create the source member in the QCLSRC source file (or whichever file you specified in the CL Program Build Style Configuration dialog). Then, enter the necessary Create Program (CRTPGM) and Create Service Program (CRTSRVPGM) commands. If a bind.clle member is found when a build is submitted, it is pushed to the associated library (along with the compile.clle member), compiled, and run.

The Command Build Style

The Command build style is much simpler than the CL Program build style. You simply provide a command, and this command is run whenever you submit a build from the project. You specify the command on the configuration dialog for the command build style, shown in Figure 11–15.

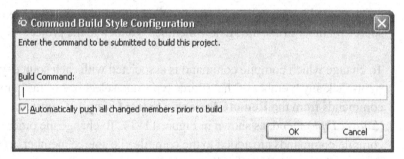

Figure 11–15: Command build style configuration properties.

This assumes you already have a build program for the application, and you wish to maintain this build program independent of i5/OS projects. Alternatively, you could copy the contents of that build program into the compile.clle member and use the CL Program build style.

Building the Project

Submitting a build is easy once the desired build style is selected and configured: right-click the project, and select **Remote Actions >**

Submit Build. This pushes all changed members from the project to the associated library and submits the build to a batch job. The batch job is added to the Job Status view. Once the job has completed, the compile results can be retrieved and displayed in the Error List view. (For more details, see the section on using the Job Status view, earlier in this chapter.)

Each of the build styles has a preference on its configuration dialog to turn off automatically pushing all changed members. If this option is turned off, you will need to use the Push Changes or Push Selected action (discussed earlier in this chapter).

To run a build, an i5/OS project uses server programs that are shipped in the QDEVTOOLS library. (This library is installed when you install 5722-WDS for V5R3 and V5R4, or 5761-WDS for V6R1 option 60.) Specifically, it uses QRBPGMBLD to run CL program builds, QRBCMDBLD for command builds, and QRBRUNCL for batch compiles. Calls to these programs will show up in the Commands Log view for each submitted build.

Certain information needs to be passed between the i5/OS project and the build programs. For example, the location of the compile.clle and bind. clle members needs to be passed for the CL Program build style. Also, the list of all compile messages resulting from the build needs to be returned. This information is passed via IFS files. The files are created in your IFS home directory under the subdirectory *.eclipse/RB*. They are given a unique identification number that is passed as a parameter to the build programs. This is similar to submitting batch compiles for RSE. It requires authority to access the IFS, as outlined in chapter 8.

The i5/OS Projects > Build and Compile preference page contains a preference that controls how many days these temporary files are kept on the remote system. The default is seven days.

Working Offline (Disconnected)

i5/OS projects are offline by their very nature. The source is stored and edited on the local workstation. A connection to the remote system is only required when changes are pushed to the associated library, or when a build is submitted. In fact, you can even disconnect immediately after the build is submitted. Later on, when you reconnect, you can update the status of the build job in the Job Status view and retrieve the compile results.

TIP You can put the RSE connection associated with an i5/OS project "offline" if you find that you keep getting prompted to connect to the remote system. Right-click the connection and select **Work Offline**. A checkmark appears next to the action when the connection is offline. This forces everything to be retrieved from the cache. If the required information is not available from the cache, actions like program verification will fail. Make sure to put the connection back online when you are done working disconnected.

Working in a Team

One of the advantages to using i5/OS projects for development is the ability to store your RPG, COBOL, CL, and DDS source in a stream-file based Software Configuration Management (SCM) system. By *stream-file based*, we mean an SCM system that is designed to manage files that are a continuous stream of bytes (typical of Windows, Linux, and UNIX files), as opposed to files based on a fixed record length (i5/OS source members).

These are the SCMs used to manage Java and Web projects, and for programming languages used on many other platforms. Examples of stream-file based SCM systems include open-source offerings such as CVS and Subversion, as well as commercial offerings such as Rational ClearCase. These systems offer features like the following:

- *Optimistic and pessimistic locking*: Pessimistic locking is the classic technique of checking out and locking a file while editing, so no one else can change it at the same time. With optimistic locking, you don't pre-lock the file. Instead, you make your changes, and then check the file back in. Some systems offer automated merging tools for cases when someone else modifies the file at the same time as you.

- *Virtually unlimited tracking of file changes*: Every change made to every file is tracked. You can always go back and see who made which changes to a file, and when those changes were made.

- *Handling multiple versions of a file*: Multiple versions of a file can be tracked, so you can work on a new version while providing fixes for previous versions.

- *Security*: Some of the systems offer integrated security, to control who has read and write access to files.

Using a stream-file based SCM system can allow organizations to store all their source code in one system, instead of implementing one system for their non-i5/OS source files, and another for RPG, COBOL, CL, and DDS.

Associating a Project with a Repository

This section assumes you have already set up a repository and configured a repository connection for it in the Workbench. How you do this depends on which SCM system you are using. Consult the documentation of your SCM system for information on how to configure a repository connection in Eclipse. The Eclipse client for CVS is included in the Workbench. You will need to install additional Eclipse plug-ins for other SCM systems. The screen shots in this section are from Subversion.

The basic instructions are the same regardless of which SCM system you are using. The first step is to associate the project with a repository. Right-click the project and select **Team > Share Project**, as shown in Figure 11–16.

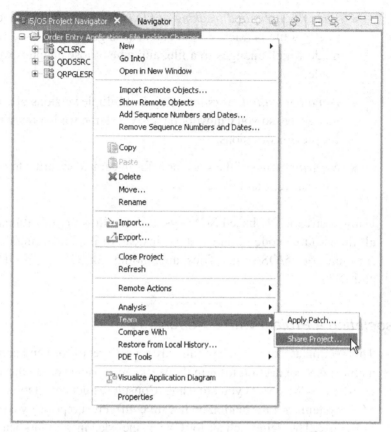

Figure 11–16: The Share Project action.

Figure 11–17: Selecting the repository type

This opens the Share Project dialog shown in Figure 11–17, where you select the repository type you will be using. Select the type and click **Next** to continue.

The rest of the wizard is specific to the repository type. Most types prompt for the repository location, along with a few parameters on how the project should be shared. For example, the Subversion (SVN) version of the wizard allows you to either use the project name as the folder name in the repository or specify a different folder name.

After a project is associated with a repository, the repository usually adds decorators to the icons and labels for the files, folder, and project. Icon decorators can show if a file is locked or if it has changes that are not committed to the repository. Label decorators often show the current version or revision number of the file, the last modified date, and the file's author.

Synchronizing, Commit, and Update

Once a project is associated with a repository, the cascading Team menu in the pop-up menu shows a list of actions specific to the repository type. This menu usually includes actions to synchronize the local project with the contents in the repository, as well as to commit, update, and lock selected files, as shown in Figure 11–18.

The Synchronize With Repository action opens the Synchronize view, shown in Figure 11–19. This view lists all local files that have changed and need to be committed to the repository. It also shows all repository files that have changed and need to be updated in the local Workspace.

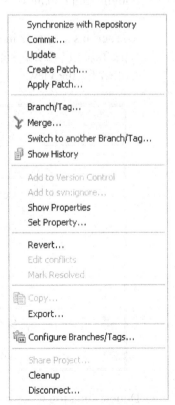

Figure 11–18: The Team menu using Subversion.

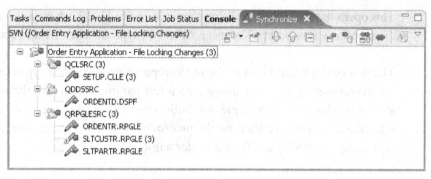

Figure 11–19: The Synchronize view.

You can tell the state a file is in by the decorator applied to its icon. An arrow pointing right means the file was changed locally and needs to be committed. An arrow pointing left means the file was changed in the repository and needs to be updated locally. A double-headed arrow means the file was changed in both locations and needs to be merged. Actions to commit and update files are available in the pop-up menu in the view.

The actions available in the Synchronize view are specific to the repository type. Table 11–2 lists some of the common actions that are shown in the toolbar for the view.

Table 11–2: Synchronize View Actions	
Icon	Action
	Go to the next difference.
	Go to the previous difference.
	Collapse the view.
	Show only incoming changes.
	Show only outgoing changes.
	Show both incoming and outgoing changes.
	Show only conflicts.

Double-clicking a file opens a side-by-side compare editor, showing the local file on the left side and the repository file on the right. Some compare editors allow changes from the repository file to be copied into the local file.

Project Metadata

Each i5/OS project is associated with an RSE connection, an associated library, and a build style. Each source physical file within a project stores its CCSID, record length, IGC data attribute, and description. Each member stores its description and the remote timestamp of the last time the member was pushed to the associated library.

These properties are referred to as *metadata*. Some metadata is considered public and is stored in files inside the project. Other metadata is considered private and is stored in a private area of the Workspace. Since public metadata is stored inside the project, it is shared with other developers when the project is shared using a SCM system. If two developers were working on an i5/OS project, they would be using the same values for public metadata properties but have their own values for private metadata properties. Table 11–3 lists each of the project resource types, along with its metadata.

Table 11–3: Project Metadata		
Resource Type	Public Metadata	Private Metadata
Project	RSE connection name	Associated library
	Build style and properties	
Source physical file	CCSID	
	IGC data	
	Record length	
	Description	
Member	Description	Remote member timestamp (to determine if the member needs to be pushed)

The public metadata files should not be modified directly. Therefore, they are not shown in the i5/OS Project Navigator view. The values stored in the metadata files can be set using the properties dialog for the corresponding resource. If you look at the project in the Navigator view, you can see the project metadata files. Here is the name and project-relative location of each one:

- Project: .iseries_project_properties

- Source physical files: *FileName*\.iseries_srcpf_metadata\.iseries_ srcpf_properties

- Member: *FileName*\.iseries_srcpf_metadata*MemberName. MemberType*_properties

Understanding how the metadata is stored is not required for individual developers using i5/OS projects. However, it does have implications for developers sharing i5/OS projects via an SCM system. When you retrieve a project from the SCM repository, you must ensure you have created the RSE connection required by the project. You will also need to go into the project properties and set the associated library.

The metadata files also have to be synchronized with the repository. For example, a member's description is stored in the member's metadata file. Changing the description changes the metadata file. The next time the project is synchronized with the repository, the member's metadata file will show it as having outgoing changes.

Troubleshooting

Below are some common problems related to the topics in this chapter, along with suggestions on diagnosing and fixing the problems:

- *I don't see my i5/OS project in the i5/OS Project Navigator.*

  This can happen if the project is closed or if it was retrieved from an SCM repository and the *.project* file was not extracted. Open the Navigator: select **Window > Show View > Other**, then select **Navigator** from the General category.

  The project is closed if it has a solid blue folder icon and does not have a plus sign beside it. To open a project, right-click it and select **Open Project**. (Similarly, a project can be closed by right-clicking it and selecting Close Project.) Otherwise, expand the project and look for the *.project* file. Synchronize your project with the repository and extract the *.project* file if it is missing.

- *Why don't I see actions to push the members from my project to the remote server?*

  These actions only show up if you have a build style associated with the project. Associate the Command build style with the project and enter a dummy command.

- *I can compile from the RSE, but my compiles don't work from i5/OS projects.*

  Compiles and builds from i5/OS projects require information to be passed between the workstation and the compile program on the server, via IFS files. The Workbench tries to write this information into files in the IFS directory *[homeDirectory]/.eclipse/RB/* (where *[homeDirectory]* is your home directory as specified in your i5/OS user profile). Make sure your home directory exists and that you have read and write access to it.

  Alternatively, you can turn batch compiles off for i5/OS projects and have the compile commands go through the RSE instead of the i5/OS projects build program. Do this by going to the **i5/OS Projects > Build and Compile** preference page and de-selecting the **Run compiles as batch jobs** preference.

- *Why are all members from my project pushed to the associated library?*

  i5/OS projects store the remote timestamp of a member every time it is pushed to the associated library. This timestamp is checked on subsequent pushes to see if the remote member needs to be updated. Timestamps are stored in the project the first time members are pushed. To turn off pushing all changed members for compiles, use the **i5/OS Projects > Build and Compile** preference page.

- *I just extracted an i5/OS project from our SCM repository, and it has a red X on it.*

  After a new project is extracted from the repository, it does not have the associated library property set yet. Open the project properties, and specify the associated library. Also, make sure the RSE connection (connection name and RSE profile name) associated with the project exists in your RSE. Create the RSE profile and connection if it does not exist.

- *How can I use a different editor with the members in my project?*

  Configure this on the **General > Editors > File Associations** preference page. Find the file extension you want to edit (for example, *.rpgle*) and add the editor you want to use in the associated editors section of the preference page. After that, you should see the editor in the cascading Open With menu in the pop-up menu for members with that file extension. Refer to the section "Handling Sequence Number and Date Fields" earlier in this chapter for details on handling sequence number and date fields, if the editor cannot handle them.

- *What are the Analysis and PDE Tools actions in the pop-up menu?*

  These actions are not applicable to i5/OS projects. Some tools contribute their actions to all project types and appear on all projects, even if they are unrelated.

- *I use hex codes in my source that causes SEU to show lines in certain colors. When I edit a member in an i5/OS project, these hex codes get corrupted.*

  Editing members with these hex codes in the RSE is not a problem because the RSE uses Unicode for transferring source members between the workstation and i5/OS. The default encoding used for i5/OS projects is the native encoding of the workstation. This causes the hex codes to get corrupted. To fix this, create an empty i5/OS project, open the project's properties, change the text file encoding from inherited to **other**, and set the encoding to **UTF-8**. Then, add the members to this project.

12

The Application Diagram

A picture is worth a thousand words. And if you happen to be maintaining a large legacy application, it might be worth even more than that! Trying to understand the structure of an application is a long, tedious, and difficult task, if you only have source code to read. A graphical representation of that source code, however, can make the task easier and faster.

This is one of the main reasons why the Application Diagram was created. The Application Diagram creates a graphical representation of a native i5/OS application, making maintenance and modernization of the application easier. Originally, the Application Diagram was only shipped in WDSC 7.0 Advanced Edition, but it is now included in Rational Developer for System i.

The Application Diagram provides two different views into the structure of an application: a source call diagram and a program structure diagram. The source call diagram scans a selection of ILE RPG, ILE COBOL, and CL source members, and shows the members, subroutines, procedures, and called programs. Connections are drawn between these resources, as shown in Figure 12–1, to represent subroutine, procedure and program calls, and copy-member relationships.

The program structure diagram takes a selection of programs and service programs and visualizes the ILE binding information. Programs and service programs are drawn with the list of modules bound into each. Relationships are drawn between programs and service programs to represent service program bindings.

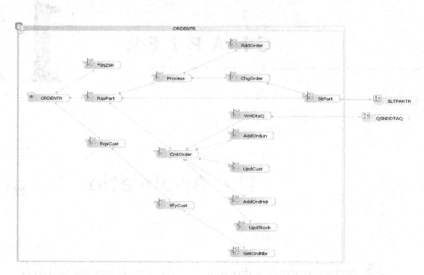

Figure 12–1: A source call diagram.

TIP

Tools like the Application Diagram can be very useful on their own, but can be even more valuable when combined with others tools. Using the Application Diagram and the Remote Systems LPEX Editor in combination is a perfect example. Using split-screen editing, you can view a diagram of a source member while you are editing the source code. Use the diagram actions, such as double-clicking on a calls relationship, to position the editor to areas of interest.

Creating a Diagram

Creating a diagram is easy. Select the resources you want to use in building the diagram, and then select **Visualize Application Diagram** from the pop-up menu, as shown in Figure 12–2.

ILE RPG, ILE COBOL and CL are applicable source types for the Application Diagram. All of the following resources are valid selections for the Application Diagram:

- *Source members*: Select source members in the RSE to include in the generated diagram.

- *Programs and service programs*: Select programs and service programs in the RSE to include in the generated diagram.

- *Member filters*: All applicable source members resolved by the filter are used.

- *Object filters*: All programs and service programs resolved by the filter are used, as well as all applicable source members in source files resolved by the filter.

- *IFS files and folders*: All applicable source files in the folders are used. Subfolders are recursively included.

- *Local files and folders*: All applicable source files in the folders are used. Subfolders are recursively included.

Figure 12–2: The Visualize Application Diagram action.

- *i5/OS projects*: All members within the project are included. Individual source files or members within a project can also be selected.

Multiple resources can be selected as input to a single diagram; however, they must be the same kind of resource. For example, you can select a combination of IFS folders and IFS files, but you can't select an IFS file and a member. You can select programs, service programs, and members together to generate a diagram that shows the source call and program structure at the same time.

The Application Diagram uses the LPEX *ILErpg, ILErpgSql, ILEcobolSqlCics,* and *cl* parser associations to determine what source types are ILE RPG, ILE COBOL, and CL. The common source types are already associated with these parsers, but if you use a nonstandard source type (like *myrpg*), you will need to associate it with the correct LPEX parser. Otherwise, the Visualize Application Diagram action will not appear in the pop-up menu when you right-click members of this type. Chapter 7 covers LPEX parsers and how to associate source types with a parser.

Before building the diagram, a check is made to see if any of the selected resources are open in the editor with unsaved changed. When launched directly from a resource, the Application Diagram uses the saved contents of a member or file, not the unsaved contents of the editor. If there are unsaved changes, you are prompted whether or not to save the editors before proceeding.

TIP

To launch the Application Diagram directly from the Remote Systems LPEX Editor while editing a source member, use the **Source > Visualize Application Diagram** menu action. When launched this way, the Application Diagram uses the contents of the editor regardless of whether they are saved or not.

A progress monitor is displayed while the diagram is being built, as shown in Figure 12–3. The monitor shows the current state of the build process above the progress bar, and the current member, file, or object being processed below the progress bar. After the diagram build completes, the Application Diagram editor opens.

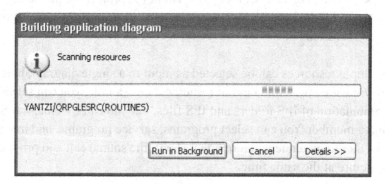

Figure 12–3: The progress monitor for generating a diagram.

The diagram might take a few minutes to build if you selected a large number of resources or have very large source members. Click the **Run in Background** button on the progress monitor to hide it, so you can continue to use the RSE while the diagram is built. The Workbench's Progress view can be opened to show the same status information as in the progress monitor. To open it, click the "progress" icon (⟳) in the bottom right corner of the Workbench window while the diagram is being built.

Reading the Diagram

A diagram consists of *nodes* and *connections*, as shown in Figure 12–4. Nodes represent resources, such as members, programs, service programs, subroutines, and procedures. Connections represent relationships between the resources, such as calls, copies, and includes.

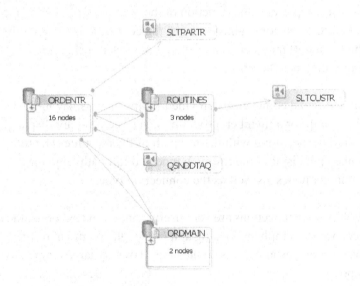

Figure 12–4: A sample diagram.

A node is drawn as a rectangular box with an icon in the top left corner and the resource name either in the middle, or along the top, of the box. The icon, color, and sometimes shape of the box can be used to visually determine the type of resource. In the sample diagram in Figure 12–4, the node labeled ORDENTR represents a source member, while the node SLTCUSTR represents a program. Table 12–1 lists all the icons and what types of resources they represent.

Table 12–1: Icon Descriptions	
Icon	**Description**
	Source member, local file, or IFS file
	Main entry point procedure
	Procedure
	Subroutine
	Program
	Service program
	Module

A connection is drawn as an arrow between two nodes. The direction of the arrow represents the direction of the relationship. In the sample diagram in Figure 12–4, for example, one of the connections between the ORDENTR and ORDMAIN members represents a copy relationship; member ORDENTR copies member ORDMAIN.

All nodes and connections provide tooltips that display more details. The tooltip for a member, program, or service program displays the resource type, along with the full path of the resource. The tooltip for a connection displays the resource type and full pathname for the source and target nodes, as well as the connection type.

Tooltips for connections are very useful, since you cannot tell the type of a connection simply by looking at it (although you might be able to guess based on the resources it is connecting). For very large diagrams, it might be impossible to have both the source and target nodes of a connection showing in the editor. Using the tooltip, you can still see what nodes are connected.

Some nodes are considered *external* to the diagram. This means the member, program, or service program was not part of the initial selection, but was added to the diagram because one or more selected resources references it. The node is added to capture the reference, but the details of the member, program, or service program are not available. External nodes contain no contents and are drawn with a dashed outer line. The SLTPARTR node in Figure 12–4 is an external node.

An Application Diagram can be built with both source and program information, by selecting source members, programs, and service programs. By default, the source call and program structure diagram are shown at the same time. To show only the source call diagram or the program structure diagram, right-click a blank area of the diagram, and select one of the views from the cascading **Switch View** submenu.

The Source Call Diagram

A source call diagram shows the main entry points, subroutines, and procedures defined in the selected source members, along with the calls between them and calls to external programs.

Figure 12–1 shows a sample diagram generated from one ILE RPG source members: ORDENTR. Inside this member, the diagram shows a collection of subroutine nodes and subroutine calls. There are two program objects shown. Connections between subroutine nodes and program nodes represent program calls.

Table 12–2 summarizes what is generated in the Application Diagram for each of the supported languages.

Table 12–2: Language Feature Mapping		
Source Language	Language Feature	Representation in Diagram
ILE RPG	Main line code	Main entry point node
	Subroutine	Subroutine node
	Procedure	Procedure node
	Subroutine call	Connection from the caller to the called subroutine
	Procedure call	Connection from the caller to the called procedure
	Program call	Connection from the caller to the called program
	/copy	Includes connection between the current member and the copied member
	/include	Includes connection between the current member and the copied member

Table 12-2: Language Feature Mapping (Continued)		
Source Language	**Language Feature**	**Representation in Diagram**
ILE COBOL	Procedure division	Main entry point node, with the name as specified on the PROGRAM-ID paragraph
	Sections	COBOL procedure node, with an implicit connection created from the main entry point node to each section node
	Paragraph	COBOL procedure node with an implicit connection created from the section node to each contained paragraph node
	COBOL procedure call (PERFORM, GO TO, MERGE, SORT, XML PARSE)	Connection from the calling COBOL procedure to the called COBOL procedure
	ILE procedure call (CALL)	Connection from the calling COBOL procedure to the called ILE procedure
	Program call (CALL)	Connection from the calling COBOL procedure to the called program
	COPY statement	Includes connection between the current member and the copied member
CL	Source member	Main entry point node with the same name as the member
	Subroutine (SUBR/ENDSUBR)	Subroutine node
	Subroutine call	Connection from the caller to the called subroutine
	Procedure call	Connection from the caller to the called procedure
	Program call	Connection from the caller to the called program
	INCLUDE	Includes connection between the current member and the copied member

If you just select source members when building a diagram, all members are assumed to be bound together when attempting to resolve procedure calls between members. If you select the programs and service programs along with the members, the Application Diagram uses the binding information from the programs and service programs to resolve procedure calls.

If the Application Diagram detects that a selected ILE RPG member is a copybook of another member, it will not generate a main entry point node for the copybook. ILE RPG members that are not determined to be copybooks will have the main entry point node generated (unless they specify NOMAIN on the control specification).

Program calls that use a variable (field) to hold the name of the called program, instead of a literal or constant, are shown as a call to a program node where the name of the program node is the variable (field) surrounded by angle brackets. Calls to programs that use *LIBL instead of a qualified library name are resolved when the diagram is built.

TIP
Switching to the Source Call Diagram view filters out all programs and service program objects, including all program calls from subroutines and procedures. This can be useful if you have a very large, complicated diagram and only want to focus on the subroutine and procedure calls.

The Program Structure Diagram

Figure 12–5 shows a sample diagram generated from some programs and service programs. The nodes on the left represent programs, and the other nodes represent service programs. Some of the service programs show module information because they were part of the initial selection (QQFUTILS). Others were not part of the selection and are external to the diagram, and are therefore shown empty (QPZOCPA).

The connections between the programs and service programs represent ILE bindings. The program or service program on the source end of the connection binds to the service program on the target end of the connection.

Inside the program or service program node is a list of the modules bound into the program or service program. When a program or service program node is collapsed, it lists the name of the first module, along with an ellipsis to indicate there are more modules. If there is no ellipsis, the program or service program only contains one module. The entire list of modules is displayed when the program or service program is expanded.

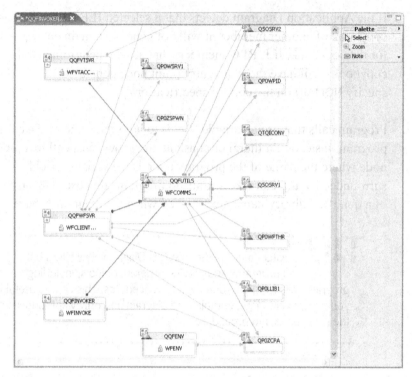

Figure 12–5: A program structure diagram.

Functional Zoom

When the Application Diagram initially opens in the editor, it only shows the top-level resources (members, programs, and service programs). A plus sign is added near the top left corner of any node that has additional lower-level details available. Clicking the plus sign (or using the keyboard shortcut Ctrl+Alt+E) expands the node to show the additional details. Clicking the minus sign (or pressing Ctrl+Alt+C) when the node is expanded causes the node to collapse again.

This ability to drill down in the diagram to examine lower level details is referred to as *functional zoom*. When the node for a source member is collapsed, it shows a text description of how many subroutines and procedures are contained in the member. For example, in Figure 12–4, the member ORDENTR says "16 nodes," which indicates this member contains 16 subroutine and procedure nodes. When the node is expanded, the text is replaced with the call graph for the subroutines and procedures inside the member.

Two types of connections are shown between top-level resources when the resource is collapsed: *direct connections* and *aggregate connections*. The connections are drawn the same, but represent different information. A direct connection represents a relationship between top-level resources. A copy relationship between two members is an example of a direct relationship.

An aggregate relationship is a connection drawn between top-level resources, but represents a relationship between nodes contained within in those resources. The relationship between the top-level resources is inferred from the lower-level resources. When the resource is expanded, the endpoint of the aggregate connection is updated to reflect the true source (or target) of the connection. If the resource is collapsed again, the endpoint of the connection is changed back to the top-level resource.

Let's look at an example involving a procedure call between two source members. Source member A contains procedures A1 and A2. Source member B contains procedures B1 and B2. Procedure A1 calls procedure B1. When the Application Diagram opens

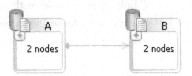

Figure 12–6: An aggregate relationship.

for members A and B, the members are initially collapsed. An aggregate connection is drawn between the members, as shown in Figure 12–6, to signify that something in member A uses something in member B.

If member A or member B is expanded, the endpoints for the connection are updated to reflect the true source and target of the relationship, which are procedures A1 and B1. This is shown in Figure 12–7.

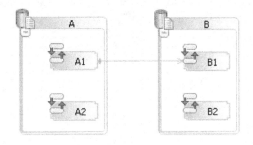

Figure 12–7: A direct relationship.

Using the Diagram Editor

There are lots of ways to view, navigate, and mine information from the Application Diagram. For example, you can print, save, and export the information contained in it.

The Outline View

Like most Workbench editors, the Application Diagram uses the Outline view to provide a high-level overview of the contents of the editor and to facilitate navigating around complex diagrams. The Outline view shows the entire diagram, shrunk down to fit inside the view. It also shows a shaded box that represents the portion of the diagram currently visible in the editor, as shown in Figure 12–8. This is referred to as the *Thumbnail view*.

The editor can be repositioned on the diagram by dragging the shaded box in the Outline view with the mouse.

The Outline view also provides a hierarchical listing of all nodes in the diagram, as shown in Figure 12–9. This is referred to as the *Text view*. Clicking on a node in the Text view positions the diagram so that the node is visible and selected. You can toggle between the Thumbnail and Text views using the icons in the view's toolbar.

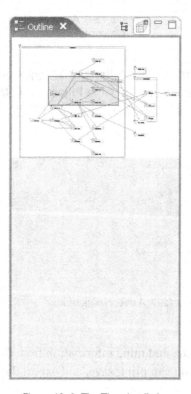

Figure 12–8: The Thumbnail view.

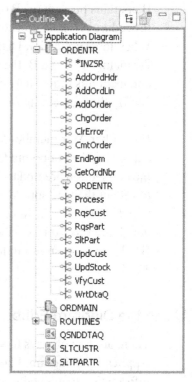

Figure 12–9: The Text view.

The Properties View

The Properties view shows details for nodes and connections selected in the diagram. Information in this view is grouped by tabs down the left side. Table 12–3 describes the properties that are shown for each resource type.

TIP

....

Don't forget, for properties that use a table view, you can always click a column heading to sort the table by that column. Clicking the column heading again toggles between ascending and descending order.

....

Table 12–3: Property Attributes		
Resource	**Properties Tab**	**What Is Shown**
Main entry point, subroutine, or procedure	General	Name, type, source language, location (member name), start and end line numbers
	Calls	A table of subroutines, procedures and programs called by the selected node
	Called by	A table of subroutines, and procedures that call the selected node
Program	General	Name, library, object type (*PGM), subtype (language), debuggable (whether the program contains debug information), and creation time
	Modules	The list of modules bound into the program, along with general information for each module
	Uses Service Program	The list of service programs used by this program
Service program	General	Name, library, type (*SRVPGM), subtype (language), debuggable (whether the service program contains debug information), and creation time
	Modules	The list of modules bound into the service program, along with general information for each module
	Uses Service Program	The list of service programs used by this service program
	Used by	The list of programs and service programs that use this service program
	Exported Procedures	The list of procedures exported by this service program, and the name of the module each belongs to

Table 12–3: Property Attributes (Continued)		
Resource	Properties Tab	What Is Shown
Module	General	Name, library, type (*MODULE), subtype (language), debuggable (whether the module contains debug information), source location, creation time, parent program/service program name, and object type
	Procedures	The list of procedures in this module, and whether they are exported or not
Connection	General	Names of the "from" and "to" nodes, connection type, and subtype; also includes the source line number for subroutine, procedure, and program call connections

Keep in mind that the information shown in a diagram is limited to the scope of the resources initially selected to build the diagram. So the Called By table shown in the Properties view for a subroutine will only list callers from within the initial selection. It won't show callers from source members not included in the initial selection.

TIP The Properties view is docked in a small area in the bottom left corner of the RSE perspective. Move the view to the right of this area (where the Object Table and Commands Log views are) to see all the information in it without scrolling. See chapter 4 for more details on customizing view locations.

The Palette (Select, Zoom and Notes)

The Application Diagram has a palette attached to the right side of the diagram, as shown in Figure 12–10. The palette contains three tools:

- Select ( )
- Zoom ( )
- Note ( )

The Zoom tool allows you to zoom in and out on the diagram. Click **Zoom** from the palette, and then click the diagram to zoom in. Hold down the Shift key while clicking to zoom out. Click **Select** when you are done zooming. (The Note tool is covered later in this chapter.)

The Workbench toolbar contains a drop-down box that shows the current zoom percentage. To change this, enter a percentage value in the entry field or select one of the predefined values from the drop-down.

Figure 12–10: The Application Diagram palette.

The palette can be collapsed by clicking the black arrow (▶) in the top right corner of the palette. Clicking the arrow again restores the palette. In addition to the palette attached to the diagram editor, the Workbench also has a stand-alone Palette view. The two palettes are interchangeable. In fact, if you open the separate Palette view, the attached palette automatically disappears. This is another useful way of freeing up space in the diagram editor. If you find yourself using the palette infrequently, just open the Palette view and stack it with some other views, or make it a fast view.

Print, Save, and Other Useful Stuff

The Application Diagram editor has lots of useful actions for quickly printing the diagram, saving the diagram, and jumping from the diagram to the source code for a specific node or connection.

Right-click any member, subroutine, procedure, module, or OPM program node in the diagram, and select the **Edit Source** or **Browse Source** action to open the corresponding source member and position to the line where the node is defined. Alternatively, double-click the node as a shortcut to the Edit Source action. The same actions are available on subroutine, procedure, and program call connections. Invoking the action opens the source member and positions to the line where the call is made.

As you would expect, the Application Diagram provides Print (Ctrl+P) and Print Preview actions, available from the Workbench's File menu. From the Print dialog, you can scale the diagram or force it to fit on a specified number of pages. Even if you use these features, however, you will probably still end up with a diagram spanning multiple pages. In this case, click **File > Page Setup** to shrink the margins as much as your printer will allow, to make it easier to tape the printed sheets back together into a complete diagram.

The next section of this chapter covers how you can add notes to a generated diagram to start documenting it. You have to save the diagram after doing this, or any other customizations, to avoid losing your changes. You might also want to save a diagram to keep it for future reference, or to send it to a colleague.

You can save a diagram in three different formats: Application Diagram file, graphic, or text. The Application Diagram file is the native format for diagrams. It allows the diagram to be reopened in the Application Diagram editor.

Diagrams are saved to a Workspace project. If you don't already have a project to store your diagrams, you can create one using the New Project wizard. Start by selecting **File > New > Project**, which opens the New Project wizard. In the wizard, select the **General > Project** project type, and click **Next**. This displays a wizard that prompts for the project name, as shown in Figure 12–11. Enter a name for your project, and click **Finish**.

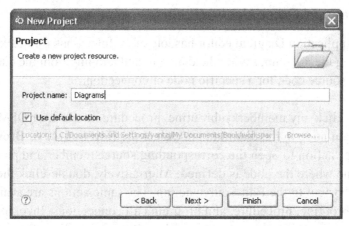

Figure 12–11: Creating a new project.

To save a diagram, make sure the diagram is in focus, and then select **File > Save As** from the Workbench menu. This opens the Save As dialog shown in Figure 12–12. Enter a filename for the diagram, and select the project you want to save it to.

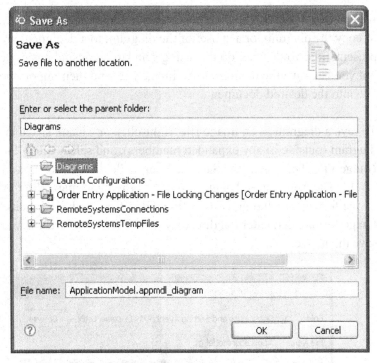

Figure 12–12: The Save As dialog.

Saving an Application Diagram creates two XML files: a model file (*.appmdl*) and a model diagram file (*.appmdl_diagram*). The model file stores information about the application. The model diagram file stores information about how the diagram is displayed, such as the layout, what nodes are expanded, and all notes and text added to the diagram.

You can open a saved diagram by double-clicking either the model file or the model diagram file. The editor looks for the other file in the same directory. You can open a diagram with just the model file and it will use a default layout, but you cannot open a diagram with just the model diagram file.

TIP •••
You can send someone else a copy of your diagram by saving it and sending them the *.appmdl* and *.appmdl_diagram* files. The recipient can open these files in Rational Developer for System i, even if he or she doesn't have access to the resources used to create the diagram.
•••

Instead of just saving the diagram to open again later, you might want to copy the diagram, or a subset of the diagram, to a document or presentation. You cannot do this using standard copy and paste actions, but you can save the diagram to an image file, and then import the image file into the desired document.

To save a diagram as an image file, right-click any blank space in the diagram (outside of any expanded members), and select **File > Save as Image File**. This opens the Save As Image File dialog shown in Figure 12–13. The Application Diagram supports saving to many different image formats, including BMP, JPEG, GIF, PNG, and SVG. Select the image format, and enter the directory and filename where you want to save the image.

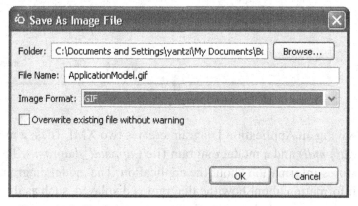

Figure 12–13: The Save As Image File dialog.

TIP

To save only a subset of the diagram to an image file, first select the nodes and connections you want to save, and then right-click one of the nodes and select **File > Save As Image File**.

The third way to save a diagram is to a text file. This writes each of the members, programs, and service programs in the diagram as a list in the text file. As you can see in Figure 12–14, under each member are "Called by" and "Calls" sections, listing who calls it and who it calls.

```
                        Application Topology
========================================================================

                              ORDENTR

Location:  \Order Entry Application - File Locking Changes\
QRPGLESRC\ORDENTR.RPGLE

Main Entry Point:  ORDENTR

Total functions:21
------------------------------------------------------------------------
Called by:
        *INZSR
                    ORDENTR
        AddOrder
                    Process
        AddOrdHdr
                    CmtOrder
        AddOrdLin
                    CmtOrder
        ChgOrder


        . . .
------------------------------------------------------------------------
Calls:
        *INZSR
        AddOrder
          AddOrdHdr
        AddOrdLin
        ChgOrder
                    SltPart
                    VfyPart
                    vfyQty
        ClrError
        CmtOrder
                    AddOrdHdr
                    AddOrdLin


        . . .
```

Figure 12–14: Sample text output.

Documenting Your Application

The generated diagram provides a great visualization to assist in understanding the application. However, there is often knowledge about an application that is not captured in the source code; it is in the developer's mind. Adding documentation to a generated diagram can tie together these two valuable sources of information.

Two different types of documentation can be added to a diagram: notes and text. Notes are designed to be attached to a node or connection in the diagram. Text is more free-form documentation that is not attached to a specific node or connection.

You can add notes to the diagram using either the pop-up menus on nodes and connections or the Note tool from the palette. It's easier to use a pop-up menu, since it adds the note and a connection to the note in a single action. Using the palette, you have to create a note and then create a connection from the source node to the note.

You must save your diagram after adding notes or text to it. Otherwise, your hard work will be lost!

CAUTION

To add a note using a pop-up menu, right-click the node or connection you want to document, and select **Add Note** from the menu. This generates a new note and adds a connection from the selected node to the note. Enter your text in the generated note. Use Ctrl+Enter to move to the next line in the note, and press Enter to complete it. Figure 12–15 shows an example of a note attached to a subroutine node.

Figure 12–15: An example of a note attached to a subroutine.

The Text tool is in the palette, in the same drop-down list as the Note and Note Attachment tools. To add a text node, select **Text** from the palette, and click in the diagram where you want to add the text.

Functional zoom (discussed earlier in this chapter) allows members to be expanded and collapsed, to show and hide contained subroutines and procedures. Notes attached to subroutines and procedures remain visible when the corresponding member is collapsed, but their connection line is hidden. When the member is re-expanded, the connection line is shown again.

Note nodes, text nodes, and note attachment connections can be deleted from the diagram by selecting them and pressing the Delete key.

Customizing the Diagram

The Application Diagram provides many options for customizing the look and layout of the diagram. When a new diagram opens, the editor determines the best layout for it, so that connections generally go in one direction (left to right, by default), and connections that cross or go through nodes is minimized.

Two aspects of the layout can be customized: orientation and line style. The orientation determines which way a diagram is drawn. The default orientation is horizontal (left to right). The other option is vertical (top to bottom).

The line style determines the type of lines used for connections. The possible values are oblique and rectilinear. The oblique line style uses diagonal lines to connect nodes. The rectilinear line style uses only horizontal and vertical lines, with 90-degree angles to connect nodes. Generally, the oblique line style (the default) creates more readable diagrams, but the rectilinear line style can be good for less complex diagrams, such as those showing only ILE bindings.

The orientation and line style can be set as global preferences on the Application Diagram preference page. To override the default settings for a particular diagram, right-click a blank area of the diagram and select **Change Layout** from the pop-up menu.

You can customize the layout after a diagram opens by manually rearranging nodes and connections. Simply drag and drop nodes, using the mouse to move them around. To add extra bends to a connection (*bend points*), place the mouse pointer on the connection where you want to bend, and then drag and drop the connection.

The Application Diagram provides grid lines, rulers, and alignment actions to assist in customizing the layout of diagrams. To toggle grid lines and rulers on and off, use the **Diagram > View > Grid and Diagram > View > Rulers** actions from the Workbench menu. To align nodes vertically or horizontally, first select the nodes, then use one of the alignment actions from the **Diagram > Align Workbench** menu. The Align Left, Center, and Right actions align the nodes vertically. The Align Top, Middle, Bottom actions align the nodes horizontally.

At any point, you can have the Application Diagram automatically arrange the diagram. To do this, simply right-click a blank area of the diagram and select **Arrange All**.

The last customization we will cover is colors and fonts. When you select a node, its incoming connection lines are highlighted red, and its outgoing connection lines are highlighted green. Likewise, if you select a connection, the source node is highlighted red, and the target node is highlighted green.

To customize the incoming and outgoing highlight colors, along with the font, go to the **General > Appearance > Colors and Fonts preference** page and look under **Application Diagram**. This makes a global change for all diagrams. You can customize the font for a specific diagram in the Properties view when no nodes or connections are selected. (Click in a blank area of the diagram.)

Troubleshooting

Below are some common problems related to the topics in this chapter, along with suggestions on diagnosing and fixing the problems:

- *The Visualize Application Diagram action doesn't appear in the pop-up menu for my selection.*

  1. Make sure you are using either WDSC 7.0 advanced edition or Rational Developer for System i. (The Application Diagram was not shipped in the standard edition of WDSC.)

  2. Make sure you have selected valid inputs for the Application Diagram. (See the section "Creating a Diagram" at the

beginning of this chapter for a list of valid selections.) The action will not appear if one of the selections is not valid.

3. If you have selected source members (or local/IFS files), make sure you have selected only ILE RPG, ILE COBOL, and CL source members. The Application Diagram uses the LPEX parser associations to determine if the selected source types are valid. If you use a nonstandard source type for any of these languages, you will need to associate your source type with the correct LPEX parser. (See chapter 7 for more information.)

- *You keep telling me to right-click a blank area of the diagram and select an action, but I don't see that action.*

When we say "blank area," we mean an empty area of the diagram that is not contained by any nodes. When you expand a member, the node for that member expands to show a call graph for the subroutines and procedures inside the member. It also shows lots of white space inside the member node. Right-clicking in this area will show the pop-up menu for the member node, not the overall diagram. Make sure you right-click a blank area outside of any member nodes.

- *My source calls procedures and/or subroutines in other source members, but these are not showing up in the diagram.*

The Application Diagram only parsers source members that are part of the initial user selection. If one of the selected source members calls procedures or subroutines from a member that was not selected, these calls will not show up.

- *Why do I see empty members in my diagram?*

1. An empty member might be a copy member of a selected member, but was not itself selected with the initial input to the diagram. When the diagram is generated, it only scans and shows information for selected source members. It will, however, show members that are copy members, along with an "includes" connection between the members.

2. The member might be a copy member that was part of the initial user selection, but the member does not define

any structural elements, like a procedure or subroutine. It might just define procedure prototypes or other definitions, or contain calculation specifications.

- *Why do I see empty service programs in my diagram?*

This is a similar reason to the previous question. The service program was not in the initial user selection, but something in the initial selection binds to the service program. In this case, the diagram includes the service program to show the binding relationship, but does not include details of the service program, such as the module list or exported procedures.

- *Why is my diagram empty?*

You have probably switched to a view that has filtered out all the nodes in the diagram. Right-click a blank area of the diagram, and select **Switch View > All**.

- *Why do I get warnings about the number of selected resources, nodes, and connections?*

There are practical limitations on the visual rendering of a diagram, in terms of how fast the editor can draw and refresh all the nodes and connections. This limit depends on the number of nodes and connections in the diagram and the speed of the workstation. A diagram with lots of nodes and no connections will draw quite easily, while one with fewer nodes but lots of connections between them will draw considerably slower.

The functional zoom capabilities added to the Application Diagram in Rational Developer for System i make this less of an issue, since the initial diagram only shows top-level resources. You can then drill down on the specific members you are interested in to see more details.

CHAPTER 13

Screen Designer

Manually coding a user interface always seems to fall under the "trial and error" coding style, regardless of whether the user interface language is DDS, HTML, or Java. You make some changes, compile, run, and see what it looks like.

The team responds, "Okay, that needs to be moved here. We're missing something there."

You make some more changes, recompile, and try again.

Now, you're told, "We're almost there. We need to add a new field here and change the length of that field there."

And on it goes.

This is exactly why you shouldn't code directly in any user interface language, unless you have some supernatural ability to mentally visualize 5250 screens as you type DDS source code. For the rest of us, including those of us who don't even know how to write DDS, there is Screen Designer, a visual editor for DDS display file source.

Like the Application Diagram tool discussed in chapter 12, Screen Designer was originally shipped only in WDSC 7.0 advanced edition, but is now included in Rational Developer for System i. As of Rational Developer for System i version 7.1, Screen Designer is a *technology preview*. This means some functions are not completely implemented yet, and Screen Designer has not had as much testing as the other RSE features.

Overview

Opening, saving, and closing Screen Designer is just like the Remote Systems LPEX Editor. To open Screen Designer from the RSE, right-click a DSPF or MNUDDS source member, and select **Open With > Screen Designer (Technology Preview)**. This locks the member and opens it in Screen Designer. On a save, changes are saved back to the remote member.

Double-clicking a source member in the RSE always opens the Remote Systems LPEX Editor, since Screen Designer is only a technology preview. The last editor used is remembered for i5/OS project members. You can change the default editor for i5/OS projects on the File Associations preference page (General > Editors > File Associations).

The design window in Screen Designer, shown in Figure 13–1, is made up of three main components:

- The design page screen controls along the top are used to define which records should be shown together in the visual design area.

- The design area in the middle renders the screen selected in the screen controls area and provides visual editing of the DDS source.

- The palette along the right side includes all the DDS *parts* (records and field types). Parts are added to a record by selecting them in the palette and dropping them on the design area.

Screen Designer includes design, source, and preview modes, which are represented by the three tabs in the bottom left corner of the editor. Clicking a tab switches the editor to the selected mode.

The design mode, shown in Figure 13–1, provides the visual editing capabilities in Screen Designer. The source mode provides an embedded copy of the Remote Systems LPEX Editor, for directly editing the DDS source. The preview mode provides the ability to preview screens as they would appear when the application runs. You can toggle between the modes, with changes made in one mode automatically reflected in each of the other modes.

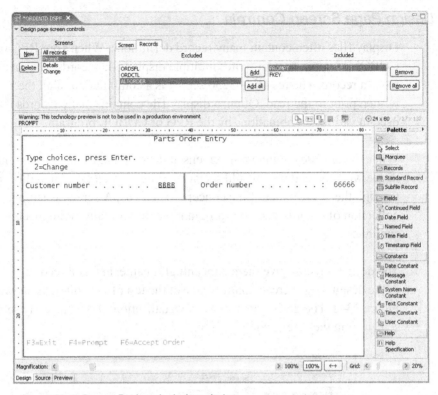

Figure 13–1: Screen Designer's design window.

Design Mode

In design mode, a new record or field is added to the DDS source by selecting it in the palette and dropping it on the screen, and then using the mouse to position it in the correct location. To modify the attributes or keywords for a field, select the part in the design area and use the Properties view to make the changes.

The Outline view displays the records, fields, and keywords used in the DDS source. The same outline is shown in the design and source modes of Screen Designer, as well as the Remote Systems LPEX Editor when editing DDS source. Using the Outline view is essential to using the design mode effectively. (You'll see why later in this chapter.)

Design Page Screen Controls

Display files often contain many record definitions. When your RPG or COBOL program runs, it writes multiple display file records, and then reads a record. The resulting 5250 screen is a combination of all the records written prior to the read. Often, a display file contains many records that are used in various combinations by the RPG or COBOL program.

When visually designing your screens at development time, it is essential to see what the end user would see at runtime. Screen Designer allows this through the development time concept of *screens*. A screen is simply a collection of records that your program would normally write together at runtime.

You define screens, give them a meaningful name, and add records to them in the design page screen controls area at the top of the editor, as shown in Figure 13–2. The design area shows a visualization of the currently selected screen from the screen controls area.

Figure 13–2: The design page screen controls.

Screen Designer always includes a screen called All Records that, as the name suggests, includes all records. You can define additional screens by clicking the New button. This creates a new screen named "Untitled," which you can (and should) rename on the Screen tab.

Figure 13–2 shows a display file source member that has three screens defined, in addition to the All Records default screen: Prompt, Details, and Change. From the Records tab, you can see that the Prompt screen (which is currently selected) includes the PROMPT and FKEY records, and excludes the ORDSFL, ORDCTL, and ALTORDER records.

Records can be added and removed from a screen by selecting the screen and switching to the Records tab. This does not add or delete records from the DDS source; it only adds and removes existing records from the screen that is visualized in the design area.

The design area shows the currently selected screen from the screen controls area. Depending on the option to draw records transparently (covered in the next section), the screen will either show all records defined in the screen or just the currently selected record. If all records are shown, fields for the current record are colored and fields for all other records are grey. Only fields for the current record can be selected in the design area. To select a grey field, you must first select the record (to make the record active in the design area), and then select the field.

As you've seen through out this book, maximizing use of the Workbench space is crucial. Once you have selected the screen you want to work with, the screen controls area can be collapsed by clicking the downward-pointing triangle in the top left corner of the editor. Click the triangle again to re-expand the area.

TIP There are various ways in which developers might use the concept of screens. Some might prefer to see only individual records in the design area, and just use the All Records screen and turn off the option to draw records transparently. Others might fully embrace the screen concept and re-create all of their runtime screens. Still others will find some middle ground to be most practical, creating definitions for frequently modified screens and using All Records for others.

The concept of a screen doesn't exist in DDS, so Screen Designer stores the screen definitions as comments at the bottom of the DDS source, as shown in Figure 13–3. Do not delete these comments, or you will lose your screen definitions.

```
A*%%RS+<record-sequences>
A*%%RS+ <sequence name="Prompt">
A*%%RS+  <record-write record-format="PROMPT" />
A*%%RS+  <record-write record-format="FKEY" />
A*%%RS+ </sequence>
```

Figure 13–3: An example of screen-definition comments. (part 1 of 2)

```
A*%%RS+ <sequence name="Details">
A*%%RS+  <record-write record-format="ORDSFL" />
A*%%RS+  <record-write record-format="ORDCTL" />
A*%%RS+  <record-write record-format="FKEY" />
A*%%RS+ </sequence>
A*%%RS+ <sequence name="Change">
A*%%RS+  <record-write record-format="ALTORDER" />
A*%%RS+ </sequence>
A*%%RS </record-sequences>
```

Figure 13–3: An example of screen-definition comments. (part 2 of 2)

CODE Designer (part of the older CODE tools package) had a similar
concept of a screen and also stored the definitions as comments, but used
a different format. If you open a source member in Screen Designer that
contains CODE Designer screen definitions, the CODE Designer definitions
are migrated to Screen Designer format. The CODE Designer definitions are
left in the source in case you want to use both tools. However, subsequent
changes to screen definitions in CODE Designer will not be migrated to
Screen Designer format.

The Design Page

The design area visualizes the screen currently selected in the screen
controls area and provides actions for editing the underlying records and
fields, as shown in Figure 13–4. The design area is made up of a toolbar
along the top, magnification and grid controls along the bottom, and the
screen rendering in the middle.

The toolbar contains the following options:

- *Draw records transparent* ( ): Toggle between showing all the
  records for the selected screen or just the currently selected record.

- *Show rectangular help specifications* ( ): When selected,
  rectangular boxes that represent the boundaries of the help areas are
  displayed in the design area. When help specifications are showing,
  it takes two clicks to select a field inside the rectangular box. The
  first click selects the box, and the second click selects the field
  inside the box.

- *Show in black and white* ( ): Toggle between showing the design
  area in black and white, or color.

- *Show grid lines* (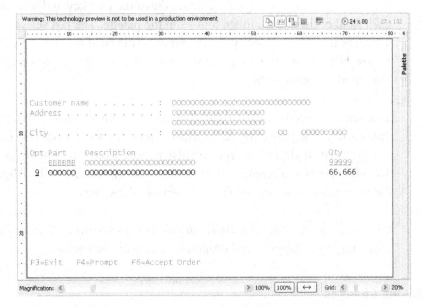): Toggle between showing and hiding grid lines in the design area.

- *Configure preferences* ( ): This is a shortcut into the preferences page for Screen Designer.

Figure 13–4: The design area.

The magnification slider along the bottom of the design area allows you to zoom from 50% to 400%. The current zoom level is shown to the right of the slider, along with a button to quickly zoom back to 100%. There is also a button that sets the zoom level to stretch (↔) the width of the design area to fit Screen Designer's window.

The font, font size, screen background color, and whether or not to show ruler bars can be customized on the Screen Designer preference page. Go to **Remote Systems > Screen Designer (Technology Preview)**.

Laying Out the Screen Just Right

Grid lines are useful to assist in reading rows and columns and to ensure that fields are aligned correctly. Next to the magnification controls is another slider that affects how the grid lines are displayed. As you move the slider to the right, the grid lines are drawn brighter and with less space between dots. We find having the grid slider somewhere around 55% to be optimal.

In addition to the grid lines, you can use special actions to align fields vertically or horizontally relative to each other or the screen. First, select the fields you want to align by holding down the Ctrl key and selecting each field or use the Marquee tool from the palette. The last selected field serves as the reference point for alignment. This field will be shown with hollow boxes in its selection outline, versus the solid boxes in the selection outline of the other fields.

To align the selected fields, right-click any of them, and select one of the options from the cascading Align menu. You can choose from left, center, or right vertical alignment. You can also choose from top, middle, or bottom horizontal alignment. Select one of the options from the Align to Parent menu to position the fields relative to the screen.

Of course, don't forget that fields can also be moved around the design area simply by dragging and dropping them with the mouse.

Making Changes

The majority of changes to records and fields are made in the Properties view (discussed in a later section). However, Screen Designer does allow some editing actions directly in the design area, such as the following:

- Editing text constants

- Moving and resizing fields

- Moving and resizing help areas

To directly edit a text constant, select the text constant field by left-clicking it, and then pause, and left-click again to switch to edit mode. Double-clicking the field does not work; there needs to be a pause between the clicks. When in edit mode, the field is shown with a blue border, and you can directly edit its text value.

To resize a field, first select the field, and then move the mouse to the edge of the field selection box at either end of the field. When the cursor changes to a horizontal double-headed arrow, hold down the left mouse button and resize the field by moving the mouse left or right. Multiple fields can be resized together this way.

To move or resize a help area, first make sure you have "show rectangular help specifications" selected from the toolbar, and then select the help area by clicking anywhere inside the box. Resize the help area by clicking on one of the drag handles and moving the mouse while holding down the left button. Move the help specification by left-clicking anywhere on the box except on a drag handle, and moving the mouse while holding down the left button. A tooltip is displayed, showing the current location of the help area while it is being moved or resized.

Of course, Screen Designer also has all the basic features you would expect from a modern editor: cut, copy, paste, delete, undo, and redo.

TIP
You can change the currently selected field in the design page using the cursor keys. To multi-select fields without using the mouse, hold down the Ctrl key, and then use the cursor keys to navigate to each field. Press the Spacebar to select the field.

Printing

That screen you just designed is a work of art. Now it's time to print it and send a copy to your mother. She always appreciated your artwork back in school. Why should it be any different now?

At the time of this writing, the File > Print menu is disabled for Screen Designer, but don't let that stop you from printing! To print a copy of the screen in design mode, right-click in the design area and select **Print** from the pop-up menu. Alternatively, you can print a copy of the source code using the LPEX print command. Press Esc in source mode to jump to the command area, type **print**, and press Enter.

The Palette

The palette, shown in Figure 13–5, is used to add new records, fields, and constants to the DDS source when in design mode. It is organized into four drawers, Records, Fields, Constants, and Help, which contain the actual parts that can be added.

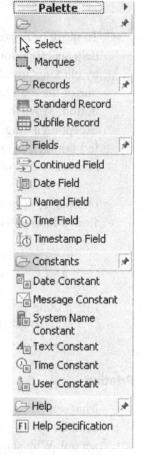

To add a new part to the DDS source, first select the record where you want the field, constant, or help specification added. Do this by selecting the record in the screen controls area or by selecting the record in the outline view. Then, select the part in the palette (with a single click), and click in the design area where you want the part inserted. Alternatively, drag and drop the part from the palette onto the design area.

Quite a few layout and customization options can be made to the palette, such as these two:

- Hide and show the palette by clicking the triangle (⏵) in the palette's title bar.

- Dock the palette on the right or left side of the design area by right-clicking the palette's title bar and selecting "left" or "right" from the Dock On cascading menu.

If neither of these options seems to work just right, you might want to use the stand-alone Palette view. To open the Palette view, select **Window > Show View > Other** from the Workbench menu, and then select **General > Palette**. The embedded palette is automatically closed when the external Palette view is opened, and automatically reopened if the Palette view is closed. The embedded palette and Palette view are functionally the same. However, the Palette view provides more layout options, such as fast view and detached view.

Figure 13–5: The Screen Designer palette.

To customize the layout and font used by the Palette view, right-click in the palette and select **Settings**. This opens the Palette Settings dialog, as shown in Figure 13–6.

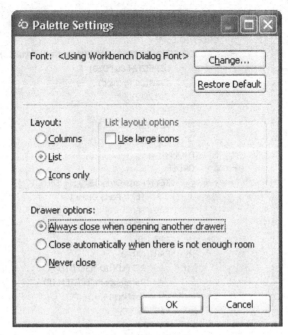

Figure 13–6: The Palette Settings dialog.

After you become accustomed to what each drawer of the palette contains, you might want to select the **Always close when opening another drawer** option. This keeps all the drawers closed, except for the one you are currently using. (You open and close drawers by clicking on their titles.) This keeps the Palette view tidy and minimizes the need to scroll in the view.

The Outline View

The DDS Outline view shows an overview of the records, fields, constants, keywords, and attributes in the current member being edited, as shown in Figure 13–7. The top entry is the file being edited. Under the file entry, there is a folder for each record defined in the member. Under each record are the fields defined in the record.

Each file, record, and field entry has a folder (📁) directly underneath it that holds the keywords associated with it. The title of the folder is a concatenation of the keywords. The individual keywords can be seen by expanding the folder.

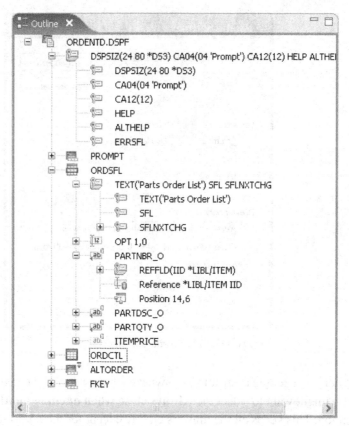

Figure 13–7: The DDS Outline view.

The icon for a record or field gives information about it, for example:

- *Record type*: Icons indicate standard ( ), subfile ( ), or subfile control ( ) records. It's difficult to tell the difference of some of them without the colors.

- *Field type*: Icons indicate character ( ), numeric ( ), or date ( ).

- *Input or output*: Icons for input fields are shown with an arrow pointing right. Icons for output fields are shown with an arrow pointing left.

- *Database reference*: Database reference fields are decorated with a cylinder in the top right corner.

The Outline view can be used in both source and design modes. In source mode, the Outline view positions the editor to a selected record, field, or keyword. In design mode, the Outline view is used to select a record before inserting a new field or constant, and as an alternative way to select fields in the design area.

The Properties View

You've already seen how fields and constants can be added to the DDS and visually arranged using the design mode of Screen Designer. However, on its own, the design page doesn't allow attributes and keywords to be changed. This is the role of the Properties view, which is used in conjunction with the design page.

Properties are available for the file as well as for each record, field, and keyword. The Properties view always shows the settings for the current selection. The selection can be made from the following:

- *Outline view*: Select a file, record, field, or keyword entry in the view.

- *Screen controls area*: Select the record from the records list for the current screen.

- *Design area*: Selecting the field in the visual design area.

- *Source page*: Selections are based on the cursor position.

Each of these selection sources is kept in sync with each other. For example, if you select a field in the Outline view, that field is also selected in the design area (or source page). The corresponding record is selected in the screen controls area, and the Properties view is updated to show the properties for the field.

TIP

The Properties view is docked in a small area in the bottom left corner of the RSE perspective. This area doesn't provide adequate space for the view to be used effectively with Screen Designer. Move the Properties view to the bigger area to the right, where the Object Table and Commands Log views are. This bigger area allows you to see more of the properties without having to scroll.

Figure 13–8 shows the Properties dialog for a DDS field. The current selection is shown as a subtitle along the top of the view. In this example, the subtitle indicates this is the ORDNBR field in the PROMPT record of file WDSCDEMO/QDDSSRC(ORDENTD) for RSE connection TORASBCC.

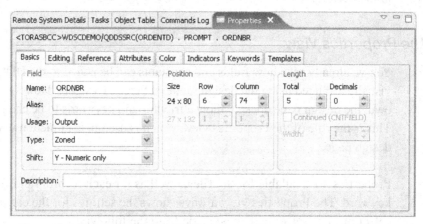

Figure 13–8: The properties for a DDS field.

Each of the attributes and keywords can be modified in the Properties view. The attributes and keywords for the current selection are grouped into categories, which are shown as tabs along the top of the view. The categories that are shown depend on the type and attributes of the field or constant. Below is a list of some of the common categories you will find:

- *Basic*: General information about the field, such as the field's name, usage, type, length, and position on the screen

- *Editing*: For edit-code and edit-word formatting

- *Reference*: For database or source reference fields

- *Attributes:* For setting display attributes, such as blinking, high intensity, reverse image, or underline

- *Indicators:* For setting conditioning indicators for the fields or constants

- *Subfile Control and Control keywords:* Settings and keywords for subfile records and subfile control records, as shown in Figure 13–9

- *Keywords*: To add and remove keywords for the file, record, or field

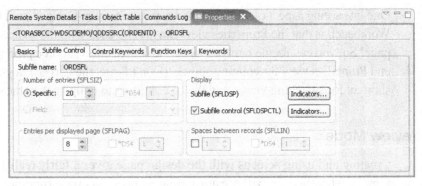

Figure 13–9: Subfile control properties.

TIP

Do you need to create a new database reference field?
Instead of adding it from the palette and then manually
entering the reference field information, you can drag and drop
the field from the RSE onto the design area. Right-click the file that
contains the referenced field, and select **Show in Table** > **Fields**.
This opens the Field Table view and lists all fields in the file. Drag
and drop a field from the Field Table to the design area to add a new
database reference field.

The Source Page

The source page of Screen Designer allows direct editing of the DDS
source. It's actually an embedded copy of the Remote Systems LPEX
Editor, so all of the features of the Remote Systems LPEX Editor, such
as prompting, syntax checking, and prefix commands are available.
(See chapters 6 and 7 for more on the Remote Systems LEPX editor.)

The design and source pages are constantly kept synchronized, so a change
made in one page is immediately reflected in the other. This allows you to
switch back and forth, using the mode that best suites your current task.

There are a few reasons why you might want, or need, to use the source
page to directly edit the DDS source. For starters, this is the only way
to delete a record from the source. (Fields and constants can be deleted
from the design page, but not records.) Some DDS experts might find
the Properties view slow and cumbersome to enter the type information,
attributes, and keywords for new fields. These users might prefer to switch
to the source page and enter them manually.

One interesting aspect of the integrated nature of Screen Designer and the Workbench is that the Properties view can also be used with the source page! So, you can toggle between using the source editor, source prompter, and Properties view for entering source. (Don't forget the Ctrl+F7 keyboard shortcut for switching views, and the F12 shortcut to jump back to the editor.)

Preview Mode

Creating and using screens with the design page gives a fairly realistic view of what the user will see at runtime. However, certain runtime aspects of the screen are not included, such as real data, the order in which screens are written, and indicators. The preview page of Screen Designer takes these things into account to provide a more realistic rendering of the screen. A sample preview page is shown in Figure 13–10.

At the time of this writing (using Rational Developer for System i version 7.1), the preview page is only partially completed (hence the "technology preview" designation). Some of the features described in this section might not work yet, unless you have a more recent version of Screen Designer that is no longer a technology preview.

Figure 13-10: The preview page.

At the top of the preview page are its screen controls. These are similar to the screen controls on the design page. This is where you select the screen you want to preview and set its runtime information, using the following tabs:

- *Records*: Specify the order in which records are written to the screen.

- *Indicators*: Define indicator sets, each of which has a name and a list of indicators that are set on. Defining an indicator set does not affect the preview area. (This is done on the Values tab.) You can use indicator sets to exercise records that have hidden fields or error messages. Indicator sets are saved as comments with the screen definitions in the DDS source.

- *Values*: Specify indicator sets and the start line for each record. Sample data can also be specified for each field.

- *Cursor*: Specify the position of the cursor.

The design area visualizes the screen selected in the screen controls area with the write order, indicators, and real data applied to the records. In preview mode, the design area is not editable, and the Properties view is not updated based on selections.

Troubleshooting

Below are some common problems related to the topics in this chapter, along with suggestions on diagnosing and fixing the problems:

- *Why is there a slight delay after Screen Designer opens?*

  In order to visually render the screen on the design page, Screen Designer needs to resolve the externally described fields in the source. Building the internal model of the DDS source, along with resolving each of the externally described fields, is the delay you notice after opening Screen Designer.

- *Why doesn't the palette show up on my design page?*

  The embedded palette on the design page and the external Palette view provide the same functionality. The embedded palette automatically closes when the external Palette view is opened. Closing the external Palette view reopens the embedded palette. If you can't find the external Palette view, try to open it again, which forces it to show. (It might be tucked away with a bunch of other views or set up as a fast view.)

- *How can I change the settings and keywords for my file on the design page?*

  You can change file-level settings and keywords in the Properties view by selecting the file entry in the Outline view (the topmost entry).

- *How do I delete a record on the design page?*

  You can't delete a record from the design page. You have to delete it from the source page.

- *I opened a DDS source member in Screen Designer for the first time, and I already see screens defined.*

  There are two reasons why this might happen. One possibility is that someone else has already used Screen Designer with this source member and defined the screens. (The screens are stored as comments in the source member.) The other possibility is that someone previously edited the source member with CODE Designer. The first time you open a source member with Screen Designer, there is a one-time migration of any CODE Designer screen definitions into Screen Designer format.

- *Some of my fields are not showing up correctly in the design page.*

  Check whether the fields are database reference fields. If they are, and the database reference file is library-list qualified, make sure the library list is set up correctly for the RSE connection, so the file can be found.

- *Why is the "screen size of 27x132" option disabled in the design area?*

  This depends on the DSPSIZ keyword in the source. If you specify this keyword with the two screen sizes, then both options are enabled.

Otherwise, the default 24x80 option is used, and the 27x132 option is disabled.

- *When I right-click and choose Open With > Screen Designer (Technology Preview), I see the file open in the Remote Systems LPEX Editor.*

  If the member is already opened with Remote Systems LPEX Editor, selecting to open with Screen Designer will just put the focus on the opened member. You will need to close the member and reopen it with Screen Designer.

- *Can I browse a display file using Screen Designer?*

  Yes, you are in luck if you are using Rational Developer for System i. Right-click the member and select **Browse With > Screen Designer**.

- *Preview mode is empty. It has some text saying it is partially functional.*

  You need to select the screen from the screen controls that you want to preview.

What's Next

Congratulations, you are now an RSE expert! By now you've realized there are lots of great features in the RSE, and you're wondering how you ever survived using just SEU and PDM. At least, we hope that's what you're wondering!

Throughout this book, you've been introduced to many features. You've probably started to use a few of them in your day-to-day job. Getting comfortable with them, to the point that they become second nature, will take time and experience. This is especially true with the little things, like remembering all the keyboard shortcuts, which help to improve efficiency using the RSE. Just remember, there was a time in your career when SEU and PDM were new and unfamiliar tools.

There are many things to explore with the Workbench beyond WDSC and Rational Developer for System i. One of the goals of Eclipse is to provide an integration platform for application development tools. There are many other IBM and non-IBM, commercial and open-source extensions to Eclipse that you might find valuable. A good place to start looking is the Eclipse plug-in central site, *www.eclipseplugincentral.com*.

Keeping Informed

Your education is far from over. We work in an industry that seems to undergo almost continuous change and advancement. There will be new features and products added to the i5/OS application development tools portfolio. Applications will need to become more and more integrated, both within and across systems and organizations. New user interface paradigms will come and go. There will be improvements to the software development process and related software tools. Hopefully, you're like us, and see these as exciting challenges to learn and grow.

We have the same challenge as you do: staying current with the latest technologies, programming languages, new language features, development tools, best practices, and methodologies, all while doing our normal jobs! There is so much information that it can be both hard to find and overwhelming, at the same time.

Social bookmarking and *feeds* are very powerful tools for finding information and keeping current on what's happening in the industry. We use them on a daily basis to stay up-to-date on what industry thought leaders are posting in their blogs, what's happening on Eclipse and Jazz.net, and recent articles on IBM developerWorks and various i5/OS-related Web sites. You can even get a feed from the WDSC and Rational Developer for System i support site!

Social Bookmarking

We can't provide an exhaustive list of resources in this book. It would be incomplete, take up too much space, and quickly become outdated. Social bookmarking is a way for everyone to associate Internet resources (essentially anything with a URL) with an arbitrary list of keywords to describe the resource. Then, others can search the keywords to find relevant resources.

The Web site http://del.icio.us is an example of a social bookmarking site. We, along with others in the industry, have been busy tagging resources we find with tags such as *WDSC*, *RDi*, *LPEX*, and *debugger*. Go to *http://del.icio.us/tag/WDSC* to find links to everything that has been tagged by at least one person as relating to WDSC. Alternatively, go to *http://del.icio.us/tag/WDSC+articles* to narrow the list down to links that are tagged *WDSC* and *articles*. The great thing here is anyone can participate. If you tag a new resource as WDSC, it instantly appears in the list for anyone who enters the above URL.

Dogear is the system we use internally at IBM to apply the same principles of social bookmarking and tagging on our internal network. It is now available as part of IBM Lotus Connections. We use this when we need to tag internal pages or external pages, but we don't want the entire world to know what we are currently researching!

RSS and Atom Feeds

The large number of resources out there, and the frequency with which they are updated, makes it a very daunting task to open your Web browser and visit each one regularly. Many of these Web sites, blogs, and podcasts provide one or more *feed*s that can be downloaded and displayed in a news reader. News readers aggregate many feeds into a single user interface (a browser or rich-client application), so the information comes to you, instead of you having to go and find the information.

Many of the Internet portals (such as Google and YAHOO!) allow you to add feeds to your portal page. The latest versions of Internet Explorer and Firefox both have direct support for feeds. There are also rich-client news readers, including some that are built on Eclipse!

When you see the symbol 🔊 or the letters *RSS* or *Atom* on a Web site, it means the site provides a feed. Really Simple Syndication (RSS) and the Atom syndication format are XML languages that define the semantics of the information sent from the Web site to the news reader.

Additional Resources

Here are some additional WDSC and Rational Developer for System i resources to help you find information about the RSE:

- The WDSC Web site, *www.ibm.com/software/awdtools/wdt400*

- The Rational Developer for System i Web site, *www.ibm.com/software/awdtools/rdi*

- The WDSC/Rational Developer for System i Development team blog, *wdsc.wordpress.com*

- The Midrange.com WDSC mailing list, *lists.midrange.com/ mailman/listinfo/wdsci-l*

- The MC Press Online Website, *www.mcpressonline.com*

- The Midrange.com wiki, *wiki.midrange.com*

- Eclipse, *www.eclipse.org*

This is just a small subset of all the resources out there. We encourage you to use del.icio.us and other social bookmarking sites to find more resources. On the flip side, if you have an article, Web site, newsletter, conference, or any other type of resource, tag it on social bookmarking sites so others can find it!

APPENDIX

Keyboard Shortcuts

Each of the chapters provides the keyboard shortcuts to drive the Workbench features that pertain to that chapter. This appendix puts them all together in one place, for easy reference.

General Windows Shortcuts

Table A–1 lists the keyboard shortcuts that work with most Windows-based applications. This includes WDSC and Rational Developer for System i.

Table A–1: General Windows Shortcut Keys	
Keyboard Shortcut	**Action**
Ctrl+A	Select all of the material in the document.
Ctrl+C	Copy the selected text and place it in the clipboard.
Ctrl+X	Cut the selected text and place it in the clipboard.
Ctrl+V	Paste the text contents placed in the clipboard.
Ctrl+P	Print the document.
Ctrl+S	Save the document.
Ctrl+Y	Redo/repeat the previous action.
Ctrl+Z	Undo typing.
Ctrl+Home	Go to the top of the document or view.
Ctrl+End	Go to the end of the document or view.
Ctrl+Right arrow	Jump one word to the right.
Ctrl+Left arrow	Jump one word to the left.
Hold down shift while moving cursor	Select text.

General Workbench Shortcuts

Table A–2 lists the Eclipse Workbench keyboard shortcuts that we find are most commonly used. Refer to the **General > Keys** preference page for a more complete catalog.

Table A–2: General Workbench Shortcut Keys	
Keyboard Shortcut	**Action**
Alt+- (minus key)	Access the view's System menu. This is the same as right-clicking on the view's tab.
Alt+F4	Exit the Workbench.
Alt+*mnemonic*	Access the Workbench menu bar actions.
Alt+Shift+Q	Get the list of views, where you can select the view to open.
Ctrl+F4 (or Ctrl+W, but not with LPEX)	Close the current editor.
Ctrl+Shift+W	Close all editors.
Ctrl+F6	Cycle among open editors.
Ctrl+F7	Cycle among open views.
Ctrl+F8	Cycle among open perspectives.
Ctrl+F10	Open the pull-down menu for the current view, if there is one. For editors, it will open the menu for the vertical ruler (also known as the marker bar) on the left of the editor area.
Ctrl+E	Activate the editor drop-down for the editor set, where you can select the editor to switch to.
Ctrl+H	Open the Search dialog.
Ctrl+M	Maximize or restore a view or editor. (This does not work in the Remote Systems LPEX editor.)
Ctrl+Shift+E	Open the Switch to Editor dialog.
Ctrl+Shift+L	Obtain a full list of the currently available keyboard shortcuts.
Shift+F10	Pop up the context menu for the current view, editor, or selected item. (This is the same as right-clicking.)
F1	Access the help system.
F10	Position the cursor on the first menu of the Workbench menu bar.
F12	Jump to the current editor from any view in the Workbench.
Esc	Close a menu. This is the same as clicking the Cancel button in a dialog.

Table A–2: General Workbench Shortcut Keys (Continued)	
Keyboard Shortcut	**Action**
Keyboard arrow keys	The arrow keys can be used to navigate through lists and tree views in the Workbench. For example, you can navigate through the entire Remote Systems view using just the arrow keys. Use the Up and Down arrow keys to navigate through items that are already showing. Use the Left and Right arrow keys to collapse and expand entries, respectively.
Position by typing	If you are in a table or tree view, and you start typing, the view attempts to position to an entry in the view that matches what you are typing. For example, if you are in the Remote Systems view, and you just expanded your library, you can quickly jump to the QRPGLESRC source file by just entering QRPGLESRC. (Chances are you will only have to enter part of the name.)

Object Table View Shortcuts

You can use the keyboard shortcuts in Table A–3 while working in the Object Table view to perform actions that are consistent with PDM actions.

Table A–3: Object Table View Shortcut Keys	
Keyboard Shortcut	**Action**
F4 (Prompt)	Prompt the command string entered on the command line. If there is no command in the command line, the Browse For Command dialog box opens, where you can select a command for prompting.
F5 (Refresh)	Refresh the current list in the Object Table view. This is the same as clicking the Refresh button.
F9 (Retrieve)	Display the last command string entered on the command line.
F14 (Display date)	Display the date and size by toggling between the "default," "customized," and "all format" settings for the Object Table view.
F16 (User options)	Invoke the Work With User Actions window, where you can modify the user actions (user options).
F17 (Subset)	Invoke the Subset dialog box, used to subset the list.
F18 (Change defaults)	Invoke the Properties for Command Execution page, where you can change the defaults to use when you run commands.
F21 (Print list)	Invoke the Print dialog box to specify the print options, and then print the list. This prints to the local Windows printer.
Just start typing	This automatically opens the Position To dialog.

Remote Systems LPEX Editor Shortcuts

Table A–4 lists the commonly used keyboard shortcuts for the Remote Systems LPEX Editor. Some of the keyboard shortcuts are language-specific, while others are generic actions that will work with any language.

Table A–4: Remote Systems LPEX Editor Shortcut Keys	
Keyboard Shortcut	**Action**
Alt+C	Copy the selected line or block of lines.
Alt+D	Delete the selected line or block of lines.
Alt+I	Change the selected text to lowercase.
Alt+J	Join the current line with the next line.
Alt+S	Split the line at the cursor position.
Alt+L	Select a single line or block of lines. To select a block of lines after Alt+L, click and drag the left mouse pointer.
Alt+M	Move the selected line or block of lines.
Ctrl+Q	Set a quick mark.
Alt+Q	Go to the quick mark location.
Alt+R, use the arrow keys, then Alt+R again	Select a rectangular block of text.
Alt +U	Deselect the text.
Ctrl+F	Find or replace a string.
Ctrl+G	Go to the Filter Division in the source member (in COBOL).
Ctrl+J	Return the cursor to the place in the editor where text was last entered.
Ctrl+L	Position the cursor to the line specified.
Ctrl+M	Select the structured block (in ILE RPG and CL).
Ctrl+Shift+O	Show the block nesting (in ILE RPG and CL).
Ctrl+N	After a search, find the next occurrence of the string.
Ctrl+S	Save the contents of the current member.
Ctrl+P	Print the member currently in focus.
Ctrl+W	Show the entire source (remove filters).
Ctrl+F4	Close the current member.
Ctrl+F5	Remove error messages, any pending actions, and any filtering.
Ctrl+F6	Cycle through all open editors.
Ctrl+2	Open a new view of the same source member.
Alt+Shift+Left/Right arrow	Move between multiple views of the same source.

Table A–4: Remote Systems LPEX Editor Shortcut Keys (Continued)	
Keyboard Shortcut	**Action**
Ctrl+0 (zero)	Close the view. This applies to multiple views of the same source member.
Ctrl+, (comma)	After a verify or compile, go to the previous problem.
Ctrl+. (period)	After a verify or compile, go to the next problem.
Ctrl+/ (forward slash)	Comment the selected code (in COBOL).
Ctrl+\ (backslash)	Uncomment the selected code (in COBOL).
Ctrl+Enter	Insert a new line.
Ctrl+Insert	Copy the selected text in the editor. This is the same as Ctrl+C.
Ctrl+Backspace	Delete the current line.
Ctrl+Up arrow	Scroll the editor up one line without changing the current line.
Ctrl+Down arrow	Scroll the editor down one line without changing the current line.
Ctrl+Space	Obtain Content Assist.
Ctrl+Delete, Ctrl+Shift+Delete	Delete all the text between the cursor and the end of current line (Field Exit).
Ctrl+Shift+A	Open a single member.
Ctrl+Shift+C	Invoke the last compile command used for the source member type.
Ctrl+Shift+D	Find the date.
Ctrl+Shift+M	Jump to the other end of a structured block (in ILE RPG and CL).
Ctrl+Shift+N	After a compare, navigate to the next mismatch.
Ctrl+Shift+P	After a compare, navigate to the previous mismatch.
Ctrl+Shift+R	Refresh the compare.
Ctrl+Shift+S	Save the contents of all open members.
Ctrl+Shift+V	Program verify the source member.
Ctrl+Shift+F5	Refresh the Outline view.
Ctrl+Alt+E	Expand the node to show lower-level details. This is the same as clicking the plus sign (in the application diagram).
Ctrl+Alt+C	Collapse the node to hide the lower-level details. This is the same as clicking the minus sign (in the application diagram).
Shift+F4	After a find or replace, search for the next occurrence of the same string.
F1	Invoke language-sensitive help.
F3	Position to an ILE RPG subroutine or procedure declaration.

Table A–4: Remote Systems LPEX Editor Shortcut Keys (Continued)	
Keyboard Shortcut	Action
F4	Invoke source prompting.
Home	Move the cursor to the beginning of the line.
End	Move the cursor to the end of the line.
Page up	Move the cursor up one window.
Page down	Move the cursor down one window.
Home, then Shift+Tab	Move the cursor in the prefix area.

Integrated I5/OS Debugger Shortcuts

Table A–5 lists the keyboard shortcuts for starting the Integrated i5/OS Debugger and controlling debug execution.

Table A–5: Integrated i5/OS Debugger Shortcut Keys	
Keyboard Shortcut	Action
F5	Step into the current execution line while debugging.
F6	Step over the current execution line.
F7	Step return.
F8	Resume execution of a suspended program.
F11	Re-launch the last program for debugging.
Ctrl+F9	Show the stopping thread. This action positions to the Debug view, to the top of the call stack, and highlights the current execution line in the editor.
Ctrl+F11	Re-launch the last program for running.

APPENDIX

B

Chapter Differences for WDSC 7.0

This book was written to the RSE features as they exist in Rational
Developer for System i 7.1. This appendix outlines the differences
between what is described in the book and what you would see if you were
using WebSphere Development Studio Client for System i 7.0 (WDSC).
This appendix does not cover the packaging differences between WDSC
and Rational Developer for System i; these are covered in chapter 1.

Differences are divided into overall differences, which affect all chapters,
and chapter-specific differences. Apart from the overall differences, there
are no specific differences for chapters 1, 3, 4, 5, 10, and 14.

Overall Differences

The biggest overall difference in the RSE between WDSC and Rational
Developer for System i is the change from using iSeries to i5/OS. (And now
we have to change it to IBM i!) So, instead of creating an i5/OS connection as
in Rational Developer for System i, you create an iSeries connection in WDSC.
Along with this name change, the names of the subsystems and some views
have also been cleaned up. Table B-1 provides a mapping between the names
used in Rational Developer for System i and WDSC.

Table B–1: Mapping Rational Developer for System i Names to WDSC Names		
Name in Rational Developer for System i	Name in WDSC	Type
i5/OS	iSeries	Connection
Objects	iSeries Objects	Subsystem
Commands	iSeries Commands	Subsystem
Jobs	iSeries Jobs	Subsystem
Commands Log	iSeries Commands Log	View
Data Table	iSeries Data Table View	View
Error List	iSeries Error List	View
Field Table	iSeries Field Table View	View
RPG Indentation	iSeries Indent	View
Jog Log	iSeries Job Log	View
Job Status	iSeries Job Status	View
Listings	iSeries Listings	View
i5/OS Project Navigator	iSeries Project Navigator	View
i5/OS Service Entry Points	iSeries Service Entry Points	View
Source Prompter	iSeries Source Prompter	View
Object Table	iSeries Table View	View

Chapter 2, Installation and Setup

Differences in the Rational Developer for System i and WDSC installs are minor and are described in the chapter.

Chapter 6, The Remote Systems LPEX Editor: The Best of Both Worlds

In the section on saving and closing, the preference to first save to a temporary member and then copy to the original member is new in Rational Developer for System i 7.1. WDSC 7.0 always saves directly to the original member.

Chapter 7, The Remote Systems LPEX Editor: RPG, COBOL, DDS, and CL Editing Features

Overall, the language features for RPG, COBOL, CL, and DDS have been updated to the V6R1 level for Rational Developer for System i 7.1. WDSC 7.0 uses the V5R4 levels. This affects the language parsers, syntax checkers, program verifiers, and language help.

In the section on ILE RPG, content assist, wizards, and Outline view have been updated to V6R1 in Rational Developer for System i 7.1. Outline view was enhanced to refresh asynchronously. In WDSC 7.0, Outline view refreshes synchronously. (You can't do anything else while it refreshes.)

In the CL section, a new line-length CL formatting preference was added in Rational Developer for System i 7.1. This is set to the record length in WDSC 7.0 and cannot be changed.

Chapter 8, Compiling and Binding

In the section on the Error List view, the options to automatically remove and automatically insert messages from the view are new in Rational Developer for System i 7.1.

Chapter 9, Running and Debugging Programs

Launch configuration names start with *iSeries* in WDSC 7.0, and *i5/OS* in Rational Developer for System i 7.1.

Chapter 11, i5/OS Project: The Other Way to Manage Your Source

In the section "Non-source Objects and i5/OS Projects," save-file support is not included in WDSC 7.0. It is included in WDSC 7.0 Advanced Edition and Rational Developer for System i 7.1.

Chapter 12, The Application Diagram

The Application Diagram is not included in WDSC 7.0. It is included in WDSC 7.0 Advanced Edition. Support for CL was added to the Application Diagram in Rational Developer for System i 7.1.

Displaying program calls is new in the Application Diagram in Rational Developer for System i 7.1. The Application Diagram in WDSC 7.0 AE only shows calls between subroutines and procedures.

In WDSC 7.0 AE, the Application Diagram does not show nodes representing source members. Instead, it opens showing all subroutines and procedures, without any member boundaries around them.

Chapter 13, Screen Designer

Screen Designer is not included in WDSC 7.0. It is included in WDSC 7.0 Advanced Edition. Screen Designer is still a technology preview in Rational Developer for System i 7.1; however, more features and fixes have been implemented.

Index

Note: Boldface numbers indicate illustrations

NOTE: Locators ending in an italic t indicate a table.

System i Books from MC Press

APIs at Work, 2nd edition

ISBN: 978-158347-069-5
Author: Bruce Vining, Doug Pence, and Ron Hawkins
http://www.mc-store.com/5085.html

IBM i5/iSeries Primer, 4th edition

ISBN: 978-158347-039-8
Authors: Ted Holt, Kevin Forsythe, Doug Pence, and Ron Hawkins
http://www.mc-store.com/5070.html

Free-Format RPG IV

ISBN: 978-158347-055-8
Author: Jim Martin
http://www.mc-store.com/5073.html

The Modern RPG IV Language, 4th edition

ISBN: 978-158347-064-0
Author: Robert Cozzi, Jr.
http://www.mc-store.com/5080.html

The Programmer's Guide to iSeries Navigator

ISBN: 978-158347-047-3
Author: Paul Tuohy
http://www.mc-store.com/5075.html

See more titles at http://www.mc-store.com